COMMUNICATING AND CONNECTING

FUNCTIONS OF HUMAN COMMUNICATION

Second Edition

Third Revised Printing

Edited by

William A. Donohue
Lisa L. Massi Lindsey with Jennifer Ann Maginnis
and Carrie M. Oliveira

Department of Communication
Michigan State University
Centers for Disease Control and Prevention

Cover design and photography by: timholl.com
Cover designed by Tim Holl
Female figure's likeness: Stevie Jaqutis
Male figure's likeness: Reyson Morales

Copyright © 2001, 2002 by Kendall/Hunt Publishing Company

ISBN 13: 978-0-7575-3327-3
ISBN 10: 0-7575-3327-2

Revised Printing 2006

All rights reserved. No part of this publication may be reproduced, stored in a retrieval system, or transmitted, in any form or by any means, electronic, mechanical, photocopying, recording, or otherwise, without the prior written permission of the copyright owner.

Printed in the United States of America
10 9 8 7 6 5

Contents

Foreword .... *viii*

Chapter One

Introducing Communication Functions 1
William A. Donohue

    The Communication Challenge 1
    The Essence of Communicating 2
    What Is Communication? 3
    How Does Communication Work? 7
    Why Do Connections Fail? 13
    Conclusions 14
    References 15
    Chapter One Case Study Quiz 17

Chapter Two

Language and Meaning 21
Laura E. Drake

    What Is Language? 21
    The Characteristics of Language 26
    Language and Effective Communication 38
    References 40
    Chapter Two Case Study Quiz 43

Chapter Three

Using Social Knowledge in Communication:
Interpreting and Forming Messages 47
Sandi W. Smith and Steven R. Wilson

    Schemas and Input Processing 48
    Goals, Plans, and Output Processing 53
    Conclusions 60
    References 61
    Chapter Three Case Study Quiz 65

Chapter Four

Communication and Self-Concept Development 69
Paul A. Mongeau

    Communication and Self-Concept 69
    Self-Concept and Self-Esteem 73
    Communication and Gender Development 74
    Where Does Our Self-Concept Come From? 76

How Many Selves Are There? 78
Effective Self-Concept Development and Change 80
Conclusions 82
References 84
Chapter Four Case Study Quiz 85

Chapter Five

Relational Development **89**
Monique M. Turner and Kimo Ah Yun

What Kinds of Interpersonal Relationships Do We Form? 90
What Kind of Lovers Are We? 98
Predictors of Relational Success 99
Why Do We Form Interpersonal Relationships? 100
A Closer Look at Self-Disclosure 102
References 105
Chapter Five Case Study Quiz 107

Chapter Six

Socialization **111**
Vernon Miller, Letticia N. Callies, and Janie Harden Fritz

How Socialization Works 116
Socialization Guidelines 124
Special Applications 126
Conclusions 126
References 127
Chapter Six Case Study Quiz 131

Chapter Seven

Communication and Conflict Management:
Trying to Keep Things under Control **135**
Michael E. Roloff

Conflict Issues 137
Origins of Conflict 139
Consequences of Conflict 140
The Nature of Conflict Management 142
Effective Conflict Management 144
Conclusions 149
References 150
Chapter Seven Case Study Quiz 155

Chapter Eight

Appreciating Cultural Differences **159**
Mary Jiang Bresnahan and Timothy R. Levine

What Is Culture? 161
Why Study Culture? 163

    How to Begin Understanding Culture 166
    Self-Construals—What Are They and Why Do We Need Them? 172
    Applying This Framework 173
    Conclusions 176
    References 176
    Applications 177
    Questions for Thought and Discussion 178
    Chapter Eight Case Study Quiz 181

Chapter Nine

Persuasion 185
Deborah A. Cai and Edward L. Fink

    Defining Persuasion 186
    Relationships among Attitudes, Beliefs, and Behaviors 187
    Persuasion without Thought 191
    Influence in Groups 193
    Persuasive Messages 194
    Conclusions about Messages 198
    Learning to Persuade 199
    References 201
    Chapter Nine Case Study Quiz 203

Chapter Ten

Coordination and Organizational Communication Structure 207
J. David Johnson and William A. Donohue

    Understanding Organizations 208
    Network Analysis 212
    Cultural Approaches 214
    Coordination: The Process of Organizing 217
    Conclusions 220
    References 220
    Chapter Ten Case Study Quiz 221

Chapter Eleven

Communication and the Decision-Making Process 225
Abran J. Salazar and Kim Witte

    Group Decision-Making and Problem-Solving 227
    Do Groups Make Better Decisions Than Individuals? 228
    The Anatomy of a Decision: Group Decision Development 233
    Group Communication and Effective Decision-Making 236
    Conclusions 238
    References 238
    Answers to the NASA Moon Survival Problem 240
    Chapter Eleven Case Study Quiz 241

Chapter Twelve
Leadership 245
Franklin J. Boster

    Defining Leadership 247
    Leaders 248
    References 255
    Chapter Twelve Case Study Quiz 257

Chapter Thirteen
Diffusion of Innovations:
Getting People to Do New Things 261
James W. Dearing

    What Is Diffusion? 262
    How Do People React to Innovations? 264
    The Case of Corn Flakes 266
    The Result of Seichi's Study of College Football in Japan 267
    Reference 269
    Chapter Thirteen Case Study Quiz 271

Chapter Fourteen
Mass Media Exposure:
Use, Negative Effects, and Theoretical Explanations 275
Stacy L. Smith and Aaron R. Boyson

    Defining Mass Communication and Types of Effects 275
    Patterns of Media Use 278
    Negative Effects 281
    Theoretical Explanations 286
    Conclusions 288
    References 288
    Chapter Fourteen Case Study Quiz 293

Chapter Fifteen
Learning from the Mass Media 297
Charles K. Atkin

    What Do People Learn from the News Media? 298
    What Is the Impact of Political Campaigns? 302
    Do Public Service Information Campaigns Work? 304
    Is Educational Programming Educational? 305
    Which People Learn the Most? 307
    How Can You Learn More from the Informational Media? .. 309
    References 311
    Chapter Fifteen Case Study Quiz 313

Chapter Sixteen
The Art of Speaking in Public 317
Monique M. Turner, Lisa L. Massi Lindsey, Leslie M. Deatrick

    Research 320
    Toulmin Model of Argumentation 324
    Speech Considerations 325
    A Guide to Informative Speaking 333
    A Guide to Persuasive Speaking 334
    Monroe's Motivated Sequence 336
    Organizing a Speech 338
    Delivering a Speech 346
    Cross-Examination 354
    Post Speech 354
    Speech Types 355
    Into the World You Go 358
    References 358

Workbook
*Leslie M. Deatrick, Alysa A. Lucas, Lisa L. Massi Lindsey
and Monique M. Turner* 359

    Homework Assignments 361
    Speech Materials 369
        Informative Speech: Tell Us about Your Major 369
        Persuasive Speech: Support My Cause 377
    Working toward Good Study Habits 385
    Key Terms/Concepts 389
    Chapter Exercises 397
    Section Leader Activity Profile Evaluation 427
        Midterm 427
        End of Semester 429

Foreword

This book is all about communicating and connecting. Connecting goes beyond communicating. If communication is the exchange of information, connecting is much more comprehensive. Computers communicate, and people connect. You will read much more about this definition in the first chapter; but this book is about people communicating, and what they use communication to do.

This book would not be possible without the efforts of so many people. We would like to thank the authors for their contributions. They gave their time to this project so that the proceeds for this book could be donated to a fund supporting graduate education at Michigan State University. We would also like to thank Tim Holl for the work he put into designing the cover. Finally, thank you to the many students who provided feedback on the first edition of this textbook which proved very useful in the preparation of the second.

Chapter One

INTRODUCING COMMUNICATION FUNCTIONS

William A. Donohue
Michigan State University

THE COMMUNICATION CHALLENGE

Much of my research focuses on intense conflict situations. How would you react in these contexts?

- A bank robber has just taken three hostages in the course of a robbery event to avoid capture by the police. The bank is surrounded. You have been called by police to negotiate with the hostage taker for the release of the hostages and for the person to give up and come out peacefully.

- A husband and wife are fighting about the custody of their children. They are going though a very painful divorce. The judge has requested that the couple try to mediate their differences with a court appointed mediator. You have been asked by the judge to step in and mediate the dispute so the couple can create a custody agreement they can live with.

- Two ethnic groups in the Middle East are fighting over land and religions freedom. The issues are unclear, the emotions are high, and violence is imminent. You are selected as the chief negotiator for the United States and must decide how to intervene, if at all, and how to structure a plan that secures your interests while decreasing the threat of violence.

These are some of the actual communication challenges that I have assumed over the years. In each case, all the negotiator or mediator has to offer are strategies and tactics capable of facilitating communication between the parties. The hostage negotiator must calm the robber, keep the person talking, and seek a remedy in everyone's interests. The divorce mediator must encourage each party to understand the issues dividing them, overcome their emotions, and develop a custody plan in the child's best interests. The international negotiator must work to understand the needs of both parties and craft an agreement capable of diffusing war while building a sustaining peace. Here are some principles that guide my work in conflict:

1. **Respect.** I always approach these challenges with respect. I recognize that these parties have a great deal of power to control the outcomes, and I respect that

power. When I think something or someone has power to influence my life, I respect it, or suffer the consequences.

2. **Preparation.** Because I respect the individuals and their power, I try to continuously learn how best to approach them. I acquire the skills necessary to harness the power and the confidence that comes with acquiring the skills. I am motivated to learn because I respect the challenge of these situations.

3. **Control.** The essence of communicating is control, or the ability to function within predictable boundaries. I continuously seek out strategies capable of reducing emotion and encouraging problem solving. I have learned to approach all conflict situations by first listening to others, being aware of their non-verbals, avoiding the need to become defensive, and above all, understanding all parties' needs. When do I fail? Failure happens when negotiators push parties inappropriately and the parties get out of control. Remember the last argument or fight you had. Chances are you neglected to listen and just yelled. You failed to respect the communication process, so you crashed and burned.

THE ESSENCE OF COMMUNICATING

Many experts cite communication as central to success in careers and relationships. For example, business leaders are convinced that communication is their primary business challenge and the key to success. If internal communication shows poor coordination and control, businesses fail to respond to customer needs. Leadership is a similar problem. Think of all the great leaders you revere. Each is probably a powerful communicator that really made you believe in him or her.

No matter what career you select, from engineering to medicine to social work, you must know how to communicate your thoughts. Technical skills are useless unless you have the ability to share them. It is no wonder that verbal ability (writing and speaking skills) is the number one predictor of success in college and career.

Communication is also central to achieving a fulfilling personal life. You will read about marriage in upcoming chapters, and how communication contributes to its success or failure. Since over 90% of college students eventually get married, understanding something about communication can make this mountain less intimidating. You see, that's our key point. Communication skills help individuals face the challenges in their lives. Look at the three principles once again:

Respect. Most students take their careers, and hopefully, their personal lives, very seriously. They respect the power of the rewarding career and solid relationships to make them happy and successful. This respect motivates them to prepare for these challenges. For example, consider the problem of survival in America's urban streets. Elijah Anderson wrote in the May, 1994 *Atlantic Monthly* about what it takes to survive in the streets. He talks about the psychology of respect in which survival on the streets depends upon knowing how to act tough. He defines a set of rules, or codes, that all street residents use to know how to gain respect for being tough and skilled. Weakness is exploited, and strength is always challenged. Above all, street players must respect the code to simply walk down the street and live to tell about it. Underestimate the code and suffer the consequences.

Preparation. What skills do you need to be productive? We have already made the case for communication as a central skill. The remaining chapters reinforce the value of communication in accomplishing many of life's most basic necessities: satisfying relationships, productive work groups, and effective organizations. But, do you really believe that? Do you respect the power of communication to make or break success in accomplishing these necessities? Most people have trouble respecting it because they feel they don't need to improve their skills. After all, they have been communicating for many years. Why prepare for something you already know how to do?

Elijah Anderson is very clear about the role communication plays in surviving on the streets. Those skilled in communication survive. They know how to act tough and send the right message at the right time. The unskilled are generally exploited and/or killed. They don't know how to communicate the tough self-image that acts as their "juice," or currency, or protection. Jackets, sneakers, gold jewelry, and other valued things are what people use to shore up their identity. In other words, the street wise person must always communicate their identity, whether through words or things, to survive; however, these skills are not learned overnight. Street players practice the street code from infancy on to prepare them for their adolescent years when they must master the code for survival. While this situation may be extreme for most students, the point is relevant for all students. Preparation is essential for control.

Control. Once you have acquired the skills, you can begin to extract what you need from your environment. The street player extracts respect from his or her peers. More preparation and more skill means more control and the ability to succeed. The same is true for the prepared communicator. This person is more persuasive in meetings, more likely to find depth and honesty in relationships, and more capable of leading others to action.

In my research on hostage negotiation, I found that a key element to success for negotiators is not allowing the hostage taker to rattle them. Typically, a hostage situation begins very emotionally. The hostage taker rants and raves and makes all kinds of demands early on. Challenging these demands right away does not force the hostage taker to back down. Quite the contrary is true. The hostage taker becomes even more angry and firm in the face of this opposition. The hostage negotiator is trained (prepared) to listen and understand, not to challenge and confront. Anyone's uncontrolled instinct is to just say "no" right away and confront the other immediately. Staying in control is necessary to calm the hostage taker and begin bargaining for the release of the hostages. The same is true for you. Staying in control when you get really mad will help you solve the problem without making it worse.

Respect, preparation, and control work together. If you disrespect communication or take it for granted, you will view preparation as unimportant. At that point, you will risk losing control. Respect your challenges, prepare to confront them, and learn to control how others respond to you. These constitute our goals. We seek to prepare your communication skills to increase your control. Preparation begins by learning some of the basic principles of communication.

WHAT IS COMMUNICATION?

Connection

The essence of communicating is **connection.** When people communicate, they want to interconnect their minds. They seek to plant ideas and thoughts into one anothers' heads. As you read these pages, I am putting my thoughts into words. And, I hope to connect with you so that you receive and understand my ideas as I intended, and perhaps want to read more. If I don't connect with you, my thoughts will get lost, and our communication will break down.

To illustrate the importance of connecting, in one of the hostage negotiations I've studied, a husband and wife team hijacked a bus shortly after it began a long trip west. You're probably asking why anyone would hijack a bus. After all, what are you going to do with a bus? This couple hijacked it to get media attention. The male believed he was the Second Coming of Christ. No one believed him, or would pay attention to him, so he hijacked the bus knowing that the media would follow the story closely. I certainly don't mean to imply that the couple was psychologically disturbed because of their religious convictions; however, this couple had a history of psychological problems.

To complicate matters, the hijacker believed that, on the day of the hijacking, he was exactly the same age as Christ when He was crucified. So, the hijacker needed to be killed by the police (as Christ had been killed) that day so he could be resurrected in three days to prove his identity. He wanted the media present to videotape the resurrection. His wife fully supported her husband's efforts. The police tried talking to the hijacker, but they were not totally successful in connecting with him. Clearly, he was in his own little world, suffering from a fairly severe psychological disorder.

After about 20 minutes of negotiating, the police connected with him enough to persuade him to release all the hostages on the bus. After the release, the police tried to persuade him that he was not Christ, and that he should give up, but the hijackers would not listen. Thus, the hijackers emerged from the bus and started firing at the police. They returned the fire, wounding the couple. The couple then committed suicide.

What's remarkable about this episode is the inability of the police to connect with the hijackers who were in great psychological distress. Sure, the police persuaded the hijacker to release the hostages; but the police could not get inside the hijacker's head to communicate the absurdity and finality of his position. Of course, the hijackers could not get inside the police officers' heads to convey that he was Christ. The hijacker simply refused to see that he was going to die; the police refused to see that he was Christ. When you can't get through to someone, it means you have failed to connect.

Connecting means influencing one another's attitudes, values, and behaviors through information exchange. Let's look at each one of these elements more closely:

Influence. Influence means change. When you really connect with someone, you change their attitudes (what they like or don't like), values (what they believe is important), and behaviors. You might strengthen or weaken familiar ways of thinking and acting, or you might move them in a different direction, but when you connect, you exercise some kind of influence over these elements of the other's thinking. When the other connects with you, that person changes your thinking, as well. Continuous communication means constant connection and mutual influence.

Information Exchange. You exercise this mutual influence through information exchange. Information is nothing more than some kind of recognizable pattern to which you attach meaning. Anything can be information as long as you attach meaning to it. The more patterns you recognize the more information you perceive.

Most of the time we communicate using language, whether it is the formal verbal sort represented by the

4 Chapter One

page you're reading, or the nonverbal kind known as body language. As you understand more languages, you become capable of attaching meaning to more patterns. Thus, language is symbolic. Each recognized pattern of information stands for, or symbolizes something else. The word "pig" stands for the muddy pink animal in the barnyard. When the word "pig" is used normally in a sentence, it becomes a meaningful symbol for you. Perhaps you now understand the phrase, "Language is our communication tool box." Through symbols, we exchange meaningful patterns of information and start the communication process rolling. We will discuss language more in Chapter 2. In general, we can conclude that communication takes place when parties exchange recognizable patterns (usually linguistic symbols) that mutually influence one another.

Can we say that the hijacker and police negotiator "communicated" with one another? Certainly, they were exchanging information. Each understood what the other was saying. Words were coming from one anothers' lips. Regarding the issue of giving up, they were talking past one another. They were not connecting. A simple act of information exchange is not sufficient to say that communication has taken place. When messages are sent and received as intended, yet fail to influence the communicators, then communication has not taken place.

To summarize, communication has four important elements:

1. Influence: the altering of one anothers' attitudes, values, and behaviors
2. Information exchange: the sending and receiving of messages
3. Meaning: the recognition and interpretation of patterns
4. Symbolic language: the system of meaningful patterns we use to communicate

The Power of Connection

These four elements have very important implications for you. When you give your presentations in class, words may come from your lips. However, if all you do is move your lips without trying to connect with the audience, you will not communicate with them. You must move them! Keep them interested in your talk. Be a force for change in their lives. Is this too difficult? I have learned time and time again that people fail as communicators because they simply go through the motions of getting the words out. They don't really try to connect with their audience. They don't try to move them.

Let's take a historical look at the power of using symbols for connection. Note these examples of how symbols and language contributed to significant changes in civilization.

The Birth of Language. The first recorded use of symbols for communication is found in cave drawings. Dated at about 25,000 BC, nomadic tribes made cave drawings of animals, some of which specified the best way to hunt and kill the animals. These drawings marked a great leap forward for humanity because they were the first known attempt to preserve technology through symbols. Certainly, oral language developed before these drawings, but the drawings demonstrated that humans were symbol-using creatures, and capable of advancing their civilization.

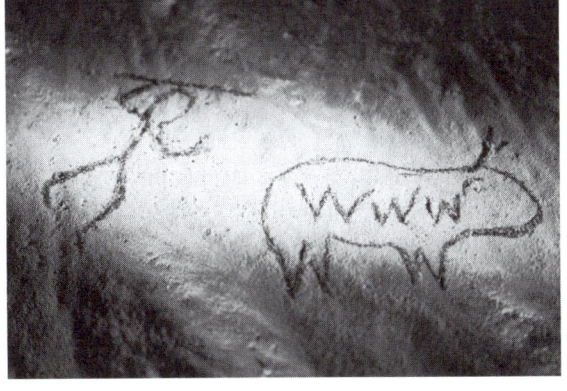

The Birth of the Written Word. An equally significant human event is the birth of the first known abstract language, Sanskrit, which dates back to about 10,000 BC. Around this period in history, humans began domesticating animals. This practice represented a very significant turning point for civilization. It meant that people no longer needed to roam the earth nomadically. They could pick a place, grow crops, and raise animals; however, this move required a lot more organization than nomadic life in which one eats what one gathers. Language is needed to store the kind of complex knowledge necessary to advance the civilization. Again, language marks a turning point in civilization.

The Birth of Mass Communication and the Nation-State. While advances in language progressed through the centuries, the western world's political landscape changed significantly with Gutenberg's invention of the printing press in 1450 in Germany. Prior to the printing press, documents were duplicated very slowly by hand, making mass communication impossible. Politically, nations as we know them today did not exist. City-states and kings dominated the political landscape because people could not communicate efficiently from village to village. The printing press changed all that. The newspapers brought villages together to form nations as people began to learn about their shared interests in culture, defense, and commerce.

The Global Village. If newspapers brought villages together, the invention of the telegraph in 1856 brought nations together. The telegraph started the electronic communication revolution. Two days after the telegraph linked the Atlantic and Pacific coasts, the Pony Express went out of business. Soon thereafter, Marconi invented wireless communication in the form of radio waves. Television quickly followed, and today we have the information highway that links the world. The ability to connect with people all over the globe significantly shrinks our world. I can communicate electronically through mail or teleconference with anyone around the world, almost as easily as I can talk to my neighbor. Make your own judgments about whether or not this means real progress, but there is no doubt that changes in communication mean big changes in civilization.

Your Personal Growth. From this historical interlude we learn that changes in communication mean changes in relationships, groups, cultures, and civilizations. In your own life, learn to control the changes by controlling the communication process. If you don't respect the communication process, and ignore its capabilities, you will suffer the consequences of letting the process control you. I see people all day long who underestimate the role of communication in their personal success. Until they lift that burden, their progress will certainly be slow.

Let me give you an example of how communication shapes who you are. I recently counseled a student who was having a very difficult time preparing her presentation, as she was afraid the other students in the class would reject her. She did not want to take the risk of getting up in front of people. As she began to reveal a little of her background, I discovered that she frequently experienced rejection by others. Because she did not feel attractive, she believed that people did not accept her or even like her. From these communication experiences, she developed a weak self-concept. She did not like herself. She felt inadequate.

So, I told her, "The first step toward a better self-concept is to improve your communication with others. As you speak more confidently, people will respond positively to you. Then, you will feel better about yourself, which builds confidence. Talk like a winner, and people will respond to you that way." Again, control the process, and learn to succeed. She took this advice to heart and delivered a great presentation. She really asserted herself. She commanded respect and people gave it to her.

Growth for Society. Society also benefits from more controlled communication. I work in many communities struggling with substance abuse and violence-related challenges. These communities are forming coalitions of individuals committed to change. They connect with each other and with community leaders and neighborhood groups, researchers, and others to help design and implement action plans to improve their communities. Connecting on a large-scale basis allows them to make better and faster decisions.

HOW DOES COMMUNICATION WORK?

I hope I have connected with you to the extent that you respect the process of communication and want to begin preparing yourself to learn to control it. Toward that end, let's look more closely at how the basic communication system works. First, we'll look at the components of the system, and then explore how it functions.

Elements of the System

The Communicators. We typically focus first on the individuals doing the communicating. As communicators everyone possesses certain qualities that affect how and what they communicate. First, consider the communicator's goals and intentions. Each of us wants to accomplish something with our communication. We might be fully aware of our intentions, or we might not know the specific reason we are talking. For example, you might call someone to persuade him or her to attend the theater with you. That call represents a specific intention or goal. While at the theater you might engage in small talk that has no apparent purpose other than just getting to know one another.

Second, all communicators possess various psychological orientations that help them filter information they receive, and structure messages they send. For example, everyone holds attitudes that define what each person likes and dislikes. I like classic rock and roll, and you might hate it. People also hold cultural values that define what they find important or unimportant. I value honesty, sincerity, and hard work—how boring. But, that's what I value, and that defines me as a typical American, I suppose.

What cultural values do you have? These values are typically reflected in your language. For example, what terms do you use to refer to someone of the opposite sex? These terms reflect values for physical attractiveness, and communicate to others that you value these individual characteristics.

Every time we receive or send information we use our filters (attitudes and values) to screen what we see or say. A less positive term for "filters" is "biases." What are your biases? Are you biased against certain people, religions, or cultural ceremonies? Or, are you aware of your biases and try to keep an open mind. The first step toward better control is understanding your biases and how they influence how you receive and send information.

The Channels. The second element of the communication system is the channel through which you communicate. The channel is the method you use to communicate. You use many channels throughout the day. For example, you might call someone on the phone. You might send a friend a letter. You could electronically mail someone a memo. If you were a television star, you could say "hi" to your mom using television. All of these methods for communicating are different channels.

Channels have two important characteristics. They are either broad, or narrow. Broad channels carry a lot of information, whereas narrow channels carry much less information. A channel is broad if it involves most of your five senses. For example, face-to-face communication has the potential of being very broad because you can see, hear, touch, kiss (if that is appropriate), and smell the other person. Five pieces of information are available to evaluate the communicators and their messages. A very narrow channel may involve only one sense, and do so on a very limited basis. A written message gives only visual, symbolic information. A written message with a picture attached broadens the channel. A phone call involves only your hearing. A phone call with visuals broadens the channel.

Most people control their channels very strategically. You might be too nervous to ask someone out on a date using face-to-face communication. You would rather do it over the phone so they can't see you sweat or be nervous. Some people break up with people they have dated with a letter because they do not want to allow for any exchange of information and risk a big argument. Channel manipulation is especially crucial in public health campaigns. What channels should health professionals use to persuade young people to engage in safe sex or wear safety belts while driving? Research will identify channels people prefer when receiving information. If you try to send information to people through a channel they do not use, or if you select a channel that inappropriately fits the message, your communication will most likely fail.

The Messages. Most people understand the need to manipulate messages to accomplish their goals. There are two main features of messages that are important to understand in controlling them. First, communicators must pay attention to the verbal and nonverbal aspects of their messages. The verbal part of the message consists of words themselves, while the nonverbal part consists of the emphasis placed on those words. Sending a note to someone saying, "I love you," contains important verbal information but little nonverbal information indicating how you really feel. The note could add nonverbal emphasis by adding an exclamation point, "I love you!" Or, you could add even more emphasis by selecting a face-to-face channel and holding the person tightly and saying "I love you," in a deep and sincere voice. Many aspects of a message can modify it and change its meaning. What if you said to someone in a casual voice, "I love you," while you were also looking at your watch? Those nonverbals say, "I don't really love you, I'm just saying that." Controlling your communication means controlling both the verbal and nonverbal dimensions of the message.

Second, communicators should also focus on the content and relational aspects of their messages. The content is the topic or substance of the message. For example, the content of this message is a discussion about messages. The content of an invitation to the theater is the invitation itself. The relational aspect of the message consists of information about what the sender believes is true about the relationship between the communicators. The sender may be the boss and want to communicate a superior relationship. Or, the sender might want to create an informal relationship with the other person.

For example, consider these two methods the boss uses to ask her assistant for a cup of coffee. The content aspect of the message stays the same, but the relational part changes. See if you can tell how it changes.

1. Get me a cup of coffee as soon as possible.
2. If you're going over to the coffee machine and have the time, could you please get me a cup of coffee?

Both statements have the same content goal: the boss wants a cup of coffee. However, the two statements communicate very different relational messages. Notice

8 Chapter One

that the first request almost requires the person to act. It is a very short and directive statement. It assumes that the boss has the right to make the request and is reinforcing her superior position. The second request is very indirect and seeks to treat the person more as an equal rather than as an assistant. The first statement draws attention to the relationship. The second statement does not make a big deal about the relationship. How do you vary the relational messages in your greetings? What's the difference between "Hey babe, what's happenin'," and, "Good morning, sir." Both are greetings, yet they send very different relational messages.

The Noise. Any communication system carries noise in it. Noise is interference. It consists of anything that might impede or prevent communicators from freely exchanging information. For example, my wife often wants me to tell other people long jokes at parties. Parties are too noisy for long jokes. People just will not pay attention to long jokes at parties. Conversations at parties are short, so short jokes are more appropriate given all the interference present at a typical party.

Perhaps you can think of many different forms of noise or interference in communication. Advertisers worry about noise affecting the receiver's understanding of their messages. They try to include elements in their messages that enhance the main message and don't distract from it. Information that distracts from the main message can be labeled noise. For example, some commercials on TV are very funny, but people have trouble remembering the product. The humor becomes "noise" for the message.

Some interesting research has been conducted to test the effect of noise on the persuasiveness of messages. Are messages more or less persuasive when receivers are distracted by noise so they can't hear the whole message? Most of these studies were conducted by having subjects view videotaped commercials for products that they disliked, and then asking them to evaluate the products after the commercials. While the commercials were playing, one group was exposed to some distracting noises while the other group received no distracting noise.

Which group was more persuaded by the commercials? The group that received the noise was significantly more persuaded. Why is noise persuasive here? It worked because the noise prevented the receivers from concentrating on, or thinking about the reasons why they did not like the product in the first place. The no-noise group was free to think about the bad features of the product. This is not to say that noise is always an effective communication device. When you simply want to inform someone about an idea, noise can hinder the accurate receipt of the message. It is important to understand when noise is effective and when it is not. Again, controlling communication also means controlling the noise level.

The Impact. Messages can have very significant or very insignificant impacts. Some scholars in communication use what they call the "Memorable Message" research methodology. The method asks people to recall memorable messages that had a big impact on them. For example, do you remember a really important piece of advice your parents gave you as a teenager?

I remember the most memorable words of wisdom my father gave me one day while we were watching a group of boaters, trying to pull their boats ashore on their trailers just

Introducing Communication Functions 9

as a big storm was breaking. They were smashing into each other, despite our efforts at helping, and the boaters were yelling at each other in ordinarily religious language. I asked my father why these people did not see the storm coming and take precautions. He criticized their lack of knowledge about safe boating, and indicated that these people were doomed to crisis because of their ignorance and lack of respect for the lake. What he told me was, "What you don't have in your head, you better have in your behind." In other words, when you do something stupid you better be strong or rich enough to pay the consequences. That message had a great deal of impact on me and has stuck with me for a long time. I'm sure you keep memorable messages in your heads that have had a big impact on you.

Communications can have many impacts. They can inform or entertain people, or persuade or deter people from doing something. They can incite emotions to make people laugh, cry, or get mad. You will learn a great deal about how communication influences people in the social influence chapter. Soft drink manufacturers are very savvy about this impact issue. They know that to persuade people to buy their products they must arouse their emotions in the product; let's face it, pop is basically boring. Recall the Mountain Dew commercial featuring a bike rider chasing a cheetah, catching it, and pulling a Dew from its throat! Emotional arousal is the key to persuasion in the soda-pop product category and advertisers know it. Research tells a great deal about what kinds of messages are most likely to have the intended impact on the audience.

The point here is that, controlling communication means having a CLEAR idea about what goals you want to accomplish with your communication. Many people fail because they do not really know what impact they want their communications to achieve.

Context. Communication always takes place within some kind of context: the context for our communication at this moment is this book, and the environment within which you are reading it. Maybe you got a traffic ticket just prior to reading this chapter. You are upset and that is affecting your attention to these words. In face-to-face communication the context of the interaction changes all the time. Someone tells a funny story, and suddenly others jump in with their stories, too. At another moment, a different person tells a tragic story, and the funny stories seem less appropriate.

Sometimes the rules of the context require you to be very polite, and other times the rules ask you to party hearty. Rules are expectations of appropriate and inappropriate behavior, and the conditions under which those behaviors are expected to be prohibited. You can think of contexts as sets of rules for behavior. When you came to college, you might not have known all the rules of the game. How should I act with my roommate? What kind of classroom rules are expected here? When should I approach people and be friendly? You learn these rules and expectations after you spend time in the context. The rules change all the time, but some remain fairly stable. Controlling your communication means understanding the rules and how to operate within them, and maybe stretch them from time to time.

I recall a hostage incident in which the hostage taker was shooting drugs during the standoff. The person was sometimes lucid and sometimes ranting incoherently. The police had difficulty with this person because the context, and then the rules, changed so frequently. They could not predict how the hostage taker might interpret one of their comments. They needed the situation to stabilize so they could learn the rules, and increase their ability to predict the behavior of the hostage taker. Bargaining with someone in a crisis situation requires a lot of predictability; crazy behavior makes that difficult. Rules act as road signs to help guide communication behavior. When people don't know, or can't read the signs, communication is very difficult.

Culture. Finally, culture is a very significant dimension of the communication process. All behavior takes place from some kind of cultural perspective. Culture consists of the shared values individuals express. Asian countries are typically viewed as collectivistic whereas Western countries are seen as being very individualistic. People in collectivistic countries value group identity over individual identity. An individual would never think of doing something that might make that person stand out in the group. Group harmony is most important. In individualistic cultures, such as the United States, we value individual success over group success. We give more weight to individual sports statistics, and pay players accordingly. We think someone is successful professionally when he or she stands out from the crowd.

We will learn a great deal about culture as we move further into this book. It is essential for everyone to understand cultural biases because they influence our interpretation and production of messages. More importantly, successful communicators understand the culture of the people with whom they are communicating. For example, health campaigns aimed at teens are difficult for public health officials because the officials are always much older. They do not relate to the teen cultures and how to communicate within them, so most of these campaigns fail. As indicated above, cultural values are very significant information filters and should never be underestimated.

System Functioning

Illustrated here is a basic model of the communication process. The model depicts face-to-face communication between two individuals.

FIGURE 1.1 The Communication Process

Communicator A:
Goals, Attitudes, Values

Noise
Message Exchange
Noise

Communicator B:
Goals, Attitudes, Values

Communication Context

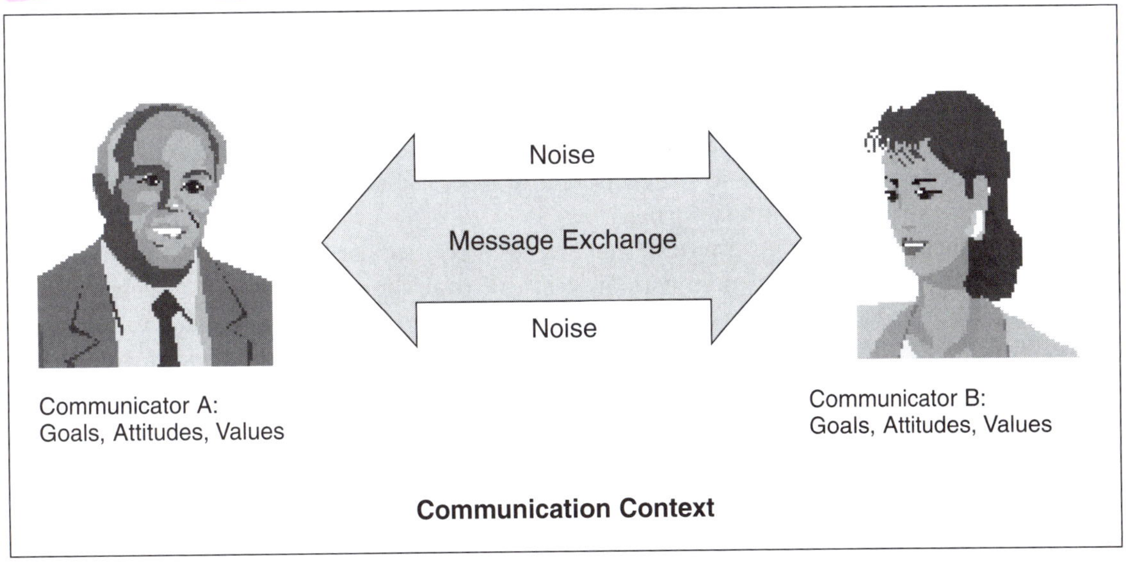

In this picture, two individuals are exchanging messages. Each person always uses his or her filters when listening to another person, or creating a message that seeks to accomplish a goal. The important point here is that each person MUST understand, or at least recognize the other's goals, attitudes, and values to communicate meaningfully. Never assume you know everything about a person because of that person's social or

cultural affiliations. Each person is unique and MUST be approached as unique. What does the person want? What does she value? What does she like? Ask these kinds of questions continuously.

For example, look at the people in the picture. If you wanted to communicate with the man on the right what assumptions would you make about him? Culturally, he may have some kind of African heritage. We might assume that he is an African American, particularly if we heard him speak using one of many African American dialects. What kind of social assumptions might you make about him? He seems well dressed with a conservative hair style, and almost "business-like" in appearance. Should we then approach him more formally in keeping with his apparent conservative orientation? Certainly, we must make reasonable assumptions about people. But if we go too far and rely only on superficial stereotypes, we run the risk of not connecting with people.

As you think about your message, you quickly predict its likely impact. Will the person be offended or delighted? Is the language I want to use appropriate for this person and this situation? Will we like each other more or less after communicating? If the answers are consistent with your goals, you deliver the message, and begin reading the nonverbal behavior of the other person. "Is my message being received as I predicted?" you might ask. If not, most people typically adjust their messages based on this feedback. Have you ever stopped yourself in mid-sentence because the other person looked puzzled or angry about your comment?

After a number of exchanges you begin to gain a sense of whether or not your messages are having their intended impact. Unfortunately, noise can negatively affect your intended impact. You might need to adjust your message or try another time. I recently consulted with a company that exhibited significant communication problems. None of the employees were receiving the boss' messages. It turned out that the middle managers were filtering the information so much that few people below them received the information. Noise can come in many forms.

When parties interact for a while, they create a context, or situation that is unique to that place and time. Successful salespeople know that the rules people develop while communicating are very informal and flexible. They can be shaped to suit your goals. Salespeople often tell jokes or other stories to make a formal sales-call situation more informal and comfortable so people will open up. They know how to shape contexts quickly and effectively.

Finally, culture becomes part of this context-shaping process. As groups of people bond together for long periods, they develop interaction customs and rituals. A custom is a standard way of communicating, or performing any behavior. A ritual is a standard practice that takes on a kind of spiritual significance. Some of the most notable customs people develop include unique languages, patterns of dress, art, religion, and mating. You must keep track of so many customs and rituals as you interact in a culture. And, still more complicated is that everyone must be multicultural. We live in national and regional cultures, city and neighborhood cultures, and work and home cultures. Each is formed through communication, and each shapes the way we interpret and form messages.

WHY DO CONNECTIONS FAIL?

The remaining chapters in this book seek to help you avoid failure. They give you the background to know how to connect with others to reduce failure. No one is ever completely communicatively successful. It is impossible to accomplish all of your goals all of the time. There are some smart things you can do to improve your chances of success. Remember, preparation improves control.

Failure to Understand

The first, and perhaps most common reason connections fail is one person not understanding another. We live in a superficial world that values speed, and quality takes a back seat. It is easier to stereotype someone rather than listen to that person and understand him or her as a unique individual.

I recently talked to a student who complained of not connecting with her father. She felt he did not understand her values, or even know her very well. I asked about their communication patterns and she reported that her father frequently tried to dominate her. He argued about everything and seldom asked her questions or sought her input on ideas. It was a classic case of perceived listening failure. The woman perceived that her father did not listen to her or respect her point of view. He simply dominated her. I asked why he might do that. She replied that he spoke to many women, particularly her mother, that way. I felt sad that something as simple as listening to someone could create these relational distances.

Was the father responding to his daughter as a female and not a person? Does he listen to men better than women? Does he dismiss the opinions of young people? Does he believe that children have little or nothing of importance to say? What are your biases in this regard? How well can you reduce your biases and respond to someone as an individual? This is a difficult task, but so many communications fail to connect because people fail to understand one another. Ask yourself about the person's values, and their knowledge about the subject? Where are they now? Where do you want them to go? You must ask the first question before you can answer the second.

Message Failure

Many messages fail because they are the wrong message for the wrong people at the wrong time. As we shall see in later chapters, successful messages must:

1. **Have realistic content and relational objectives.** Don't try to do too much too fast. If political campaign experts want to persuade voters to support a candidate from a party the voter detests, they typically first try an interim step. They try to soften support for the party so the voters will be more neutral. Neutral voters are easier to persuade than voters committed to the opponent. Failure to form realistic objectives often makes messages fail.

2. **Be targeted to specific individuals or groups.** As we suggested above, the more information you know about the other communicator, the better you can tailor your message to that person. So many campaigns fail because they do not target their message properly. For example, I recently attended a seminar in which the speaker was describing a campaign to persuade poor, rural farmers in South

Africa to use condoms. The rural farmers in this country were generally illiterate because they were not permitted to become educated. Yet, the campaign relied heavily on brochures and written signs that the people could not read. The medium of communication was not tailored to the audience's needs.

3. **Be sensitive to context and culture.** So often a message is targeted properly, but it is delivered at the wrong time. The context simply will not support the message. In one hostage situation, a group of Cubans held in a US prison rioted because the Secretary of State said the Cubans had to go back to Cuba. They rioted to stay in the US prison since prison conditions in the US were better than prison conditions in Cuba. They took several hostages during the riot. The second day of the riot, the Secretary announced that he would not deport any Cubans after all, hoping this would end the riot; however, the riot gained a life of its own, and the Cubans wanted more. The message was not suited to the context and it failed to connect with the prisoners. But, after several days, rioting took its toll on the Cubans, and they ultimately agreed to the negotiator's final offer. The offer was nothing more than what the Secretary offered on the second day—a right to stay in the US. After several days, they were ready to hear the message, but they had not been ready to hear it on the second day.

In this situation, the negotiators failed to analyze the prisoners, the context, and the noise evident in the information exchange. The chaos and noise associated with the riot made negotiations difficult. The cultural and identity needs of the Cubans were also neglected. Generally, this kind of violence means that communication and connections have failed. Lack of communicative control often leads to loss of social control.

CONCLUSIONS

This book is about connections. It seeks to answer some very important questions about how to use connections to improve your communicative control. To accomplish this goal, we have divided each chapter into three sections:

Why Do We Connect?

What needs drive our connections? Humans must satisfy some very basic needs in connecting with one another. In subsequent chapters we will learn that people connect to form language. Language is the toolbox for communicating. Failure to connect as children makes language impossible to learn. We will also discuss connecting to develop social knowledge. Social knowledge is important to understanding how to communicate. Can you imagine trying to communicate in a place in which you had no knowledge of people, situations, rules, or events? Other chapters build on the observation that connection is needed to develop our self-concept. Who we are as individuals is an issue that underlies our ability to take risks, form relationships, and interact competently. Each chapter begins by defining and illustrating a need and exploring its dimensions.

How Do We Connect?

Each chapter identifies the processes that we go through to satisfy our needs. For example, we need to know what stages relationships go through as they develop.

Research in relational communication indicates that couples go through fairly definitive stages in the escalation and de-escalation of their relationships. It is important to know these stages because as you progress through them, you need to reflect on the stages. Are you in a stage that is appropriate to your needs? Or, have you escalated the relationship too far to be comfortable for you?

What Strategies Control Connections?

Finally, what strategies can we use to control how we connect? Research in communication provides many insights about more constructive strategies to help control your connection. For example, in the conflict chapter, you will learn how to move conflicts into more constructive interactions. One of the most troubling consequences of conflicts that escalate out of control is that parties often GET STUPID. The blood rushes from the thinking part of their brain to the "get even" emotional part of their brain. They get stupid and do things they later regret. I hope you avoid getting stupid and stay in control of yourself when in conflict.

Respect, Preparation, Control

Good luck reading this book. It has been enjoyable to construct. It represents our best attempt to bring you some general concepts to help prepare you for your future. If I did not feel so strongly about the role of communication in your future, I would not be so excited about this book. Writing has been a very personal challenge for me and all the authors contributing to this text. We hope you find it interesting as it prepares you for your future.

REFERENCES

Anderson, E. (1994). The code of the streets. *The Atlantic Monthly,* May, 80–110.
Donohue, W.A., & Roberto, A.J. (1993). Relational development as negotiated order in hostage negotiation. *Human Communication Research, 20,* 175–198.
Yates, J. (1989). *Control through communication: The rise of system in American management.* Baltimore: The Johns Hopkins University Press.
Zaleznik, A. (1989). *The managerial mystique: Restoring leadership in business.* New York: Harper & Row.

Chapter One Case Study Quiz— Communication Function

Instructions:

Please read the following case study carefully and select the best answers to the questions. This quiz is an individual assignment. Remember: sharing answers is a form of plagiarism.

It is a busy time at the university's library as the semester comes to an end and students begin to return library books in high volume. Extra employees are scheduled to work during peak times so that all the books can be checked in and shelved in the library. In the meantime, the supervisor of the Circulation department has changed a procedure for checking in books. Normally, when paperback books are checked in, they are sent to a division of the library that binds paperbacks with hard book covers. The new procedure is to separate paperback books ONLY if they are clearly damaged. The supervisor mentions this new procedure to one employee in passing during peak hours and asks that they deliver the information to the employees who check-in books. Erin has just arrived to her shift at the library and there are several bins of books that need to be checked in. The few paperback books she has in her bin, she sets aside to forward to the other division. As Erin delivers the paperback books, the Circulation supervisor pulls her aside and chastises her for not following the new procedure. When Erin explains that she was unaware of the new procedure, the supervisor chastises her again. Erin apologizes, returns to her desk and proceeds to create a sign indicating the procedure change so no other employees will make the same mistake.

Student's Name _____

Section Number _____

Section Leader's Name _____

Chapter One Case Study Quiz— Communication Function

1. This scenario offers an example of a supervisor intending to relay a new procedure to her employees during peak hours at the Library. This situation made it extremely difficult for the message to be understood because of the _____.
    a. Noise
    b. Culture
    c. Symbolism
    d. Context

2. The supervisor was communicating a message face-to-face to Erin. In this case, face-to-face serves as the:
    a. Channel
    b. Message
    c. Noise
    d. Communicator

3. The supervisor was trying to influence the employees':
    a. Attitudes
    b. Beliefs
    c. Behavior
    d. Values

4. In this case study, there is message failure. The supervisor intended that Erin learn about the new task and then pass along the information to other employees, but this did not happen. Why did this message fail?
    a. The message did not have realistic content
    b. The message was not targeted to specific groups or individuals
    c. The supervisor was not sensitive to the context
    d. All of the above

5. All of the following are important elements of communication EXCEPT:
    a. Influence
    b. Symbolic language
    c. Respect
    d. Information exchange

Case Study **19**

Chapter Two

LANGUAGE AND MEANING

Laura E. Drake
University of Maryland

The movie *Nell* features Jodie Foster as an adult who speaks a bizarre and unintelligible language. Growing up in the woods of North Carolina, Nell was socially isolated and had known only her mother and twin sister her entire life. She had never met a man or woman from the "outside" world. She lived in a rustic cabin with no running water or electricity. With both her family members now deceased, Nell was "discovered" by law enforcement officials and a doctor (Liam Neeson). Nell rejected their efforts to communicate with her. Her moans, screams, and physical force frightened them and they worried about her health and safety. A consultant speech pathologist (Natasha Richardson) assumed Nell's wild behaviors and idiosyncratic speech meant Nell had been abused, perhaps even tortured, as a child.

The doctor is intrigued by Nell's seemingly irrational behavior and inability to communicate, especially when contrasted with her competence in daily chores like cooking and chopping wood. Therefore, he blocks the speech pathologist's attempt to forcibly commit Nell to a psychiatric hospital. Instead, the physician and speech pathologist study Nell in her own environment and eventually de-code much of Nell's language. "Arna" means big. "Messa" means little. "Evede" means evil-doers. They discover that Nell is a highly intelligent and loving person, perfectly capable of caring for herself. Their problem lies in convincing officials, researchers, journalists, and nosy townspeople, who assume Nell is developmentally delayed or mentally ill. Using the doctor as an interpreter, Nell finally stands up for herself. In court, she explains in Nell-language that although she has lived a sheltered life and knows small things, she is not to be pitied. People in the big world know big things, but also have big problems. In comparison, Nell's worries are no worse than anyone else's.

This movie provides an excellent illustration of the vital functions language serves for human beings, as well as the pitfalls of our reliance on language as a tool for communication. Using the movie as a background, we will explore the characteristics of language, then describe what it does for us as communicators. We will then discuss the relationship between language and perception, in terms of gender and racial differences in language use. Finally, this chapter will offer ways to improve your effectiveness as a language-user and communicator.

WHAT IS LANGUAGE?

Language is a tool. Like most tools, language has multiple uses and functions. Humans use language to establish identities, form relationships, comfort others, persuade parents to loan out the car, or create team spirit and productive work environments. Perhaps the most important function of language is helping us make sense of the world. It is our means for interpreting events for others and sharing our ideas and feelings. You, as a student, depend on the properties of language for gaining knowledge. Language is the vehicle through which instructors and texts enlighten your view of the world by relaying their experiences and insights to you. As you learned in Chapter One, language is the primary means of connecting us with each other. Humans without social contact and healthy relationships are at risk for disease and early death. Therefore, we could think of language as a necessary, not just a convenient tool.

Language Is a Unique Communication System

Our ability to use language to accomplish tasks sets humans apart from other animals. While other species communicate, humans alone use language. Defleur, Kearney, and Plax (1993) describe a common romantic idea that humans can communicate with animals. Grizzly Adams was a movie character who kept a huge grizzly bear as his pet and could drink mountain water beside deer and other creatures. *Flipper* was a television show that centered on the relationship between two boys and a dolphin. The classic television show, *Lassie*, featured America's favorite collie rescuing humans from disaster. Most of us who have pets would not deny that communication takes place between pets and their owners; but animal communication systems differ in significant ways from human communication.

Many animals can use **inherited communication,** genetically determined patterns of behavior like those used by insects. Ants, bees, flies, and spiders are born with genetic codes for helping others of their kind find food or a mate. Their communication is the result of instinct. For example, we've all seen bees congregate over a trash bin filled with pungent scraps of barbecued chicken. Bees are initially attracted by the scent, then return to the hive and communicate the exact location and distance of a food source through movement patterns and the orientation of their bodies to the sun.

Other animals use **learned communication.** Through experience, they associate signs in the environment with events or meanings. They also develop ways to manipulate their own behavior to act as a sign to other animals or to people. For instance, birds do not produce the songs characteristic of their breed unless they hear other birds sing the song (Defleur et al., 1993). My dog, Suds, uses learned communication. We have a cowbell hung beside the back door. When she was a puppy, I always rang the bell prior to opening the door. Soon, I forced Suds to ring the bell with her nose. Following every ring of the bell, I pushed her outside. In only a few weeks, she learned to associate bell ringing with going out. Now she communicates to me by ringing the bell herself. In effect, she is "asking" to go out.

Suds also has learned words, like "dinner." Does this mean she can use language? Communication researchers argue no. A better explanation is that by the same associative process described above, she has learned that a particular sound pattern I make will always be followed by food. It's unlikely that she knows that the particular sound pattern, "dinner," refers to the food.

This unique ability to refer to objects, events, people, and ideas constitutes communicating via language, a symbol system put together according to rules. Humans, like animals, can use inherited and learned systems of communication. What sets us apart from insects and mammals is language—our ability to select symbols to represent the objects or ideas we want to share with others. Languages are as diverse as the people who use them. Not all languages employ words as symbols. Morse code is a language made up of short and long electronic buzzes, clicks, or flashes of light. Each set of long and short flashes represented a letter or word. Computer binary codes like ASC II are also languages. A series of 0's and 1's represents a letter, space, comma, and so on.

Language Is a "Game," Governed by Rules

Learning to use language, in many ways, resembles learning a game, like Tag, Monopoly, or Poker. Learning a new game can be difficult, confusing, or exhilarating as we master a complex set of rules and procedures. Once we've learned the game, we no longer think about the rules, at least not consciously. Instead we concentrate on strategy, "playing to win." Language is a game in the same ways. It has rules, norms, and principles for play. By the time we are adults, we internalize the rules and norms, so that they operate below our awareness. We may only become aware of the rules and norms when others violate them. Yet we may have difficulty explaining to violators why their language use is "wrong."

Rules. Language uses four sets of rules. The first is **phonemic** or sound rules. Phonemes are the sounds we produce for letters or groups of letters. In the English language, for example, we have 26 letters, but about 44 sounds. Communication practitioners in Speech Pathology help speakers correct the sounds they make, by diagnosing phonemic disturbances. Phonemic rules tell us that a letter makes different sounds, based on the letters preceding or following it. For example, the letter *c* in "ice" has a different sound than in the word "case." Phonics is a reading technique based on strategies for memorizing phonemic rules in ways that make reading easier.

FIGURE 2.1

Phonemics
Sound Rules
ice
case

Next, **semantic** rules refer to the meanings for sounds, words, or letters. The smallest unit of meaning in a language is called a **morpheme.** Morphemes can be very small, as in the case of prefixes and suffixes. These units of language have meaning because adding a particular prefix or suffix changes the meaning of a word. The word "call" can be changed by adding *-ed.* The word "called" now means that the calling occurred in the past. The prefix *dis-* changes the meaning of a word by negating it. "Dissatisfied" means that satisfaction did not occur.

FIGURE 2.2

Semantics
Sounds, Words, or Letters
dis + satisfied = dissatisfied
⊗ + ☺ = ⊗ or ☹

Most of us are so proficient with morphemes, we fail to realize how intricate and complicated semantic rules are. Think how difficult these rules can be for children and second language learners. They "know" some of the semantic rules of English, but sometimes apply morphemes incorrectly. They learn that "-ed" creates past tense. But with words like "go," children mistakenly say "goed." In this case semantic rules require not just a suffix, but an entirely different word, "went." Rules like this are seemingly endless. Examples like these should enhance your appreciation for the expertise you've gained in language use during your lifetime. The fact that you can understand what others mean and they can understand you is a major accomplishment.

General semantics is a division of communication theory devoted to diminishing misunderstandings between people. General semanticists argue that communication research should repair or prevent misunderstandings by discovering how words distort or complicate meanings. One of the techniques they advocate is adding "etc." to show our communication partner that we haven't said (and can never say) all there is to say about a topic. For example, "I've been having a lot of trouble at school, etc." tells the listener that your situation at school involves more feelings and worries than you're able to describe with words. Perhaps part of the problem is a class that's more difficult than you expected. Another problem may be your roommate. Still another part of the problem may be that you're overloaded. "Etc." acknowledges this multitude of meanings for "trouble at school."

Another general semantics technique is **indexing**, subscripting or dating words to show that their meanings can change over time. Indexing helps communicators avoid **static evaluations**, mistaken assumptions that people or things are consistent and never change. Everyday language encourages us to make static evaluations with words like "is." For example, "Mike is a jerk," "Larquetta is smart," and "Mel is shy." Each of these examples implies permanence. It is more accurate to realize that Mike can be a jerk, but other times can be very helpful. Larquetta may have terrific insights in philosophy, but know nothing about changing a tire. Mel may be shy around crowds, but a chatterbox with her closest friends. We can show this change by indexing: "Mike was a jerk," "Larquetta was smart," and "Mel was shy." While indexing may seem impractical for our everyday conversations, it alerts us to the fact that language can affect our perceptions of people, events, and objects.

A third set of rules exists for putting meanings together into coherent patterns—**syntax**. Like the other rules of language, syntactic rules are rarely noticed until we break them. If we're sitting down to dinner and I say, "Pass the please me salt," you'll recognize this as incorrect, even though my utterance has all the necessary elements of a correct sentence in the English language. Even when we can't analyze the mistake, we tend to see utterances like this one as incoherent, irrational, and nonsensical. If I keep it up, others may begin to question my mental state. Using language "properly" is the domain of our declarative social knowledge, as you will read in the chapter on social knowledge. We have expectations for situations and people, and language use is one way to meet those expectations. Just like the police and doctor who first discovered Nell, we typically feel uncomfortable, frightened, or worried around people who use language in unusual ways.

FIGURE 2.3

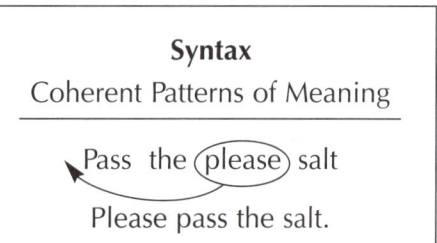

The final level of rules in language is **pragmatic**. Pragmatic rules describe how ordinary people use language to accomplish everyday tasks. For instance, if I want you to tell me the time, I might ask, "Do you know what time it is?" If you were wearing a watch and answered my question literally, you'd say "yes." I'd likely see your remark as sarcastic or inappropriate, because pragmatic rules should tell you that my question actually functions as a polite request that you "tell me the time."

FIGURE 2.4

Pragmatics

Use of Language

"Do you know what time it is?"

means

"Tell me the time."

Speech Act Theory explains the pragmatic rules for accomplishing such tasks as requests, commands, promises, questions, and compliments. Nofsinger (1991) writes that

24 Chapter Two

our knowledge of pragmatic rules allows us to determine when a question is merely a question and when it is, in fact, a request. There is an important difference between what we say, and what we do by what we say. Speech Acts are these "doings." That is, we use language to do a compliment or request, and others understand and respond to what we're doing. When my step-daughter asks, "do you want half of my candy bar?" she is not only forming a question, but also doing an act, called an offer. If I say, "yes," I've not only answered the question, I've also done an acceptance. Even the question, "how are you today?" can count as doing a greeting.

Norms. If rules were all we had to learn of a language, our task would be difficult enough. In addition, we must adhere to the norms of language use in a culture or group to which we belong. Norms are the "shoulds" and "should nots" of language. Norms are closely tied to procedural social knowledge, in that they tell us how to behave in a given situation. These simple "do's and don'ts" are learned through interacting with parents and older children as we grow up. For example, a norm in our culture requires that you respond to a greeting like "Hi!" with a reciprocal greeting of your own, like "How ya doin'?" Part of the initial fear experienced by the doctor in *Nell* came from Nell's failure to respond in this expected way. Instead, she ignored his efforts to obtain mutual recognition between them.

Many times, we learn language norms through mistakes or modeling others. For instance, we learn that to avoid disapproval (especially from parents) we should say "please," "thank you," and "excuse me." We also learn to not interrupt adults. When interacting with our peers, we learn that we shouldn't say too much (don't be a "blabbermouth") or too little (don't be so shy). We also learn we should not inform grown-ups about other kids' behavior (don't be a "tattle-tale").

One way to distinguish language rules from norms is through how others respond. Rule violations typically bring correction, such as when we mispronounce a word. Others let us know when we've pronounced a word incorrectly, especially if it's the listener's name. Violating norms usually elicits a different response. If you violate a norm, people assume you are aware of, but have chosen to break it. You are held accountable for your behavior if you swear in church, for instance. If you continue to break norms, others may label you "incompetent" or "bad." Rather than correcting us, people will simply avoid our company or decide they don't like us. This reaction in part explains the popularity of Howard Stern, syndicated radio personality based in New York. Those who listen to Stern on the radio or have seen his movie, *Private Parts,* know that Stern loves to violate norms. He makes human excrement a topic of discussion, and interrupts others (what we've learned we should *not* do). He refuses to use polite terms like please and thank you (what we've learned we *should* do). As a result, he's radio's "bad boy" and people either love or hate him. Those who like him perhaps vicariously enjoy the freedom of his disregard for norms, but those who hate him describe him as rude, crude, and ridiculous.

It is important to be aware of the repercussions of norm violation. In some cases, being "different" makes us more interesting or flamboyant. The down side is that breaking too many norms, or breaking the really important ones, can lead others to dismiss or dislike us.

Standard and Non-standard Language. The most prominent set of norms for language centers on the use of standard versus non-standard speech. Standard English is the kind spoken by Ted Koppel on *Nightline*. Its grammar is conventionally "correct." It is crisply enunciated, does not include slang, and is delivered in carefully modulated tones.

TABLE 2.1 Standard and Non-Standard English

Standard English	Non-Standard English
He is sick	He sick
He has been angry	He be angry
Hello	Hey
You All	Y'all
Everyone	All Y'all
th sounds (like "that")	d sounds (like "dat")
th sounds (like "think")	t sounds (like "tink")
She never does anything	She never does nothin'

Standard English is so labeled because it is the social gauge for achieving "perfect" language use. In Great Britain, the standard is called "received pronunciation" (Dodd, 1995). Non-standard English typically involves other dialects of English. For example, in the United States, we can distinguish Southern English, East Coast English, Midwestern English, Latino English, and Ebonics. These dialects are language systems in their own right, but are governed by syntactic, semantic, and phonemic rules which differ in identifiable ways from standard English. Table 2.1 provides only a few examples of the differences between standard and nonstandard English.

Notice that labeling one kind of language as the standard of perfection sets up an inevitable comparison. The implication here is that those who speak non-standard language may be labeled as non-standard *people*. This is precisely what happens in social interaction. Research shows that we feel greater trust for people who speak as we do (Infante, Rancer, & Womack, 1993). Therefore, it is a natural, and perhaps unconscious response, to dislike those who speak differently.

These kinds of judgments encourage racism, sexism, and class distinctions in our culture. We judge others' intelligence, economic standing, and worth based on their language. These judgments can have serious positive or negative consequences. For instance, many Americans assume someone with a British accent is more intelligent than average. On the other hand, non-standard language users are more likely to be labeled "dumb," "low-class," "rude," or even "redneck." The current debate over the use of Ebonics (previously known as "Black English") in elementary school classrooms illustrates people's implicit understanding of this impression-making process. Some educators object to Ebonics and feel that children should be forced to use standard English so they will be socially accepted. Other educators argue that if teachers can use Ebonics to understand children and teach them the appropriate equivalents in standard English, the children will have a greater potential to succeed in our society.

THE CHARACTERISTICS OF LANGUAGE

Knowing the rules and norms of language won't always prevent misunderstandings. The character of language makes misunderstanding an omni-present threat. This is, in part, because we mistakenly assume that language holds some objective meaning. As we'll see in this section, the process by which we acquire meanings is highly personal and sometimes unique rather than shared. You may conclude that no objective meanings exist. Because language is symbolic, abstract, arbitrary, and conventional, meanings are instead "negotiated" between communicators. Understanding this negotiation process gives us the power to decrease misunderstandings, even if we can't erase them entirely.

Language Is Symbolic

Language is a symbol system. A symbol is anything which stands for, or signifies, something else: an object, person, idea, place, etc. Religious symbols like a crucifix or star of David stand for a complex system of beliefs about humans and the universe. Uniforms, like those of law enforcement personnel, may signify authority. Historically, in our culture a black dress stood for mourning. The word "book" stands for the object from which you are now reading. Money is also symbolic. We use it to buy groceries and gasoline, but in reality, money is a scrap of paper. Paper money represents its equivalent in gold. In our colonial era, gold had direct worth as a precious metal and was exchanged for goods and services. In the modern day, we don't put gold in a vending machine. Instead, we insert coins that stand for gold. On some college campuses, even coins and paper money are becoming obsolete. Now, money is represented by a magnetic strip on a debit card, similar to a credit card, which tells the vending machine how much money you're permitted to spend.

The symbolic quality of language makes it a powerful force in triggering our emotions and thoughts. Words can produce the same responses we would feel if we were actually experiencing an event. Have you ever come across an old letter you wrote, or someone sent to you? Perhaps it was tucked away in your keepsakes. Re-reading the words brings back a flood of memories long forgotten, and feelings like those we experienced back then. Poetry and fiction have this power for many people.

If you need more evidence of the power in symbols, visit any local museum or art gallery. Humans exert tremendous time and effort preserving old symbols. Museum curators carefully treat and mount original documents and clothing. When my husband and I visited Mary Todd Lincoln's girlhood home in Lexington, Kentucky, we saw a glass case full of letters written by Abraham Lincoln. It was chilling to see the actual paper which he held in his hand and the actual words he scrawled out with a quill and ink. The chill probably comes from my ability to imagine Abraham Lincoln sitting at a desk producing this document. The symbol evokes the same awe I would feel if I had the opportunity to stand in his presence.

Language Is Abstract

As a symbol system, language uses letters and words to represent things in the physical world, like rocks, trees, and birds. These are **referents, the thing a symbol refers to.** We also use words to symbolize referents in the psychological or emotional world, like fear, jealously, pride, or anger. Language is **abstract** because we can use it to talk about referents we can't see or point to. Abstractness is a useful characteristic of language. What would happen if we couldn't refer to "love," for example? The abstractness of language allows us to understand concepts like "cool" or "individualistic" even though they have no referent we can touch; not in the way I can touch a "computer," the machine on which I am currently typing.

Language is abstract for a second reason; a single symbol can refer to any number of specific referents in a whole class of items. For example, the symbol R-O-C-K can refer not just to the stone I am holding in my hand, but to any stone, of any size, in any location. This aspect of abstraction can contribute to misunderstandings. Have you ever made plans to meet a friend "in front" of the communication building at a particular time, only to be stood up? They may understand "front" as the parking-lot side of the building, while you meant the circle intersection side.

Language Is Arbitrary

Because language is composed of symbols, it is necessarily **arbitrary.** Arbitrary assignment means two things. First, the symbol we assign to an object, person, event, or idea was originally chosen by whim, without relying on any particular rule for assignment. The vessel I fill with coffee in the morning could have easily been called C-H-A-I-R rather than "cup." Translating from one language to another gives us a perfect example of the arbitrariness of language. In English we say "house." In Spanish, it's "casa." Which is correct? Neither. Both were arbitrarily chosen symbols that represent a residential dwelling.

Those who have studied a second language may argue that many words are adapted from other languages, not chosen by whim. It's true that many words in the English language evolved from French or Latin. In turn, some Latin words came from Greek which may have come from Sanskrit, the oldest known language. Originally, someone chose a sound to represent or stand for an object, idea, or person. Later, those sounds were translated into written form. Thus, even if we follow the evolution of a word back to its origin, some person had to be the first to assign a particular sound or written symbol to a referent. That person could have picked any sound or written symbol as easily as any other.

Second, arbitrary assignment means there is no necessary connection between a symbol and its referent. Nothing in the character of the universe requires all drinking vessels to be called "cup," or even "glass." We tend to mistakenly believe that some characteristic of the referent calls for, or makes logical, a particular symbol instead of others. Our mistake comes from the fact that with frequent use, we imbue the symbol with some special quality or essence of the referent. To say, for example, that "school" is called school because it is where we learn, is to confuse some quality of the referent with a quality in its symbol. Symbols have only the qualities we give them in our minds. There is nothing inherent in the symbol "school" that forces it to refer to learning.

In the movie *Nell*, researchers were intrigued by Nell's habit of sitting in front of a mirror, gesturing toward it and saying "Nay 'n May." They thought that perhaps she was referring to herself via two personalities, Me ("May") and Nell ("Nay"). Thus, her bizarre behaviors were the result of a personality disorder. The researchers were fooled by the arbitrary nature of language. They later discovered that "May" was the name of Nell's twin sister, now deceased. When talking to the mirror, Nell was talking to her identical twin, not to herself.

Language Is Conventional

To communicate with others, we must share symbols among people. That is, the symbols in language must be **conventional**. A convention is a norm—a pattern for behavior which we implicitly agree to follow. In the case of language, we "agree" to call a referent by a given name. For instance, we agree among ourselves to refer to the act of pedaling a two-wheeled aluminum frame over some distance as B-I-K-I-N-G. Conventionality is easily illustrated in the fact that we change symbols for referents over time. The word "gay" used to refer to a lively, happy, exciting event. Now, it refers to sexual orientation.

Nell's adventure in getting acquainted with her researchers represents the process of "conventionalizing" language. As the doctor began to understand some of the referents for Nell's speech, he employed them as well, so that the two of them could share ideas. For example, Nell symbolized the doctor as "guy ange." The doctor finally learned that this meant "guardian angel." He later used these same symbols to persuade Nell to leave her home and escape the helicopters descending on the forest. The doctor said, "Jay guy ange. No ta-ta." which meant, "I'm your guardian angel. Don't be afraid." As a result of their conventional (shared) understanding of these symbols, Nell complied with his request.

Conventionality is also illustrated in the special "codes" we have with intimate friends, called **idiomatic communication** (Bell & Healy, 1992). Personal idioms are the words, phrases, or gestures that have unique meanings (not understood by outsiders) between friends or romantic partners. Based on shared experiences, relational partners can use idioms to refer to activities, emotional states, objects, places, people, greetings, goodbyes, insults, or sexual matters (Bell & Healy, 1992). Idiomatic communication helps relationship partners demonstrate their solidarity to themselves and to others. For example, my husband and I humorously refer to one of our female acquaintances as "Gotta bag?" This code includes a lot of unspoken characteristics of and experiences with this woman, as well as our feelings about her. Because we agree on the meaning for this phrase, we can convey all this information in a simple, two-word code that others don't understand. Thus, we can communicate about this topic, even in public, without offending others.

Meanings

Meanings are the images, ideas, and feelings we associate with a symbol and its referent. Two kinds of meanings apply to language. **Denotations** are the conventional definitions we give symbols. These are listed in texts like *Webster's Dictionary*. On a personal level, however, a symbol rarely evokes exactly the same ideas, images, and feelings in any two individuals. Thus, to some degree, meanings are idiosyncratic. Our unique, subjective responses to events, objects, people, and situations are **connotations**. When I was little, my grandmother and I had very different connotative meanings for the referent "dog." For me, all dogs were furry, cute, fun, wriggly, affectionate beasts. Whenever we saw one, I wanted to pet it. My grandmother feared for my life on these occasions. She would hold both my hands and tell me to keep walking, fast! Somehow, grandma's negative experiences gave her connotations like ferocious, big, aggressive, unpredictable, and mean.

FIGURE 2.5 The Semantic Triangle

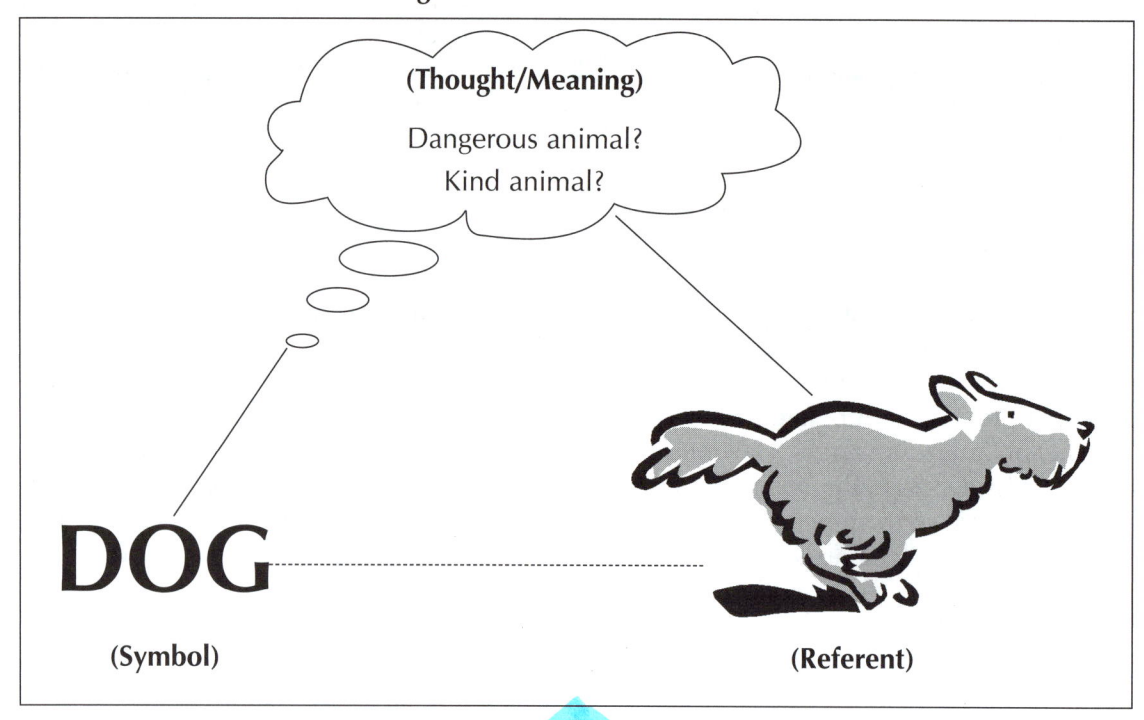

(Thought/Meaning)
Dangerous animal?
Kind animal?

DOG
(Symbol)   (Referent)

The Semantic Triangle. I. A. Richards developed a theoretical perspective for understanding the tie between symbols and the referents they represent, as well as the meanings we apply to them, called the **semantic triangle** (Foss, Foss, & Trapp, 1991). In Figure 2.5 you see that symbol and referent make up two corners of the triangle. To illustrate the abstract, arbitrary, conventional tie between symbols and referents, the line between them is dotted. In contrast, the lines from symbol to meaning and referent to meaning are solid, indicating that our meanings are directly affected by the referents we encounter in life and can be called up through symbols just as effectively as through experiences.

The semantic triangle reminds us to avoid assuming that our conversational partner has the same thoughts and reactions (meanings) we have for symbols. Richards developed the term "proper meaning superstition" to describe the mistaken belief that words or symbols have meanings (Foss et al., 1991). He argued that it is more accurate to understand that meanings are in people, not words.

Acquiring New Meanings. Given that people have their own personal connotations for symbols, how can we learn and share "new" meanings and symbols with others? If we acquire meanings only from personal experiences, how can you, as a student, learn new ideas in a classroom? Richards explained that we acquire new meanings by associating well-understood symbols for ones which are less understood (Foss et al., 1991). As children, we asked endlessly about the meaning of new words. If our parents were clever, they'd explain a new concept using words we already understood. We would then pair the new word with bits and pieces of the known words' meanings (Liska & Cronkhite, 1995). Johnson (1991) describes this as the **inferential process, using the context and responses of others to interpret the connotations and denotations for new symbols**. From experience, we all know how delicate the inferential process is, and how easily it can go wrong. For several Christmases as a child, when our church would sing "Tidings of Comfort and Joy" I would be thinking that a group of angels called "Tidings" have come for a man named "Tanjoy," to take him away somewhere, perhaps to heaven.

Coordinated Management of Meaning (CMM) is a theoretical perspective that describes how communicators construct inferences. In our relationships, whether romantic or familial, we implicitly develop norms or acceptable interaction patterns. For example, I have observed on many occasions that male friends tend to develop a repertoire of acceptable insults they throw at each other as playful banter. While many sets of friends do this, each set develops their own list of "approved" insults. Between them, this kind of banter becomes a rule, or expected form of behavior. Relationship participants "coordinate" by developing shared notions of what these language habits mean, called "constitutive rules." Constitutive rules are employed by communicators to determine what an act or word constitutes or counts as. For example, dual career couples may develop rules that talking during dinner about events in their respective work days counts as "sharing" or "quality time."

Language Is Self-Referencing

Because meanings are subjective, our choice of symbols says as much about us as the referents we discuss. This makes language **self-referencing,** or reflective of a speaker's character and experience. My grandmother lives in Arizona, and typically visits me in Chicago for a week in early spring. When she complains in the morning that "it's cold," those symbols and their meanings indicate important information not only about the objective temperature, but about my grandmother as well. Her choice of language tells me that her blood has grown thin living in such a warm climate. After a winter in Chicago, 59 degrees feels positively balmy to me, not cold. Grandma's comment says a lot about her life and her point of view.

Language Shapes Our Identity

Symbolic Interactionism Theory explains how the ability to share symbols with others helps us come to know ourselves. This theoretical perspective was developed by George Herbert Mead during the 1930's and 40's. Mead was concerned with the human ability to "create" individuals and societies through symbols (Wood, 1997). In the process of learning our native language, we also learn our culture's values and morals through the special connotations given to symbols. By learning what our society is about and locating ourselves within it, we come to know who we are. Additionally, we learn to see our "self" as others see us. The significant people in our lives interact with us in ways that express their vision of us as "outgoing" or "shy," "smart" or "funny." As he was growing up, if Kim's parents gave him art supplies and complimented his drawings and other creative efforts, over time these messages may have led Kim to see himself as "artistic" or "creative." In *Nell*, the main character's interaction with her mother and sister probably contributed to her perceptions that she was a "normal" language user. According to the doctor's records, Nell's mother was partially paralyzed; she spoke in an eerie, droning tone, from only one side of her mouth. Modeling her mother's speech would contribute to Nell's odd pronunciation. In addition, Nell's sister was an identical twin. Her remaining "odd" words could be explained as "twin-speak," the idiomatic communication that develops between identical siblings.

Speech Community Theory explains that groups of people develop distinctive ways of using language. These characteristic language techniques distinguish "insiders" from "outsiders." Gerry Philipsen (1992) defined a speech community as "a universe of discourse with a finely organized, distinctive pattern of meaning and action" (p. 10). He examined the language norms of two groups, one in California and another in a southern suburb of Chicago. His analysis explained that language norms act as a code, indicating to others of your speech community that you hold their values and beliefs: what it means to be a man or a woman, how to get a job, what kinds of talk are acceptable in which situations. Philipsen's analysis suggested that language is not merely used for conveying information, but also for linking speakers together in particular social relationships within their group.

The Impact of Language on Social Life

We've defined language and discussed which characteristics make it both a useful tool and a rather tricky one. The rest of this chapter focuses on how language is associated with effective communication. For instance, the growing concern in the United States for political correctness is really a debate about language. Can changing our use of language help change our perspective of social groups? We'll discuss theories which suggest that concern over the power of language is well-founded. As our world becomes smaller through global connections, our need for effective communication becomes greater. Understanding the link between language and communication effectiveness prepares you for life in the twenty-first century.

Early investigations of language asked, "What makes speakers credible (persuasive, believable, dynamic, and effective)?" **Opinionated language** indicates the speaker's attitude toward a topic and toward listeners who either agree or disagree. For example, "Any idiot who doesn't believe the environment is endangered is too dumb to see the obvious" shows that the speaker is concerned about environmental issues and doesn't respect those who aren't. Infante, Rancer, and Womack (1993) summarized research on opinionated language and audience response. Findings suggest that if you have some expertise or credentials relevant to the topic, opinionated language is more persuasive than neutral language. When listeners already have strong negative or positive attitudes toward the topic, neutral language is more credible.

Language intensity is the degree to which speakers deviate from neutrality on a topic. More intense language uses more emotional or vivid words, stronger expressions, and sex or death metaphors. For example, environmental activists who complain of the US government "raping" our environment are employing more intense language than if they accused the government of "taking advantage" of natural resources. Findings regarding the effectiveness of intense language have been inconsistent, depending on whether listeners already had strong arousal regarding the topic, whether the speaker was perceived as credible, whether the speaker was male, and whether the listeners already support the speaker's position. In general, when these factors are present, highly intense language is credible.

Intensity is sometimes associated with "objectionable" language, the kind that is typically censored from television or mentioned in a warning on CD covers. Just like other forms of intensity, obscene language can be effective for some speakers, in some situations. The trouble is that people have difficulty agreeing on what types of language are truly objectionable, rather than merely "indelicate." Liska and Cronkhite (1995) distinguish between three kinds of objectionable language: **obscenities** are sexually explicit slang, **profanity** refers to religious terms used as slang, and **scatology** refers to using vocabulary for bodily waste and functions as slang.

Language Affects Perception and Thought

Do we all live in the same world? Some scholars argue that we don't, at least psychologically. The **Sapir-Whorf hypothesis** explains that the language we speak affects how we perceive the world. Because languages are developed by groups to deal with their particular experiences and problems, different languages reflect different world views. Language then perpetuates this view. Therefore, members of different linguistic communities see, feel, hear, and experience the world differently, in that they are sensitized to some phenomena, and desensitized to others.

The Sapir-Whorf hypothesis argues that language not only expresses our ideas, but also shapes them. This can have two implications for language users. First, languages may not be truly "translatable," since cultures have specialized connotations for particular words. Those connotations may be difficult to capture in another language. Dodd (1995) gives us several examples: The Bororo tribe of the Amazon has several words for the bird, "parrot." The Hanunoo language of the Philippines has 92 words for "rice." Eskimos have many words for what we call "snow." In North American English, we have only one word for each of these concepts. Does this mean that because I speak English I am incapable of perceiving differences among types of rice or snow? Probably not. Occasionally I cook brown rice with chicken because I think it tastes more complimentary than white rice. Having lived all my life calling this food by a single name, with no other distinction than its color, I am likely less sensitive to differences in rice than someone with Asian influence.

If our language allowed greater distinction, we might also have slightly different connotations for each word, as other languages do. What happens when we want to make an important distinction, but our language has no word for noting a contrast? We must then invent new terms. The term, "sexual harassment" evolved because we did not have a means for distinguishing appropriate from inappropriate, complimentary from demeaning, and appreciative from degrading sexual advances.

A second implication then, is that changing our language can transform our appreciation of the world (Carroll, 1956). Language changes can affect our perceptions of other races, sexes, and ages positively, helping us develop respectful and tolerant connotations for women, African Americans, or people over 60.

Political Correctness. Political correctness advocates argue that changing our labels for people and events will help us change our perceptions and increase sensitivity to the views of non-dominant groups in our society. However, those who oppose political correctness warn us that re-labeling can be carried too far, if the new labels in fact silence some perspectives. A few short years ago, political correctness made it preferable to say "Happy Holidays" instead of "Merry Christmas." The new phrase was meant to acknowledge that not everyone celebrates Christmas. But in at least one case, the new greeting had detrimental effects: One of the hallmarks of the holiday season is the arrival of Santa Claus in the Macy's Thanksgiving Day Parade. One year, the parade ended with Santa shouting out, "Happy Holidays" rather than "Ho, Ho, Ho, Merry Christmas!" The following year, Santa merely waved. He said nothing at all. When Santa was no longer allowed to say "Merry Christmas," his role in American history and culture was silenced, not acknowledged, by political correctness.

On the other hand, there are examples of language in our culture that support bigotry, sexism, or ageism, and ought to be discouraged. Using history as a lesson, communication scholars note that employing dehumanizing, degrading language makes it easier to dismiss or dispose of those who differ from us. One of the factors responsible for the holocaust in Nazi Germany was the use of terms that dehumanized the Jews. Referring to the Jews as vermin or disease encouraged people to perceive Jews as less than human. Therefore, it became acceptable psychologically to steal from them, enslave them, put them in ghettos, and finally, exterminate them. Similar cases exist in United States history: "niggers" were easier to enslave than African people; "savages" were easier to detain on reservations than Native American People; "Japs" were easier to detain in relocation camps during WWII than Asian People; it was easier to trivialize the perspectives of "girls" or "broads" than women. One way to discourage these kinds of controlling, overbearing social views is to find words that don't dehumanize, demoralize, or devalue others.

Sexism. Spender (1980) describes sexism as a language bias toward males, both in syntactic and semantic rules. For example, some scholars consider the generic use of "man," "he," and "his" to be exclusionary and suppressive to women. "He" and "his" were not recognized as generic and all-inclusive until the mid 1500's (Spender, 1980). These terms were eventually adopted as a conventional rule of grammar in the early 1700's. Prior to this time, "they" and "their" were the conventions for gender-inclusiveness. Recent trends in our grammar are returning to this usage, to avoid excluding women. In addition, people employ "s/he" and "her/his" to indicate non-sexed descriptions.

The effect of sexist language is to discourage acceptance of females in various roles in our society. For instance, the tendency to "mark" traditionally male jobs occupied by females (stewardess, seamstress, janitress, chair-woman, woman doctor, woman lawyer) identifies these workers as not only different, but somehow inferior to male workers in the same positions. Traditionally male names (Sidney, Leslie, Shirley, Evelyn), once they become popular for females, are somehow no longer flattering for males (Spender, 1980). Connotations for a word like "aggressive" are positive when applied to men, but negative when applied to women. While this language problem was once trivialized in our society, growing evidence of language effects has made this view more accepted. Words like chairman, fisherman, and councilman are perceived as men, by males and females alike, in grade schools and college classrooms (see Spender, 1980 for a summary of empirical evidence).

The danger of sexist language lies not in words themselves, but in perceptions and connotations attached to those words. Because of their semantic inequalities, sexist words support social inequality. The same problem applies to racist language. Notice the frequency with which speakers mark terms like "Black man" and "my Asian friends," without even realizing the negative comparison they have made to white males as the standard in our culture. The goal of effectively correcting these negative comparisons should be kept in mind when evaluating the worth of social movements like political correctness.

Language and Accountability

In addition to racist and sexist language, we need to be aware of language that avoids, rather than claims personal responsibility for our own feelings and attitudes. For example, no one can "make" you angry. Instead, we each have the choice to respond angrily or calmly in any situation. You've experienced this when, on different days in the week, you've either yelled at another driver for making a stupid mistake, or ignored the

TABLE 2.2 "I" Versus "You" Statements

Avoiding Ownership	Taking Responsibility
"You stay up way too late and keep me up at night."	"I can't sleep when you're up past midnight with the stereo on."
"You drive like a maniac. Slow down."	"I get really scared when you take corners so fast."
"You never leave me enough information about these telephone calls."	"I don't understand these phone messages. I need to know the caller's question."

other driver, realizing s/he just didn't notice their error. Was it other drivers who changed from one day to the next? Probably not. More likely, it was you who changed. Perhaps on the day you yelled, you were already tense at the thought of coming deadlines for papers and projects. Stress makes an angry response more likely on your part. Your comparatively calm day may have occurred just after turning in the reports and other projects. At that point, you are now too tired or too relieved to be angry with other stressed-out drivers.

"I" statements illustrate willingness to take responsibility for our own feelings and actions by describing our feelings, rather than evaluating others'. In contrast, **"you" statements** avoid responsibility and blame others. Beebe and his colleagues (Beebe, Beebe, & Redmond, 1996) remind us that no one likes to be judged or criticized. "You" statements are likely to trigger defensiveness in our relational partners, because they sound like attacks. We are more likely to solve problems with "I" language. For example, "You don't care about keeping this place clean!" is accusatory. "I'm uncomfortable living in a place with dirty dishes in the sink and books piled on the floor" acknowledges (a) the speaker's accountability for his/her feelings, (b) that the speaker's response to a messy house is not the ONLY response, and (c) other people (including the listener) may feel differently about it. The same principle applies to the contrasts in Table 2.2:

Language Clarity

Because language is abstract, it can become a barrier rather than a useful tool for connecting humans. Abstractness contributes to vagueness in language. Vague terms muddy language, making it even more abstract, less concrete, and less understandable than it needs to be. If shared understanding and connection are our goals, we must strive for clarity in language. You've experienced the vagueness of language if you've ever asked someone to give you a "straight answer." We can have the feeling people are taking advantage of the abstractness of language to avoid taking any definitive stand on an issue. For example, is "termination of pregnancy" the same as "abortion?" These labels may have the same referent, but very different connotations. The same effect is achieved by referring to "war" as a "police action" or "peace-keeping mission." In Sarajevo, the religiously-motivated conflict between Croats, Serbs, and Muslims, was called "ethnic cleansing" not "genocide." In the United States, "ghettos" have become "low income neighborhoods." The point is that controversial issues can be dealt with very persuasively by using **doublespeak**—substituting vague terms for concrete ones; saying, but not saying, what we really mean.

Euphemisms. We also deal with controversial or undesirable topics through **euphemisms,** conventionally "polite" terms substituted for straightforward ones. Ironically, we use euphemisms in social situations or "mixed company" to discuss topics which *aren't socially appropriate*. While we can't bring ourselves to talk directly about human waste, reproduction, or death outright, we must still grapple with our need to share feelings and thoughts on these topics. For example, "bathroom" was once a taboo term. Instead, we asked for the "powder room" or "rest room." If someone is obese, we refer to them as large, not fat. When someone dies, we prefer to say s/he has "passed on," or less delicately, "kicked the bucket," "bought the farm," etc. Reproductive activities are a source of numerous euphemisms, including "humping," "the nasty," "doing it," "knockin' boots," and "the wild thing." Used cars are "previously owned." "Diet" foods are less popular than "light" ones. "Vintage" clothing seems cooler than "second-hand" or "resale" clothes.

Equivocal Language. Equivocation means purposely using words which are subject to two or more interpretations. Thus, equivocating is a way to allow your listener to believe one thing when in fact you may mean something else. McCornack (1992) argues that equivocation is a significant source of deception in relationships. His **Information Manipulation Theory** explains that we can supply information equivocally when we don't want to disclose the full truth. For example, if a friend asks you about a new hairstyle you think is awful, you can equivocate by saying it's "unusual," "interesting," or "different."

Sex and Language Differences

Do women and men use language differently? Early research suggested they do. Lakeoff (1977) argued that men use dominant, and women deferential language. Language differences are also suggested by popular book titles about men's and women's relationships like *You Just Don't Understand* (Tannen, 1990). Until recently, we accepted the notion that men use forceful, efficient, blunt, or authoritative language while women use gossip, more euphemisms and trivial, tentative, or hesitant language (Spender, 1980). A dominant stereotype held that women talk more than men. However, more investigation challenged these notions and yielded further insight. For example, Fishman (1983) found that consistent with prior research, women did ask more questions in mixed-sex dyads; however, contrary to prior findings, she argued against viewing this as evidence of insecurity or tentativeness. Rather, questions constituted the "work" of keeping interaction alive, as in responding to male-initiated topics. Men and women change their language styles depending on the context and their audience. Men used more dominating language when in the company of same-sex friends, but more deferential language in mixed company or when talking with women (DeFleur et al., 1995). When all contexts are considered (not just domestic ones), researchers find that on average, men speak more frequently and speak longer than women (Tannen, 1990).

Spender (1980) argues convincingly that sex differences in language are complicated by **gender roles,** our social expectations for the behaviors of each sex. Socially constructed genders include stereotypes about male behaviors and female behaviors (Markus, Crane, Bernstein, & Salidi, 1982). When our ideas about gender roles are inflexible, we perceive women and men as speaking differently, even when they use language in exactly the same ways. For instance, Fishman (1983) finds that both women and men initiate new topics for conversation. However, she argues that when women attempt to control conversations, they are perceived as "arguing," while men may be perceived as merely stating a point of view. As explained in the chapter on social knowledge, our gender knowledge influences how we interpret and what we remember in others' messages.

One of the concerns in comparing men's with women's language centers on the distribution of "power" between them. **Interactional Theory** (Wood, 1997) describes how power is evidenced in our messages. For instance, **one-up messages** are those which illustrate the speaker has power over the receiver. Commands, orders, and interruptions can function as one-up messages. In contrast, **one-down messages** show that the speaker accepts an inferior social position by giving the receiver power. Complying with requests, allowing interruptions to go by, and asking for advice might count as one-down communication.

Code Switching

Changing your language in different contexts is like using a different "code," with its own rules and norms. The ability to switch from one language code to another is labeled **code-switching.** You've code-switched if swearing was a habit you consciously tried to control around your parents or pastor. Most of us use language differently with friends than with elders, bosses, or small children. There is evidence of significant code-switching across races and cultures as well (Harvey, 1992). The changes you make may be subtle or profound, conscious or not conscious. When I visit my girlhood home in Alabama, I unconsciously revert to what I call "southern speak." I begin to say "y'all" and use a long "a" sound rather than a Chicago, short "a" sound. The movie *Nell* ends five years after Nell's speech in court. Nell's closest friends, including the doctor and speech pathologist, are gathered for a party at her home. We see from the interaction among these characters, that Nell has successfully learned the language codes of standard English. However, she switches to her old code to teach a little girl the rhyme Nell and May recited as children.

Being a successful code-switcher is something like being bi-lingual, or even tri-lingual. Skillful code-switchers reach their communication goals more often because their ability to code-switch makes them more flexible. They have a greater range of communication strategies to employ across social situations. However, code-switching should not be confused with insincerity. Rather, it should be seen as evidence of our implicit social knowledge: If we understand that language (a) leads others to judge us, (b) identifies us as "insider" or "outsider," and (c) helps others recognize what we're "doing" as we talk, then we can employ the kind of language most likely to be accepted in a particular situation, at a particular time, with particular listeners.

The Hudson Report, "Work Force 2000," suggests that in the next century, code-switching will be an important skill on the job. Latino and Black dialects will become more prevalent, as only 58% of new entrants to the work force will be White Anglo Americans. 22% are expected to be immigrants from various other cultures, and the remaining 20 % African and Latino Americans. Thus, as our living and working environments become more diversified, we need flexible language skills to build relationships and communicate effectively with neighbors and co-workers.

Communication Accommodation Theory (CAT) explains our tendency to code-switch. Accommodation means adjusting to our conversational partners in speed, tone, volume, pitch, rhythm, use of profanity, formal, or informal language, etc. There are three ways to accommodate: **converging** involves adapting your own verbal and nonverbal communication to be more similar to your partner; **diverging** means accenting or emphasizing the differences between communicators; **maintaining** refers to keeping your own style, without any recognition of the differences between you and your partner. For example, you'll notice a lot of convergence between people who've become good friends. After a period of time, they begin to laugh similarly, use the same inflection or stress on certain syllables, and use the same slang. When I first moved to Alabama as a 4th grader, I exhibited a lot of divergence. When my girlfriend, Leslie, would ask if I wanted "funilla" ice cream, I would correct her by enunciating very crisply, "Vanilla."

According to CAT, the more we rely on our own language group for our identity, norms, and values, the more we tend to diverge or maintain. This is especially likely when we see our conversational partner as an "outsider," since diverging emphasizes our identity to outsiders. Divergence can also occur when we perceive that our language group is under attack. On these occasions, divergence functions as a show of strength. On the other hand, convergence is more likely when we are not dependent on our own language group for our identity, or when we see our conversational partner more as an individual than a representative of some outside group. Under these circumstances we are more likely to converge in an effort to establish common ground.

LANGUAGE AND EFFECTIVE COMMUNICATION

We have seen that language can be both a useful tool and a potential barrier to connecting humans. As our global population continues to expand at incomprehensible rates, the importance of language for promoting understanding grows. One way to synthesize the characteristics and functions of language described in this chapter is through an analogy. Rubin (1988) thinks of communication as an iceberg. Spoken symbols (language) are only the tip of the iceberg. That means language is an aspect of communication that we see above the water line. Underneath the surface, language is attached to the aspects of communication we don't see: meanings, values, experiences, culture, needs, and goals. This makes language a powerful, but often unrecognized force in maneuvering successfully through life.

Now that you understand the role of language in shaping our views of the world, it is your job as a communicator to use language responsibly, just as you would use any tool. Using language effectively means employing language that's (a) clear, (b) appropriate for you, and (c) appropriate for the situation (Liska & Cronkhite, 1995).

Clarity

Remember that language is symbolic. It is therefore abstract and ambiguous. Because meanings are in people, not words, language is always subject to varied interpretations. As effective communicators, **we must strive to use more concrete, not more abstract language.** Concrete language tries to directly identify a referent, whereas abstract language uses generalities.

We can clarify language by avoiding doublespeak. Similarly, euphemisms, while they may spare embarrassment, can also make meanings more obscure and should be used sparingly. Avoid equivocal language whenever possible. If you ask your hairstylist for "a little off the top" you may or may not be happy with the results. "Take off half an inch" is a more precise request. Also clarify equivocal language you receive from others.

Check your perceptions to be sure you've understood what the speaker intended. This takes only a moment and is usually worth the effort. If you ask a friend how they like your new casserole recipe and you his/her response is, "It's different," it may be worth your time to ask, "Is that different *bad*, or different *good*?"

Finally, remember that language follows semantic and pragmatic rules. **Are you following the same rules as those around you?** If not, you may be contributing to misunderstandings. Again, checking your perceptions is the key to identifying rules. For example, "In my book, smiling just means being friendly. Did you think I was flirting with you?" Encourage others to ask similar questions of your rules.

Appropriateness for You

Language is self-referencing. Are you creating impressions of yourself you want others to have? **Consider how your language contributes to your image.** Using language that is inconsistent with the identity you're building sends others conflicting signals. For example, your language may be linking you with a particular group or speech community. Using language others find objectionable or "non-standard" may lead them to judge your class, intelligence, or qualifications incorrectly. Remember that effective communicators have the flexibility to switch codes when necessary, to be an accepted and productive member of work groups, family groups, neighborhood groups, or political interest groups, each of whom have their own language rules and norms. Further information on pursuing goals in social situations is provided in the chapter on social knowledge.

Because language is self-referencing, it can provide us with information about others and our relationships with them. Oftentimes, we find ourselves distracted or hurt by others' offhand comments. However, we should **remember that comments from others may say more about their feelings or state of mind, than about objective reality.** When you encounter a co-worker who consistently makes negative or hurtful remarks, understand that you might not be at fault. Rather, his/her negative language may tell you that the person is a chronic complainer, overly judgmental of others, or perhaps jealous of someone else's skills and accomplishments.

Remember too that language can enhance relationships, or hinder them. Competent communicators should be cautious to **use language for relationship-building.** We need connections with others for a variety of reasons. Therefore, we must be on guard against language which excludes or alienates others. For example, using idiomatic communication, while it enhances your closeness and solidarity with intimate relational partners, may also serve to exclude and alienate non-intimates. It can make them feel left out, like a "third wheel." In most cases, it is in our best interests to make our language as inclusive as possible.

Changing to more inclusive language can expand our perceptions of the world. Therefore, **we should be open to new ways of expressing ideas.** Experimenting with new terminology for events, people, groups, and other phenomena may increase our knowledge and enhance the precision with which we perceive these phenomena. It can also increase our sensitivity to the perceptions of others.

Appropriate to the Situation

Language is a code system governed by rules and norms. **You must be aware of these rules and norms to use them competently.** As explained in the chapter on social knowledge, norms are usually situationally determined. Procedural knowledge tells you how to handle yourself in particular situations. Increase your sensitivity to procedural norms by watching others. Check your perceptions of their behavior by asking why they do "X." Monitor your language to be sure it conveys what you want it to convey in your current context, whether a funeral, wedding, or Super Bowl party. For example, if you hope to be seen as credible, then opinionated, objectionable, or intense language may or may not be appropriate for achieving your goal.

Making a plan for achieving your goals means having in mind the kind of language you want to use, not just the ideas you want to get across. For example, at my first job I was nearly fired over what I perceived to be a simple discussion. When I said, "I don't see why we have to trade off carrying this stupid beeper from week to week!" my boss felt I was threatening her authority. That wasn't at all what I intended. I would have achieved my goal more effectively with more neutral language, such as, "I'm wondering if there's some better system we could adopt for dealing with this beeper."

Breaking norms can have devastating consequences, as it can lead others to dismiss or dislike us. **Be aware of the judgments and stereotypes people apply to the language you use.** Abiding by conventional norms and rules is less crucial with our friends than with strangers or acquaintances. As you'll read the chapter on social knowledge, friends interpret and respond to our language based on personal knowledge about us. For example, if you use profane language with a friend, s/he may perceive you as temporarily crabby or depressed. An acquaintance or job interviewer however, is more likely to interpret your language as unprofessional and an indication that you're not mature enough to handle the job.

Similarly, you must be on guard for your own tendency to judge others. Your language choices can evoke positive or negative responses. We can offend without meaning to, by employing sexist and racist language, or static evaluations. Be aware that the terms with which we label others shape evaluations of their status and credibility. Communication accommodation reminds us to be sensitive to others' reactions and to adjust our language when necessary.

In some ways, we're all like Nell. While we may be independent and relatively self-sufficient, the practical requirements of work, school, and family life force us to learn and follow others' norms and rules. Language is our primary means for building connections with others. Establishing, then maintaining those connections from day to day depends on your understanding of the characteristics and functions of language.

REFERENCES

Beebe, S. A., Beebe, S. J., & Redmond, M. V. (1996). *Interpersonal communication: Relating to others.* Boston: Allyn & Bacon.

Bell, R. A., & Healey, J. G. (1992). Idiomatic communication and interpersonal solidarity in friends' relational cultures. *Human Communication Research, 18,* 307–335.

Carroll, J. B. (1956). *Language, thought, and reality: Selected writings of Benjamin Lee Whorf.* Cambridge, MA: MIT Press.

DeFleur, M. L., Kearney, P., & Plax, T. G. (1993). *Fundamentals of human communication.* Mountain View, CA: Mayfield

Eisenberg, E. M., & Goodall, H. L. Jr. (1993). *Organizational communication: Balancing creativity and constraint.* New York: St. Martin's Press.

Fishman P. M. (1983). Interaction: *The work women do.* In Thorne, Kramarae, & Henley (Eds.), Language, gender, and society (pp. 89–101). Cambridge: Newbury House.

Foss, S. K., Foss, K. A., & Trapp, R. (1991). *Contemporary perspectives on rhetoric* (2nd Ed). Prospect Heights, IL: Waveland Press.

Gallois, C., Franklyn-Stokes, A., Giles, H., & Coupland, N. (1988). Communication accomodation in intercultural encounters. In Y. Y. Kim & W. B. Gudykunst (Eds.), *Theories in intercultural communication* (pp. 157–185). Newbury Park, CA: Sage.

Infante, D. A., Rancer, A. S., & Womack, D. F. (1993). *Building communication theory* (2nd Ed). Prospect Heights, IL: Waveland Press.

Lakeoff, R. (1975). *Language and woman's place.* New York: Holt, Rinehart, & Winston.

Harvey, P. (1992). Bilingualism in the Peruvian andes. In D. Cameron, E. Frazer, P. Harvey, MBH Rampton, & K. Richardson (Eds.), *Researching language: Issues of power and method* (pp. 65–89). New York: Routledge.

Liska, J., & Cronkhite, G. (1995). *An ecological perspective on human communication theory.* New York: Harcourt-Brace.

Markus, H., Crane, M., Bernstein, S., & Siladi, M. (1982). Self-schemas and gender. *Journal of Personality and Social Psychology, 42,* 38–50.

McCornack, S. A. (1992). Information manipulation theory. *Communication Monographs, 59,* 1–16.

Nofsinger, R. E. (1991). *Everyday conversation.* Newbury Park, CA: Sage.

Pearson, J. C. (1985). *Gender and communication.* Dubuque, IA: Wm. C. Brown.

Philipsen, G. (1992). *Speaking culturally.* Albany, NY: State University of New York Press.

Ruben, B. D. (1988). *Communication and human behavior* (2nd Ed). New York: Macmillan.

Spender, D. (1980). *Man made language* (2nd Ed). New York: Routledge & Kegan Paul.

Tannen, D. (1990). *You just don't understand: Women and men in conversation.* New York: Ballantine Books.

Wood, J. T. (1997). *Communication theories in action: An introduction.* New York, NY: Wadsworth.

Chapter Two Case Study Quiz—Language Acquisition

Instructions:
Please read the following case study carefully and select the best answers for the questions. This quiz is an individual assignment. Remember: sharing answers is a form of plagiarism. This quiz is worth 10 points.

In the National Bestseller "Odd Girl Out," the author focuses on the role popularity plays in the lives of young girls (those in middle school and early high school). The author describes in great detail the experience of Brianna, Mackenzie and Jenny. After arriving at a new school, Jenny found that the most popular girls in school, Brianna and Mackenzie, had a mission in life (or at least the seventh grade) to make Jenny's life unbearable. The popular girls felt that their status was threatened by Jenny and to respond they spread rumors about Jenny going all the way with several boys in the grade and they dubbed her: "Harriet the Hairy Whore." Brianna and Mackenzie then pooled other girls in the grade to create the club Hate Harriet the Hore Incorporated. For short, the girls called the club "HHHI," otherwise pronounced as "Hi." To the teachers, parents and oblivious students, Brianna, Mackenzie and their cronies were nice by always saying hi to Jenny in their cute, sing-songy way, but the girls' said "HHHHHHHiiiii," as a way to sound out all the letters in their club name. Jenny felt embarrassed, fearful by the behavior of her peers, and that their behavior was her fault. Exhausted by their tactics, Jenny finally called them on the phone and asked, "Why do you hate me? Why do you have the Hate Harriet club?" Brianna and Mackenzie swore the club did not exist and Jenny was pleased by this discovery. She looked forward to school the next day, but when she walked down the hall she was greeted by students with, "HHHiii," and smirks on their faces. Jenny hated herself for believing these girls actually liked her.

Simmons, R. (2002). *Odd girl out: the hidden culture of aggression in girls.* New York: Harcourt.

Student's Name _____
Section Number _____
Section Leader's Name _____

Chapter Two Case Study Quiz—Language Acquisition

1. Brianna and Mackenzie's creation of "HHHI" is best described as:
   a. A Euphemism
   b. Idiomatic Communication
   c. Code switching
   d. Opinionated Language

2. Which characteristic of language best describes Brianna and Mackenzie's use of "HHHI"?
   a. Semantics
   b. Syntax
   c. Pragmatics
   d. Indexing

3. Jenny believes "HHHI" has what type of meaning?
   a. Referent
   b. Connotative
   c. Denotative
   d. Arbitrary

4. Teachers might believe "HHHI" has what type of meaning?
   a. Referent
   b. Connotative
   c. Denotative
   d. Arbitrary

5. The Symbolic Interactionism Theory would infer what about this case?
   a. The girls created "HHHI" to show their dislike for Jenny without saying it directly
   b. "HHHI" indicates to other people in their grade that Jenny is someone to hate
   c. "HHHI" indicates to Jenny that there something about her to hate
   d. That calling peers a hairy whore is acceptable due to the cute "HHHI" symbol

Case Study

Chapter Three

USING SOCIAL KNOWLEDGE IN COMMUNICATION:

INTERPRETING AND FORMING MESSAGES

Sandi W. Smith
Michigan State University

Steven R. Wilson
Purdue University

One of the most exciting learning experiences during your college years can be a Study Abroad program. Imagine yourself in a foreign country where you are unfamiliar with the language, customs, and culture. You, as a sojourner, are armed with a dictionary, so you know the words typically used in the country that you are visiting and the meanings typically associated with them. You do, however, still have trouble making sense of the messages that others send to you and knowing what kind of messages to send back to them that are appropriate and effective. You, as this sojourner, are lacking in **social knowledge.** The social knowledge that we gain throughout our lives allows us to understand and to achieve goals with other people who share our culture, who interact with us in common situations, and with whom we may form personal relationships.

In a sense, you were a little like this sojourner when you first came to college. If your roommate came from a different cultural background than you did, you probably found it difficult to predict what he or she would do in different situations. You also probably found it difficult to know how to interpret his or her messages and how to get your responses across in a way that he or she would understand. This is because you each held different social knowledge about cultural norms that governed your interactions, roles, situations, and the unique nature of each of your personalities. This knowledge of culture, roles, situations, and people is called **declarative knowledge.**

You were also a bit like the sojourner in that you did not know the specific steps to take in order to realize your goal of graduating from college. You probably did not know the steps that you needed to take to fulfill this goal. You needed to learn the specific courses that you are required to take; how to choose the best professors for the classes you needed; how to register for these classes; how to get from one class to another once you were registered; and how to approach your professor about a questionable grade that you might receive. Knowledge of how to meet goals by using plans of action is called **procedural knowledge.**

In order to understand how we use social knowledge as we communicate, we will cover three basic areas in this chapter. First, we will discuss how social knowledge is used to interpret the messages that others send to us. We will describe how this type of social knowledge is stored in "schemas," as well as the different stages of "input processing" that we go through in order to decide what other people mean. Second, we will clarify how we use social knowledge to decide what messages to send to others. We will explain how this second type of social knowledge is stored in "plans," as well as the different stages of "output processing" that we go through in order to decide what to say to others. Both of these sections include guidelines for using social knowledge. Finally, we will show how social knowledge relates to other topics in this book, including personal development, social integration, organizational management, and societal enrichment.

SCHEMAS AND INPUT PROCESSING

What Are Schemas?

Social cognition concerns "how people make sense of other people and themselves" (Fiske & Taylor, 1984, p.1). To do this, each of us must learn a body of social knowledge about culture, roles, situations, and people (including ourselves). We store this information in knowledge structures that are known by various names (Planalp, 1989), the most common of which is the schema. The knowledge that is held in schemas is unique to each of us in that it represents the information that is believed to be true about a particular domain, the relationships among the attributes of the domain, and specific instances or examples of the domain (Smith, 1995; Wilson & Kramer, 1986). For example, we have self-schemas that hold the information we believe to be true about ourselves, such as our biological sex and our level of friendliness, among other things. This schema also holds the relationships among these attributes for us, such as what our biological sex has to do with our level of friendliness. It also holds specific instances and examples of these attributes such as how we were more or less friendly in a particular situation because we felt that our sex-role dictated that action (Fiske & Taylor, 1991).

Types of Schemas

There are three different levels on which different categories of social knowledge exist (Miller & Steinberg, 1975). First, we have social knowledge at the cultural level for attributes such as gender and ethnicity. Next, we hold social knowledge at the sociological level for entities such as roles and situations. Finally, on the psychological level we have knowledge representations of personality traits, the self, and close relationships. Each of these levels and categories of social knowledge have implications for the ways that we interpret the communication that we receive from others, as well as the ways that we form the messages that we send in response.

Cultural level social knowledge. At the cultural level, social knowledge about ethnicity and gender may affect communication. "These aspects of people are so prominent and central that virtually everyone develops at least rudimentary schemas for them" (Markus, Crane, Bernstein, & Saladi, 1982). Rao (1994) conducted a study of ethnic schemas held by undergraduates at Michigan State University and the ways that they behaved based on that social knowledge. He investigated conceptions of foreign teaching assistants, and he found that students had common expectations that the T.A.s could not speak English clearly, that they would be hard to talk to in and out of the classroom, and that they were smart. When Rao showed a 10-minute videotape of a foreign teaching assistant that confirmed the expectation that he or she could not speak English clearly, over 50% of the students reported that they would drop the class that the foreign teaching assistant was conducting.

Markus, et al. (1982) conducted a study of gender schemas. Gender is different from biological sex in that it involves the sex-role stereotypes that are associated with biological sex. We each have a preferred gender category as well as a biological sex category. For example, Bill may see himself as masculine, in which case he is likely to have the masculine attributes commonly associated with males. Or Bill may see himself as feminine and, therefore, would likely have female attributes; or he may see himself as androgynous, in which case he is likely to have a combination of masculine and feminine attributes. In this study, Markus et al. (1982) investigated the content of gender schemas. People who were feminine were more likely to be seen and to see themselves as soft-spoken, tender, gentle, cheerful, warm, and yielding. On the other hand, people who were masculine were more likely to be seen and to see themselves as taking a stand, defending their own beliefs, and being ambitious, competitive, assertive, and individualistic. Androgynous people were likely to be seen and to see themselves as a combination of masculine and feminine attributes. In addition, people with each type of gender identity were more likely to remember, endorse, and supply examples of the behaviors and attributes associated with their gender.

What this means in terms of communication, then, is that when you are a receiver of communication, your gender schema will influence how you interpret and what you remember about other people's messages. For example, if you are a masculine male or female you may be most likely to think well of and to remember messages that are direct and to the point. Whereas, if you are a feminine male or female then you may be most likely to endorse and remember messages that are tactful and reserved. If you are androgynous, you may endorse and remember either kind of message best depending on the situation. In addition, one of your secondary goals when you send your own messages will be staying true to your conception of gender.

In summary, cultural level social knowledge includes knowledge of central and prominent aspects of people such as their ethnicity and gender. We have expectations about how people should and will communicate based upon this social knowledge. In addition, we determine how we will communicate with others based upon the ethnicity and gender of ourselves and the other in the situation.

Sociological level social knowledge. The types of knowledge we have about various roles and situations are critical components of communication. Role schemas include knowledge organized into sets of expectations that govern how persons holding certain social positions should behave (Trenholm & Jensen, 2000). The roles of student, professor, friend, romantic partner, parent, and child should be particularly salient for you while you are in college.

One of us asks our classes to generate the knowledge held in the role schema for the typical professor. Along with poor personal hygiene and out-of-date clothing, students frequently mention communication attributes such as boring, speaks in a monotone voice, speaks a different language, mumbles, no sense of humor, aloof, and speaks down to us. In order to determine how social knowledge about the typical professor differs from that of the outstanding professor, Smith and her graduate students (Smith, Medendorp, Ranck, Morrison, & Kopfman, 1994) conducted research on Michigan State students. They found that their collective role schema for the outstanding professor included attributes such as being a good speaker, encouraging interaction in class, moving while speaking, varying vocal tones, giving and requesting feedback, providing examples and stories, making eye contact, and smiling. The different information contained in the schema for a typical versus an outstanding professor should allow you to get a sense for how you could identify one or the other in terms of their communication behavior, and how you would be likely to communicate with them differently based on your social knowledge of professors.

We have social knowledge about situations as well, and this knowledge affects the ways we interpret and produce messages (Miller, Cody, & McLaughlin, 1994). Cantor, Mischel, and Schwartz (1982) found that people have different situation schemas for different social events, such as being at a religious ceremony, being at a party, and being at a job interview. These situation schemas consist of knowledge of the different types of people and proper activities for each social setting. You can imagine that you would interpret a loud greeting accompanied by a kiss and hug quite differently if it occurred at a religious ceremony, a party, or a job interview. Situation schemas also affect the ways that we produce messages. For example, you would likely go about introducing yourself differently in these different situations.

In summary, sociological level knowledge allows us to assign meaning to role related behavior in different social situations and to produce communication behaviors that are seen as appropriate to the role and situation. In addition, we need knowledge on the psychological level if we want to be able to have close relationships and to be seen by others and ourselves as individuals.

Psychological level social knowledge. Person, self, and relationship schemas are the structures in which we hold the knowledge that allows us to know others as individuals, to have a sense of self that is unique, and to form close relationships such as friendships and romances. **Person schemas** allow us to answer the question "What kind of person is he or she?" (Cantor & Mischel, 1977, 1979a, 1979b). Whether our answer is "studious," "wild," or "withdrawn," the person schema we have called to mind that corresponds to this label contains knowledge that allows us to make sense of the messages that this person is likely to send us. This knowledge also helps us decide how to frame the messages that we send in return. For example, suppose that a person came up to you and said, "I'm just exhausted because I didn't sleep at all last night." You might make the inference that the studious person was up all night preparing for an exam, that the wild person was up all night having fun, and that the withdrawn person was up all night worrying. You might respond by asking the studious person a question about something that is unclear to you about the upcoming exam, by asking the wild person how he or she feels today, and by avoiding asking the withdrawn person anything at all about their experiences last night.

The most well-developed body of knowledge we have is the **self schema** because we are always gathering information about the ways we act and respond. The self schema is similar to the person schema in that we are asking "What type of person am I?" Self categories are similar in kind to those we hold for other people, and these categories of self affect the ways we communicate with others. Fong and Markus (1982) found that people who were extroverts, and who were asked to find out about another person, asked significantly more questions about whether that person was talkative and outgoing, while introverts did the opposite and asked more questions about whether that person was shy and reserved. In other words, we tend to seek information about others that is related to our own self schemas. The study also found that once we have information about others that is related to our own self schemas, we are more likely to have confidence in the judgments and inferences we make about them based on that information.

In addition to person and self schemas, we have **relational schemas** (Planalp, 1985). Relational schemas can exist for any type of interpersonal relationship such as friendship or romance (Smith, 1995). Davis and Todd (1985) showed that depending on the presence or absence and weighting of seven attributes (success, viability, intimacy, spontaneity, stability, support, and enjoyment), different types of friendships could be distinguished from one another. People's ratings of these attributes served to distinguish best friends, close friends of the same sex, close friends of the opposite sex, casual acquaintances, and former friends. Once we categorize a person as a friend, we are likely to interpret their messages and form our messages to them in ways that are different than we would with an acquaintance. Planalp (1992; 1993) found that conversations between friends had more mutual knowledge of one another, laughter, profanity, interruptions, intimacy, relaxation, and spontaneity than did conversations between acquaintances. Therefore, we might interpret the interruption of a close friend as "excitement about the topic," while we might interpret the interruption of an acquaintance as "rude." We would be likely to tell a close friend about a fight with a romantic partner in great detail, while we would be unlikely to do this with an acquaintance.

You should now be able to see that we communicate with others based upon the cultural, sociological, and psychological social knowledge that we hold. No matter whether this knowledge is held in ethnic, gender, role, situation, person, self, or relational schemas, it affects the ways we interpret the messages others send to us. In order to understand more fully the way in which this social knowledge operates in the interpretation of messages, we need to examine stages of input processing that occur during communication.

Stages of Input Processing

Input processing refers to the different ways in which we use social knowledge to understand other people's messages. The stages of input processing are selective exposure, selective attention, decoding, interpretation, and inference.

Selective exposure. When we go out of our way to place ourselves in or to avoid situations where we will be certain to encounter a certain event or person, we have engaged in selective exposure (Trenholm & Jensen, 2000). The decision to enter or to avoid is based on your social knowledge of what you believe is likely to happen in the situation. For example, the Rao (1994) study of Michigan State undergraduates found that when a foreign teaching assistant seemed to conform to their expectations that he or she could not speak English clearly, over 50% of them reported that they would drop the class. In other words, they decided to avoid the situation involving the class because information they held in their ethnic schema about foreign T.A.s was confirmed during a 10-minute exposure.

It is also likely that you would go out of your way to enroll in a course that all of your friends said is taught by an outstanding professor. Once you decided to enter this situation, your social knowledge of outstanding professors would probably cause you to focus on certain aspects of the professor's behavior.

Selective attention. We selectively attend to, or focus on, some aspects of a situation, while we ignore other aspects of that situation completely (Fiske & Taylor, 1991). The schema that is currently invoked in our mind determines where we will search for the information that we do attend to in the situation. An example of selective attention might occur in a class that all your friends said was taught by an outstanding professor. You would have the role schema of outstanding professor in mind, and this schema would likely direct your attention to those behaviors commonly held in the schema. You might notice his or her sense of humor, that he or she encouraged interaction in class, and all the other attributes that Smith, et al. (1984) found in the role schemas of Michigan State students for outstanding professors. At the same time, you would likely ignore those times when this professor spoke in a monotone voice and was boring because the social knowledge that would lead you to expect to find these behaviors was not activated.

Decoding. The information to which you did selectively attend would then be decoded. This means that you would transform the actual object or event you observed into a mental picture (Fiske & Taylor, 1991). The information that you decoded would then be mixed together with the knowledge that you already had in your currently invoked schema so that you could assign meaning to the object or event.

Interpretation and inference. People interpret, or make sense of new information by matching it with social knowledge held in the schema activated at the time of processing. If this match is ambiguous or incomplete, inconsistencies are resolved and missing pieces of the puzzle are filled in by inference (Wilson & Kramer, 1986). Interpretation involves classifying and labeling ambiguous behavior so that its meaning is clear. Often the same behavior is interpreted differently depending on the person schema we have in mind (Srull & Wyer, 1979). For example, if Ron talks to his instructor after the first day of class, we might label his behavior as "outgoing" or "brownosing." Inference making is simply going beyond the information that is known, by making a judgment about an unknown based on what is known (Smith, 1995). If you classify Ron as outgoing shortly after meeting him, then you also may infer that Ron is funny (because you associate these two qualities in your extrovert schema), and you may do this even though you've never heard Ron say anything funny.

A second example of interpretation and inference might occur when a freshman meets his or her roommate for the first time. If the roommate shares many features with the student's best friend, the student is likely to interpret their first interaction in a very positive way because a match between the new information and the social knowledge held in a friend schema would occur. Because we all want to predict future behavior, especially of a person with whom we will be living, it is necessary to make inferences during this first encounter. The freshman must go beyond the information that he or she currently knows about the roommate. In the case that a relational schema of "best friend" is operating, the inferences about future behavior are likely to be highly positive. This will not be the case if the new roommate caused a "hated enemy" schema to be invoked.

Guidelines for Input Processing

As you can see, social knowledge plays a critical role as we talk with strangers, roommates, professors, family, and close friends. We bring an abundance of cultural, sociological, and psychological-level information to every communication situation. Without this knowledge we would start each conversation like the sojourner in a foreign country for the first time failing to understand other people's meanings or norms for interaction.

On the other hand, our social knowledge can get in the way when it leads to stereotyping, self-fulfilling prophecies, or conflicting interpretations and memories of events.

1. Our first guideline, then, is to **realize that our snap judgments or first impressions can be inaccurate, and that we should give others the opportunity to violate our expectations.** Stereotyping occurs when we assume that every member of a social group possesses all of the attributes we associate with that group. We stereotype by rigidly adhering to our schemas regardless of what another person does. For example, if we make a snap judgment that our new professor is aloof, boring, and out-of-touch based on our "typical professor" schema and never give our new professor a chance to disprove this impression, then we are stereotyping.

2. The second guideline builds upon the first in that **we must realize that when we act based upon our perceptions, we can cause others to behave as we expect them to.** Self-fulfilling prophecies occur when we expect another person to behave in a particular way, and then do things that make it likely that the person will behave as we expect (Schneider, Hastorf, & Ellsworth, 1979). This can cause either positive or negative outcomes.

    For example, based on their ethnic schema, most students expect that foreign TAs have difficulty speaking English clearly (Rao, 1994). Now imagine that "Nagesh," a foreign TA, arrives on the first day to teach his class. As he walks into class his students groan "Oh no," roll their eyes, and whisper back and forth. Normally Nagesh speaks English clearly, but now he is nervous because his new students are upset about having a foreign TA. Because he is nervous, Nagesh stumbles a few times as he introduces himself. His students get more upset; some get up and leave. Nagesh becomes more nervous and makes more mistakes. Unknowingly, these students have helped create the very behavior in Nagesh that they feared.

3. The third guideline is that we should **realize that most behaviors are open to multiple interpretations, and that others may not label a behavior or recall a situation in the same way that we do.** If you recall a recent conflict you had with a close friend, family member, or romantic partner, the chances are great that the root of this conflict was a different interpretation of a behavior or memory of a situation. "When you said that, it meant that you did not care about me." "No, that is not what I meant at all." When your conflict is about an important issue or with a person who is very important to you, try to take another's perspective and think about how they might see things differently than you do.

The results of input processing are the mental representations of the actual event, as well as interpretations and inferences about the event. This social knowledge forms the basis of our subsequent judgments about the event, as well as the messages we form in response to the event. When deciding what to say in situations, we rely on goals, plans, and output processing.

GOALS, PLANS, AND OUTPUT PROCESSING

Aside from knowledge about culture, roles, situations, relationships, and people, you also have social knowledge about how to communicate effectively in everyday situations.

This special type of social knowledge is called **procedural knowledge,** which is your understanding about how to communicate in order to get things done (Anderson, 1985). Procedural knowledge includes the goals that you try to accomplish by communicating as well as your plans for accomplishing those goals.

What Is a Communication Goal?

A goal is a state of affairs that you want to attain or maintain in the future (Hobbs & Evans, 1980). You probably have a long-term goal of earning a college diploma and pursuing a career. You do not yet have the diploma or career, but these are goals that you currently desire and are striving to attain. A communication goal is a desired state of affairs that can be attained only by interacting with others (Cody, Canary, & Smith, 1994; Wilson, 1995). Getting your car washed is not a communication goal since you can do it without talking to anyone. Persuading your professor to give you a higher grade on a paper assignment or convincing someone that you find attractive to go on a date are communication goals, since you must talk to people in order to accomplish them.

Types of Communication Goals

Communication goals can be divided into primary and secondary goals (Dillard, 1990; Dillard, Segrin, & Harden, 1989). The **primary goal** is what compels you to say something in the situation; it tells what the situation is about. Imagine that you worked very hard on an essay for your English composition course, only to receive a grade of "C" for your effort. You decide to discuss this grade with your English professor during her office hours. If you were interrupted during the middle of this conversation and asked, "What are you trying to accomplish in this situation?" you might reply "I'm trying to get my professor to raise my grade." Persuading the professor to raise your grade is your primary goal. Both you and your professor realize that this is what the conversation is about.

Aside from primary goals, people also pursue **secondary goals** during conversation (Dillard, 1990; Hample & Dallinger, 1987). Secondary goals arise from concerns that are common across individuals and situations. In most cases, you want to avoid becoming too anxious, to make a positive impression, to act consistently with your values, and to maintain important friendships. These secondary goals often hold you back from saying certain things, or lead you to say them with tact. For example, you want to convince your English professor to raise your grade (primary goal) but you also may want to keep a favorable impression in the professor's eyes (secondary goal), especially if you are going to have this professor for several additional classes in the future.

Let's consider another example to make sure that the distinction between primary and secondary goals is clear. Imagine that you are attracted to another student who sits close to you in this class. You had never met this person before this class, and you have only talked to him/her a few times before class. You decide to ask this person out on a date in order to get to know him/her better. You hope the person will say "yes" to your request because you will be embarrassed if s/he turns you down. Getting the person to go out with you is your primary goal, while avoiding embarrassment is your secondary goal. Notice that the primary goal motivates you to talk to the other person, while the secondary goal holds you back or leads you to say some things rather than others.

As this "date request" situation illustrates, tension can exist between primary and secondary goals. Goal conflict occurs when the actions that help you accomplish one goal hinder you from accomplishing another goal (O'Keefe & Delia, 1982; Wilson & Putnam,

1990). To understand goal conflict, imagine that you work part time as a shift manager in a fast food restaurant. One of your close friends also works at this restaurant. Although your friend generally is a good worker, recently s/he has made a habit of coming back from breaks five minutes late when you are in charge. Other employees have noticed what your friend is doing. In this situation, you may want to tell your friend that s/he needs to return from break on time when you are in charge, because you want to fulfill your role as manager. However, you also may fear saying something that will get your friend upset at you for "making a big deal out of nothing." Pursuing the primary goal of changing your friend's behavior has the potential to conflict with the secondary goal of not upsetting your friend. Situations involving goal conflict can be tricky to handle. Planning is needed to manage such situations successfully.

What Is a Communication Plan?

Aside from your goals, procedural knowledge also includes your plans for how to accomplish those goals. Plans are people's knowledge about available means for overcoming obstacles and accomplishing goals (Berger, 1995; Dillard, 1990). You may have the goals of graduating from college in four (or five) years and landing a desirable first job. You also know that there are potential obstacles to achieving these goals: you may have difficulty getting into classes required for graduation, and there are a limited number of desirable jobs and a large number of graduates competing for them. Given this state of affairs, you probably have begun to develop plans for overcoming these obstacles to your goals. For example, you may plan on taking at least 15 credits per term, going to summer school if necessary, and doing an internship to build your resume.

A communication plan is your knowledge about how to accomplish one or more communication goals. A plan is similar to a schema in that both contain social knowledge. The difference is that a schema stores information about people, roles, and situations, while a plan stores information about what to do in order to accomplish goals. People develop plans for achieving a variety of communication goals, such as plans for ingratiating a new roommate, finding out sensitive information about others, getting a date, persuading a friend about a controversial issue, and selling textbooks back to a bookstore (Berger, 1995; Roloff & Jordan, 1992; Waldron, 1990).

People rely on several sources of information to develop their plans, including knowledge at the cultural, sociological, and psychological levels that we discussed earlier (see Berger & Jordan 1992). At the cultural level, we all receive instructions at a young age about how to achieve social goals. In our culture, people often introduce themselves by issuing a greeting such as "Hi," stating their name, and offering a handshake. You may remember your parents teaching you these steps when you were young. Such a plan could be modified and used in almost any situation in our culture. People in all cultures appear to develop communication plans, although individuals from different cultures may have different ideas about how to plan effectively (Cai, 1994; Kim & Wilson, 1994).

At the sociological level, people learn plans by observing role models. As a graduate student, one of the authors developed his own plans for teaching a large-lecture class by observing one of his professors who had taught such classes for many years. Elements of the plan included how to communicate main ideas clearly, encourage class discussion, and use audio-visual equipment to hold students' attention. After becoming a professor, the author has developed and used this plan with many different classes.

At the psychological level, people also develop plans for communicating with well-known others such as close friends or romantic partners. For example, if you want to convince your best friend to go see a movie this Friday, you may use a plan that you learned from having asked your best friend to do things together in the past. In other words, you may develop specific plans for persuading your best friend because you now have a lot of knowledge about what works with him/her. Regardless of whether your plan is based on cultural, sociological, or psychological-level knowledge, it can vary in three ways.

Qualities of Communication Plans

Communication plans can have three important qualities: differentiation, completeness, and contingencies (Berger & Bell, 1988; Dillard, 1990). A **differentiated plan** contains several elements or steps, while an undifferentiated plan contains only one or a few steps. Imagine that two people, Serena and Sam, both decide to ask other students in their class for dates. Serena plans to ask a third party questions about the man she wants to ask out, to start conversations with this man before class and find out what they have in common, to "accidentally" bump into him in another situation, and then to ask him out. In contrast, Sam simply plans to ask out the woman he likes after the next class. Serena's plan is more differentiated than Sam's plan, since her plan has four steps while Sam's has only one.

A **complete plan** has each of the steps or elements worked out in detail, while the steps in an incomplete plan are vague or unspecified. When Serena asks out the man she likes, she may plan to start off the conversation by talking about the test they just took in class and then ask him if he would like to go out to dinner on Friday night. When Sam asks out the woman he likes, he may not plan the specific details of what to say, but rather just "see how things go." Serena's plan is more complete than Sam's since she has decided exactly how she'll ask for a date, while Sam has not planned the details.

Finally, a **contingent plan** includes back-up elements in case some of the original steps do not work. Imagine that both Serena and Sam ask their prospective dates out for dinner on Friday night. What if both prospective dates say that they would like to go but they have to work Friday night? Serena already has planned in advance to ask about Saturday night if her prospective date is busy Friday, while Sam has not considered the possibility that his prospective date might be busy on Friday. Serena's plan includes contingencies while Sam's plan does not.

Developing differentiated, complete, and contingent plans does not guarantee that you will always accomplish your communication goals, but planning in detail can help. Charles Berger and Robert Bell (1988) conducted an interesting study of the communication plans developed by lonely and shy college students. Lonely students agree with statements such as "I lack companionship" and "There are very few people that I can turn to." Shy students agree with statements such as "I feel tense when I'm with people I don't know well" and "I am often uncomfortable at parties and other social functions." Berger and Bell had groups of lonely and shy students write plans for requesting a date and making a good impression on a new roommate, and then compared these plans with those written by other students. On average, the lonely and shy students wrote less differentiated and contingent communication plans than did other students, and the plans written by lonely and shy students were judged as less effective by peers. The authors suggest that training college students to develop more detailed communication plans might be one way of helping them overcome loneliness and shyness.

To this point we have discussed plans for accomplishing a single goal, such as asking someone out on a date or getting your roommate to give you a ride to class. As we noted earlier, however, people often have more than one goal at a time, and these primary and secondary goals can come into conflict. We also develop plans for managing conflicting goals.

Plans for Managing Conflicting Goals

Situations that contain goal conflict can be difficult to handle. Developing a plan for such situations requires extra effort if you are to be successful (Greene, 1995). Remember the situation where you were a shift manager at a fast food restaurant, and your close friend and fellow employee has made a habit of returning five minutes late from break? There are three types of plans for managing goal conflicts like this: selection, separation, and integration (O'Keefe & Delia, 1982; O'Keefe & Shepherd, 1987).

Selection involves prioritizing one of the conflicting goals and ignoring the other. For example, you could plan to say whatever is necessary to get this person back from break on time, even if it means not being friends anymore. In this case you have selected the primary goal. Alternatively, you could plan not to say anything at all to this person about being tardy for fear of losing him/her as a friend. In this case you have selected the secondary goal. Although it is simple, selection rarely works well when both conflicting goals are important. You need to say something, or the other employees will think you are playing favorites, but you also don't want to lose a close friend.

Separation involves attempting to pursue each of the conflicting goals at different times or places. For example, you might plan to tell this person that you want to remain close friends outside of work, but say that you have to put your professional relationship first at work. In this case you have tried to separate your relationships with the other person into different places: professionals at work, friends outside of work. Alternatively, you could plan to initially tell this person how close you feel to him/her and how much you value your friendship, but then say that s/he has to start arriving back from break on time. In this case you have tried to separate the conflicting goals in time: first you say things to maintain the friendship, then you say things to try to change your friend's tardiness.

Integration involves attempting to redefine the situation so that the two goals are no longer in conflict, and both goals can be pursued at the same time. As an example, we have defined the manager situation as having the primary goal of "persuading your friend to start coming back from break on time." What if you instead defined the situation as having the primary goal of "getting your friend to help you with a sticky situation at work?" You might plan to tell your friend: some of the other employees are being a little petty. They have noticed that you have come back from break five minutes late a couple of times. Now I know that five minutes is no big deal, and it doesn't bother me, but some of the others are beginning to say that I'm playing favorites because I wouldn't let them be late. Could you help me out here? I'd really be grateful if you could make sure to be back on time, so that these other employees will stop complaining.

By redefining the situation as "asking for help," you no longer are faced with a conflict between telling your friend what to do and upsetting your friend. If this approach succeeds, then you can get your friend to stop being tardy and maintain your friendship at the same time. Integration requires considerable creativity and effort. You not only have to plan what to say, but you also have to plan how to redefine your goals in the situation so that they no longer conflict. Taking the time to develop an integrative plan, however, can be worthwhile if both the primary and secondary goals are important. Plans that integrate conflicting goals generally are rated as more effective than those that separate or select conflicting goals (O'Keefe & Shepherd, 1987; Bingham & Burleson, 1989).

You should now be able to see that we develop plans for accomplishing a variety of communication goals, and for dealing with situations that contain goal conflict. Regardless whether this procedural knowledge comes from cultural, sociological, or psychological levels, we rely on it to decide what to say to others. In order to more fully understand the way in which we translate this procedural knowledge into action, we need to examine stages of output processing.

Stages of Output Processing

Although having detailed plans can be helpful, we still have to be able to use those plans effectively. Output processing refers to the different steps in translating a plan into action (Berger, 1995). The stages of output processing are generating and selecting, implementing or decoding, and modifying plans.

Generating and selecting plans. People may generate plans prior to entering into conversation, but they often generate and select plans "on-line" or during the conversation itself. For example, if you are preparing for a job interview then you may develop detailed plans about how you will present yourself and answer various questions, but this differs from a situation in which you are flying on an airplane and the passenger in the next seat mentions she is hiring for a new position in public relations. If you are interested, you will have to do a lot of planning on the spot.

Vincent Waldron (1990) conducted a study that illustrates how planning goes on during conversation. Waldron brought together pairs of unacquainted college students and told them to have an "initial" conversation. Prior to the conversation, Waldron instructed one of the students to find out information about the second student's religious beliefs, and the second student to find out information about the first student's political views (neither student knew that the other had received these instructions). All of these initial conversations were videotaped. Immediately after each conversation, Waldron separated the students and had each one watch a videotape of their conversation. As they watched their videotape, students wrote down everything they could remember thinking during the conversation. Students were doing a good deal of "on-line" planning, since 44% of the thoughts they later recalled having had during the conversation were concerned with the goals they were pursuing or with the plans they were using to attain their goals.

If you generate more than one possible plan for accomplishing a communicating goal then you also may need to select which plan to carry out. People may rely on simple decision rules to select plans, such as "use the same plan that I used the last time" or "use the plan that I typically use" (Greene, 1990; Wilson, 1995). When they have more time, people also may consider which plan is most appropriate and most likely to work (Canary & Spitzberg, 1987; Kim & Wilson, 1994).

Implementing or encoding plans. Once you select a plan, you have to put it into action. Encoding is the process of transforming your mental plan into words. Implementing plans involves several related decisions, including what topics to talk about, what words to use, and how loudly to speak (Greene, 1984a). We often make these choices mindlessly, with little conscious attention.

Modifying plans. After implementing your initial plan you may discover that you still have not accomplished your goal. You might ask another student out on a date for Friday night only to find out s/he has to work that evening, or you might give another stranger directions only to find out that s/he didn't understand them. When you encounter obstacles to achieving your goals, you may decide to modify elements of your original plan, generate and select a new plan, or give up on accomplishing your goals (Dillard, 1990). Plans can be modified in several ways. For example, if a stranger does not understand your directions the first time, you might speak slower and louder while repeating the same directions, describe the same route but add additional landmarks along the way, or describe an entirely different route (Berger & DiBattista, 1993).

Guidelines for Output Processing

As you can see, social knowledge plays a critical role as we talk with strangers, acquaintances, family, and close friends. We bring an abundance of procedural knowledge about how to accomplish a wide range of communication goals to every situation. Without this knowledge we would not know what to say to be an effective and appropriate communicator.

On the other hand, the best made plans can go awry. We must be able to generate, select, implement, and modify our procedural knowledge to carry out plans successfully. Remember the following three guidelines for output processing:

1. **When possible, prepare and practice your plans in advance.** People may not perform effectively when they must develop and carry out communication plans in completely new or novel situations. John Greene and his colleagues have carried out a series of experiments in which they hand students an index card and tell them to give an extemporaneous speech about the topic written on the card (Greene, 1984b; Greene, Smith, Smith, & Cashion, 1987). One group of students is given 60 seconds to generate a plan before they start speaking, while a second group must start speaking immediately after they receive their card. As you would expect, students who are given time to develop and mentally rehearse their plan beforehand speak more fluently than those who must develop their entire plan as they speak.

   Greene also has carried out a variation of this experiment, in which one group of students initially is taught to use a vague plan that can be applied to most topics (e.g., first discuss the problem, then discuss potential solutions) while a second group is given no training. After this, both groups are given an index card and told to start speaking immediately. Even though neither group can anticipate the specific topic on their index card, students who have practiced using the vague plan beforehand still speak more fluently than students who have not been trained to use any plan at all. These experiments illustrate that people get better at implementing communication plans when they practice the specific topic, or at least the general task, beforehand.

2. **Keep your arousal at a comfortable level as you implement plans.** Arousal can impede your ability to carry out plans effectively. People feel aroused when they experience intense emotions such as strong anxiety, fear, or anger (Metts & Bowers, 1995). Physiological signs of arousal include sweaty palms, increased blood pressure, and increased heart rate (Cappella, 1995).

   People make more errors carrying out plans when their level of arousal is very low or very high rather than when they are moderately aroused (Greene, 1988). That is, either too little or too much arousal can be a problem. If you are trying to persuade your English professor to raise your paper grade, you may carry out your plan more effectively if you stay involved but calm rather than if you don't care how things turn out or if you get very anxious or angry during the conversation. Indeed, people include fewer logical arguments in their plans to persuade others when they are highly aroused (Dillard et al., 1989).

3. **Finally, be mindful about whether your initial plan needs to be modified.** People may not carry out plans effectively when they do so mindlessly, especially when plans have to be modified. Mindlessness refers to a mental state where people fail to pay attention to relevant details, think in terms of categories rather than exceptions, and assume there is only one way to accomplish a goal. Mindfulness occurs when people create new categories and are open to new information and perspectives (Benoit & Benoit, 1986; Langer, 1989). Acting mindlessly means being on "automatic pilot," while acting mindfully requires mental effort. Imagine that you are coming out of the place where you live and a stranger asks you for directions to the Communication Building. You have walked from where you live to the Communication Building a hundred times, and you have given several other people directions to the building. Without much thought, you give this stranger the same directions that you have given many times before. You have acted mindlessly in this situation.

Acting mindlessly works fine as long as your communication plan has worked well in the past and the current situation is similar to those prior situations, but what if that stranger says that s/he didn't understand your directions and asks you to go through them again? Charles Berger and Patrick DiBattista (1993) had students give directions to either an Asian or European-American stranger. After each student completed his/her directions, the stranger said s/he didn't understand the directions and asked the student to try again. How would you adjust your directions the second time? Very few students in the study changed the route they had described the first time or mentioned more landmarks along the way. Most students simply repeated the same directions while talking slower and louder. Students did this even when it was obvious that the stranger had no difficulty understanding English (i.e., when the stranger was European-American). Rather than paying attention to why the stranger was having difficulty understanding their directions, students in the study simply altered their plan in a mindless fashion. If your initial plan fails, that's a good clue that you need to be more mindful as you modify your plan or develop another one.

CONCLUSIONS

Social knowledge is a critical component of communication in personal development, social integration, organizational management, and societal enrichment. As you read the chapters that follow, think about the ways that social knowledge is used. In personal development, self and relationship schemas are of primary importance. In social integration, we have cultural and role schemas that affect socialization and cultural development, and in organizational management and social influence, goals and planning are key issues. The entire section on societal enrichment addresses how we learn social knowledge through cultural institutions such as the media and education. Social knowledge is the foundation for the interpretation and production of messages in the variety of contexts that make up our lives.

REFERENCES

Anderson, J. R. (1985). *Cognitive psychology and its implications* (2nd ed.). New York: W. H. Freeman.

Benoit, P. J., & Benoit, W. L. (1986). Consciousness: The mindlessness/mindfulness and verbal report controversies. *Western Journal of Speech Communication, 50,* 41–63.

Berger, C. R. (1995). A plan based approach to strategic communication. In D. Hewes (Ed.), *Cognitive bases of interpersonal communication* (pp. 141–179). Hillsdale, NJ: Erlbaum.

Berger, C. R., & Bell, R. A. (1988). Plans and the initiation of social relationships. *Human Communication Research, 15,* 17–235.

Berger, C. R., & DiBattista, P. (1993). Communication failure and plan adaptation: If at first you don't succeed, say it louder and slower. *Communication Monographs, 60,* 220–238.

Berger, C. R., & Jordan, J. (1992). Planning sources, planning difficulty, and verbal fluency. *Communication Monographs, 59,* 130–149.

Bingham, S. G., & Burleson, B. R. (1989). Multiple effects of messages with multiple goals: Some perceived outcomes of responses to sexual harassment. *Human Communication Research, 16,* 184–216.

Cai, D. A. (1994). *Planning in negotiation: A comparison of U.S. and Taiwanese cultures.* Unpublished doctoral dissertation, Michigan State University, East Lansing, MI.

Canary, D. J., & Spitzberg, B. H. (1987). Appropriateness and effectiveness perceptions of conflict strategies. *Human Communication Research, 14,* 93–118.

Cantor, N., & Mischel, W. (1977). Traits as prototypes: Effects on recognition memory. *Journal of Personality and Social Psychology, 35,* 38–48.

Cantor, N., & Mischel, W. (1979a), Prototypes in person perception. In L. Berkowitz (Ed.), *Advances in experimental social psychology* (Vol. 12, pp. 3–52). New York: Academic Press.

Cantor, N., & Mischel, W. (1979b) Prototypicality and personality: Effects on free recall and personality impressions. *Journal of Research in Personality, 13,* 187–205.

Cantor, N., Mischel, W., & Schwartz, J. C. (1982). A prototype analysis of situations. *Cognitive Psychology, 14,* 45–77.

Cappella, J. N. (1995). The management of conversational interaction in adults and infants. In M. L. Knapp & G. R. Miller, Eds.), *Handbook of interpersonal communication* (2nd ed., pp. 380–418). Thousand Oaks, CA: Sage.

Cody, M. J., Canary, D. J., & Smith, S. W. (1995). Compliance-gaining goals: An inductive typology of actors' goal types, strategies, and successes. In J. Daly & J. Wiemann (Eds.), *Communicating strategically* (pp. 33–90). Hillsdale, NJ: Erlbaum.

Davis, K. E., & Todd, M. J. (1985). Assessing friendship: Prototypes, paradigm cases, and relationship description. In S. Duck & D. Perlman (Eds.) *Understanding personal relationships: An interdisciplinary approach* (pp. 17–38). Beverly Hills, CA: Sage.

Dillard, J. P. (1990). A goal-driven model of interpersonal influence. In J. P. Dillard (Ed.), *Seeking compliance: The production of interpersonal influence messages* (pp. 41–56). Scottsdale, AZ: Gorsuch Scarisbrick.

Dillard, J. P., Segrin, C., & Harden, J. M. (1989). Primary and secondary goals in the production of interpersonal influence messages. *Communication Monographs, 56,* 19–38.

Fiske, S. T., & Taylor, S. E. (1991). *Social cognition* (2nd ed.). Reading, MA: Addison-Wesley.

Fong, G. T., & Markus, H. (1982) Self-schemas and judgments about others. *Social Cognition, 1,* 191–204.

Greene, J. O. (1995). Pursuit of multiple social goals: Action assembly theory contributions to the study of cognitive encoding processes. In B. Burleson (Ed.), *Communication yearbook 18* (pp. 26–53). Thousand Oaks, CA: Sage.

Greene, J. O. (1990). Tactical social action: Towards some strategies for theory. In M. J. Cody & M. L. McLaughlin (Eds.), *The psychology of tactical communication* (pp. 31–47). Clevendon, UK: Multilingual Matters.

Greene, J. O. (1988). Cognitive processes: Methods for probing the black box. In C. H. Tardy (Ed.), *A handbook for the study of human communication: Methods and instruments for observing, measuring, and assessing communication processes* (pp. 37–66). Norwood, NJ: Ablex.

Greene, J. O. (1984a). A cognitive approach to human communication: An action assembly theory. *Communication Monographs, 51,* 289–306.

Greene, J. O. (1984b). Speech preparation processes and verbal fluency. *Human Communication Research, 11,* 61–84.

Greene, J. O., Smith, S. W., Smith, R. C., & Cashion, J. L. (1987). The sound of one mind working: Memory retrieval and response preparation as components of pausing in spontaneous speech. In M. McLaughlin (Ed.), *Communication yearbook 10* (pp. 241–258). Newbury Park, CA: Sage.

Hample, D., & Dallinger, J. M. (1987). Individual differences in cognitive editing standards. *Human Communication Research, 14,* 123–144.

Hobbs, J. R., & Evans, D. A. (1980). Conversation as planned behavior. *Cognitive Science, 4,* 349–377.

Kim, M. S., & Wilson, S. R. (1994). A cross-cultural comparison of implicit theories of requesting. *Communication Monographs, 61,* 210–235.

Langer, E. J. (1989). *Mindfulness.* Reading, MA: Addison-Wesley.

Markus, H., Crane, M., Bernstein, S., & Siladi, M. (1982). Self-schemas and gender. *Journal of Personality and Social Psychology, 42,* 38–50.

Metts, S., & Bowers, J. W. (1994). Emotion in interpersonal communication. In M. L. Knapp & G. R. Miller (Eds.), *Handbook of interpersonal communication* (2nd ed.) (pp. 508–541). Thousand Oaks, CA: Sage.

Miller, G. R., & Steinberg, M. (1975). *Between people.* Chicago, IL: Science Research Associates.

Miller, L. C., Cody, M. J., & McLaughlin, M. L. (1994). Situations and goals as fundamental constructs in interpersonal communication research. In M. L. Knapp & G. R. Miller (Eds.), *Handbook of interpersonal communication* (2nd ed., pp. 162–198). Thousand Oaks, CA: Sage.

O'Keefe, B. J., & Delia, J. G. (1982). Impression formation and message production. In M. E. Roloff & C. R. Berger (Ed.), *Social cognition and communication* (pp. 33–72). Beverly Hills, CA: Sage.

O'Keefe, B. J., & Shepherd, G. (1987). The pursuit of multiple objectives in face-to-face persuasive interactions: Effects of construct differentiation on message organization. *Communication Monographs, 54,* 398–419.

Planalp, S. (1985). Relational schemata: A test of alternative forms of relational knowledge as guides to communication. *Human Communication Research, 12,* 3–29.

Planalp, S. (1989). Relational communication and cognition. In B. Dervin, L. Grossberg, B. J. O'Keefe, & E. Wartella (Eds.) *Rethinking communication: Paradigm exemplars* (Vol. 2, pp. 269–279). Newbury Park, CA: Sage.

Planalp, S. (1992). Friends' and acquaintances' conversations: I. Perceived differences. *Journal of Social and Personal Relationships, 9,* 483–506.

Planalp, S. (1993). Friends' and acquaintances' conversations: II. Coded differences. *Journal of Social and Personal Relationships, 10,* 339–354.

Rao, N. (1994). *The oh no! syndrome: A language expectation model of undergraduates' negative reactions towards foreign teaching assistants.* Unpublished doctoral dissertation, Michigan State University, East Lansing, MI.

Roloff, M. E., & Jordan, J. M. (1992). Achieving negotiation goals: The "fruits and foibles" of planning ahead. In L. L. Putnam & M. E. Roloff (Eds.), *Communication and negotiation* (pp. 21–45). Newbury Park, CA: Sage.

Schneider, D. J., Hastorf, A. H., & Ellsworth, P. C. (1979). *Person perception* (2nd ed.). Reading, MA: Addison-Wesley.

Smith, S. W. (1995). Perceptual processing of nonverbal-relational messages. In D. E. Hewes (Ed)., *The cognitive bases of interpersonal communication* (pp. 87–112). Hillsdale, NJ: L. E. Erlbaum.

Smith, S. W., Medendorp, C., Ranck, S., Morrison, K., & Kopfman, J. (1994). The prototypical features of the outstanding professor. *Journal of Excellence in College Teaching, 5,* 5–22.

Srull, T. S., & Wyer, R. S. (1979). The role of category accessibility in the interpretation of information about persons: Some determinants and implications. *Journal of Personality and Social Psychology, 37,* 1660–1672.

Trenholm, S., & Jensen, A. (2000). *Interpersonal communication* (4th ed.). Belmont, CA: Wadsworth.

Waldron, V. R. (1990). Constrained rationality: Situational influences on information acquisition plans. *Communication Monographs, 57,* 184–201.

Wilson, S. R. (1995). Elaborating the cognitive rules model of interaction goals: The problem of accounting for individual differences in goal formation. In B. Burleson (Ed.), *Communication yearbook 18* (pp. 3–25). Thousand Oaks, CA: Sage.

Wilson, S. R., & Kramer, K. K. (1986). Attitude object prototypicality, attitudinal confidence, and attitude-behavioral intention consistency: A cognitive view of the attitude-behavior relationship. *Central States Speech Journal, 37,* 225–238.

Wilson, S. R., & Putnam, L. L. (1990). Interaction goals in negotiation. In J. A. Anderson (Ed.), *Communication yearbook 13* (pp. 374–406). Newbury Park, CA: Sage.

*The authors would like to thank Kate Pieper and Brandon Brown for their helpful comments on a previous version of this chapter.

Chapter Three Case Study Quiz—Social Knowledge

Instructions:

Please read the following case study carefully and select the best answers to the questions. This quiz is an individual assignment. Remember: sharing answers is a form of plagiarism.

When Sidney was first hired to tutor athletes at a large university, she was very nervous about the actual one-on-one sessions with the different athletes. First, there are dozens of NCAA (National Collegiate Athletic Association) rules that tutors must follow and Sidney was concerned about violating any of these rules. Second, she wasn't sure how to interact with the athletes since she had never been an athlete herself. And finally, Sidney was uncertain about all the procedures within the tutoring center including where to file her timesheet each week. On her first day, a veteran tutor showed her where to get her timesheet, how to file paperwork, and where to meet her assigned athletes. Her first session was with a high-profile football player. Instead of accepting the feeling of uncertainty about the tutoring, Sidney decided to ask the football player what his expectations of tutoring sessions were. Once the two had decided on the guidelines of their sessions, the football player spoke about his life as an athlete on the campus. Sidney left the introductory session feeling very comfortable and looking forward to the next session. Over the semester, she learned the policies of both the NCAA and the tutoring center with ease as well as generated a positive working experience with the football player. The experience was so positive that the football player requested her again for the next semester and she became the veteran tutor that introduced the new tutors to the tutoring center.

Student's Name _____

Section Number _____

Section Leader's Name _____

Chapter Three Case Study Quiz—Social Knowledge

1. Sidney has many concerns about her role as a tutor. What type of knowledge is she concerned about?
    a. Procedural knowledge
    b. Declarative knowledge
    c. Social knowledge
    d. Career knowledge

2. Sidney's concern for tutoring procedures such as filling out her timesheet is called:
    a. Procedural knowledge
    b. Declarative knowledge
    c. Social knowledge
    d. Career knowledge

3. The football player was impressed with Sidney as a tutor. He not only liked the way she approached the situation, but she was helpful in explaining difficult concepts to him. Because of this, he requested her to be his tutor the next semester. This is:
    a. Selective attention
    b. Interpretation and inference
    c. Relational schema
    d. Selective exposure

4. Sidney believes the football player to be hard-working, loyal to his sport, and friendly. What type of schema is displayed here?
    a. Self schema
    b. Relational schema
    c. Person schema
    d. Sociological schema

5. Sidney's communication plan for the introductory tutoring session with the football player was very detailed. She first wanted to know his expectations of the sessions, what it was like to be an athlete, and finally, to gain information about him as a person. Sidney has a:
    a. Differentiated plan
    b. Undifferentiated plan
    c. Complete plan
    d. Contingent plan

Case Study

Chapter Four

COMMUNICATION AND SELF-CONCEPT DEVELOPMENT

Paul A. Mongeau
Arizona State University

There came a quiet Sunday morning. He walked out on the countryside and turned onto a small farm. He went behind the barn, and concealing himself . . . he pulled out a revolver and shot himself in the chest. With his hand pressed against the wound to control the bleeding, he staggered back to the Ravoux cafe where he was staying, climbed the stairs to his room and collapsed. Soon after the innkeeper found him near death and rushed to get the local doctor. The bullet could not be removed, and there was little to do (Meissner, 1992, pp. 673–674).

From Kurt Cobain to Michael Hutchence and many others, contemporary stories of a suicide are distressingly familiar. What makes this account particularly compelling is that it describes the suicide of Vincent van Gogh, perhaps the greatest painter in recent Western history. What could lead a person with such enormous talent to take his own life?

Although Vincent (as he preferred to be called) struggled with mental illness all his adult life, this chapter will try to use his life to discuss the self-concept. This chapter will first attempt to define self-concept and differentiate it from self-esteem. Second, factors that influence both self-concept and gender development will be reviewed. Third, the factors involved in the presentation of various identities will be discussed. Finally, both suggestions for, and pitfalls of, changing the self-concept will be presented.

COMMUNICATION AND SELF-CONCEPT

Communication is performed to connect one person with one or more people. We connect with others to satisfy various individual, social, organizational, and societal needs. Calling a friend to alleviate loneliness might fulfill an individual need. Asking a person out on a date might fulfill a social need. Asking a coworker for information you need to complete a project might fulfill organizational needs. Finally, trying to persuade people in your neighborhood to oppose a proposed toxic waste incinerator might fulfill societal needs.

Self-concept (also known as self-identity) can be thought of as what a person thinks about him or herself. Caputo, Hazel, & McMahon (1994) refer to self-concept as "a subjective collection of your attitudes and beliefs about yourself built up over all the years of your life" (p. 77). Five aspects of self-concept deserve attention. First, self-concept presumes a personal identity. Second, the self-concept is subjective. Third, the self-concept is relatively enduring. Fourth, the self-concept has social origins. Finally, self-concepts have both content and structure.

Self-concept presumes personal identity. The self-concept is a very important part of the communication process. The self-concept makes communication possible because without it, connecting with another person would be impossible. The self-concept is so important to communication because it implies a sense of personal identity. This means that each person is aware of him or herself as a social object (Scheier & Carver, 1980).

Infant humans are not born with a separate personal identity. Instead, each person *develops* the ability to differentiate him/herself from other people and the surrounding environment. A sense of personal identity gives each person a sense of "self" and without this, connecting with another person would be both impossible and unnecessary. Whether it is giving strangers directions, expressing our love for another person, or giving an order to a child, it is our sense of personal identity that makes human connection possible.

Self-concepts are subjective. Your self-concept is your own creation; that is, your own private view of who you are. Put another way, self-concepts are subjective. Because your self-concept is a large set of subjective perceptions and evaluations, it may not be consistent with reality or with how other people perceive you.

Because the information in your self-concept is subjective, it is important to remember that it can be biased. What one person thinks of him or herself may differ from what other people think of him or her. I remember a good example of this point. I was a student in a graduate class at Michigan State several years ago and we were discussing how to measure shyness. In the course of this discussion, the class was surprised to find that our professor considered himself to be shy. We were surprised because the professor was a very prominent scholar and was generally considered to be quite sociable and outgoing. While it was not consistent with others' views of the professor, it was still a part of his self-concept.

Because the self-concept is subjective, it is difficult to say that a particular view is "right" or "wrong." My view of myself may not be the same as how others view me. This is not to say that I am right and everyone else is wrong (or vice versa). For the most part, no view is better or worse than any of the others.

Another, more dangerous example of the subjective nature of self-concepts can be seen in people with eating disorders. People who suffer from eating disorders (such as anorexia nervosa or bulimia) have a view of their own body that is inconsistent with both reality and with others' perceptions. You might look at a victim of an eating disorder and see a person who is dangerously thin. The victim may look in the mirror and evaluate him or herself as being too fat. This biased self-perception, in turn, may lead to further attempts at weight loss to the point of potentially having devastating physical consequences.

Self-concept is relatively enduring. While definitions of self-concept differ widely, most scholars agree that self-concepts are relatively enduring. This means that self-concepts are relatively stable and/or resistant to change. I wake up each day feeling pretty much like the same person I was the day before. People who are considered mentally stable don't wake up one day with an identity that is significantly different from the one they had the day before. The key term in this entire discussion, though, is *relatively*; self-concepts are *relatively* enduring. Self-concepts can and do change both through the natural process of maturation as well as through intentional effort. Change, whether natural or intentional, happens slowly and gradually.

Consider the person that you were five years ago. Where were you? What were you doing? What was your view of yourself? Is your view of yourself the same now as it was then? Most people will say no. Change over a long period of time is quite normal. It is less likely, however, that a person's self-concept will change dramatically over a very short period of time.

Our memories make the enduring nature of the self-concept possible. Each person has experienced a unique and unified sequence of life events. I can think back to the sequences of events that have happened to me and recognize that they happened *only* to me. I recognize that these events have happened to the same "me" even though my body, attitudes, and values may have changed since some of these events took place.

Self-concepts have social origins. Much of the information (i.e., beliefs and evaluations) in the self-concept comes from communication with others. We literally cannot see ourselves except in mirrors or photographs. The primary way that we can "see" ourselves is through others' actions and reactions toward us. The concept of the "looking glass" (an old-fashioned term for mirror) self implies that our view of ourselves is developed through how others respond to us in our daily interactions. People provide us with feedback that indicates what they think of us. Over time we integrate this feedback into our picture of ourselves. This feedback could be positive, as when a teacher tells us that we are a good student. This feedback, however, can also be negative as when others refer to us as "worthless" or "losers." Through repeated exposures to this feedback over time, these labels are likely to become part of what we think of ourselves.

Communication scholar William Wilmot (1995) suggested a similar idea in the residual self. Wilmot argues that we enter every interaction with a certain sense of self. This sense of self is developed from previous interactions that we had with others. If people react positively to the self that we present in the interaction, our self-concept is reinforced.

There are interactions, however, where the self-concept we project is *not* reinforced. In this case, there are two views of the self, one that we projected and a different one reflected in the other person's feedback. In this case, Wilmot contends that we have to rectify the two views of the self by adjusting our self-concept to more closely match the feedback we receive from others. As a consequence, each interaction leaves some residue on our self-concept. In Wilmot's view, the self-concept is a result of all the residues left from all the interactions that we have been part of.

In summary, what we think of ourselves is determined, in part (and perhaps in *large* part), by how others react to us. How do you know that you are attractive or funny or artistic or intelligent? These are difficult judgments to make about ourselves, in part because it is quite difficult to be objective in such matters. We come to know these things about ourselves through repeated feedback from others. This feedback might be very explicit, as when someone tells me that I am funny immediately after I told an amusing joke. This feedback might also be implicit as when people laugh heartily (and at the appropriate time) after I told that joke.

That the self-concept has social origins implies that the relationships that we are part of are important to the self-concept. We care about some people's feedback more than others. If you are traveling in an unfamiliar area and a gas station attendant doesn't pay attention to you, it might not bother you very much. The same feedback from a significant other (e.g., family member, good friend, or romantic partner) might have you wondering what is wrong.

The value of relationships and feedback recalls the tragedy of Vincent van Gogh. It is in the difficulty in forming relationships and in the feedback from others where Vincent felt most let down. Vincent had considerable difficulty initiating and maintaining relationships with women. His first few attempts at initiating a romantic relationship were not reciprocated. In the years that he painted (fewer than 10 years), his most consistent female acquaintances were prostitutes (including one to whom he presented his freshly severed ear).

In the last decade of his life, Vincent's personal identity was clearly wrapped up in being a painter; however, the feedback he received from others did not validate this view. While Vincent was alive, only one of his paintings was sold. He would trade his paintings in return for other artists' work or give his paintings as gifts to those who had treated him well. These gifts were often not appreciated. One portrait he painted of the doctor who treated him after he sliced off his ear was immediately hidden and eventually used to repair a hole in a chicken coop (Sweetman, 1990). Even his own mother sold several of his early paintings to a junk dealer for a pittance.

The feedback that Vincent received from others (including his own mother) was that they did not value him as a painter. The lack of validation of the center of his self-concept must have made his struggles with mental illness that much more difficult to deal with.

Self-concepts have content and structure. The self-concept has been compared to a set of mental photographs that you have of yourself. When I think of my personal photographs that make up my self-concept I see myself with my wife and son. I also see myself teaching class and talking with students. I also see myself with my brother and sister (though this doesn't happen as much as it should). My self-concept would include my time as a student (both when things were going well and when they went poorly) and with my family and friends as I grew up.

The mental photographs in this analogy represent the collection of beliefs that I have about myself. In other words, the beliefs (or photographs) represent the content of my self-concept. Put simply, the self-concept contains information about the self.

The information I have about myself is not a random collection of images, like a bunch of photographs that have been randomly piled into shoeboxes. So my self-concept has **structure.** The information I have about myself is organized in particularly complex ways like a large number of photographs that are systematically organized into several photo albums. Each photo (i.e., belief and/or evaluation about the self) is placed in an album with other similar photos (beliefs or attitudes) and is cross-referenced with other, similar photographs in other albums.

In technical terms, the self-concept can be considered a system of what Smith and Wilson (in the previous chapter) called the **self-schema.** A schema represents how we organize the information that we have about an object, so a self-schema represents the information each person has about his- or herself. In all likelihood, the self-concept is too large and complex to be contained in a single schema. The fact that the self-concept is a complex system of schemas (Berger, 1987) focuses attention on the structure of the self-information.

Scholars argue that the self-concept contains several facets. There is the physical self, the moral-ethical self, the family-oriented self, the personal self, and the social self. Each of these parts of the self-concept contains a large number of individual beliefs and attitudes. These parts of the self-concept are not mutually exclusive; instead, they are overlapping and interconnected. For example, it would be hard to fully consider the social self without also considering how a person interacts with, and fits into, their family (i.e., the family-oriented self).

Many scholars agree that the self-schema is different from other kinds of schemas. For example, research indicates that we can recall information about ourselves more quickly than information about other people, objects, or events. We can access self-information so quickly because we have used this information so often in the past. This is particularly true of information that we evaluate as being important to us. So I can probably recall information about my job or family more quickly than I can access my attitude toward reducing the federal budget deficit.

The speedy recall of self-information is particularly true for positive self-information. It takes us longer to recall negative self-information than positive self-information. If this is the case, then, I should be able to recall my junior year in college (when I got a 4.0 GPA) or successes in graduate school more quickly than I can recall details about my four years as a college freshman.

SELF-CONCEPT AND SELF-ESTEEM

Now that I have defined and discussed several important aspects of the self-concept, it is important to differentiate it from self-esteem. As we discussed above, the self-concept can be thought of as the content and structure of the information (i.e., beliefs and attitudes) you have about yourself. Self-esteem, on the other hand, can be defined as your positive or negative **evaluation** of that self-information. To use the photo analogy again, the self-concept is like an interconnected collection of photographs of yourself. Self-esteem, on the other hand, represents your evaluation (i.e., the extent to which you like or dislike) of what you see of yourself in those images.

Like the self-concept, self-esteem is subjective. As a consequence, it is possible that two people can have similar self-information but evaluate that information quite differently (i.e., have different levels of self-esteem). This can happen because self-esteem has frequently been defined as the difference between two perceptions: that of the real-self and that of the ideal-self. Our real self is simply how we see and evaluate ourselves as we are. Our ideal self, on the other hand, represents our perception of the best person that we could be. The closer the real comes to the ideal, the more positive self-esteem will be.

For example, take two students, Sandi and Chuck. Being a student is an important part of both their self-concepts and they both have 3.00 grade point averages (GPAs). Sandi and Chuck's self-esteem will be influenced by how close their real self (reflected in their GPAs in this example) comes to their ideal self (i.e., the best GPA they could have earned given the circumstances they are in).

Sandi is quite happy with herself and her grades. She feels that a 3.00 GPA is the best she can do because she has to work two jobs to pay for her own education. In Sandi's case, her real self and her ideal self are very close (as far as grades are concerned at least). As a consequence, we might expect Sandi to have relatively high self-esteem.

Chuck, on the other hand, is quite unhappy with himself and his grades. Perhaps because of a strong high school record or pressure from home, he can accept nothing less than perfect grades. Every time he receives a grade of less than an 'A' (or 4.0), he feels a bit worse about himself. In Chuck's case, his real self is quite far from his ideal self and his self-esteem is likely to suffer as a consequence.

The disparity between the real and the ideal self must have been quite evident in Vincent's life. He wanted to be successful and accepted as a painter. Success and acceptance, however, did not come his way. In many ways, Vincent's real self fell far short of his ideal self. As his mental illness grew, perceived differences between his real and ideal self must have grown as well.

Self-esteem can also be determined by comparing one's self to others (i.e., social comparisons). These social comparisons help to form self-esteem by allowing us a chance to see how we stack up in relation to relevant others. Knowing that I scored 78 of 100 on an exam is hard to interpret, but knowing that many of my classmates scored in the 50's or 60's tells me much more about how I performed. If most of my classmates scored in the 80s or 90's, however, that says something quite different about my performance on that test.

I remember a great example of this from my time in the Communication doctoral program at MSU. A number of my colleagues and I were in a very difficult Communication statistics class and we were receiving our midterm exam grades. The professor told us that the exam was very difficult and that the grades ranged from 10 (yes, 10!) to 95 points out of a possible 100. When a particular friend received her exam, she responded very positively. When I asked her how she did, she replied "I GOT A 30!" She was happy in this case not because a 30 was a particularly good score, but because she did not receive the 10! She evaluated the failing grade positively because she performed better than at least one other person in the class.

These social comparisons may also be the source of sibling rivalries. Older siblings are frequently bigger, faster, and seem to know more than the younger siblings. Younger siblings never seem to come out positively in these comparisons. (But then again, I'm the youngest child in my family!)

COMMUNICATION AND GENDER DEVELOPMENT

One of the most important outcomes that arises from communication and the creation of self-concept is gender development. Before discussing how communication influences gender development, however, it is important to differentiate gender from sex. This is a particularly important task because the terms are often used interchangeably even though they are clearly separate constructs.

Sex and gender. Sex, according to communication scholar Julia Wood (2001), "is classified by biological characteristics" (p. 20). A person's sex (i.e., male and female) is defined by biological characteristics such as genitalia, chromosomes, and hormones.

While sex is a biological characteristic, gender is psychological. Wood (2001) claims that culture determines which behavior is masculine (i.e., associated with males) and which is feminine (i.e., associated with females).

What are considered appropriate behaviors for men/boys and women/girls can and does vary across cultures. For example, modern rules guiding behavior for women are quite different in the United States when compared to Afghanistan. Moreover, appropriate behavior for men and women vary within the same culture over time. As an example, modern U.S. gender norms differ from those enacted in 1900 or 1950.

Contemporary North American gender norms maintain that masculine behavior is to be "strong, ambitious, successful, rational, and emotionally controlled" (Wood, 2001, p. 22). Feminine behavior, on the other hand, is to be "attractive, deferential, unaggressive, emotional, nurturing, and concerned with people and relationships" (Wood, 2001, p. 22). A person's sex (male or female) is determined by their biological and physiological characteristics. A person's gender, on the other hand, is determined by the extent to which a person acts in a stereotypically masculine or feminine manner. The healthiest choice is when a person exhibits a combination of both masculine and feminine behavior, called androgyny.

While a person is born with his or her sex, gender is learned and socially reinforced. How do we learn masculine or feminine behaviors? Whether learned from our parents, siblings, peers, the media, or other role models, communication plays an important role in gender development.

Exactly *how* communication influences gender development is a relatively controversial issue. Three sets of theories have been developed to explain how communication influences gender development. These include psychodynamic theories, social learning theories, and cognitive development theories.

Psychodynamic theories. Psychodynamic theories assert that gender development is determined early in life. For example, by 18 months, infants can correctly differentiate boys from girls and have a rough sense of what behavior is appropriate for each. In these theories, gender development is determined most directly by the early relationships with family. The most important family relationship is with the primary caregiver (usually the mother). Gender differences that are observable in adulthood can be traced back to the mother having different kinds of relationships with sons and daughters during infancy.

According to psychodynamic theories, relationships between mothers and daughters are characterized by similarity and identification. This identification occurs because mothers and daughters share the same sex. Because the identification occurs at a very early age, it helps to form both the child's personal and gender identities. Daughters raised in a close, nurturing, environment will tend to associate their own self-concept with a close relationship. This early association with the primary caregiver sets the stage for women's later gender-identity as relationally oriented.

Relationships between mothers and sons, on the other hand, are characterized by difference because they do not share the same sex. In order to establish himself as a male, a boy cannot identify with the mother as girls can. Boys instead must differentiate themselves from the primary caregiver/mother. Thus, the male's gender identity is based upon establishing himself as an individual. This differentiation from the primary caregiver sets the stage for the boy's later gender-identity as independent and individually oriented.

The process of gender identification described by psychodynamic theorists occurs during infancy (i.e., the earliest stages of life). Gender development, however, continues throughout one's lifetime. As a consequence, other theoretical formulations must be developed to describe how communication assists in the development of gender identity in later life stages. Two such theories will be described: social learning theories and cognitive development theories.

Social learning theories. The second set of gender development theories is called social learning theories. These theories posit that an individual's gender develops from positive and negative reinforcements that are received for engaging in certain behaviors. As children grow they imitate the behavior of everyone and everything they see. They are reinforced, however, for only some of the behavior they engage in and are punished for some others. These theories assert that boys are typically rewarded for engaging in stereotypically masculine behavior and punished for engaging in stereotypically feminine behavior. The opposite, of course, would be true for girls.

As I was preparing this chapter, my 4-year old son did something interesting that made me think of social learning theories. While at day care, he took lipstick out of a girl's purse and applied it to his face. What could have caused this behavior? We had recently been to a circus so perhaps he was emulating a clown. On the other hand, he could have been engaging in a stereotypically feminine behavior (i.e., applying makeup). While the first explanation is gender-neutral, the latter is gender-inconsistent (i.e., a boy engaging in a feminine behavior).

My wife and I did not know how to react to this behavior. On the one hand, we did not want to discourage gender-inconsistent behavior (and indirectly encourage gender-stereotypical behavior). On the other hand, if he was emulating a clown, no discipline was needed (except, perhaps, for taking the lipstick without asking). Given that the day-care provider had already scolded him for taking the lipstick, we decided to do nothing.

Cognitive development theories. Social learning theories present individuals as passive receivers of reinforcement. A third set of theories, cognitive development theories, posits that people actively engage in behavior that they think will be rewarded and avoid behavior that they think will be punished. Rather than passively imitating other social actors, cognitive development theories presume that individuals make choices depending on *expected* rewards or punishments.

Certain television shows are popular with high school students, for example, because they exhibit attractive models of adult behavior. Students might watch certain movies or read certain magazines because they provide descriptions of how today's college student is supposed to act.

WHERE DOES OUR SELF-CONCEPT COME FROM?

The self-concept has now been defined, differentiated from self-esteem, and linked to gender development. An important issue to consider at this point is where the self-concept comes from. We are not born with a fully functioning sense of self. Our individual identity and self-concept develop gradually over time. The development of self-concept is made possible and is influenced by both internal and external sources. Two internal factors have already been noted earlier in this chapter. Specifically, the self-concept is made possible by the development of an individual identity and a stored memory of continuous life events. These internal forces help make the development of self-concept possible.

There are also a number of important external forces that shape self-concepts. External influences of self-concept that will be discussed include culture, family, and the roles we play.

Culture

Culture strongly influences the development of self-concepts. As I alluded to in the discussion of gender development, culture is one of the primary factors that determine what is 'proper' behavior for men and women within their bounds. Even though men and women have achieved greater equality in the U.S. over the past several decades, there are still expectations that men and women will act in different ways. These expectations and the reinforcement we receive for meeting them (or punishment we receive for violating them) have a strong impact on our self-concepts.

An example of American culture influencing self-concepts has to do with a concept called individualism. American culture emphasizes individualism and uniqueness over conformity and a group focus. Individual rights and concerns are considered more important in the U.S. and other individualist cultures than are group or collective concerns. This cultural focus on individualism can be seen in old Western movies were the lone cowboy rides against tyranny and injustice.

In many Eastern cultures, however, the reverse is true; i.e., the group or collective is seen as more important than the individual. There are greater pressures to conform to social expectations in these cultures. There is a greater concern expressed over protecting and maintaining "face." Exhibitions of individuality in collectivist cultures are perceived as rude and self-centered.

Family

The family is one of the most important factors in self-concept development. The family is such an important influence on our life that it is often called a **primary group**. The family is likely one of the primary ways that cultural norms are actually enforced. As I noted in the discussion of gender development, several theories presume that our early familial relationships (especially with the mother or primary caregiver) have an important impact on our adult personality and self-concept. These theories presume that the relationship with the primary caregiver has an important impact on how an infant sees him/herself and relates to others. If a mother treats her child in a nurturing way, the child will likely have a strong sense of self-worth. If the mother does not treat the child in a loving and caring way, it is less likely that the child will exhibit feelings of self-worth. Those feelings about the self are thought to influence adult self-concept and influence the nature of adult relationships.

Vincent had a difficult family life. His father was a relatively distant and unapproving Calvinist minister. Vincent's mother gave birth to a stillborn boy (also named Vincent) one year to the day before the Vincent that we know was born. According to Meissner (1992), Vincent's mother treated Vincent as a "replacement child" for her first, stillborn, son. In short, Vincent did not receive much in terms of overt expressions of love and support from his parents early in life. Later in life, his parents did not understand his career choice in art. Initially, at least, the parents cannot be blamed for being skeptical about Vincent's choice because he tried his hand at selling art, selling books, and the clergy (Vincent's father's occupation) and failed at all of them before turning his attention (at the age of 27) to art. The lack of support from his parents may have had a strong impact on Vincent's mental problems.

Roles

The roles that we play have an important impact on the development of self-concept. In the family we might be the mother or father, son or daughter, sister or brother, stepbrother or stepsister. On the job, you might be a boss, trainee, or an employee. If you are reading this chapter, you are almost certainly a student.

Each role that is enacted comes with a set of behavioral expectations. As a consequence, each role that is played demands that we behave somewhat differently. How are college students supposed to dress? Spend their free time? Engage in conversations? Now consider each of these questions for a college professor. It is unlikely that your behavioral expectations are the same for both roles. We expect students and professors to act differently both inside and outside the classroom (whether they actually do is another question).

The roles that we play and the behaviors we are expected to perform become part of our self-concept. The influence of roles on the self-concept is hard to see sometimes because we have learned our roles and their required behaviors so well. But consider when you first came to college. The role of a college student isn't the same as the role of a high school student. As a consequence, you may have experienced a period of anxiety or uncertainty because you did not know how others expected you to dress, act, talk, and even think. After a while, though, the behavior expected from the role came more naturally. You don't have to think about it now because you have integrated the new behaviors and role into your self-concept.

Each role you play comes with a number of communication expectations. For example, what sorts of communication rules were there at your home regarding communication at the dinner table? In some homes, children are meant to be "seen but not heard." At other homes, children are expected to actively participate in family conversations. How are students in class expected to communicate? The president of the Campus Republicans Club? What about the social chair of a fraternity? A professor?

Finally, it is important to remember that roles come in pairs. Each role comes with another, linked role. To be a child implies that there is a parent. To be a protégé implies that there is a mentor. To be a student, there must be a teacher. Roles, and the behaviors that are expected from those who enact them, do not exist in isolation but instead are linked to the roles and behavioral expectations of others. So again, our sense of self developed from our social interactions and the relationships that we have with others.

HOW MANY SELVES ARE THERE?

In the immediately preceding discussion, I made the point that each person plays a number of roles. For example, I have to play the roles of teacher, father, advisor, husband, professor, and journal editor. Each role that I play may require that a different "me" be presented. In other words, it is an oversimplification to think of the self-concept as depicting a single entity. There are many "selves" that are enacted in the various roles that each person plays.

Even within a single role, let's use the example of being a student, there are many "selves" that you might present. Assume that you have to do three things in a particular afternoon: go to class, meet with a professor about an independent study, and chair a student government committee meeting. First, as a student in class, you may choose to act one way. Second, after class, when you meet alone with that same professor in his or her office, you might engage in different behaviors than you did in class. Third, after your meeting with the professor, you have to go to a student government committee meeting that you chair. This context will likely demand that you enact an entirely different set of behaviors than what you performed in the first two activities. Finally, after the meeting, you might visit a friend who just returned from a family funeral and take them to a mutual friend's twenty-first birthday party. These last two activities will likely force you to present a different self in part because you have shed the role of student and taken on the role of caring friend (and partier).

Because of these variations in behavior that we exhibit across situations and roles, we tend to describe ourselves in very general ways. When answering the question, "Who am I?" most people will respond with general terms (e.g., "helpful and fun loving"). We use general terms because

78 Chapter Four

how these characteristics are specifically enacted will differ across contexts. Consider the trait of being helpful. Being helpful might require one set of behaviors during a holiday dinner with your family, while being helpful might require an entirely different set of behaviors at your friend's twenty-first birthday party.

Your behavior (and your self-descriptions) may also differ depending on the person or people you are with. While you would describe yourself in one way with your parents (e.g., helpful, serious, and controlled), you might describe yourself quite differently to your friends (e.g., helpful, fun-loving, and caring).

There are times, however, when these various behavioral descriptions and expectations come into stark contrast with one another. When I was a teenager, I remember sneaking into an East Lansing High School football game with some friends. The "self" being presented was of a reasonably rebellious member of a friendship group. As I turned and ran away from our favorite spot to hop the fence, I ran (almost literally) into my stepbrother who was an East Lansing police officer at the time. He was in uniform and providing security for the game. (This, of course, required a specific set of behaviors for him as well.) In the blink of an eye, my communication expectations went from rebellious teen to that of a law-abiding family member. After a few minutes of uncomfortable small talk, I left by stepbrother to again become my other (and preferred) "self" for the evening.

In summary, it is clear that our behavior will vary depending on the role that we are playing, the context we are in, and the people we are with. We have little trouble, though, fitting all these different "selves" into our self-concept. Put another way, our self-concept is relatively enduring, yet at the same time allows for quite a bit of variation.

Self-Monitoring

While it is true that most people act like different people in different situations, some people do this to a greater extent than do others. Put another way, people differ in the extent to which they exhibit different 'selves' in varying situations. Take Mike and Nancy for example. Mike's behavior is relatively consistent across situations. You always know where he stands on an issue and you can tell how he is feeling by looking at his actions. He acts the way that he feels. Because Mike's behavior is determined by how he is feeling, he doesn't fit into some situations as well as other people do.

Nancy's behavior, on the other hand, varies quite a bit from situation to situation. Nancy fits in well in just about any situation she finds herself in. She is able to easily determine what behaviors are right for any situation and can do what it takes to fit in. Because of her ability to see what is appropriate and her ability to change her behavior, Nancy fits in well in most situations. There are times, however, when you have a hard time figuring out exactly what she is feeling. For example, there are times when Nancy appears to be happy but you have found out later that she actually felt quite sad (or vice versa).

Do Mike and/or Nancy sound familiar to you? They are fictitious, of course, but they were constructed to help describe a concept called **self-monitoring** (Snyder, 1987). People are generally described as either being high or low self monitors. Both low and high self-monitors want to act in a socially appropriate manner, however, they make judgments of what is socially appropriate based on different criteria. High self-monitors base their judgments of appropriateness on external factors. Those external factors might be other people's behavior or aspects of the context. High self-monitors base appropriateness judgments on cues they observe from the situation. Low self-monitors base social appropriateness judgments on internal factors including their own attitudes, moods, and values.

High self-monitors, like Nancy in our example, have two important skills. First, they have a cognitive skill in that they are very adept at scanning the social situation to determine what behaviors are appropriate. Second, high self-monitors have an ability to change their behavior in order to act in a way that they think is appropriate in that situation. High self-monitors fit into many social situations because they can determine what is appropriate behavior for the particular context and modify their behavior to meet the situational constraints. They act the way that they are supposed to act in whatever situation they are in.

Low self-monitors, like Mike, do not pay as close attention to the social setting they find themselves in. The low self monitor's behavior is generated internally, by their feelings and attitudes. They are also not as adept at modifying their behavior to meet changing situational demands. They act the way they feel.

Self-monitoring makes some important differences in communication behavior (see Snyder, 1987 for a review of early research on self-monitoring). High self-monitors are highly skilled at presenting whatever image they consider appropriate. That is, high self-monitors are good at effectively presenting a variety of "selves" (and, as a consequence, should be better liars). Low self-monitor's behaviors are generally true reflections of underlying beliefs, attitudes, or feelings. Not surprisingly, then, low self-monitors exhibit stronger correlations between attitudes and behaviors than do high self-monitors. Low self-monitor's actions, thus, are likely to be more strongly based on their self-concept than is true for high self-monitors.

In social interactions, high self-monitors talk more and tend to control conversation to a greater extent than do low self-monitors. High self-monitors also make a greater effort at ensuring that the conversation works smoothly. High self-monitors seek more personal information from their partner than do low self-monitors. It should come as no surprise, then, that high self-monitors are perceived as more competent communicators than are low self-monitors.

EFFECTIVE SELF-CONCEPT DEVELOPMENT AND CHANGE

Your self-concept, in a sense, has already developed. You cannot go back and build an entirely new one. Advertisers will try to convince you that buying a new car or toothpaste, or losing weight can create a "new you." An entirely new you isn't possible; however, changing aspects of your existing self-concept is.

As has been noted several times, your self-concept has developed gradually over the course of your lifetime. This means that your self-concept can and does change over time. This change does not have to be random. You can take charge and make some intentional changes in your self-concept. There are some common mistakes, however, that people make in trying to change their view of themselves. Two of these mistakes are shooting too high and expecting change too quickly.

Shooting too high. Self-esteem (as noted above) can be determined by making social comparisons (i.e., comparing yourself to others). One common mistake that people make in trying to change their self-concept is shooting too high. For example, presume that you are just learning to play the guitar. It would be a mistake to compare your guitar playing to Eric Clapton's. No matter how much you practice you will never come off looking like a good guitar player using this comparison. Such a comparison would make it hard to notice any improvement. You might become discouraged and quit before you get a chance to improve. If you were just learning how to play the guitar, a more appropriate target of social comparison would be someone else who has also just started to play the guitar.

For all of the difficulty and discomfort in Vincent's life, he was fortunate to have good social comparisons throughout his artistic career. When Vincent turned his energies to art, he began drawing rather than painting. In Brussels, Vincent made the acquaintance of Anton Van Rappard, a student at the Brussels Academy. In an excellent biography, Sweetman (1990) commented that Van Rappard "was just what Vincent needed, someone slightly in advance of himself, not so far as to assume the unwanted role of teacher, but just far enough to nudge him onward" (p. 140). In his late career, Vincent's closest artist friends included Henri de Toulouse-Lautrec and Paul Gauguin who were also struggling (and nearly starving) artists at the time.

There are times when the *target* of your social comparison may be appropriate but the person is not honest. Several years ago, one of my former students was in her first year in a very good communication doctoral program. She told me that she was struggling and felt like a failure. One reason for these feelings was that she thought that she was having a more difficult time adjusting to the rigors of the doctoral program than were her peers. The problem in this case was not her trouble in adjusting, but in the veracity of the information she was receiving from other first-year doctoral students. As it turned out, the other students were having just as much trouble adjusting to their program, but they were unwilling to admit it. Until they all talked and admitted their difficulties it seemed as though my student was having a harder time adjusting than everyone else. Under those circumstances she felt as though there was something wrong with her.

Expecting change too quickly. I have made the point several times that your self-concept has been in the making your entire life. The corollary to this point is that your self-concept is going to be slow in changing. Many times people become frustrated because change doesn't come quickly and naturally. Take weight loss as an example. Magazines, newspapers, television, and the Internet are full of quick weight loss schemes. When people try these schemes and don't get the quick results that are described, they get discouraged and stop trying to lose weight. When this happens, people generally gain back whatever weight they originally lost.

Slow gradual change gives you a better chance to get used to the "new you." Trying to change your self-concept is like taking on a new role. It feels strange at first but over time you get used to it. If you don't expect all of the change all at once, you are going to find that the new behavior fits better.

Taking the change process relatively slowly will give those around you time to adjust to the "new you." You have to remember, though, that not everyone around you is going to be happy with the changes you might be making. If you feel that you are too timid and submissive, you might decide to become more assertive and to stand up for your rights more often. Some alleged friends, however, may have benefited from (i.e., been able to take advantage of) your past timidity. These friends may not like the fact that you are starting to stand up for yourself because it interferes with their rewards.

Slow and gradual change while a good strategy is hard to see. As a consequence, it might be useful to have others compliment you on the change that they can see. A good social comparison can help here as well. While you may not be able to see your own improvement, you can see how you are doing in comparison to someone else (who may also be improving).

In short, effective change of your self-concept should be done slowly and gradually. But what else can be done in helping change your self-concept? There are at least two things that can be done; build confidence in yourself and practice, practice, practice.

Build confidence in yourself. While your self-concept can be changed, it may not be an easy thing to do. One of the important parts of changing your self-concept would be to build the confidence in yourself that such changes can be successfully performed. Setting and reaching realistic and reasonable goals and maintaining them can build confidence in yourself. If you want to make a major change in yourself it doesn't make sense to try to make the entire change all at once.

A more effective strategy might be to break the change up into chunks. It is important that you make the first chunk a small one that you are confident that you can attain. Sometimes the hardest thing about changing yourself is getting started. Starting with a small task that you can perform gets the change process off to a good start and may give you the confidence to take on the larger tasks. After you make these changes it is important that you reward yourself. Part of the reason for changing the self-concept is to feel better about yourself. Once you get going, you can take on larger tasks; however, be careful not to take on too much at once.

Practice, practice, practice. One key in changing your self-concept is to give yourself enough time to change. Let's say that you feel that you are too shy and need to be more outgoing. It is highly unlikely that you can go from shy to gregarious overnight. Such a change will require that you repeatedly enact a new set of behaviors. You might decide to begin one conversation every day. It could be in the cafeteria at lunch, before or after class, or in a grocery store or a laundromat. For a while, it will feel strange to act in a new way. It won't seem like yourself who is starting the conversation. You are taking on a new role, though. Just as you have to give friends and family a chance to get used to the "new you," it is important to give yourself the same chance.

CONCLUSIONS

In summary, the self-concept is a personal characteristic that makes communication possible. Without a sense of self-identity and a cumulative memory of life events, communicating with others would be impossible. Self-concepts develop over the entire life span. Certainly, childhood is the time when self-concepts change most dramatically and quickly, however, changes in self-concept can and do occur at all life-stages.

Your self-concept has been developed, molded, and changed by a large number of factors. Relationships with parents, other family members, friends, teachers, and others influence how you think of yourself. Much of the impact that these others have on your self-concept occurs through the feedback you receive. How others react to us goes a long way in developing and changing the way that we think of ourselves.

There is a very close and important relationship between the self-concept and communication. Our self-concept exerts a strong impact on how it is we present ourselves to others. The feedback we receive during interactions with others in turn, influences how we think about ourselves.

Before I close this chapter, however, let me consider three contexts where the relationship between self-concept and communication is particularly important. These contexts are conformity versus independence, job interviews, and personal relationships.

Conformity Versus Independence

There comes a time in each person's life where others try to make him or her do something they don't want to do. It might be some friends wanting you to smoke or experiment with drugs when you don't want to. It might be a boyfriend or girlfriend who wants you to go further sexually than you are ready to go. It might be members of an organization who want you to engage in initiation rituals that you think are wrong.

You face an important choice in all three of these cases. On the one hand, you could act in a way that is consistent with your beliefs; on the other hand, you could go along with what the others want you to do. Will you be independent (and stand up for your beliefs) or will you conform (and go along with the crowd)?

Self-concept and self-esteem are important to these choices. Take two students, Ron and Janet. Janet has thought a lot about the negative consequences of drug use. She has been part of several campus groups fighting drugs in elementary and junior high schools. In other words, the part of her self-concept relating to drugs is organized and well supported. Janet's self-esteem is quite high as she feels very positively about herself.

Ron, on the other hand, hasn't really thought about the use of drugs very often. He hasn't sought any information about it and has pretty much ignored any anti-drug activities in school. Moreover, his self-concept is pretty low. He doesn't really think that highly of himself.

Now consider Ron and Janet who find themselves in a situation where a friend offers them ecstasy at a party. Assume their friend tries to put pressure on them to take the drug. What do you think Ron and Janet will do? It is likely that Janet will be more willing and able to resist the pressure. Given her more clearly organized schema on drugs and stronger self-concept she should be able to stand on her own two feet and act on her beliefs. Given a lack of self-esteem and self-confidence, Ron may be less able to resist the pressure, even if he doesn't feel that it is the right thing to do.

Job Interviews

A second context where the self-concept is particularly important is the job interview. There are at least two reasons why the self-concept is relevant to this context. First, a job interview may force you to take on a new role. Take Tim, a college senior looking for a job. Tim went directly from high school to college and is finishing college after four years. Tim has spent almost his entire life as a student. In the job interview, Tim has to present a "self" that says that he would be a good employee. Since Tim's self-concept is wrapped around being a student, projecting this new "self" can be very awkward. It's no wonder that job interviews are difficult for people!

The self-concept is also important in the job interview because the questions that are being asked tend to focus on the self. Many times, interviewers will ask interviewees to describe their best and worst qualities. Such interview questions are difficult because they tap parts of our self-concept we don't generally think about (or maybe do not *want* to think about).

Relational Development

A final context where the self-concept is important is the development of close relationships. Several theories of relational development predict that what makes a relationship work is that partners provide mutual rewards. You can be rewarding to others in many ways. You might be a good listener, humorous, or help improve others' mood. Rewarding relationships will be more successful than costly relationships.

Given these theories, self-concept and self-esteem are important to relationships. The more positively you view yourself, the more rewarding a person you will likely be to others. Those with high self-esteem will be better friends and romantic partners than are those people who are constantly down on themselves.

REFERENCES

Berger, C. R. (1987). Self-conception and social information processing. In J. C. McCroskey & J. A. Daly (Eds.), *Personality and interpersonal communication* (pp. 275–304). Newbury Park, CA: Sage.

Caputo, J. S., Hazel, H. C., & McMahon, C. (1994). *Interpersonal communication: Competency through critical thinking.* Boston: Allyn and Bacon.

Meissner, W. W. (1992). Vincent's suicide: A psychic autopsy. *Contemporary Psychoanalysis, 28,* 673–694.

Scheier, M. F., & Carver, C. S. (1980). Individual differences in self-concept and self-process. In D. M. Wegner & R. R. Vallacher (Eds.), *The self in social psychology* (pp. 229–251). New York: Oxford University Press.

Snyder, M. (1987). *Public appearances, private realities: The psychology of self-monitoring.* New York: Freeman.

Sweetman, D. (1990). *Van Gogh: His life and his art.* New York: Touchstone Books.

Wilmot, W. W. (1995). *Relational communication.* New York: McGraw-Hill.

Wood, J. T. (1999). *Gendered lives: Communication, gender, and culture* (3rd ed.). Belmont, CA: Wadsworth.

Chapter Four Case Study Quiz—Self-Concept

Instructions:

Please read the following case study carefully and select the best answers to the questions. This quiz is an individual assignment. Remember: sharing answers is a form of plagiarism.

A community in California was shocked when several pre-teen and teenage girls pressed charges of sexual molestation to rape against eight of the most popular teenage boys from a local high school. Even more shocking was that these eight teenage boys were members of the "Spur Posse," a group of twenty-five high school teenage boys who participated in a competition. Each member earned a point for each girl they slept with. When the authorities found out that all, but one case included consensual sex, the charges were dropped. The one Spur Posse member who was charged with rape, participated in 100 hours of community service yet served no jail time. Another shock wave went through the community when the Spur Posse was supported and what happened was seen as the fault of the girls. One girl admitted to a counselor at school that she slept with one guy and his friends because she thought that this is what would make her popular. One mother of a Spur Posse member believes that it "...sad for the girls that they have such low self-esteem that they would..." participate in such behavior. Further, a Spur Posse father defended his son by saying, "Nothing my boy did was anything any red-blooded American boy wouldn't do at his age."

Smolowe, J. (1993, April 5). Sex with a scoreboard. *Time, 141, 41.*

Student's Name _____

Section Number _____

Section Leader's Name _____

Chapter Four Case Study Quiz—Self-Concept

1. A Spur Posse member believes that he is a good-looking person who is popular, athletic, and charming. This is an example of his:
   a. Self-esteem
   b. Self-monitoring
   c. Self-concept
   d. Social schema

2. If this Spur Posse member (described in question one), believed he was a good-looking person because other people told him he was, this would exemplify that:
   a. Self-concepts have social origins
   b. Self-concepts are subjective
   c. Self-concepts are relatively enduring
   d. Self-concepts presumes personal identity

3. As described by the case study, one freshman girl who was involved with a Spur Posse member thought that sleeping with him was the socially appropriate thing to do. If she learned that this was socially acceptable based on observing the behavior of other girls who were involved with these popular guys, she would be labeled as:
   a. Having low self-esteem
   b. Having feminine qualities
   c. Being a low self-monitor
   d. Being a high self-monitor

4. One father believed that the Spur Posse members did nothing wrong. The Posse's behavior was not only defended by the community, but, in a way, rewarded. If the Spur Posse members' continued to actively engage in the behavior, this would exemplify the:
   a. Social learning theories
   b. Schematic theories
   c. Gender theories
   d. Cognitive development

5. After the girl had sex with the members of the Spur Posse, she might not have felt good about herself. If her real and ideal self are very different, she likely has:
   a. Low self-esteem
   b. High self-esteem
   c. A relatively enduring resistance to change
   d. An objective self-concept

Chapter Five

RELATIONAL DEVELOPMENT

Monique M. Turner
University of Maryland

Kimo Ah Yun
California State University, Sacramento

Brant and Sarah are new communication students at Michigan State. As luck would have it, Brant and Sarah are enrolled for the same section of Communication 100. On the first day of class, Brant and Sarah arrive early. Not only are they eager to hear Dr. Donohue's first lecture, but they want to make sure that they get a good seat. The first to arrive to class, Brant and Sarah take the middle two seats in the first row of the class. To guarantee that he is ready to take notes as soon as class begins, Brant begins to prepare for the note-taking that is sure to follow. To his surprise, Brant discovers that he failed to bring either a pen or a pencil to class. Sheepishly, he asks Sarah if he could borrow a pen. Sarah obliges and as she hands him a pen they begin a conversation. For the next hour (they showed up especially early), they begin to reveal information about themselves. Sarah reveals that she is from Kingsley, loves the Redwings, and lives in Akers Hall. Brant reveals that his parents are MSU graduates, he grew up in Kalamazoo, and enjoys spending time with his dog, Sparky.

In this example, Brant and Sarah have initiated what is known as an interpersonal relationship. In particular they have revealed information that describes unique characteristics about themselves that make them who they are. While only time will reveal whether Brant and Sarah's relationship will continue, what we do know is that many of our interpersonal relationships develop in a similar manner. We meet people, we share information about each other, we evaluate whether we desire future interactions, and finally, we decide if we want to pursue a relationship.

One area of communication that focuses on relationships between close others is known as interpersonal communication. Specifically, **interpersonal communication is the process in which two or more people interact, and in this interaction meaning is mutually derived.** More simply, interpersonal communication is that type of communication that is directed at an individual and illuminates the personal element of a relationship.

WHAT KINDS OF INTERPERSONAL RELATIONSHIPS DO WE FORM?

Most of us are involved in several interpersonal relationships. For example, I (Monique) am involved in so many interpersonal relationships that I can hardly keep them straight! I have two sisters, two step-sisters, a brother, two foster brothers, one niece, two nephews, two brother-in-laws, a significant other who has a three-year old daughter, several colleagues, hundreds of students, and many good friends. Without counting, I know that I am involved in many relationships which require different kinds of communication. When I talk to my partner's three year old, it requires a much different kind of interaction than when I talk to my friend and co-author, Kimo.

This chapter will examine three kinds of relationships that most people are involved in: families, friendships, and intimate relationships. While all three areas are of considerable interest, much of the current attention among communication scholars has been given to intimate partners. Consequently, this chapter will primarily focus on intimate relationships.

Family

The American family has undergone rapid changes. While it was once realistic to define a family as two parents and a few children, this is no longer accurate. At present, there are single mothers and fathers who are divorced, never been married, estranged, or widowed. There are adopted children, foster children, and step children. In fact, the definition of family has been expanded to include people who are not related through any legal connection. Some people even refer to their close friends as "family."

Galvin and Brommel (1991) recognized the problems of the evolution of the word family. Consequently, they define family as "Networks of people who share their lives over long periods of time; who are bound by ties of marriage, blood, or commitment, legal or otherwise; who consider themselves as family; and who share future expectations of connected relationship." This definition encompasses countless variations of interactions we share with people we consider family.

One method that has been used to better understand the different types of families is to categorize them into independent groups, often referred to as typologies. Kantor and Lehr (1975) and Constantine (1986) developed a method to categorize family communication interactions. Constantine's approach to understanding family dynamics is based on four views which can be distinguished on the basis of their goal-directed behavior. Kantor and Lehr (1975) distinguished the first three paradigms: open, closed, and random. Constantine (1986) distinguished the fourth, synchronous.

Closed. The guiding image of the closed family system is **stability, security, and belonging.** Closed families express affection and caring based on tradition. Consequently, expressions of closed families are limited, reserved, and regulated. Members belonging to a closed family typically hold traditional family roles. Energy of individuals are directed toward the family. Also, families of this type have rigid rules. Not only are the rules known, but people are expected to follow the rules. In the closed family, negotiating is out of the question; conflicts are solved through predetermined rules. With this family type, a parent may respond to a child's question about why they must do something by telling them, "because I said so!"

Random. The random system is guided by **novelty, creativity, and individuality.** Families guided by the random view express affection in spontaneous, enthusiastic and public fashion. Members belonging to a random family vary in their time commitment to the family. At times, considerable amounts of time will be expected of participants. While some rules are established, the rules are not rigidly enforced.

Open. The open family is an image of **adaptability, efficacy, and participation.** Open families express affection candidly, share feelings openly, and are not constrained by rules or tradition. Negotiation is seen as a positive and useful tool in the open family. Members belonging to an open family are not constrained by traditional family roles. Also, families of this type rarely have rigid rules. Each person is encouraged to provide new and unique information to their family. If conflict occurs, everyone involved is allowed to discuss the matter and put forth their views. If a child in an open family were to break a rule, he or she would be likely to hear "What do you think we should do about this?"

Synchronous. The synchronous family is guided by images of **harmony, tranquility, and mutual identification.** Expressions of affection are limited and reserved. Persons in synchronous families rarely communicate openly. Discussions are seen as unnecessary because family members "know" how the others would react. Communication is implicitly known and understood.

Friendships

Although it is likely that each of us are involved in some type of friendship, it is a difficult concept to define. Even when we limit our definitions to within the United States, "what a friend is" differs from person to person. When I (Monique) was in high school my friends tended to be my schoolmates who were on the track and cross-country teams with me. Since I spent a majority of my time in and out of school with them (e.g., in class and at practice) we were a close-knit group of friends. These friendships developed out of **proximity.** Now that I am older, most of my friendships have developed due to **attitude similarity.** I become friends with people who share my values, priorities, and likes.

People refer to others as "acquaintances," "close friends," "best friends," or "like family." This final distinction causes a further concern with defining friendship. Often it is the case that our sisters, brothers, mothers, fathers, and cousins are our friends too—maybe even our best friends. Nevertheless, research has indicated that there are distinctions between our friends and other kinds of relationships we have (Adelman, Parks, & Albrecht, 1990).

Distinctions of Friendship

Voluntariness. While many of us are born into our families, we choose our friends. We spend time with certain people because we want to. As friends, we are not obligated to spend time with each other. This is not always true of family. Frequently, my partner hears from his parents, "You need to visit your grandmother!" On the other hand, I rarely tell my friends "You really need to visit me, you know."

Equality. Most friends are considered our social equals (Reisman, 1979, 1981). We develop friendships with those who are like us financially and socially. For example, rarely do wealthy people develop close ties with poverty stricken others. Verbruggel

(1977) found through his research that equality in social status was a major factor in the choices we make of close friendships.

Assistance. We tend to develop friendships with people who can help us. Think of how you define "friendship." Do phrases like "I like people who I can count on" or "I want to be friends with people who are there for me" come to mind? If so, then you are not alone. Human beings tend to be very social animals. We recognize that we cannot exist alone, and it is not surprising that we seek to surround ourselves with people who can help us.

Activity Sharing. We develop friendships with people that we can do things with (Argyle & Henderson, 1985). For example, one of my favorite pastimes is watching sports. I especially like to watch Michigan State University play sports since MSU is my alma mater. Because I do not like to watch alone, I surround myself with friends who will share this activity with me. Friends are an outlet for us to enjoy the activities we do. This does not mean that we do not like people who are not just like us, but that we enjoy spending time with people who do similar activities.

Confidentiality and Emotional Support. At times we need someone to listen to our problems and successes, someone who will not divulge our secrets, and support us. There are traits that we seek in our friendships. You may be asking "Why wouldn't you go to your family for this type of support?" First, some of us might not have highly-connected families, which would make it possible to turn to them for emotional support and confidentiality. Second, there are other motivations for seeking out friends with these traits. For example, friendship circles tend to be less densely connected than families. Therefore, you can feel more secure that if you tell a secret it will not escape. That way, if the disclosure becomes too emotionally disruptive for the friendship, one can get out. This is not so true for families. Additionally, friendships are much easier to get out of than families. It is highly common in our society to break off a friendship, dating relationship or marriage; however, we rarely hear of divorcing from family members. In fact, it is so rare that when such occurrences exist, it is dramatized by the media.

Intimate Relationships

How do you know when a friendship turns into a love relationship? Do you know anyone who has been intimate with someone yet claims, "we're just friends." Sternberg's (1987) concluded that intimate relationships can be examined by discussing three components: intimacy, commitment, and passion. **Intimacy** involves feelings of closeness, sharing, communication and support. **Passion** involves physiological arousal and an intense desire to be with another person. **Commitment** involves both the short-term decision to love another person, and the longer term commitment to maintain that love.

According to Sternberg the extent to which the relationship emphasizes the above components will define what kind of relationship it is. Most of our relationships that we engage in on a daily basis do not emphasize any of these components, and would be known as **non-love**. When intimacy is the only component there is the kind of closeness we encounter when we **like** someone. On the other hand, when passion is the only component, there is a high desire to be physically close with another, but no intimacy or commitment. This is known as **infatuation.** You may know other people who have a high degree of commitment, but no intimacy or passion; Sternberg would refer to this as **empty love.** When we have intimacy and passion, but have not established a sense of commitment yet, this is known as **romantic love. Fatuous love** is the combination of commitment and passion, while **companionate love** combines commitment and intimacy. Finally, **consummate love,** the kind most people are ultimately seeking, combines all three components. For a visual understanding, refer to Figure 5.1. Think of each side of the triangle as either intimacy, commitment, or passion. The first side can be thought of as commitment, the second side as intimacy, and the bottom of the triangle as passion. If the line is dotted, that means that component is missing in the relationship.

FIGURE 5.1 Sternberg's Triangular Theory of Love

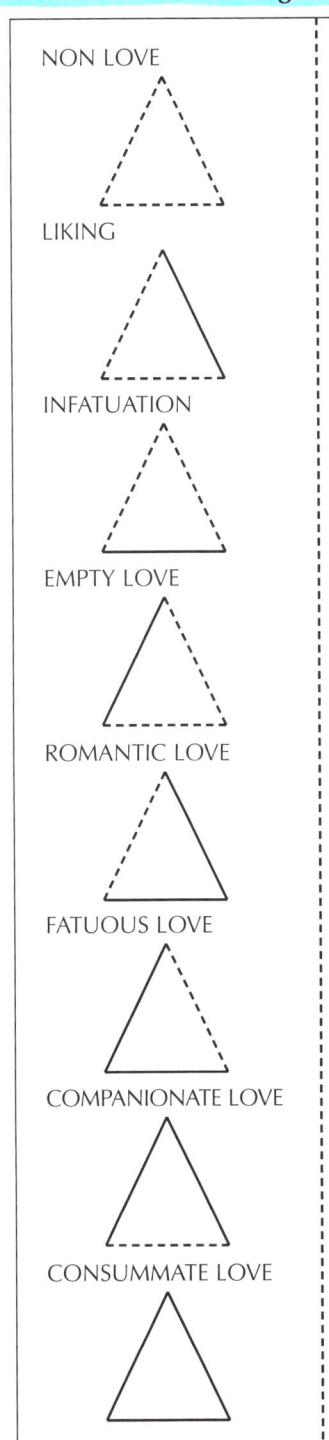

NON LOVE

LIKING

INFATUATION

EMPTY LOVE

ROMANTIC LOVE

FATUOUS LOVE

COMPANIONATE LOVE

CONSUMMATE LOVE

*Think of each side of Sternberg's triangle as indicative of commitment, intimacy, or passion. The side(s) that is dotted illustrates that this particular component is **missing** from this type of relationship.*

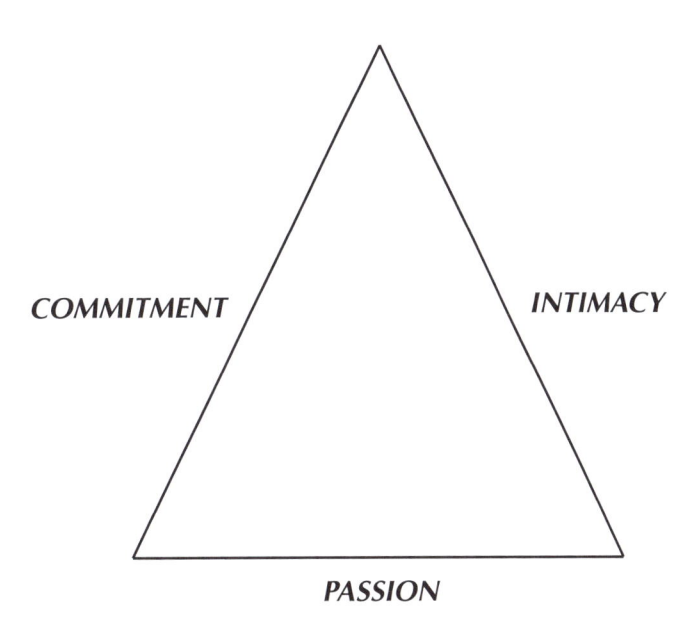

COMMITMENT   INTIMACY

PASSION

In what kind(s) of relationships are you currently involved? Are your relationships missing key components that could enrich them or make them more serious?

Adapted from Hendrick and Hendrick (1990a).

Relational Development 93

Marital Relationships

In many societies, the most intimate kind of relationships are marital ones. Mary Anne Fitzpatrick (Fitzpatrick, 1988) has undertaken the task of classifying couple types. Heavily influenced by Kantor and Lehr's work (1975), she isolated eight factors which describe important relational characteristics. These characteristics include: conflict avoidance, assertiveness, sharing, ideology of traditionalism, ideology of uncertainty and change, time regularity, undifferentiated space, and individuality (autonomy). Fitzpatrick defined four types of couple relationships: traditionals, independents, separates, and mixed (of which there are six combinations). Through her research, she found that 20% of couples are traditionals, 17% are separates, and 22% are independents (Fitzpatrick, 1988). Hence, 59% of couples are classified as pure types while 40% of couples are mixed.

Independents. Independent couples accept uncertainty and change, but do not pay as much attention to schedules and traditional values. Independents are the most autonomous of the types, confront conflict, are willing to negotiate autonomy, and do considerable amounts of sharing. In terms of sex role orientation, independents are more likely to support androgynous and flexible sex roles than are separates or traditionals.

Separates. Separates tend to maintain more distance between each other than other couple types. Separates experience little togetherness and sharing. In contrast to independents, separates avoid conflict, have differentiated space needs, and maintain schedules. Separates usually oppose androgynous and flexible sex roles.

Traditionals. The hallmark of the traditional couple is a need for routine. Consequently, traditionals hold conventional belief systems and resist change. Additionally, traditionals are prone to physical and psychological sharing, and have high degrees of interdependence. While couples of this type will engage in conflict, they prefer to avoid it if possible. Uncertainty and change upsets the traditional couple. Similar to separates, traditional couples demonstrate strong sex-typed orientations and oppose androgyny.

Mixed. As previously stated, 40% of couples represent some mixed type. Mixed couples include: traditional/separate, separate/traditional, independent/ separate, separate/independent, traditional/independent, and independent/ traditional (the husband is designated by the first term) (Fitzpatrick, 1988).

A large body of research has been written on couple types and the extent to which they experience relational satisfaction and cohesiveness. The results of some of this research has been summed in Table 5.1. In general, couples who agreed on relational definitions tended to agree with each other on a greater number of issues. Moreover, those who agreed were also more cohesive. Interestingly, couples who disagreed on their relational definitions were as relationally satisfied as those who agreed on their relational definitions (Fitzpatrick, 1988).

TABLE 5.1 Couple Type Differences On Relational Measures

Couple Types	Marital Satisfaction	Cohesion	Consensus	Affectional Expression	Sex Roles	(Wives only) Gender
Traditionals	High	High	High	Moderately High	Conventional	Feminine
Independents	Low	Moderately High	Low	Low	Nonconventional	Sex-typed
Androgynous Separates	Low	Low	Moderately High	Low	Conventional	Feminine Sex-typed
Separates/ Traditionals	Moderately High	Moderately High	Moderately High	High	Conventional	Feminine Sex-typed
Other Mixed Types	Moderately High	Low	Low	Moderately High	Depends on Type	Depends

The Stages of Intimate Relationships

Dr. Mark Knapp, a noted interpersonal scholar, developed what is known as the stages of interpersonal relationships. These stages are important to examine when speaking of love relationships. These stages reveal the different communication patterns we use depending on the level of the relationship we are in.

Initiating

Like the term denotes, this is the beginning stage of interaction. Usually, when we meet people for the first time we try to portray ourselves as someone who is likable, friendly, understanding, and socially adept (Knapp & Vangelisti, 1992). We are also careful to reduce any uncertainty we may have about the stranger, hoping to gain clarification of the other's mood, interests, feelings about us, and an understanding about the other's public self.

As we take in information about the other person during an initial interaction we also bring much information with us. Stereotypes, prior knowledge about the person, or previous interactions we have had with this person will mold our interaction. We consciously or subconsciously ask ourselves if we like this person, if we think s/he is physically attractive, and/or whether we should continue this conversation.

Relational Development

Experimenting

It is common for students at Michigan State University (I am sure it holds true for any school) to ask two questions when they are speaking with a new person, "What's your major?" and "Where did you grow up?" As a matter of fact, it is typical for people to ask, if they know someone else in your hometown, "Oh. Do you know . . . ?"

The hallmark of experimenting is small talk. Although most people dislike engaging in this form of communication, it is necessary when meeting new people. Knapp and Vangelisti (1992) note that during the beginning of new relationships we spend a lot of time experimenting. Seeking potential similarities, we search for a breadth of information about the other person. Miller and Knapp (1986) reveal that there are three types of information we seek out from others. The first type is **cultural information.** By knowing what culture another person is from we can use stereotypes we have developed in order to predict their behavior. In addition, if the other person is from the same culture as you, you may share predictable ways of behaving (Miller & Knapp, 1986). The second type of information is **sociological information.** This kind of information deals with a person's membership or reference groups. If we hear that a person is a doctor, fraternity member, or tuba player in the marching band we can begin to scan all of the information and associations we may have with such labels. The final type of information we seek out is **psychological information.** Here, we recognize the differences we may have with our conversational partner. This type of information-seeking is more likely to occur with people who are more familiar to us.

Intensifying

When we have moved beyond being an acquaintance with another person there are indicators that the relationship is **intensifying.** This stage tends to work in increments, as people are often more cautious about intensifying than they are about initiating or experimenting. For example, we may sit close to someone before we hold hands, and hold hands before we hug. Requests for psychological and physical favors are often indicative of a relationship that is intensifying (Knapp & Vangelisti, 1992).

Additionally, the amount of self-disclosure increases greatly during this stage. In particular, as people intensify relationships they begin to share secrets. For example, in this stage it might be revealed that a person is afraid of being a failure, or that their parents are divorced. Disclosures may be related to any subject, but the personal disclosures are particularly relevant to intensifying.

Several communication patterns typically take place during the intensifying stage (Knapp & Vangelisti, 1992). First, forms of address become much more informal; we tend to use first names, nick names, or terms of endearment more frequently. People also tend to unify the relationship more by using plural forms of the couple. "Let's go to the movies," or "We should study for exams," are more common while the use of "I" was more common in initiating and experimenting. Third, the couple also begins to share slang or private jokes more often. People they know, or funny occurrences they've shared may be the subject for exchanges unique to the relationship. Fourth, the couple will use a greater number of verbal shortcuts. Saying "salt" instead of "Please pass me the salt" may take place due to the couple's accumulated source of knowledge, shared assumptions, expectations, interests, interactions, and experiences. Fifth, the couple will use more direct expressions of commitment. You may find yourself saying "We are really lucky to have each other." Finally, the partners will find each other helping the other with understanding. One might say "Oh, what you mean is . . . " or "In other words . . . ".

Integrating

When the relationship has reached a point where two persons in a relationship are combining to form one unit, we can say they are **integrating.** During this stage, couples typically share some kind of physical symbol of their unification. In high school for instance, you may have worn your partner's class ring or Varsity jacket. Another example of integrating is when my step-mother changed her religion when she became close with my father. During integration, social circles may merge, couples may refer to things as "theirs" (e.g. "our song," "our restaurant").

Bonding

Bonding is the public ritual which reveals that the relationship exists. There are many kinds of bonding rituals, dependent on the kind, the depth, and the length of the relationship. The most obvious form of bonding is marriage, however, going steady, engagement, or using the term "dating" are other kinds of bonding.

Differentiating

Differentiating is the first stage in coming apart. Like the term indicates, it means to become distinct or different in character. Similar to how integrating is a form of fusing the relationship, differentiating is an ungluing of the relationship. Here, previously joint possessions become separated, "My TV," "My sofa," "My dog," etc. When couples differentiate, it does not guarantee that they will break up. It may simply follow some form of conflict that the couple will overcome.

Circumscribing

The second stage of coming apart is termed **circumscribing.** The hallmark of circumscribing is the constricted (circumscribed) communication forms. In other words, the communication that takes place is better described by quantity than quality. I (Monique) recall that about a year before my parents decided to divorce, circumscribing could have described their communication patterns. Instead of discussing the family, their relationship, or other "touchy" topics, their communication was "What's for dinner?" or "Did the repair man come by?" My parents discussed surface-level, non-controversial, non-affectionate, superficial topics. Correspondingly, during the circumscribing stage phrases like "Let's not talk about that anymore," "I don't want to hear it," or "It's none of your business" can be heard.

Stagnating

When people in a relationship are **stagnating** they go through the motions of the relationship, doing the routine gestures. This stage of coming apart shows us that instead of trying to work through the conflict we settle (for some amount of time) for doing the usual thing. My parents went through the stagnating stage before their divorce. Every

Sunday morning our family would get up at 9:00 a.m., go to church, then rush home to eat pancakes and sausage. My mother, who isn't particularly religious, went through this routine week after week without ever saying a word to my father.

Avoiding

Clearly, **avoiding** is the constant wish to be away from your relational partner. Sometimes, instead of getting out of the relationship or talking with our partner, we find it easier to avoid them. You may find yourself saying, "I would come over tonight, but I have to study."

Terminating

Terminating is the final stage of coming apart, because it is when we decide to end the relationship. While the parting may be an overt act, such as a statement by one of the partners that the relationship is over, sometimes we terminate relationships through avoidance. For example, I (Kimo) was dating a person named Maria when I first started college. Maria and I had dated for nearly a year when we stopped calling each other. After about a month of not talking, I decided to call. We didn't have much to say, so I never called again and she never called me. It's been 12 years since we last talked. Maybe I should call and officially break things off.

WHAT KIND OF LOVERS ARE WE?

People who become involved in relationships often bring individual differences with them into the relationship. For example, partners may differ on how much they like to go out dancing, spend their time shopping, or the types of political beliefs that they hold. One individual difference which can influence whether intimate relationships are successful include the type of lover individuals can be labeled. In particular, it has been suggested that there are six types of lovers (Hendrick & Hendrick, 1990b). The six types of lovers have been referred to as: passionate, playful, companionate, realistic, obsessive, and altruistic. If you want to know what kind of lover you are before reading about them, complete the Love Styles Profile. The Love Styles Profile can be found in the exercises at the end of this chapter.

Passionate Love. Lovers of this type are often attracted to physical beauty. Immediate relational disclosure and physical intimacy is expected. When either relational disclosure or physical intimacy is withheld by a partner, these types of lovers quickly lose interest in the relationship and typically believe that the partner does not love them as much as they love their partner. Because lovers of this type have particular expectations of how a relationship should progress, they experience intense emotional highs and lows.

Playful Love. Lovers of this type view love as a game. New relational partners are viewed as targets to be conquered. Because love is a game to these types of lovers, relationships which progress further then they want will be immediately terminated. Lovers of this variety enjoy action in relationships. Because they are very calculating, rarely do lovers of this type do things without a particular reason. It is common for playful lovers to have more than one lover at a time.

Companionate Love. Lovers of this type believe that love should evolve from a friendship. Lovers of this type believe that relational problems can be easily solved. Stability and predictability describe these types of lovers well. Because love evolves, lovers of this variety let love grow naturally and peacefully into a solid relationship. It is rarely problematic when these type of lovers are apart. Due to their ability to build solid relationships, these type of lovers are very sure of their relationships.

Realistic Love. Lovers of this type base their partnerships on practicality. That is, how practical is it to be in a particular relationship. If the relationship is no longer practical, e.g., their partner moves to another state to go to school, then the relationship is likely to be terminated. Because lovers of this type are concerned with practicality, these lovers are concerned with compatibility. If compatibility is not apparent, these types of lovers will abandon potential partnerships. Newly forming relationships with these types of lover are similar to being on a job interview.

Obsessive Love. Lovers of this type are manipulative and jealous lovers. It is important for lovers of this type to believe that they are the center of their partner's world. For these lovers, love is like a drug addiction, with their partner being the drug. If a partner denies attention to an obsessive lover, the obsessive lover will take actions to regain attention. An obsessive lover seeks to spend all of their time with their partner. Because being involved with an obsessive lover requires a lot of attention, these lovers often go through multiple partners until they find another obsessive lover.

Altruistic Love. Lovers of this type are often described as being unselfish and kind. Wanting to make their partner happy, these types of lovers are often willing to do whatever their partner wants as long as it avoids conflict. It is rare for these types of lovers to take initiative in a relationship. Preferring to make sure that their partner supports a particular activity before they engage in it, these types of lovers often take the "wait and see" approach to relationships.

The type of love style that we take is rarely fixed. As we move from relationship to relationship people often become different types of lovers. Factors such as how much we like our partner, why we are in a particular relationship, and our prior relational experiences all influence how we will behave in a given relationship.

PREDICTORS OF RELATIONAL SUCCESS

When I (Kimo) was an undergraduate, I had a roommate named Kevin. Kevin was an interesting man, and besides the enjoyment I got out of sneaking handfuls of his beloved Cheezit™ crackers when he was at school or asleep, I was also very amused by Kevin's interpersonal interactions. Kevin enjoyed the social aspect of college. Rarely did a weekend pass when I did not receive a lecture on how to be an undergraduate. We had to go to the bar and we had to at least look like we were having fun. Frequently, to the amusement of myself and our friends, Kevin would engage in another failed relationship. The story was always the same. Kevin would meet someone, he would fall in love, and she would initially appear interested. In time, she would quit returning his phone calls. While often amused by his relational sagas, I soon learned that some relationships were destined to fail.

In their work on exploring the factors which determine whether or not people would maintain a relationship once they started dating, Parks and Adelman (1983) conducted a

FIGURE 5.2 Predictors of Relational Success

- greater certainty
- communication between partners
- support from family members
- support from friendship networks
- similarity

study which examined predictors of relational success. According to Parks and Adelman, five major predictors influence whether or not partners would maintain their relationship. The predictors included: certainty, communication between partners, support from family and friends, and similarity.

Specifically, greater certainty, communication between partners, support from family members, support from friends, and similarity were all positively related to people staying together. In fact, Parks and Adelman report that these characteristics were able to correctly classify 90% of those people who stayed together and 83% of those who did not stay together over a three month period. In total, the above characteristics correctly predicted the outcomes of relationships with nearly 88% accuracy.

WHY DO WE FORM INTERPERSONAL RELATIONSHIPS?

Now that you understand what interpersonal relationships are, and the different types of interpersonal relationships we develop, it is important to ask "Why do we form interpersonal relationships?" While communication scientists have been exploring these reasons for decades, Adler and Rodman (1994) discuss the following as the major reasons we form interpersonal relationships.

We Form Relationships with Those Whom Are Similar to Us—Most of the Time

It is not surprising that we form relationships with people who are similar to us. This is not to say that we want to be around people who are just like us. Our lives would be boring if we only associated with people who liked exactly what we like, thought exactly like us, and talked exactly like us. On the other hand, it is also difficult to form relationships with those who are nothing like us. We can associate ourselves, and understand people with whom we share similarities.

We Form Relationships with People Who Complement Our Personalities

Although we are attracted to people who are similar to us, the old saying "opposites attract" remains true. We tend to form relationships with people when their personality traits, which are different from ours, satisfy our needs. For example, I (Monique) am extremely pragmatic and realistic, while my partner is romantic and optimistic. While it is easy for me to point out why a plan will not work, he keeps me from becoming depressive. These differences in our personalities complement each other. You may like to cook, while your best friend hates to cook, but loves to do the dishes. Again, these differences are the kind that work in a relationship.

We Form Relationships with People Who Are Physically Attractive

Hard to believe isn't it? Most people believe that we like, and form relationships with people based on values and beliefs—not physical attractiveness. Nevertheless, research has repeatedly found that we form relationships with persons we find attractive. Shelly Chaiken has completed a number of studies examining the effects of physical attractiveness on other variables we like in people. Chaiken's (1979) research revealed that individuals who were perceived as physically attractive were found to have better social skills. Moreover, Chaiken's study revealed that physically attractive people are more fluent, faster speakers, report having higher SAT scores, and are more confident. In addition, people are more likely to date physically attractive others. According to Dion et. al (1972) attractive individuals have been found to date more than those who are unattractive. Furthermore, in dating situations individuals have been shown to show significant preferences toward dating others who are perceived as physically attractive (Hadjistavropolous & Genest, 1994).

Why do we do this? Chaiken offers the **Social Reinforcement Explanation.** This explanation suggests that persons who are attractive are taught from an early age that they are "cute" (Chaiken, 1979, 1986). For instance, research has revealed that children who are physically attractive tend to receive less harsh punishments when they do wrong than their less attractive counterparts. Coined the "halo" effect, attractive children are often excused from their mis-doings because their mis-doings are viewed as something that will pass over; their wrong is "cute." Unattractive children's mis-doings, however, are not overlooked. Children who are unattractive are punished more than attractive children. Later in life, unattractive people are viewed more negatively in general, and are viewed as less interesting and less successful than people who are attractive. Therefore, as research has revealed, those who are physically attractive receive far more social rewards than those who are not. Moreover, society views attractive people as being able to provide social benefits; thus, we prefer to be surrounded by attractive others (Chaiken, 1979, 1986).

Interestingly, people have a strong tendency to deny that they value attractiveness in other people (Hadjistavropolous & Genest, 1994). This denial may be viewed as taboo within our societal norms. Thus, by admitting that physical attractiveness is important one may be viewed as admitting that he or she is shallow. Furthermore, another study showed that people tend to make negative evaluations of those who rely heavily on physical attractiveness in choosing a dating partner (Hadjistavropoulos & Genest, 1994). In general, it appears that individuals want to date physically attractive others, but do not want to admit that physical attraction has an effect on their date's desirability.

We Form Relationships with People Who Like Us

When we spend time with people who like us, it bolsters our opinions of ourselves; it raises our self-esteem. Of course we don't always like people simply because they like us, but notice that you probably don't spend time with people that do not like you.

We Form Relationships with People Who Can Help Us

You have probably heard the old saying "You scratch my back, I'll scratch yours." This is the basic premise of this reason for why we form relationships. Thibaut and Kelly

(1959) called this economic relationship model the **Social Exchange Model.** This model views relationships in terms of their costs and rewards. According to this model, we seek relationships with people who give us more rewards than costs. Rewards are both physical and emotional. When we begin relationships with people we may unconsciously think, "Is this worth the effort?" For instance, the term "emotional baggage" is often used with people who take more (emotionally) than they give back. It is difficult to maintain a friendship with a person who takes, and rarely gives.

While at its most basic level social exchange theory seems selfish, it is not. For example, I work for a local charity. An important aspect of this charity is receiving corporate sponsorship. The charity offers free advertising (we put their logo on the back of our T-shirt) in exchange for gifts or money. Think how crazy it would sound to the sponsors if I said, "Please give us your money, but we will not give you anything back." In some ways friendships are like business relationships.

We Form Relationships with People Who Are Competent

People tend to be attracted to talented others. This may be because we wish that their talents will rub off on us. It is also no surprise that we are not as attracted to "perfect people" because they do not appear to be human beings—they have no flaws.

We Form Relationships with People Who We Encounter Often

Proximity, or the degree to which we are near someone, has a substantial influence on forming interpersonal relationships. This is not surprising given that if we see someone frequently, it is more likely that we will learn more about them. In addition, the more we learn and know about someone, the more likely attraction will build. Moreover, it is easier to build strong relationships with persons that are close by.

We Form Relationships with People We Can Disclose Ourselves To

Self-disclosure is a means to become close with other people. When we share intimate and important information about ourselves, we tend to develop a greater sense of liking for the other person. Furthermore, sharing personal information with other people is a sign of trust and regard; we tend not to share information with others that we do not like, and as we have already learned we tend to be attracted to others who like us.

A CLOSER LOOK AT SELF-DISCLOSURE

Earlier in this chapter we discussed self-disclosure because it is one of the key reasons we develop relationships. Self-disclosure is paramount in our relationships because it is the way in which we reveal who we are, and helps us understand others. Americans have a need to seek information about others so that we can predict their behaviors and thoughts. This is called uncertainty reduction (Berger & Calabrese, 1979). Self-disclosure is a way of reducing uncertainty. This section of this chapter will take a closer look into self-disclosure. We will discuss what exactly self-disclosure is, what kinds of information people self-disclose, what the benefits of self-disclosure are, what blocks us from self-disclosure, and, finally, strategies toward effective self-disclosure.

What Is Self-Disclosure?

Self-disclosure is the process by which we verbally reveal information about ourselves. By revealing this information, which could include our thoughts, feelings, and experiences, we advance relationships. Self-disclosure is the key to relationship development, thus the emphasis we put on it is evident (Dindia et. al., 1997). Although most people realize that they need to reveal information about themselves in order to begin and maintain intimate relations, it doesn't cease to be frightening. Telling another person your most embarrassing moment, what you are afraid of, or your intimate thoughts is intimidating. Nevertheless, we cannot help but disclose ourselves; even without words, our nonverbal communication can reveal to people how we feel or what we are thinking. Recall the last time you saw a person slink into class, slump into his/her desk and place his/her hands over her face? This is a good example of how people tend to disclose information without even saying anything.

Every person discloses themselves differently. The **Johari Window** in Figure 5.3 is an excellent model which explains how each communicator discloses or is aware about information about them. The window features four quadrants (metaphorically, one can think of them as the window panes). Quadrant one is the **open quadrant.** The open quadrant depicts the extent to which the information you are revealing is known to yourself, and known to others. Simply, it is the information that people openly share. Many people are not intimidated about sharing information. For example, a friend of mine teaches a class on human sexuality. Every semester he is surprised to learn how many people are willing to share their most intimate sexual stories in class, in front of their classmates! People such as this would be said to have large open quadrants.

FIGURE 5.3 The Johari Window

	KNOWN TO SELF	NOT KNOWN TO SELF
KNOWN TO OTHER	Quadrant 1 (Open)	Quadrant 3 (Blind)
NOT KNOWN TO OTHER	Quadrant 2 (Hidden)	Quadrant 4 (Unknown)

Quadrant two is the **hidden quadrant.** The hidden quadrant reflects the information that is known to you, but is hidden from other people. Everyone has certain pieces of information that are extremely personal. On the other hand, we are unique to the extent that we share that personal information. The more information you keep to yourself (i.e. the less you self-disclose) the larger your hidden quadrant.

Quadrant three is the **blind quadrant.** This quadrant includes the information that we fail to recognize. It is the information that is unknown to ourselves, but known to others. This can include your habits, mannerisms, and defense mechanisms. For instance, my friend, Kelly, is a third grade teacher. After she began this job, whenever we would talk she would speak to me as if I was in the third grade. It was clear that she didn't realize this, but nevertheless it was true. This information is in Kelly's blind quadrant.

Finally, the fourth quadrant is the **unknown quadrant.** This is the information that is unknown to ourself and to others. Sometimes our subconscious hides information from us. You may feel that you are unsure how you feel about someone. If someone says, "I've always loved you, I just didn't know it," this is a good example of unknown information.

As we get more involved in intimate relationships, the more we know about the other person. Therefore, the more intimate the relationship, it is likely that your hidden quadrant and unknown quadrant will become smaller.

FIGURE 5.4 An Ideal Intimate Relationship

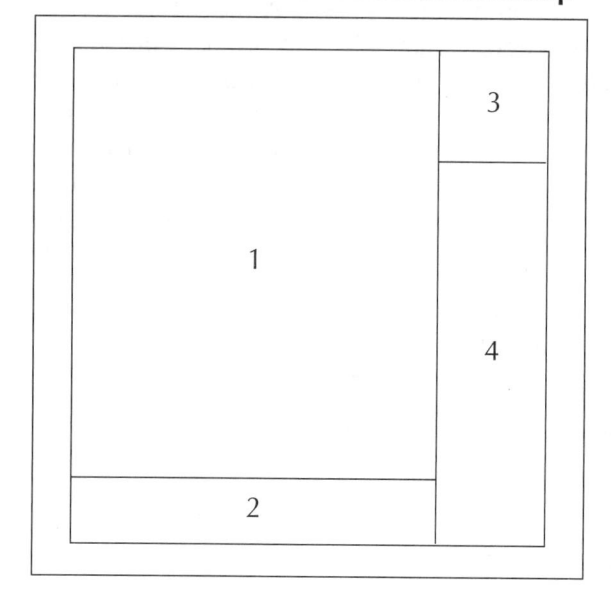

Every individual has a unique Johari Window dependent on how much information he or she will share, and how much information he or she knows about him/herself. For example, a person who is highly self aware in a healthy relationship might have the window depicted in Figure 5.2. According to Beebe, Beebe, & Redmond (1996) this window would be considered ideal in an intimate relationship. A couple with such a window is not afraid to share information, as revealed by the small hidden quadrant and the large open quadrant. In addition, the blind and unknown quadrants are small, showing the people understand themselves as well as the other. Consider your level of self-awareness and openness. What would your window look like?

What Kinds of Information Do We Reveal?

Although it is important to define self-disclosure and understand how each individual is unique with respect to self-disclosing, it is also important to understand what kinds of information we disclose. Not all self-disclosures are equally revealing. I may be perfectly willing to tell you how much I weigh and where I received my masters degree, while never disclosing information about my childhood. Altman and Taylor (1973) developed a model which helps us understand these differences. It is called the **Social Penetration Model.** The first dimension of their model deals with the breadth or amount of information one shares. More specifically, breadth deals with the range of topics one can discuss. For example, in the classroom I typically discuss only academic issues with my students. They do not know if I am in a relationship, where I live, who my parents are, or what my religion is. On the other hand, Kimo and I can discuss a vast array of topics, from gambling to religion. The breadth of topics I discuss with Dr. Ah Yun is much greater than that which I discuss with my students.

The Social Penetration Model can be helpful in allowing us to understand how communication can be more or less disclosing. As previously mentioned the breadth of information we share deals with the amount of information we discuss. Depth, on the other hand deals with the degree to which the information we reveal is personal. The outermost layer of information we share is termed **cliché**. Clichés are ritualized, stock information that we would share with most anyone. You might even think of it as the opposite of self-disclosure. "How's it going?" or "Nice day, isn't it?" are examples of clichés. The next layer of the model deals with **facts**. Not all facts are disclosing; in order to be thought of as so, they must be intentional, significant, and not otherwise known. For example, if I told you that I went to a community college in Traverse City before attending Michigan State University, I have shared a fact. The third level of the Social Penetration Model is

opinions. Opinions reveal what you think about a subject. Sharing your opinions gives other people around you valuable information about yourself. If I tell you that "Michigan State's communication Ph.D. program is the best in the nation," I am sharing my opinion. The fourth, and most personal level of self-disclosing, according to Altman and Taylor, is **feelings.** Feelings can be sharing opinions, but they are necessarily personal, while all opinions are not. Furthermore, while feelings tell what you think about a topic, feelings allow us to understand what you feel about it. For example, "I don't think you treat me very well, and *I am very hurt by that.*"

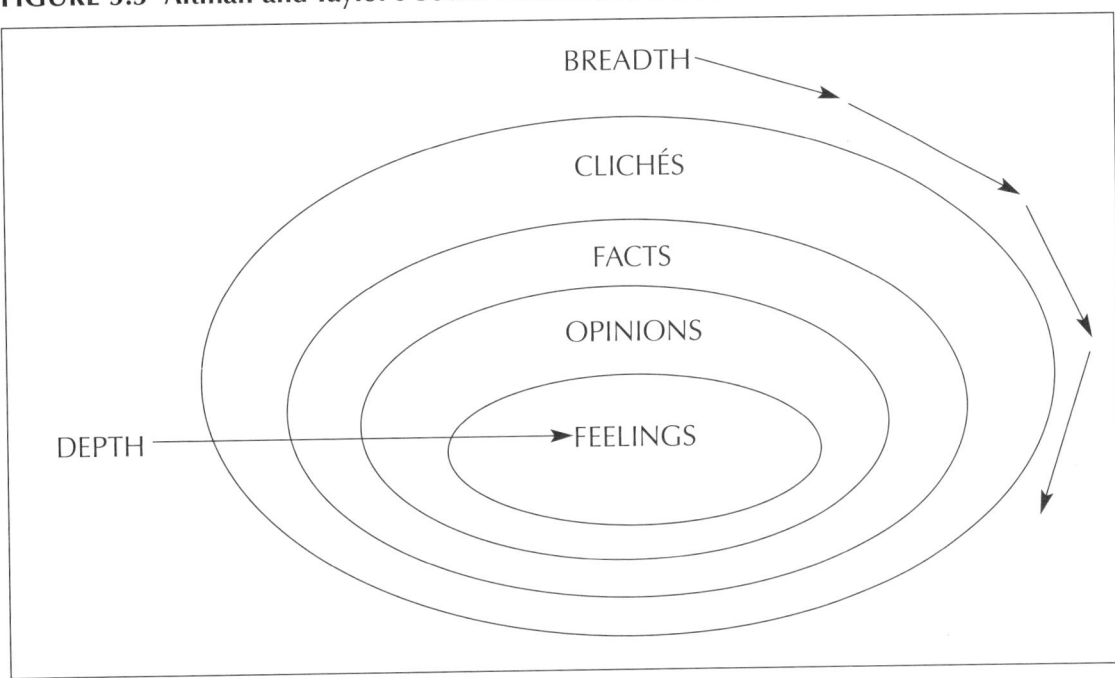

FIGURE 5.5 Altman and Taylor's Social Penetration Model

Interpersonal communication is relevant in every facet of your life. Clearly, we all have to deal with and communicate with our families, our friends, and our lovers. While this chapter only touches on some of the foundations and keys to interpersonal communication, it should provide you with an understanding of these intricacies. Good luck and communicate well!

REFERENCES

Adelman, M. B., Parks, M. R., & Albrecht, T. L. (1990). The nature of friendship and its development. In J. Stewart (Ed.) *Bridges not walls* (5th ed., pp.283–291). New York: McGraw Hill.

Adler, R. B. & Rodman, G. (1994). *Understanding human communication* (5th ed.). Fort Worth, TX: Harcourt Brace.

Altman, I. & Taylor, D. A. (1973). *Social Penetration: The development of interpersonal relationships.* San Francisco: Jossey Bass.

Argyle, M. & Henderson, M. (1985). *The anatomy of relationships.* London: Heinemann.

Beebe, S. A., Beebe, S. J., & Redmond, M. V. (1996). *Interpersonal communication.* Boston, MA: Allyn and Bacon.

Chaiken, S. (1979). Communication physical attractiveness and persuasion. *Journal of Personality and Social Psychology, 37,* 1387–1397.

Chaiken, S. (1986). Physical appearance and social influence. In C. P. Herman, M. P. Zanna, & E. T. Higgins (Eds.) *Physical appearance, stigma, and social behavior: The Ontario symposium,* (vol. 3, pp. 143–177) Hillsdale, NJ: Lawrence Erlbaum.

Constantine, L. L. (1986). *Family paradigms: The practice of theory in family therapy.* New York: The Guilford Press.

Dindia, K., Fitzpatrich, M., & Kenny, D. A. (1997). Self disclosure in spouse and stranger interaction: A social relations analysis. *Human Communication Research, 23,* 388–412.

Dion, K. K., Berscheid, E., & Walster, E.(1972). What is beautiful is good. *Journal of Personality and Social Psychology, 24,* 285–290.

Fitzpatrick, M. A. (1988). *Between husbands and wives.* Newbury Park, CA: Sage.

Galvin, K. M. & Brommel, B. J. (1986). *Family communication: Cohesion and change* (2nd ed.). Glenview, IL: Scott, Foresman.

Galvin, K. M., & Brommel, B. J. (1991). *Family communication: Cohesion and change* (3rd ed.). New York: Harper Collins.

Hadistavropoulos, T, & Genest, M. (1994) The underestimation of the role of physical attractiveness in dating preferences: Ignorance or taboo? *Canadian Journal of Behavioral Science, 26,* 298–318.

Hendrick, C. & Hendrick, S. (1990a). A relationship specific version of the love attitudes scale. In J. W. Newliep (Ed.), *Handbook of replication research in the behavioral and social sciences. Journal of Social Behavior and Personality, Special Issue, 5,* 239-254.

Hendrick, C. & Hendrick, S. (1990b). A theory and method of love. *Journal of Personality and Social Psychology, 50,* 392–402.

Kantor, D., & Lehr, W. (1975) *Inside the family: Toward a theory of family process.* San Francisco: Jossey-Bass.

Knapp, M. L. & Vangelisti, A. L. (1992). *Interpersonal communication and human relationships* (2nd ed.). Needham Heights, MA: Allyn and Bacon.

Miller, V. D., & Knapp, M. L. (1986). Communication paradoxes and the maintenance of living relationships with the dying. *Journal of Family Issues, 7,* 255–275.

Reisman, J. M. (1979). *Anatomy of friendship.* New York: Irvington.

Sternberg, R.J. (1987) Liking versus loving. *Psychological Bulletin, 102,* 331–345.

Thibaut, J. W. & Kelley, H. H. (1959). *The social psychology of groups.* Minneapolis, MN.: John Wiley & Sons, Inc.

Verbrugge, L. M. (1977). The structure of adult friendship choices. *Social Forces, 56,* 576–597.

Chapter Five Case Study—
Relational Development

Instructions:
Please read the following case study carefully and select the best answers to the questions. This quiz is an individual assignment. Remember: sharing answers is a form of plagiarism.

Ronald has always been a romantic. He fell in love quickly with one girl and he wondered what it would be like to date her, the most popular girl in school. Unfortunately, most people know him as the dork that mows everyone's lawn. By the end of summer, Ronnie has saved over $1,000 mowing lawns and he is now excited to purchase a telescope. When arriving at the mall to buy the telescope, he observes Cindy Mancini, the most popular girl in school, in a money bind. She needs $1,000 to replace a leather outfit of her mother's which she has spilled wine on. Ronald, taking advantage of opportunity, offers to give Cindy the money IF she pretends to date him for a month. He knows that dating Cindy would instantly make him popular. Cindy, who is a little less certain that the ploy will work, agrees to walk with him down the hall, sit next to him at three lunches per week, and to attend a football game with him for ONE month only. They first start out as friends and as their relationship progresses, Cindy begins to call him "Ronnie," eating pizza after school becomes a habit, and everyone believes that the two are a couple because they are always seen together. As the month comes to a close, Ronnie believes it is time to set-up a public break-up so everyone can know that he and Cindy are no longer a couple. The fight takes place on the quad and Ronnie concocts a story about Cindy spending all his money. She slaps him and runs off. Soon after, the guys ask for permission to date Cindy and Cindy's friends set up dates with Ronnie. Ronnie has become popular just how he had imagined. All the girls want to date him and he has no real interest in settling down with one girl. In the end, Ronnie is not happy dating several different girls, but rather he wished he was back with Cindy.

Student's Name _____

Section Number _____

Section Leader's Name _____

Chapter Five Case Study Quiz—Relational Development

1. According to the scenario, what love style would BEST reflect Ronnie BEFORE he dated Cindy?
   a. Companionate
   b. Altruistic
   c. Passionate
   d. Obsessive

2. Ronnie's love style changed once he and Cindy broke up. He started dating several girls with no real commitment. What love style is this?
   a. Realistic
   b. Obsessive
   c. Companionate
   d. Playful

3. Ronnie particularly enjoyed his short relationship with Cindy because it caused Ronnie to become one of the most popular guys in school. This illustrates which reason why we form relationships?
   a. We form relationships with people who are similar to us.
   b. We form relationships with people who can help us.
   c. We form relationships with people who like us.
   d. We form relationships with people who are competent.

4. Ronnie and Cindy are seen eating lunch together. What relational stage are they in?
   a. Initiating
   b. Intensifying
   c. Bonding
   d. Experimenting

5. Ronnie and Cindy have a public break up in the quad. What relational stage are they in?
   a. Differentiating
   b. Stagnating
   c. Terminating
   d. Avoiding

Chapter Six

SOCIALIZATION

Vernon Miller
Michigan State University

Letticia N. Callies
Michigan State University

Janie Harden Fritz
Duquesne University

How do you learn to "fit in" as a member of a group, organization, or society? We learn the requirements of membership through socialization, the process by which others teach and reinforce the elements of membership. One of the chief means of socializing others is through the use of stories, and stories can likewise teach us about socialization.

To understand the relationship between communication and socialization, consider the following stories. The first story comes from a friend of the authors who joined the Seals in the United States Navy. From what he learned in regular Navy basic training and heard before joining the military, he expected Seal training to be one of the most intensive, rigorous mental and physical experiences in the world. His expectations were exceeded as every moment was scheduled for his induction class of 40 distinguished Navy seamen, with harsh physical training regimens (e.g., running sprints all morning, 12-mile runs, treading water in a swimming pool for hours) designed to boost endurance, brake down barriers of individualism, and instill Seal values. Soon after arriving on the training base following a demanding physical workout with instructors constantly yelling such things as, "Pain is weakness leaving the body," and "You can rest when you're dead," his drill instructor (the Chief) barked, "Hey, you *!#*&! new meats, get your %&^* over to #%#%# Administration." At the Administration department, the inductees were given a checklist of places to go to get uniforms, supplies, paperwork, diving qualifications, jump qualifications, and guns. The inductees formed sub-groups and gave each other encouragement in an effort to hang in and complete the first phase of the training. After completing the checklist (which took a week to show competencies and to be approved), our friend reported to the Submersible Operations (Sub-Ops) department.

The Chief of the Sub-Ops department served as the socialization agent in terms of teaching and assigning tasks to the "new meats." This chief seemed particularly harsh and unbearable to the new meats assigned to his unit. Every error by new meats was criticized and corrected. Given the potentially fatal costs for errors in the field, the need for precision and accuracy carried over into the running of the departments. As a new meat, our friend constantly had to prove himself before receiving assistance. "I learned how things run in the Sub-Ops department, as well as other departments in the Seal teams, by going into each department and saying 'Hey, I'm a new meat, what do I need to do?' After I was harassed I was allowed tidbits of information from the "old salty frogmen" who looked down on me as if I were a peon." Our friend reported that it took years to complete the training, learning daily from salty frogmen and observing others in higher ranks. Now, as a Navy Seal Chief Petty Officer, he is responsible for socializing new meats and implements the very same standardized socialization tactics that he experienced.

Another friend of ours always wanted to be a banker. She grew up admiring how her father, a financial analyst, had effortlessly used a 10-key calculator. However, finishing college with a Business Administration degree convinced her that banking would be boring and that she would have a more interesting career in sales. Finding a job interview through a recruiting agency, she knew little about the company except for its name. She quickly collected more information about the firm from the library and the Internet, and then learned how the business was run when she interviewed. Still not knowing much, her first day on the job was quite startling. The supervisor of the Sales department gave her a tour and briefly introduced her to those she would be interacting with on a daily basis. Next, the supervisor instructed her on how to produce "sell-thru reports" which involved numerous equations, lots of numbers, and precise calculations of various products stocked in stores. With her head already swimming from trying to remember names and instructions, the pressure to perform or be terminated began to emerge. Fortunately, several coworkers arrived at her desk and took her to lunch. With the prospect of coworkers who might be friends and, as it turned out, were willing to share tips on selling, getting along with the supervisor, how to dress, and important rules and regulations, the first week went by quickly. She was still figuring things out on her own, but she grew in confidence knowing that she was not left to "sink or swim." In addition to her coworkers answering her questions, in time she was able to seek out information from her supervisor (who really had little other involvement in her acclimation to the company).

The last story is from Douglas Hyde's (1966) famous account of the training of communist cell members in post World War II London. Jim, a new communist cell recruit, was unpromising with a rather unsightly appearance, severe stutter, and poor educational training. Applying a four-step process, Hyde first taught Jim how to interpret recent and historical events emphasizing societal differences from the Communist Party's viewpoint. Importantly, Jim also learned how to teach this material to others which reinforced his learning. Second, Jim was introduced to other recruits who comprised his "cell" and became his close supporters and friends. Third, Jim was required to publicly recruit others to his new political views. Fourth, Hyde always debriefed Jim about his teaching and recruiting experiences and evaluated Jim's performance. This debriefing provided essential moral support and training so that Jim could learn to persuade others more effectively. Eventually, Jim overcame his lack of self-confidence and stutter and became an important industry leader and spokesperson for the Communist Party.

These stories demonstrate several communicative aspects of socialization. First, **entry into a group or organization can create conditions where incumbents' messages can have their maximum influence on newcomers' opinions and behaviors.** In some cases, successful socialization relies on leaders to instruct their followers. In other settings supervisors must advocate behaviors and provide prompt feedback following newcomer performance in order to socialize the newcomers.

Second, **the achievement of attitudinal and behavioral changes in newcomers often requires supportive messages from group members.** We will later point out that socialization can be accomplished just as successfully in one-on-one encounters as in a group setting. However, individuals are more likely to adapt the norms of a particular group when incumbents become their friends and are supportive (Van Maanen & Schein, 1979).

Third, **these examples stress the importance of the purposeful imparting of specific knowledge and values.** Setting specific goals allows groups and organizations to determine what messages should be conveyed, how they should be conveyed, who should convey them, and what conditions require controlling. To achieve socialization goals, leaders must devote their own time (instead of delegating the assignment) to teach skills, nurture growth, and inculcate values in each recruit (Brim, 1966).

Fourth, **we receive socialization messages throughout our lives, from childhood through adulthood.** Socialization messages help us understand incumbents' expectations regarding what we should or should not do and the way or manner in which we are expected to perform our duties. The following sections define socialization and its basic elements, illustrate some of the processes that enable socialization to work, present guidelines for effective socialization, and discuss the implications of being socialized and socializing others.

Socialization Defined

Socialization generally refers to the ways in which individuals learn skills, knowledge, values, motives, and roles appropriate to their position in a group or society (Bush & Simmons, 1981). On a **societal** level, socialization is a means of perpetuating the group or society and transmitting culture (Gecas, 1981). Emphases are placed on learning others' expectations of how the individual should act, what norms should be upheld, and to which values one should adhere. On an **individual** level, socialization assists self-concept development and individuals' learning to negotiate their identities. So, on a societal level socialization facilitates adaptation and conformity to a group's values whereas socialization on an individual level is an integral part of our development as distinct human beings.

Socialization benefits both individuals and groups by promoting and facilitating new members' acceptance of normative values and behaviors. For example, the stories of the Navy Seal and Jim both illustrate how individuals' self-images can be transformed through socialization experiences.

Socialization provides individuals with cues by which they can make sense of themselves in relation to society. For instance, teaching a 12-year old to shake hands when being introduced to adults facilitates the youth's transition into larger society and contributes to the development of the youth's self-image as a member of that society. Since we experience new socialization experiences each time we enter new educational, work, and community settings, it is not unreasonable to suggest that socialization messages and experiences contribute to the continuing redefinition and elaboration of our self-identities.

Socialization also provides markers by which individuals can test themselves to know the extent to which they are fitting in and have a place in society. Whether you are a member of the military, a fraternity or sorority, or a service organization, those teachings which become internalized during entry provide self-regulating guidelines for what is acceptable behavior for yourself and others. Similarly, parents attempt to inculcate values into their children so that the children will act in a responsible manner when they are on their own.

In short, socialization is a means of influence, and messages from incumbents have both important societal and individual outcomes. The next section more closely examines those outcomes, with particular attention given to individuals' assimilation into groups and organizations.

Socialization Functions of Communication

Socialization messages from one person to another serve at least five broad functions. First, **communication is a means of inculcating the values of one group to another.** Some organizations depend on the transference of values from one generation of members to another. In the extreme case, many volunteer-type organizations (e.g., charitable, political, religious, social, and athletic groups) must recruit and train a new generation of members, lest there be no one to carry on their cause. Leaders of such volunteer organizations are always vigilant to find and develop new members as they know they are only one generation away from extinction. On a less dramatic note, organizations of all types seek to instill their values in newcomers so that the newcomers will be loyal to the cause and be able to pass on its norms and values to others. Companies find the training and socialization of newcomers to be a good investment of their resources.

Second, **socialization messages assist in individual cognitive and sex-role development.** The learning of language allows us to develop cognitive representation of ourselves and others and facilitates individuals' control over their environment (Baldwin, 1969; Clausen, 1968; Kohlberg, 1969). Socialization influences cognitive development by providing a particular view of individuals and events. Symbols (e.g., words) are a chief means of conveying cultural elements. In turn, language helps classify socially significant objects and events. Whether it is the representation of furniture (e.g., chairs, tables) or positions in society (e.g., mayor, principal, teacher), the acceptance of language provides children with a classification system and an understanding of its function in society (Elkin & Handel, 1984). For example, children learn to recognize adults' use of authoritative language and learn that they, as children, are expected (in most cases) to obey commands from their parents and other adults who are caring for them.

Likewise, sex-role development evolves under the influence of others. From the moment a child is received into a family and is wrapped in a pink or blue blanket, socialization to a sex role begins (Bem & Bem, 1976). Sex-role socialization attempts to conform the self (as a male or female and the convictions about what membership in a group implies) to society's expectations (Elkin & Handel, 1984). Expectations regarding how boys or girls should act begin in the home and continue through public communication in school, friendship groups, and the mass media (Eshleman & Cashion, 1983). For instance, researchers report that at one time mothers of six-month old infants expected female babies to be relatively quiet, clean, and restrained whereas male babies were expected to be more noisy and adventurous (Goldberg & Lewis, 1972). Throughout our lives, we receive messages regarding appropriateness of play, expression of feelings, competitiveness, and rule-following from our parents and other authority figures, our peers, and the media (Jablin, 1987).

Third, **socialization messages are a means of conveying behavioral norms and roles.** Norms and roles enable us to live ordered lives together. Social interactions go more smoothly when we know the rules that constitute our culture and can predict what others will do (Bilton, Bonnett, Jones, Sheard, Stanworth, & Webster, 1987). Norms are expectations for behavior learned in interaction with others and passed down from generation to generation (Eshleman & Cashion, 1983). In essence, norms are general expectations to which all individuals within a culture or organization adhere. There are norms regarding how to greet strangers, starting meetings at the designated time, returning phone calls, and appropriate manners when eating at a restaurant.

Social roles embody expectations for how one ought to behave in a given social position (Bilton et al., 1987). Within the framework of a role of, say, a soccer coach, individuals enact their expectations of what they think a soccer coach should say and do. There are three categories of social role expectations: **pivotal, relevant,** and **peripheral** (Schein, 1968). **Pivotal** role behaviors are critical to the successful enactment of the role. For instance, if players and parents perceive that establishing a lineup and good passing are the most important aspects of coaching, they will be quite upset if the coach does not set players in positions and improve their passing skills. **Relevant** role behaviors are important to role success, but individuals can act on certain expectations and not others and still be successful overall. Parents may also want the soccer coach to (a) scout the opposing team, (b) be up-to-date on the latest offensive schemes, and (c) attend meetings with other coaches, but the parents will probably be happy if the coach does one of these tasks and ecstatic if the coach does two of three. **Peripheral** role behaviors are equivalent to "window-dressing," and their enactment (e.g., hosting an after-the-season party) has little bearing on role success. Our expectations of new employees', family members', and even college roommates' social roles can also be divided into these three categories.

The violation of pivotal and relevant expectations disrupt our lives. We schedule our coming and going around the expectations that particular norms and roles will be followed. However, the truth is that we are often not very skillful at picking up on others' role expectations or at stating our own expectations. The bottom line is that we are responsible for communicating our expectations to others, whether the expectations concern what a soccer coach should accomplish and how these accomplishments will be reached, responsibilities for covering and presenting materials in a study group, the cleanliness of your dorm room or apartment, or the use of your time during your first week on a job.

Consider your expectations of your roommate and how you communicate those expectations. Most individuals are easily able to construct a list of expectations. "Clean the shower or bathtub when you are finished, we will each buy and be responsible for our own food, be respectful of my things and I'll be respectful of yours. . . ." Yet, we often fail to convey those expectations in such a way that they are clear. (You might try making a list of ten expectations that you have communicated to your roommate and then see how many your roommate can name without any prompting. We are not suggesting that you act miserly by classifying all of your expectations. We just know from experience that you ought to let your roommate(s) know your pivotal expectations and the rationale for their importance.)

Fourth, messages during socialization are a means to develop commitment to group and ideology (values) of the group. One powerful element of socialization is the differentiating of one's group from other groups, which can develop a strong social identity and solidarity among members (Levine & Moreland, 1991). Contributing to a culture of unique, shared thought are a knowledge of the group's history, routines, accounts for itself and its performance, special language or "jargon," and rituals (Levine & Moreland, 1991). Shared socialization experiences shape members' worldview and attitudes, enable friendships to blossom, and facilitate social support by members who know what you are going through. Referring back to our earlier examples, the Navy Seal trainees sought the experience to become different and indeed discovered that they were different from their contemporaries. However, these individuals relied on their buddies who were supportive of their goals and believed in their potential.

During entry into a new organization, incumbents often stress the advantages of membership by showing how affiliation with the group and its societal views will improve newcomers' personal and economic situation. Law schools present and reinforce an ideology of individualism, hierarchical social relations, and attitudes consistent with the needs of a capitalist system (Granfield, 1986) through lectures, the testing system, and inculcating a professional vocabulary (Stelling & Bucher, 1973).

Established union members often take new employees aside and enlist their allegiance, telling them how membership will benefit them—in effect starting their own socialization process before management can begin the official organizational socializing process (Fullager, McCoy, & Shull, 1992). Universities and affiliated groups such as fraternities, sororities, and professional organizations also seek to establish group identity through messages that reinforce the group's uniqueness and the relative advantages of group membership.

Communication's role in developing commitment to a group or organization and its ideology or belief system is critical to groups and organizations. Organizations that rely on highly committed members to remain productive devote their resources to interpreting organizational events through language, establishing rituals for membership, and conducting ceremonies (Harrison & Carroll, 1991). Soeters (1986) argues that social movements (such as Right-to-Life or Pro-Choice) and organizations with "strong" cultures (i.e., explicit social norms and rewards for compliance) have many similarities. Both transfer values, require interaction between members, and have intense indoctrination and reinforcement programs.

Fifth, **messages are a means of altering behavior and resocializing a person**. Resocialization attempts to correct deficiencies in earlier socialization (Wheeler, 1966) or to control deviant behavior (Brim, 1966). Prisons and mental wards are examples of attempts to bring members' unacceptable behaviors back in line with society's expectations. Resocialization may also take place in more "ordinary" settings. Groups are known to pressure (and at times ostracize) members to behave appropriately by identifying their shortcomings, sanctioning their misdeeds, and on occasion cutting off their interactions with other group members (Moreland & Levine, 1989). Organizations often resocialize new members who have worked for other organizations or even for different departments within the same organization since role expectations and norms differ among departments and organizations (Feldman, 1976).

HOW SOCIALIZATION WORKS

Whether you are responsible for socializing others, for instance, as a leader of a student organization or a manager of a local restaurant, or making sense of recent socialization experiences, you might be interested in how various elements of the socialization work. This section examines the agents of socialization, content of socialization messages, and processes by which individuals are socialized.

Agents of Socialization

In terms of your selection of a career and general orientation toward work, your family is probably the most important socialization influence (Jablin, 1987). Your family significantly (a) affects how you view yourself, others, and the world through social comparisons, labeling, and reinforcement, (b) provides role models for relationships, dealing with society, and work, and (c) emphasizes important personal attributes that are later instrumental in your career success, such as decisiveness or concern for nurturing intellectual growth. It is usually in the home that you receive instruction and reinforcement regarding tasks such as making up your bed or taking the dog for a walk. Your family purposefully seeks to socialize you into their norms and values, and, in a larger context, society expects your family to teach you manners and how to "behave." Your family shapes the types of jobs that you seek and the levels of achievement to which you aspire.

Educational institutions in turn have an explicit mandate to socialize students into society. In elementary school, the classroom setting teaches students to follow rules, anticipate instructions, and respect hierarchical figures. (And you wondered why you were always practicing standing in a straight line!) Classroom experiences also provide informal training regarding what to do when group projects are in danger of failing, what to say to classmates who do not complete their share of the work, and how to figure out which behaviors and/or outcomes will be rewarded by those in authority. School settings also assist in vocational socialization by teaching skills that will qualify you to get a position and the norms and values elemental to success in a particular field. In this respect, school serves as a transition from the influence of family to the job.

Peers are a concomitant socialization influence such that you likely influence your friends at the same time and about as much as they influence you. Throughout our lives, we compare our values and activities to others. Peers' disclosure of their activities and the goals to which they aspire function as normative information to direct us to the norms to which we might adhere. These social comparisons enable us to validate our past behaviors and future aspirations. Peers also serve as a sounding board for our ideas and as a source of social support as we seek to test our conception of our "self" against potential jobs and careers.

The mass media (e.g., television shows, movies) also conveys information about normative behaviors in society. In general, images of work norms in television shows and movies are generally stereotypic and sex-role stereotyped. For instance, Jablin (1987) reports that television portrays successful employees as aggressive communicators who spend the majority of their time giving orders or advice, performing in boardroom debates, and conniving. Nonetheless, television programs such as and "ER" may influence the career aspirations of young viewers and create a new generation of doctors who believe that they ought to act in ways similar to the major characters in these shows.

Finally, part-time jobs, summer jobs, and internships provide introductory experiences into the workplace. Lower level part-time jobs provide low wages and generally exclude part-time employees from full-time employees' social system (Jablin, 1987). Yet, part-time jobs (a) provide high school and college students with direction for or confirmation of their career aspirations, (b) shape individuals' views of how employees ought to act at work, (c) serve as a breaking-in period with regards to working for pay, and (d) provide further opportunities for individuals to test the fit between their self-concept and a potential vocation.

In sum, there are many events and persons who have influenced your decisions to attend college, the selection of a degree program, the kind of roommate you try to be, how you seek to act in social situations, and possible jobs that you may pursue. We only name five prominent influences. However, it is important to understand who is influencing your worldview, career aspirations, and notions of the ideal family life (to name a few) so that you can evaluate the appropriateness and satisfaction with the received influence.

Content of Socialization Messages

Socialization messages often center on how individuals ought to act and why. For instance, newcomers often receive messages regarding an industry's or organization's history in an effort to impart a knowledge of the history and traditions, specialized language (i.e., slang and jargon), and politics—a knowledge of the influential members and understanding of the how things "really work"—of the organization (Chao, O'Leary-Kelly, Wolf, Klein, H.J., & Gardner, 1994). They also receive messages regarding their acceptance into the work group, the organizational goals and values, and proficient performance or how to master tasks and perform efficiently (Chao et al., 1994). However, Brim (1966) points out that long-term socialization influence is possible only when newcomers' behaviors and values are the target of change. Behaviors refer to what individuals are supposed to do, and values refer to the reasons why they are supposed to enact these behaviors. In addition, Brim suggests that it is important to consider the needs of newcomers. Specifically, newcomers have knowledge (What is the person supposed to do?), ability (Can the person do it; does the person know how to do it?), and motivational needs (Does the person desire to do it?).

To appreciate the challenge of creating appropriate socialization messages, consider the following outcome goals and corresponding training messages that a supervisor would convey to a recent college graduate entering a position in computer software sales:

1. **Knowledge and Behavior** or "What does s/he need to know?"—Instruct the new employee on the various applications of computer hardware and software and their different capabilities.

2. **Knowledge and Values** or "Why should s/he know it?"—Explain why the knowledge of computer programs is important in order to understand and maximize their use.

3. **Ability and Behavior** or "What skills must s/he master in order to perform the required tasks?"—Instruct new employees in software use and provide practice in using different software systems.

4. **Ability and Values** or "Why must s/he want to perform the tasks correctly?"—Emphasize the importance of using software correctly and designing programs to certain specifications.

5. **Motivation and Behavior** or "What will motivate her/him to perform properly?"—Explain the rewards for new employees using appropriate computer programming skills.

6. **Motivation and Values** or "What beliefs can serve as a basis for continued, enhanced performance?"—Identify rewards from the organization and society linked to the development and use of appropriate computer programming skills.

In short, supervisors face numerous challenges in discerning which socialization outcomes to seek and how to construct messages to accomplish the desired behavioral and value changes. The next section considers some of the processes by which newcomers are socialized in the workplace.

Process of Organizational Socialization

Stage models. Socialization is often described as taking place over a number of stages. Anytime that you join a group or an organization there are periods where you have comparatively little knowledge of its customs, informal status relationships, and specialized way of doing things, and incumbents often lend a helping hand or are accepting of mistakes that you might make out of ignorance. The "oldtimers" might also design "tests" to see how you react under pressure or to see if you will fit in socially. After you've been accepted into the task and social circles, you are likely to face a new set of challenges. Full membership into the group or organization might take between several weeks to several months, and in some cases several years. Of course, the ideal outcome of any socialization process is a productive organizational member who understands the job, the values of the organization, and the relationship of the job to other employees' jobs (Louis, 1980).

Numerous stage models of organizational socialization exist (e.g. Buchanan, 1974; Porter, Lawler, & Hackman, 1975; see Wanous, 1980, for a synthesis of several stage models), but one of the most popular is Feldman's (1976) anticipatory socialization, accommodation, and role management model.

In the first stage, **anticipatory socialization** (sometimes known as "getting in"), both the organization and the employee develop expectations about the other. During the interview or selection process, candidates develop ideas about the benefits of group/organization membership, the nature of their role, and their relationship to others. Organizational members also develop expectations about candidates' contributions and the ease or difficulty of working with the person. Expectations develop in the anticipatory socialization stage which shape the behaviors of newcomers and "oldtimers" toward each other. For instance, the expectations of our friend who became a Navy Seal were based on reputation and hearsay from his basic training experience and from family friends. In turn, the "old salty frogmen" knew nothing of our friend, except that they had seen thousands of would-be Seals and remembered their own Seal training. In other cases, recruits have many opportunities to ask questions of organizational representatives, read published materials, and talk to active members. Greater familiarity by both parties is anticipated to result in a smoother transition for recruits from "outsider" to "insider."

The second stage, **accommodation** (or "breaking in"), focuses on the importance of interpersonal relationships in the work group. New hires are confronted with the expectations of others. They also discover the extent to which their expectations match the reality of membership and the workplace (Louis, 1980; Wanous, 1980). At this point, new hires begin learning the nuances of their organization role while established members begin to cope with the expectations of new hires. For most individuals, their first week of college classes has some elements of shock, no matter how much preparation you have for dorm living and large lecture classes. Similarly, while you may spend several years in educational settings preparing for a vocation, your first month or two at work still requires considerable adjustment and assistance from others.

In Feldman's third stage, **role management** (or "settling in"), employees resolve two types of conflict: conflict between work in the new organization and life interests outside of work (e.g., commuting, childcare arrangements); and conflicts in the workplace itself (e.g., getting along with coworkers or the supervisor). For all practical purposes the honeymoon period has long been over, and the problems associated with the (sometimes) harsh realities of the supervisor's personality, work conditions, and time demands must be resolved or managed.

Contextual strategies. Contextual strategies refer to those experiences with which organizations purposively greet new members. Organizations' orchestration of experiences for new members range from scheduling every minute during the day and night (as in a military boot camp or pledging some fraternities or sororities) to only a brief introduction to other members (as in service and social clubs).

Van Maanen and Schein (1979) suggest that organizations use up to six sets of strategies to integrate new members (see Table 6.1). The use of each strategy is on a continuum (little use to extensive use). Consider **investiture-divestiture strategies**. Investiture occurs when organizations positively reinforce new members' existing skills, values, and attitudes. Essentially, organizations using investiture tactics tell new members, "We are glad that you are here. We believe that you can begin contributing to our organization immediately and without considerable revamping of your outlook or skills." Divestiture occurs when organizations seek to erase recruits' self-identities and recreate the identity in the organization's image. With divestiture, incumbents tell new members, "You are not yet ready to become a member of our organization. You must radically change if you are to contribute to our organization." While divestiture may be cruel in some instances, it is necessary in others. For instance, how else do you transform individualistic recruits into a tightly-knit group that will act cohesively under pressure or extreme threats? Many organizations, from the military to accounting firms rely on divestiture experiences to create comradely interdependence and feelings within their units.

Formal-informal strategies refer to the extent to which newcomers are segregated (physically or symbolically) from members and undergo a set of experiences designed specifically for them. So, new hires experiencing formal socialization are likely to undergo training and learn a fixed set of materials (that all other recruits have learned), and they may not be allowed to integrate with incumbent members until they've completed their training or passed certain tests. In contrast, those experiencing informal strategies are less likely to receive training, are more likely to learn how the organization works, and learn about job-related materials on their own (i.e., the "sink or swim" approach!). **Collective-individual** strategies address the extent to which newcomers undergo common learning experiences as a group. New hires undergoing collective socialization often eat together, go through training together, learn to help each other, and form close bonds.

With **serial-disjunctive** strategies, the question is whether newcomers have experienced coworkers or predecessors to serve as role models. Van Maanen and Schein (1979) believe that newcomers will solve problems in a more innovative manner when they cannot rely on others for answers or copy what another is doing (i.e., disjunctive). However, learning the job is often much easier when you can ask for assistance or model your behavior after someone who is successful (Miller & Jablin, 1991). **Fixed-variable** strategies concern the extent to which a definite timetable is attached to the socialization process. Fixed strategies provide a timetable and cause less anxiety among new hires. Yet, variable strategies at times create more openness among newcomers for learning new skills/values as they are unsure when their training or indoctrination period will be completed. **Sequential-random** refers to the extent to which each stage follows another in a predictable, consecutive order sequence and is made known to newcomers.

TABLE 6.1 Summary of Organizational Socialization Tactics*

Collective versus Individual

Collective socialization occurs when newcomers undergo common learning experiences as a group.

Individual socialization provides newcomers with unique, individualistic sets of learning experiences.

Formal versus Informal

Formal socialization refers to the segregation of newcomers from regular members while newcomers undergo a set of experiences designed explicitly for them.

With informal socialization, newcomers are not rigidly differentiated from incumbents and learn primarily through trial and error.

Sequential versus Random

Sequential socialization refers to a sequence of discrete and identifiable steps leading to role competence which are made known to newcomers.

Random socialization occurs when the steps leading to role competence are unknown, ambiguous, or continually changing.

Fixed versus Variable

Fixed socialization occurs when there is a definite timetable attached to steps within the socialization process.

In variable socialization processes, newcomers have few clues to how long a certain indoctrination will take.

Serial versus Disjunctive

In serial socialization, experienced members service as role models for newcomers who are about to assume similar kinds of positions.

Disjunctive socialization occurs when newcomers have neither role models nor recent predecessors to guide their role learning.

Investiture versus Divestiture

Investiture socialization involves the positive reinforcement of recruits' skills, values, and attitudes.

Through negative reinforcement, divestiture socialization processes attempt to strip away personal characteristics from a recruit.

*Adapted from Van Maanen & Schein (1979).

Not all organizations place a high priority on or are as explicit in their desire to shape members' values and behaviors (Pascale, 1985). Organizations may decide that they do not have the resources to shape new members' values and attitudes. Yet, other organizations may decide that they cannot afford to neglect learning opportunities and attitudes that are instilled into new members during this period. Consider the difference between private and public universities. Private universities often have distinct sets of values that are central to the universities' missions (Arnett, 1992; Ashby, 1983). Since the continuation of their identity depends, to a large extent, on the outcomes it produces (students who graduate and carry the university's name), many private universities structure students' socialization experiences to instill its values. In some cases, even professors are socialized (Arnett, 1992) as they play an important role in producing the "outcomes" (that is, graduates of the university). In contrast, public universities subscribe to general values that most of society holds, have less overt concern about instilling particular attitudes and values in their students, and rely on society to instill and reinforce values in their students.

Regardless of the deliberateness or casualness of the socialization experience, or where the experience takes place, socialization will produce outcomes for the individual and the group or social system of which that individual is a member. The next section considers various outcomes of socialization.

Outcomes of Socialization

What are some of the outcomes of socialization? We will consider how socialization affects personal values and identity, individuals' responses to socialization efforts by groups and organizations, and how individual socialization contributes to the development of culture.

Personal development. As mentioned at the beginning of this chapter, some researchers believe socialization messages and experiences create a unique self or individual. Others argue that socialization only serves to fit the individual into society. This "individual versus society" argument is quite extensive and is the subject of considerable debate. We take a broad view of socialization. Namely, socialization shapes the individual and enables the individual to fit into society.

Learned values and identities are integral to individuals' growth and development. Values are organized mental structures composed of cognitive, evaluative, and prescriptive components (Inkeles, 1969). They tell us how to judge something to be good or bad, as well as what we should do about it (Kluckhohn & Strodtbeck, 1961). In other words, values are the criteria by which we judge the world, and they tell us what ought to be (Ball-Rokeach & Rokeach, 1987). Values are one of the set of characteristics that your family, organization, or even society considers elemental for membership. Our families, friends, social groups, and places of employment socialize us to have a particular set of values (Gecas, 1981; McCandless, 1969). For example, your family may have stressed to you the importance of considering others' feelings when you speak. Those values—politeness and consideration - become a guide for your behavior.

In addition to values, we learn our identities—who we are in society, what roles we are to play (Elkin & Handel, 1984)—through socialization processes. Symbolic interaction theorists (Mead, 1934; Cooley, 1902) and psychologists (Cottrell, 1969; Higgins, Bond, Klein, & Strauman, 1986) suggest that we develop a sense of self in part from how we think others see us. Are you a smart, attractive, shy person who is good at math? A leader? People will tell you! Friends, parents, and teachers construct an identity which we can appropriate as a framework for who we are in relation to others. These messages also inform us if we are acting in an acceptable manner to our families, friendship groups, and the society of which we are a part.

Group development. Groups socialize their members to a particular way of thinking and behaving. Newcomers to groups must learn the appropriate norms and their particular role in order for the group to function effectively (Moreland & Levine, 1989; Bormann, 1986). As in personal development, groups seek to impart their values. Thus, if you belong to a group that values taking certain kinds of risks (e.g., consuming large quantities of liquor, evangelizing classmates), group members will expect you to engage in these behaviors. If you refrain, you may fall out of favor and/or be excluded from group membership. It is important to recognize the values of the groups to which you aspire membership (whether they be social circles or formal business organizations) in order (a) to decide if you desire to conform to the values (and remain a member) and (b) to "fit in" and succeed quickly by exhibiting behaviors reflective of the group's core values (Miller & Jablin, 1991).

Naturally, we are not always accepting of others' socialization efforts. In organizational settings, individuals generally respond to socialization efforts in one of three ways. A **custodial** response occurs when individuals accept the pivotal, relevant, and peripheral expectations for the role without modification (Schein, 1968). A new employee with a custodial response follows all the rules and guidelines presented in training and by the supervisor. **Innovative** responses are those in which individuals adhere to the pivotal expectations, accept some of the relevant expectations, and reject most of the peripheral expectations. In this case, a new hire completes the critical tasks as taught, but innovates on less important tasks, and tries to get out of peripheral tasks. Groups innovate and successfully adapt to their surroundings when most newcomers adhere to the basic values and norms of the group, but escape the trap of rituals and routines of peripheral norms. Newcomers who reject pivotal, relevant, and peripheral role expectations are demonstrating a **rebellion** response. Breaking away from the guidelines for the role and failing to accomplish the purpose of the role, these individuals disagree with all of the organization's goals. Although it is good to have a few newcomers who respond in a custodial manner for stability, as well as a few who respond rebelliously (on occasion) to shake up a few norms, organizations usually prefer compliant newcomers over difficult ones.

Cultural development. It is also through the process of socialization that a culture (whether national, ethnic, or organizational) perpetuates itself (Levine, 1969). Culture consists of explicit and implicit "patterns of . . . behavior acquired and transmitted by symbols, constituting the distinctive achievement of human groups, including their embodiments in artifacts . . . (Kroeber & Kluckhohn, 1951, p. 181; cited in Williams, 1972, p. 1). A culture maintains its relevance when current members teach new members its values, norms, and symbols. As noted by Montagu (1968), the human capacity to use symbols enables culture to be created.

A principle means of transmitting symbols and establishing culture is communication among family members. Families socialize their members to be productive societal members (Turner, 1978; Williams, 1972). Families also emphasize (and at times enforce) ethnic identity (e.g. Knight, Bernal, Garza, Cota, & Ocampo, 1993), political orientation (Tims, 1986), and consumer patterns (Wackman, Wartella, & Ward, 1977). Thus, the stories that your grandparents, aunts and uncles, and parents tell and retell about their experiences (or those of their ancestors) provide frameworks for anticipating acceptable behaviors and values and aligning or differentiating yourself from others.

On a societal level, the segmentation of cultures results from geographical, economic, or social barriers that prevent the cross-fertilization of ideas and debates on values. Although they share general values with the larger culture, each subculture within a larger society has its own distinct patterns, values, and norms. We are socialized into distinct subcultures, not into culture as a whole (Elkin & Handel, 1984). For example, if you grew up in a farming community, you experienced a subculture distinct from the subculture of urban Chicago. Similarly, the subculture of one neighborhood in Chicago may differ from other neighborhoods to the observant eye just as the subculture of your university major probably differs from the subcultures of your roommates' majors.

SOCIALIZATION GUIDELINES

From time to time, you will be responsible for the socialization of new group or organizational members. If you are like the authors of this chapter, you will not have sought out most of these responsibilities, and many of these will not be welcomed given your other time demands. Nonetheless, socialization of new members can be critical to your group's or organization's success. So, when these intrusive demands hit you, here are six guidelines to facilitate your efforts and keep you on the right track.

First, **identify the expectations developed during the anticipatory socialization stage that your newcomers are bringing with them.** It is critical to recognize that your prospective or new members already have expectations about what it will be like to be a member of your group. These expectations may be inaccurate, and the lack of fulfillment of these expectations may cause much frustration and spur an early exit from your group. In contrast, accurate expectations may speed up their transition from outsiders to full, functioning members. In either case, it is well worth your time to discover what their expectations are in terms of (a) what it takes to become a member of your group, (b) what are the positive (and negative if any) aspects of group membership, and (c) what life will be like as a group member. You may be able to correct some of their erroneous expectations. You may be able to identify the sources of incorrect information and work to avert similar problems in the future.

Second, **identify the behaviors and values that you want the newcomers to learn.** As noted earlier, effective socialization involves far more that just telling individuals what you expect of them. It is vital to know what behaviors and values you want new members to acquire (Brim, 1966). Thus, you need to determine what you want the newcomers to learn. They will probably catch on to many other important aspects of group membership, but at least you will be able to judge your success in passing on those skills, norms, and values which you have determined to be critical to group membership. (By the way, our experience has been that unplanned socialization in groups and organizations results in a variety of membership surprises which is okay for social clubs and other groups where there is little at stake. So, if it is important to develop a membership highly socialized to certain values and rituals, you'd better spend some time planning what newcomers need to learn and the most effective ways to enhance their learning.)

It is also vital that leaders recognize that they will not be able to judge the success of their socialization efforts until the **third** generation. For example, imagine you are evaluating four year's worth of socialization efforts by a student organization on campus. In particular, you are considering the transference of information from James to Pat to Cynthia and to Sam. James is a founding member of the organization and is responsible for socializing Pat (among others) who joined the following year. In the following years, Pat is responsible for socializing Cynthia who in turn is responsible for socializing Sam. So, James is passing on key concepts and skills to Pat, but James will really not know his success in socializing Pat until Pat has finished working with Cynthia. Only when Cynthia is transferring the key concepts and skills (originating from James) to Sam will James understand the success or failure of his socialization efforts. If Cynthia is teaching Sam the proper materials, then James can consider his socialization efforts to be successful. Too often, we count socialization success in terms of how much effort we expended and not in the lasting results from those efforts.

Third, **determine the best method to achieve the desired socialization outcomes.** With the Navy Seal, New Job, and Communist Cell stories, those in charge of the training had a prepared set of materials that they wanted to teach. In the Navy Seal and Communist Cell cases, socialization agents decided that the newcomers would best learn the material and reinforce each other's learning if they were taught as a group and had many experiences in common. Using Van Maanen and Schein's (1979) classification, these outcomes could best be achieved by using **formal** socialization processes (where planned experiences and a set body of knowledge were prepared). In addition, those in the Navy Seals experience **collective** (i.e., the recruits felt that they were all in the same boat and underwent the same experiences at the same time) and **divestiture** (where the events are purposefully designed to enhance the reframing of their self-images and orientations and rebuild their values and pattern of behaviors) socialization experiences.

However, this menagerie of tactics may not be appropriate for *your* new members or socialization goals. If you desire your new members to develop unique ideas and ways of solving problems, then you should consider using individual (where newcomers are socialized in isolation from other newcomers) and disjunctive (where newcomers do not have contact with others doing the same task or with the member who previously did the task) socialization processes. In other words, if you go through the effort of planning your socialization outcomes, it also makes sense to determine the socialization processes which will enable you to achieve those outcomes.

Fourth, **use socialization agents who are likely to have the most influence on newcomers and can work within your chosen array of socialization strategies.** While this guideline seems obvious enough, some individuals are better communicators in one-on-one contexts. Other group members will be nervous about socializing newcomers one-on-one and will prefer the detachment of speaking to a group of new members where questions will be fewer and less personalized. Further, some agents are better at tearing down and reshaping newcomer identities (e.g., drill sergeant) while others are better in supportive roles (e.g., guidance counselors). Many organizations have been effective in their efforts only when they've carefully selected and then resocialized the agents who will be socializing new members. As we pointed out earlier, there is often a relationship between the criticalness of socialization outcomes to organizational success and/or survival and the effort and resources expended on socializing new members.

Fifth, **keep in mind that many groups and organizations are only one generation from extinction.** Most religious groups, social organizations, and cultures must rely on the continuous recruitment of members and the passing on of values and norms for their survival. The groups and organizations into which you are now being socialized (i.e., university major, social or service organization, synagogue) would either cease to exist or experience a radical change in mission if the pivotal and relevant norms and values were not passed on. Thus, you are performing a vital service in evaluating your group's or organization's socialization efforts and in possibly restructuring its efforts.

Sixth, **strive for balance.** You must always manage the tension between incumbent members who desire fanatical alterations within newcomers and those who resist any change in newcomer attitudes. It is helpful to solicit advice from individuals representing these extreme positions, but recognize that lasting change in norms and values within groups occurs incrementally through the introduction of new members who embody the desired innovative changes (Schneider, 1987). At the same time, be aware of attempts to mimic "total institutions" where every moment of a new member's day is scheduled, contacts outside of the group are rigidly restricted, and sanctions for non-compliance are extreme. We accept that governmental military units must socialize recruits in this manner. However, mainstream organizations veer into cult-like problems when their new members are controlled in this fashion.

SPECIAL APPLICATIONS

A few final thoughts are in order with regard to some less desirable applications of socialization in our society: gangs and hazing. Gang membership continues to pose a serious problem for communities around the nation (Hagedorn & Macon, 1988). While many gangs are linked with crime and the disintegration of neighborhoods, gangs provide their members with a form of social support. Gangs provide members with an identity, a buffer from the rejection of family members or society, and rewards. Considerable research and work with gang members indicate that attempts to replace a gang member lifestyle must be accompanied by a substitute for gang member social support (Ellis, 1991, 1992; Howell, 1994). For example, resocialization efforts through boot camps may have success when they focus on changing the individual's identity, instill new norms and values, and provide camaraderie with others desiring similar changes.

Finally, hazing is a ritual marking the passage from outsider to insider in some organizations. Hazing includes physical abuse through initiations such as sleep deprivation, forced alcohol consumption, or physical punishment. Those inflicting the abuse believe that recruits who are willing to put up with the anticipation of the abuse and the abuse itself so desire membership that they will be loyal members. Hazing as a rite of passage has a long history in some organizations (e.g., Baier & Williams, 1983). However, willingness to suffer abuse does not guarantee loyalty (Hautaluoma, Enge, Mitchell, & Rittwager, 1991). In fact, it often triggers hostility toward the abusers and cruelty in the vengeance taken upon other recruits when the abused have their chance to haze. Universities are adamantly opposed to hazing and attempt to deal with reported cases of hazing as a college student dies needlessly every year as a result of such practices. Given the history and the potential for injury to new members, you should seek alternative ways to build member commitment if you are a member of an organization that hazes its members.

CONCLUSIONS

Communication is an integral part of the socialization process. Communication messages assist in creating new identities, signify acceptable behaviors, and reinforce group norms. Socialization messages are at times deliberately communicated as illustrated by the indoctrination of Jim and the training of new employees in the New Job story. Deliberate socialization messages are also conveyed by grandparents telling a family story, by professors and administrators in presentations at new students' orientation at universities, and by school teachers teaching rules and guidelines in the elementary classroom. At other times, we learn the expectations of a society or an organization by observing others, watching television, and participating in structured games at school.

Socialization is fundamental to any society. We've tried to identify some of its prominent processes and suggest guidelines for using socialization in your home, school, and work place. We hope the information will serve as a basis for understanding some of your experiences. We encourage you to think through your socialization goals for others and be conscientious in your socialization efforts.

REFERENCES

Arnett, R. C. (1992). *Dialogic education.* Carbondale, IL: Southern Illinois University Press.

Ashby, R. (1983). The public image of a small college. In Falender, A. J., & J. C. Merson (Eds.), *Management techniques for small and specialized institutions* (pp. 41–47). San Francisco: Jossey-Bass.

Baier, J. L., & Williams, P. S. (1983). Fraternity hazing revisited: Current alumni and active member attitudes toward hazing. *Journal of College Student Personnel, 24,* 300–305.

Baldwin, A. (1969). A cognitive theory of socialization. In D.A. Goslin (Ed.), *Handbook of socialization theory and research* (pp. 325–346). Chicago: Rand McNally.

Ball-Rokeach, S. & Rokeach, M. (1987). *The Great American Values Test.* New York: The Free Press.

Bem, S., & Bem, D. (1976). Training the woman to know her place: The power of a nonconscious ideology. In S. Cox (Ed.), *Female psychology: The emerging self* (pp. 180–191). Chicago: SRA.

Bilton, T., Bonnett, K., Jones, P., Sheard, K., Stanworth, M., & Webster, A. (1987). *Introductory sociology* (2nd ed.). London: MacMillan Press LTD.

Bormann, E. G. (1986). Symbolic convergence theory and communication in group decision-making. In R. Hirokawa & M.S. Poole (Eds.), *Communication and group decision-making* (pp. 219–236). Beverly Hills: Sage.

Brim, O. G., Jr. (1966). Socialization through the life cycle. In O. G. Brim, Jr., & S. Wheeler (Eds.), *Socialization after childhood: Two essays* (pp. 1–49). New York: Wiley.

Buchanan, B. (1974). Building organizational commitment: The socialization of managers in work organizations. *Administrative Science Quarterly, 19,* 533–546.

Bush, D. M., & Simmons, R. C. (1981). Socialization processes over the life course. In Rosenberg, M., & Turner, R. H. (Eds.), *Social psychology: Sociological perspectives* (pp. 133–164).

Chao, G.T., O'Leary-Kelly, A.M., Wolf, S., Klein, H.J., & Gardner, P.D. (1994). Organizational socialization: Its content and consequences. *Journal of Applied Psychology, 79,* 730–743.

Clausen, J. H. (1968). A historical and comparative view of socialization theory and research. In J. A. Clausen (Ed.), *Socialization and society* (pp. 18–72). Boston: Little, Brown & Co.

Cooley, C. H. (1902/1964). *Human nature and the social order.* New York: Schocken Books.

Cottrell, L. S. (1969). Interpersonal interaction and the development of the self. In D.A. Goslin (Ed.), *Handbook of socialization theory and research* (pp. 543–570). Chicago: Rand McNally.

Elkin, F., & Handel, G. (1984). *The child and society* (4th ed.). New York: Random House.

Ellis, A. L. (1991/1992). Urban Youth Economic Enterprise Zones: An Intervention Strategy for Reversing the Gang Crisis in American Cities. *Urban League Review, 15*(2), 29–40.

Eshleman, J. R., & Cashion, B. G. (1983). *Sociology: An introduction.* Boston: Little, Brown & Co.

Feldman, D. C. (1976). A contingency theory of socialization. *Administrative Science Quarterly, 21,* 433–452.

Fullagar, C., McCoy, D., & Shull, C. (1992). The socialization of union loyalty. *Journal of Organizational Behavior, 13,* 13–26.

Gecas, V. (1981). Contexts of socialization. In M. Rosenberg & R.H. Turner (Eds.), *Social psychology: Sociological perspectives* (pp. 165–199). New York: Basic Books.

Goldberg, S., & Lewis. M. (1972). Play behavior in the year-old infant: Early sex differences. In J. Bardwick (Ed.), *Readings on the Psychology of Women* (pp. 30–34). New York: Harper & Row.

Granfield, R. (1986). Legal education as corporate ideology: Student adjustment to the law school experience. *Sociological Forum, 1,* 514–523.

Hagedorn, J. M., & Macon, P. (1988). *People and folks: Gangs, crime, and the underclass in a rustbelt city.* Chicago: Lake View Press.

Harrison, J. R., & Carroll, G. R. (1991). Keeping the faith: A model of cultural transmission in formal organizations. *Administrative Science Quarterly, 36,* 552–582.

Hautaluoma, J.E., Enge, R.S., Mitchell, T.M., & Rittwager, F.J. (1991). Early socialization into a work group: Severity of initiations revisited. *Journal of Social Behavior and Personality, 6,* 725–748.

Higgins, E. T., Bond, R. H., Klein, R. H., & Strauman, T. (1986). Self-discrepancies and emotional vulnerability: How magnitude, accessibility, and type of discrepancy influence affect. *Journal of Personality and Social Psychology, 51,* 5–15.

Howell, J. C. (1994). Recent Gang Research: Program and Policy Implications. *Crime and Delinquency, 40,* 495–515.

Hyde, D. (1966). *Dedication and leadership: Learning from the Communists.* Notre Dame, IN: University of Notre Dame Press.

Inkeles, A. (1969). Social structure and socialization. In D.A. Goslin (Ed.), *Handbook of socialization theory and research* (pp. 615–632). Chicago: Rand McNally.

Jablin, F.M. (1987). Organizational assimilation. In F.M. Jablin, L.L. Putnam, K.H. Roberts, & L.M. Porter (Eds.), *Handbook of organizational communication* (pp. 679–740). Newbury Park, CA: Sage.

Kluckhohn, F. R., & Strodtbeck, F. L. (1961). *Variations in value orientations.* Evanston, IL: Row, Peterson.

Knight, G. P., Bernal, M. E., Garza, C. A., Cota, M. K., & Ocampo, K. A. (1993). Family socialization and the ethnic identity of Mexican-American children. *Journal of Cross-Cultural Psychology, 24,* 99–114.

Kohlberg, L. (1969). Stage and sequence: The cognitive-developmental approach to socialization. In D.A. Goslin (Ed.), *Handbook of socialization theory and research* (pp. 347–480). Chicago: Rand McNally.

Kroeber, A., & Kluckhohn, C. (1951). *Culture: A critical review of concepts and definitions.* Cambridge: Harvard University, Peabody Museum Papers, Vol. 47, No. 1.

Levine, J. M., & Moreland, R. L. (1990). Progress in small group research. *Annual Review of Psychology, 41,* 585–635.

Levine, J. M., & Moreland, R. L. (1991). Culture and socialization in work groups. In L. B. Resnick, J. M. Levine, & S. D. Teasley (Eds.), *Perspectives on socially shared cognition* (pp. 257–279). Washington: American Psychological Association.

Levine, R. A. (1969). Culture, personality, and socialization: An evolutionary view. In D.A. Goslin (Ed.), *Handbook of socialization theory and research* (pp. 503–541). Chicago: Rand McNally.

Louis, M.R. (1980). Surprise and sense-making: What newcomers experience in entering unfamiliar organizational settings. *Administrative Science Quarterly, 25,* 226–251.

McCandless, B. R. (1969). Childhood socialization. In D.A. Goslin (Ed.), *Handbook of socialization theory and research* (pp. 791–819). Chicago: Rand McNally.

Mead, G. H. (1934/1962). *Mind, self, and society.* Charles W. Morris (posthumous ed.), Chicago: University of Chicago Press.

Miller, V. D., & Jablin, F. M. (1991). Information seeking during organizational entry: Influences, tactics, and a model of the process. *Academy of Management Review, 16,* 92–120.

Montagu, A. (1968). Brains, genes, culture, immaturity, and gestation. In A. Montagu (Ed.), *Culture: Man's adaptive dimension.* New York: Oxford University Press.

Moreland, R. L., & Levine, J. M. (1989). Newcomers and oldtimers in small groups. In P.B. Paulus (Ed.), *Psychology of group influence* (2nd ed.) (pp. 143–186). Hillsdale, NJ: Lawrence Erlbaum.

Pascale, R. (1985). The paradox of corporate culture: Reconciling ourselves to socialization. *California Management Review, 27*(2), 26–40.

Porter, L. W., Lawler, E. E., & Hackman, J. R. (1975). *Behavior in organizations.* New York: McGraw-Hill.

Schein, E. H. (1968). Organizational socialization and the profession of management. *Industrial Management Review, 9,* 1–15.

Schneider, B. (1987). The people make the place. *Personnel Psychology, 40,* 437–453.

Soeters, J.L. (1986). Excellent companies as social movements. Journal of Management Studies, 23, 299–312.

Stelling, J. & Bucher, R. (1973). Vocabularies of realism in professional socialization. *Social Science and Medicine, 7,* 661–675.

Tims, A. R. (1986). Family political communication and social values. *Communication Research, 13,* 5–17.

Turner, J. H. (1978). *The structure of sociological theory.* Homewood, IL: Dorsey.

Van Maanen, J., & Schein, E. H. (1979). Toward a theory of organizational socialization. *Research in Organizational Behavior, 1,* 209–264.

Wackman, D. B., Wartella, E., & Ward, S. (1977). Learning to be consumers: The role of the family. *Journal of Communication, 27,* 183–151.

Wanous, J. P. (1980). *Organizational entry.* Reading, Massachusetts: Addison-Wesley.

Wheeler, S. (1966). The structure of formally organized socialization settings. In O. G. Brim, Jr., & S. Wheeler (Eds.), *Socialization after childhood: Two essays* (pp. 51–116). New York: Wiley.

Williams, T. R. (1972). *Introduction to socialization: Human culture transmitted.* St. Louis: The C.V. Mosby Company.

Chapter Six Case Study Quiz—Socialization

Instructions:

Please read the following case study carefully and select the best answers to the questions. This quiz is an individual assignment. Remember: sharing answers is a form of plagiarism.

Jamon has been very impressed with his new job. He has worked at the local movie theater for just three days, but already he feels comfortable in his position. On his first day, a seasoned employee gave him a tour of the theater, explained the different rules that employees must follow, as well as gave him hands-on training for his role as the projectionist (i.e., the person who starts the movies). Because of the one-on-one attention and explicit details he has received, he believes that the company really cares about their employees and values a team-based perspective. In comparison to his last job, Jamon actually looked forward to working at the movie theater. He was at his last job for just two short months. He was hired to work at a governmental office, but received no training about his job. There was no seasoned employee to welcome him, no discussion of company policies, and they even failed to show him where the bathroom and break room was! Because he was not taught how to do his job and because he was not aware of the office's policies, Jamon would get yelled at by a supervisor. He finally decided to leave the job and find one with a more positive environment.

Student's Name _____

Section Number _____

Section Leader's Name _____

Chapter Six Case Study Quiz—Socialization

1. With regard to decisions Jamon has made about his jobs, the most important socialization influence is:
   a. Media
   b. Friends
   c. Family
   d. Teachers and educational resources

2. While training for his new job at the movie theatre, Jamon was part of the buddy system in which a seasoned employee showed him the ropes. What type of contextual strategy was used to train Jamon?
   a. Informal
   b. Serial
   c. Disjunctive
   d. Variable

3. Jamon's experience being trained at the governmental office was completely different than the movie theatre. At the governmental office, his role and job expectations were not clearly stated, leaving Jamon confused about what he was supposed to do. What type of contextual strategy was used to train Jamon?
   a. Sequential
   b. Random
   c. Divestiture
   d. Formal

4. Socialization messages instruct employees how to act and why. Which of the following socialization messages was delivered to Jamon at his governmental job?
   a. Knowledge
   b. Ability
   c. Motivational
   d. None of the above

Case Study

5. When Jamon left his governmental job to look for a new job, he was immediately given an interview at the movie theatre. The interview process Jamon experienced exemplifies what stage of the socialization process?
    a. Accommodation socialization
    b. Role-management socialization
    c. Information Exchange socialization
    d. Anticipatory socialization

Chapter Seven

COMMUNICATION AND CONFLICT MANAGEMENT:

TRYING TO KEEP THINGS UNDER CONTROL

Michael E. Roloff
Northwestern University

My wife and I got married in September of 1974. I was in my last year of the doctoral program in Communication at Michigan State. Because I was a graduate student and my spouse had not yet found a job, we were as poor as the proverbial "church mouse." However, after much searching, we were able to rent a small house in northwestern Lansing. After paying the rent and buying food, we didn't have enough money left for a honeymoon. Instead, we decided to buy something that would be a symbol of our love and devotion. My wife's family had owned Shetland Sheepdogs and we decided to purchase one of these miniature "Lassies." Appropriately, we named our puppy Legitimate.

My father built Legitimate a doghouse which we put in our fenced backyard. Although we kept our puppy inside our house at night and when we were not at home, the rest of the time he romped and played in the backyard. All went well for about two weeks. One afternoon, I went to bring Legitimate inside. I did not see him in the yard and he was not in the doghouse. I checked everywhere and couldn't find him. My wife and I panicked. For days, we called, searched, and checked the dog pound. We announced to the neighborhood kids that we would pay a reward if they found him. As a result, they brought us every stray canine and a few felines they stumbled across within a mile of the house. But alas, no Legitimate.

About four weeks later, one of the kids came to the door and told us that Legitimate was lying dead on the side of the road about two blocks away. I was skeptical but went to check it out. They were right. Apparently, he had been hit by a car. We could not figure out how he could have been so close and not have been discovered by our band of determined bounty hunters. None of the kids wanted to talk about it.

Regardless, we bought a replacement Sheltie which we named Sparty. This time, we would be more vigilant. When Sparty went outside, so did one of us. However, after six uneventful months, we became overconfident. We figured that what had happened to Legitimate was a fluke. We were wrong.

One afternoon, a neighbor lady came to the backdoor and screamed, "Some kid just stole your dog!!!" The adrenaline shot through my body like a lightning bolt and I tore out of the backdoor to find this dog thief. As I sprinted down the alley, my wife said she would follow in the car. Some kids told me that the dog thief was riding a ten speed bicycle and heading to the west. One of the kids offered me his Schwinn Stingray bike.

Looking like a crazed motorcycle outlaw, I peddled off on my 15 inch bike with huge handlebars.

I saw the thief in the distance surrounded by neighborhood kids who were trying to kick him off his bike. All of a sudden, a flash of blue shot by as my wife and the eyewitness drove by in hot pursuit. I saw the dog thief and his pursuers turn a corner. By the time I got there, I noticed people standing on their porches shaking their heads and laughing. To avoid my wife, the dog thief had turned onto a sidewalk which ran alongside a one way street which blocked my wife. Undaunted, my wife jumped the curb and with the terrified neighbor lady, drove after him on the sidewalk honking the horn ferociously. To escape again, the dog thief rode into oncoming traffic and my wife had to stop.

By that time I had caught up, with my posse in tow. The kids took me to the thief's home. As luck would have it, I saw him walking into his backyard carrying Sparty under his arm. I skidded my Stingray to a halt and sprinted toward him. In those seconds that seemed like hours, I plotted my revenge. I had played football in high school and intended to lay down a perfect roll block. After I took out his knees, I figured I could do even greater damage. Suddenly the thief looked up and saw this long-haired, bearded madman bearing down on him. He did something rational. He held out the dog. I slowed up and took the dog in my arms. Because my hands were full, I could not hit him. I yelled and he mumbled something. I turned to see his two brothers (ages 20 and 21) coming out of their house. Realizing that it was me and five 12-year olds, I decided that I should beat a hasty retreat and find a cop. For the first time in my life, I found one when I needed one. The officer knew the dog thief and quickly told me about his criminal past. We went to the house where the brothers claimed the thief had been gone for several weeks visiting relatives. The officer told me not to worry because we had witnesses and the thief was just old enough to be tried as an adult. Since Sparty was a purebred dog, his monetary value made the theft more serious.

I returned home with a dog who was in shock and whose leg had been broken. The kids said the thief had dropped him while getting off the bike. But the story gets worse. After returning home, we thanked the neighbor lady who saw the theft. Without her, we would have lost another dog. At that point, her young daughter said, "Yeah, it is too bad those people down the street stole your other dog." I said, "What?" She replied, "You know, the family just down the street." She pointed to the house where we had found Legitimate's body. It suddenly dawned on me that different people had stolen the two dogs and that my neighbors had known who had taken Legitimate. I yelled, "Why didn't you tell us?" Her mother looked really uncomfortable and dragged her daughter off saying, "I told you to keep your mouth shut about that."

After several weeks, my wife and I pieced together the details of the dirty little secret. Our neighbors knew who had taken Legitimate. It was a family who had lived in the neighborhood for years. Because my wife and I were new to the neighborhood and "university hippies," they protected the family with their silence. By the time Sparty was taken, we had made some friendly contacts with the neighbors. We were more or less accepted. More importantly, the second dog thief was an outsider. He was a member of a different ethnic group than that of my neighbors. There had been a great detail of ethnic tension in the neighborhood and prejudice was rampant. Turning him in was easy.

My wife and I felt angry and betrayed. To make matters worse, the police officer called us to say that the dog thief was too young to be charged as an adult. He said nothing could be done by the juvenile officials except to enter this incident into the kid's lengthy list of prior offenses. This was far short of the justice we wanted and expected.

Upon the completion of my doctorate the following summer, I left the neighborhood sadder but wiser. I had learned that conflict is arousing and potentially violent. In writing this, I discover that the details and anger remain vivid even after 20 years! It is especially so when the incident is personal. Furthermore, people do not approach conflict in an unbiased fashion. Their attitudes, emotions, and self-interest cloud their judgments. Finally, the rules and laws that we create to control conflict do not always seem fair to those who have been victimized.

I suppose this incident solidified my interest in conflict management and I have spent the last two decades studying it. Although not all conflicts are as arousing as the one I just described, it is clear that disputes are a pervasive and inevitable part of life. As a result, it is essential that we understand how to effectively manage conflict. To pass on some of what I have learned, I will do three things: define conflict, describe the nature of conflict management, and set forth some ideas about how to effectively manage disputes.

Defining Conflict

In his classic book, Morton Deutsch (1973) defines conflict as the existence of incompatible activity. This definition is quite broad and can include disagreements within interpersonal relationships, organizations, or between nations. Regardless of whether we are studying individuals, groups, or cultures, conflict occurs whenever the behavior of one being interferes with the actions of another. Because the definition is so general, we need to clarify several key features. I will focus on three: conflict issues, origins of conflict, and consequences of conflict.

CONFLICT ISSUES

Conflict results from some "triggering event." Although it may seem that we have done nothing to provoke a dispute, people in conflict with us can usually point to an incident that set them off. We are perceived to have done something that is unacceptable. In some cases, the conflict stimulus is a statement. We said something that another doesn't like. In other instances, the triggering event is entirely nonverbal. Even if we said nothing, others can be angered by a look, gesture, or action. Indeed, we can provoke others by speaking kind words in an insulting manner. Such communication is called sarcasm (Slugoski & Turnbull, 1988).

Regardless of whether the triggering event is verbal or nonverbal, Deutsch (1973) argues that conflict centers on five basic issues. First, **conflict may be focused on values.** Values are a person's thoughts about what "should be." In a sense, values are goals that we want to achieve and we often expect others to pursue them as well. This means that when another's behavior is perceived to be inconsistent with our own value system, conflict will occur.

Value conflict can take several forms. One form results from the priorities we place on values. My wife and I share the values of equality and individual freedom for our children but we do not always prioritize them the same way. I am a first born in my family. I was raised to think that each child should have the individual freedom to engage in actions that are appropriate for his or her age. Although I love my three daughters equally, their different ages mean that older ones should be allowed to do some things that the younger ones are not yet mature enough to do. My wife is a second born. She believes strongly in equality. One child should not be afforded "special privileges." If one is allowed to do something, all the others must also be allowed to do so. As a result, my older daughter often complains that she is not permitted to do things that her friends can do, simply because her sisters are too young. My wife and I share similar values, but rank order them differently in part because we had different experiences as children. I recall not being allowed to do things because my sister was too young, and my wife remembers watching her older brother do things that she could not because she was too young! This often leads to conflict since I am sympathetic to my older daughter's arguments, while my wife sides with the younger's ones.

Value conflict may also arise from the way a value is carried out. Values may be expressed as rules of behavior. They are expectations for how we think a person should act. Even if two people agree that a value is important, they may still disagree as to how well their behavior conforms to that value. For example, two individuals may view themselves as equally religious but engage in very different actions. For one, being religious means being a member of an organized religion, regular attendance at services, and strict adherence to doctrine. Another equally religious person might personalize his or her convictions without any involvement in an organized religion. Thus, their different actions could cause these two individuals to disagree as to how religious they are.

Conflicts over values are difficult to manage. They are deeply held and influence many aspects of a person's life. Therefore, people view values as non-negotiable. Moreover, we often imagine that individuals who hold different values from our own are extremist and biased. As a result, groups with conflicting values often find that they have trouble managing disputes even when the issue is not directly related to their value (Keltner & Robinson, 1993).

Second, **conflict occurs over different beliefs.** Deutsch views beliefs as statements of fact or reality. Whereas values are focused on what should be, beliefs concern what is. In a sense, conflicts over beliefs should be easier to manage than are disputes over values. By their very nature, beliefs can be tested. If you differ over which of two cars gets the better gas mileage, you can look up the statistics in consumer magazines.

However, this is not to say that disputes over beliefs cannot be hotly contested. One can argue about the credibility of the source of the information, as well as the way in which it was collected. In some cases, people cannot agree over what a given piece of information means.

Third, **conflict may be about resources.** Uriel and Edna Foa (1974) argue that people need to get six basic resources from others. Some of these resources are concrete, like money, goods, and services, but others are more abstract, such as love, status, and information. When people have too little of a resource, they become motivated to find more of it. In times of prosperity, resources are readily available, and people trade their resources with each other. When times are tough, individuals may not have anything to trade, or others may demand too much in exchange for their resources. In such cases, individuals may have to do without or try to meet their needs by taking resources from others. Conflict emerges from being denied resources that others have and that people feel that they need or deserve. When people feel they have been deprived relative to others, they can respond aggressively (Tedeschi, Gaes, & Rivera, 1977). Those who have resources will likely defend their right of ownership and resist giving them up without compensation.

Fourth, **conflict may be over the nature of a relationship.** Such disputes can occur when individuals define their relationship in different ways. For example, one person may see a relationship as a friendship, while his or her partner views it as a romance (Baumeister, Wotman, & Stillwell, 1993). Even if two people agree about the kind of relationship they have, they may differ in what they expect from it. One spouse may see marriage as an equal partnership of shared roles and responsibilities, whereas the partner views marital activities as being divided into those activities that are expected of the husband and a different set of activities for the wife (Scanzoni, 1978).

Finally, **conflict may focus on preferences or habits.** People have a number of distinct tastes or routines for doing things. They include colors, foods, places to vacation, and routes to drive somewhere. Although many of these things seem minor, they can be deeply held. These idiosyncrasies give us a feeling of control over our lives. When they are challenged and we resist, the results can be comical. A classic example occurred in the television situation comedy, *All in the Family.* Two of the characters got into a fight over the appropriate way to put on shoes and socks. One argued that one should first put on both socks and then both shoes. The other preferred to put on a sock and then the appropriate shoe, followed by the remaining sock and shoe. These two characters fiercely debated the merits of the "sock, sock, shoe, shoe" sequence versus the "sock, shoe, sock, shoe" pattern. I have heard similar arguments about whether toilet paper should be positioned so that the sheets unroll from the back or front.

In some cases, a given conflict may involve more than one issue. This means that people may see a triggering event as being incompatible at several levels. For example, forgetting to pick up your lover after work not only denies him or her valuable resources (wasted time waiting for you), but may also violate relational expectations to be supportive and sensitive to each other (Baxter, 1986). To you, the matter is easily taken care of through an apology. No big deal. Your lover sees things differently. The issue is not just lost time but your apparent lack of concern. The interpretation of the event as a relational transgression is a more serious and difficult matter to resolve (Roloff & Cloven, 1994). Given that people do not always talk about all of the issues associated with a triggering event, one must be sensitive to other interpretations. What seems to you to be the sole issue is not always shared by others (Baumeister, Stillwell, & Wotman, 1990). Obviously, if you can't figure out the issue then it is difficult to manage the conflict.

ORIGINS OF CONFLICT

Conflict seems like an inevitable part of life. Even people who are in happy marriages report that their spouses do things on a daily basis that anger them (Kirchler, 1988). Why is conflict so common? One can identify five causes.

First, **individuals are raised in social environments in which they learn different ways of thinking and acting.** When people come in contact with others from different cultures, they become aware of the distinct ways in which humans approach ordinary, everyday activities. Moreover, even individuals raised in the same family often develop their own ways of doing things. When these learned habits are incompatible, individuals find themselves in conflict.

Second, **conflict is more likely when people are interdependent.** Interdependency means that the behavior of one person or group affects the behavior of another and vice versa (Folger, Poole, & Stutman, 1993). Interdependency results from several things. One is shared space. When you drive a car, the actions of other drivers can have grave consequences for you. As you may have found out, your roommate's behavior can directly influence your well-being and sanity! In general, people are more likely to be in conflict when they are physically close rather than distant from each other.

Interdependency may also arise from social norms and laws. Parents are expected to care for their children and to make sure that they are properly socialized. Some states even allow parents to be charged with a crime if their children violate the law or quit coming to school. Part of the parental role is to set and enforce limits that may be resisted by children. Of course, interdependency may come about because of our attachment to another. Most parents do not have to be forced by law to care for their children. They are concerned for them and worry about what might happen to them. To protect them, parents may restrict the freedom of their children, which can turn into a battle over control (Steinmetz, 1977).

Third, **conflict may result from tension.** We live in a stressful world. When people are sick, unemployed, crowded, hot, or subjected to loud noise or an offensive odor, they become irritable (Berkowitz, 1990). Such factors increase the likelihood that people will become sensitive to the actions of others and become intolerant. Indeed, stressors have been linked to interpersonal violence (Barling & Rosenbaum, 1986; Marshall & Rose, 1987).

Fourth, **conflict may result from our inability to forecast the impact of our behaviors on others.** This is especially true for others who are far removed in time and space. We cannot always know that our current actions will prove to be harmful for future generations or for those individuals who live in other geographical areas. Unfortunately, interdependency is not always apparent. As a result, our actions may unintentionally interfere with those of others.

Finally, **conflict may result from our commitment to our own world view.** Most of us are comfortable with our own way of doing things. To change would require a big adjustment in our lifestyle. Therefore, we follow the old saying, "If it isn't broken, don't fix it." Hence, alternative viewpoints are not sought out or are dismissed when making decisions (Janis, 1972). We continue doing what we have always done without considering the impact it has on others.

CONSEQUENCES OF CONFLICT

When people describe their conflicts, they often compare them to warfare, natural disasters, or hopeless situations (McCorkle & Mills, 1992). These descriptions reflect the generally negative attitude that most people have toward conflict. Surprisingly, most scholars who study conflict write about its benefits (Coser, 1956; Hocker & Wilmot, 1985). Consequently, when I lecture on the functions of conflict, I often look out across a class of "unbelievers." In this section I want to consider the good and bad consequences associated with conflict.

Benefits of Conflict

Conflict is thought to serve a variety of purposes. First and foremost, **conflict makes individuals aware of problems and forces them to respond to them.** It is a force for change. Just as pain makes us aware that we are sick or in danger, conflict signals that something is wrong in our social environment. It alerts us to take action before things worsen.

Second, **conflict can serve as a release for tension** (Coser, 1956). Some of you may have experienced frustrating times in your life. Your grades are suffering. Your parents are on your back and your lover runs off with someone else. When you try to deal with all of them by keeping them "bottled up inside," you run the danger of an explosion.

Berkowitz (1962) observed that frustrating experiences add together so as to produce aggression. Eventually, you will attack somebody and the tiniest, most insignificant thing can set you off. Confronting problems as they occur can help let off steam before you explode.

Third, **conflict can make us aware of alternative and better ways of doing things.** The more unique ideas that are considered, the more likely individuals will find innovative solutions to their problems (Nezu & D'Zurilla, 1981). The expression of diverse and often conflicting viewpoints is a necessary ingredient for effective decision-making (Schweiger & Sandberg, 1989).

Finally, **conflict has the potential to strengthen relationships.** The willingness to confront a problem signals a commitment to the relationship (Courtright, Millar, Rogers, & Bagarozzi, 1990). Confrontation indicates sensitivity to difficulties and a desire to work with another to solve them. Even if individuals are unable to completely solve the dispute, they cared enough to try. People who don't care about a relationship are unwilling to expend the energy that is required to solve a problem. They would rather avoid the issue until a better alternative comes along (Rusbult, 1987). Such neglectful behavior can be the prelude to the end of a relationship.

Given these benefits, one might ask, Why do people view conflict so negatively? We turn to that next.

Drawbacks to Conflict

People have good reason to fear conflict. At its heart, conflict involves interference with one's goals. Hence, it can be frustrating (Berkowitz, 1962). Just hearing someone express an opinion that is contrary to our own can increase our arousal level (Gormly, 1974). Although arousal could motivate us to take any variety of actions to deal with a conflict, it often sets a destructive course. Conflict is often associated with mean-spirited and negative interactions. People describe their arguments as loud, fast-paced, insulting, sarcastic, and profane (Resick, et al., 1981). Negative statements such as those often expressed during an argument are better remembered than are positive statements (Kellermann, 1989). Moreover, individuals mull over negative statements after a dispute, which makes the dispute seem worse (Cloven & Roloff, 1991). Therefore, it should not be surprising that people report that criticism and verbal attacks toward others are things they wish they had never said (Knapp, Stafford, & Daly, 1986). Unfortunately, it is difficult to take them back and the conflict may spiral out of control. Uncontrolled conflict can lead to three negative outcomes.

First, **conflict can lead to physical aggression.** Research on physical assaults and murder clearly indicates that violence emerges from arguments (Felson, 1984; Luckenbill, 1977). When individuals confront others in an insulting manner, verbal aggression often results which escalates into violent reactions (Felson, 1982). Even minor issues have the potential to lead to beatings and attacks.

Second, **conflict can destroy a relationship.** Although a relationship may simply wear out over time, more frequently partners split up over disputes. A single dispute or a series of disputes occur which threaten the desire to stay in the association (Baxter, 1984).

Finally, **conflict can seriously affect your psychological and emotional well-being.** People who are in frequent conflict often report lowered self-esteem and trust in others, as well as the feeling that they cannot control what is happening to them (Lakey, Tardiff, & Drew, 1994).

To gain the potential benefits from conflict, we must understand how to manage its potential destructiveness. To do so, requires that we explore the nature of conflict management. As you may have noted, many of the drawbacks of conflict stem from the way we try to handle our disputes rather than from the triggering event itself. Triggering events can be dealt with constructively or destructively.

THE NATURE OF CONFLICT MANAGEMENT

The term *conflict management* is a relatively new one. When I first became interested in conflict, the term of choice was *conflict resolution*. The switch in terminology is a significant one. With time, scholars have come to realize that disputes are rarely resolved. To be "resolved" implies that the issue is dead and gone. In reality, many conflicts do not come to such a neat conclusion and often result in a standoff (Benoit & Benoit, 1987; Vuchinich, 1987). In some cases, parties back off without having reached any agreement as to what to do. They are tired or fearful of what will happen next, so they just quit arguing before reaching a resolution. In other cases, an agreement is forced upon one side by a more powerful party without any change in the underlying causes of the dispute. In still other circumstances, the problems are so complex that they cannot be resolved after a single encounter. More time is needed. Hence, unresolved arguments may flair up in the future (Trapp & Hoff, 1985).

Conflict management is focused on the ways in which individuals try to control their disputes. In some instances, the aim may indeed be to completely resolve it. However in others, the goal is simply to keep the dispute from worsening. In effect, to keep it at a tolerable level. To manage a dispute, one must recognize that a conflict can go through three stages: pre-confrontation, confrontation, and post-confrontation.

Pre-Confrontation Stage

The pre-confrontation stage constitutes the time between first discovering a triggering event and initially confronting the person about it. In some cases, this stage is very short. You see a person do something and you immediately tell him or her about it. A quick response often occurs when you are in charge of someone else's behavior. Parents who are watching their children will often confront any real or even anticipated behavior that is considered to be wrong or dangerous. Impulse may also cause a person to react quickly. Sometimes another person makes you so frightened, angered, or irritated that you speak without hesitating or thinking.

However, people also wait lengthy periods of time before they confront another (Baumeister, Stillwell, & Wotman, 1990). It is useful then to distinguish between two types of delayed confrontation: temporary avoidance and long-term avoidance. When engaging in **temporary avoidance,** one anticipates confronting another at some point, but not right now. People may delay confrontation until they calm down. A triggering event may so upset you that a confrontation could be damaging to you or another person. Conversely, you may decide to hold off until the other person is in a calmer or more sober state of mind.

Temporary delay may allow individuals to plan for the confrontation (Stutman & Newell, 1990). In some cases, they may not clearly understand the triggering event. More information is needed before talking to the other person. Once he or she understands the event, he or she can consider how best to approach the other person, what to do, and how the other person will respond.

Although delaying a confrontation is often a reasonable thing to do, it does carry risks. In some cases, circumstances change so that the problem is harder to resolve. When my dog, Sparty, was stolen, my wife and I immediately tracked down the thief. Had we waited, we might not have been able to find him. Moreover, the police told us that unless the dog had been tattooed with an identifying mark, they could not have taken the dog from the thief. It would have been his word against ours.

But perhaps the greatest risk is that temporary delay may turn into **long-term avoidance.** A person may decide to never confront another. If the problem is small or unlikely to ever happen again, the decision to let it drop may not be bad (Rahim, 1986). However, without a confrontation, the problem may occur again and could grow worse. Moreover, long-term avoidance can be an exhausting means of conflict management. We often think of avoidance as a passive response. You don't say or do anything. To the contrary, it is extremely active and effortful. Gelles and Straus (1988) found that abused wives who stay with their husbands often use conflict avoidance to prevent attacks. To do so, they must identify what sets off the abuse and construct situations so that nothing will provoke the husband. This may mean steering conversations away from dangerous topics or making sure that nobody does anything that will irritate their husbands. None of this is easy to do and not surprisingly, long-term conflict avoidance typically fails.

Why then do people choose to avoid? In some cases, people are fearful of their partner's response to the confrontation. The partner might leave. If a person is very dependent upon his or her partner, the loss of the relationship is frightening (Roloff & Cloven, 1990). Individuals may also fear that the partner will respond to their complaints with verbal or physical aggression (Cloven & Roloff, 1993b). Indeed, instances of physical abuse usually result from a verbal confrontation that has gotten out of control (Gelles, 1972). Finally, people may avoid a confrontation because they do not believe it is their responsibility or right to complain. Parents will often criticize the behavior of their own children but not confront someone else's children who do the same thing (Halverson & Waldrop, 1970).

Thus, people are often faced with a tough decision. Do I avoid confronting another and silently cope with the problem or do I confront the person and hope that the conflict does not escalate?

Confrontation Stage

Although it may seem that our arguments go on forever, there is evidence that they are typically brief and end in a matter of minutes (Benoit & Benoit, 1987; Vuchinich, 1987). In many cases, a person says something, the other responds, and it's over. Perhaps because people have a sense that prolonged arguing can be damaging, they try to keep disagreements short (Vuchinich, 1986).

Although they are usually brief, a confrontation can be viewed as a sequence that moves from an opening statement through extended responses to a closing (Gottman, 1979). The opening of a confrontation typically involves a statement about what you wish the other to do or stop doing. The way one phrases the opening statement can be critical because it sets the tone for the rest of the confrontation. Starting a confrontation with an insult, command, or accusation attacks the positive image that most people have of themselves and can prompt defensiveness (Stamp, Vangelisti, & Daly, 1992). People react much better to openers that are phrased as requests or that include some information about why they are upset (Benoit & Benoit, 1990).

Once the issue has been raised, both parties react to each other's statements. In some cases, an explanation is provided for the negative behavior (Wolf-Smith & LaRossa, 1992). In effect, the person gets the opportunity to explain his or her side of the story. However, there may also be defensive reactions. A person may respond to the opening statement by denying that anything happened, stating that he or she was not responsible for anything that might have happened, or by blaming the person who is complaining (Donohue, 1981). Even more destructive, the person may countercomplain by stating that the confronter has engaged in other actions that are equally bad (Gottman, 1979). In effect, the tables are turned on the confronter. Equally upsetting, the person may simply ignore the confronter's complaint (Alberts, 1989). Generally, confrontations are more productive when individuals acknowledge rather than ignore complaints and when they provide information about the problem, rather than trade accusations.

At some point, people in a confrontation must bring it to a close. One or both parties may admit some degree of guilt and apologize, promising never to repeat the action (Schlenker & Darby, 1981). In other cases, the two individuals may agree to drop the topic until some other time, or may even agree to never talk about it again (Baxter & Wilmot, 1985). Or, the parties may simply stop talking and leave the interaction hurt, confused, and/or angry. Simply because the initial confrontation has ended does not mean that the conflict is over.

Post-Confrontation Stage

Even though a confrontation may be very short, the effects can be long-lasting. Individuals carry with them memories of what was said that they can replay later. They can dwell on perceived insults and become angrier (Sadler & Tesser, 1973). They can think of things that they should have said or done and plan their attacks for the next confrontation (Edwards, Honeycutt, & Zagacki, 1988). Furthermore, conflict may cause individuals to actively question the viability of their relationship (Booth & White, 1980). When the confrontation has not gone well, this mulling makes matters worse.

If, however, the confrontation ended with the possibility of a resolution, the post-confrontation stage may be positive. The individuals may repair any damage to their relationship and work to prevent any future instances. Or, they may simply quit thinking about it. The issue is over.

Obviously, it is critical that we identify factors that prevent conflict from reaching a constructive conclusion. I will do that next.

EFFECTIVE CONFLICT MANAGEMENT

Although a multitude of things can go wrong during a conflict, there are seven problems which are frequently encountered: directness, singular perspectives, commitments, hidden linkages, personalization, relationships, and unresponsiveness. Unless individuals address these, conflict management will be more difficult.

Directness

When confronting another, one faces a dilemma arising from how directly one should express the complaint. The most efficient method is to directly tell the person what you want. You might command them to stop. Parents often use imperatives to control their children. "Eat your food." "Turn that thing down!" Such statements are clear, but in some contexts are offensive (Donohue & Diez, 1985). They imply a right to tell someone to do something, as well as a willingness to force them to comply (Wilson, Meischke, & Kim, 1991). Such inferences often cause the individual to feel stigmatized and may cause resistance.

On the other hand, if one is too indirect, the person who is being confronted may not understand what you want. For example, Sillars (1980) found that college roommates most frequently employ passive-indirect strategies to resolve their problems. At the most extreme, these include avoiding the issue or the roommate, but also a technique called "setting a good example." Instead of directly confronting a sloppy roommate, some individuals clean up after him or her with the hope that the slob will reciprocate. Of course, this technique often fails. The roommate may assume that you clean up after him or her because you like doing it. Why deny you your pleasure? The point being that indirect techniques do not clearly express your concerns and may not be interpreted as a complaint (Newell & Stutman, 1989/1990).

Hence, the first guideline: **You must communicate in a manner that is sufficiently direct so that your concern is clear, but not so direct that it is offensive.** To do so, you may need to address the person in a polite fashion ("please turn down the stereo"), include reasons ("I have to study tomorrow and the noise from the stereo is making it hard for me to concentrate"), and pre-apologies ("I'm sorry to bother you, but the stereo is too loud"). If those fail, you can move to more direct language, but avoid offensive language (like saying, "You suck!"). Offensive language tends to inflame people, as you probably know.

Singular Perspective

When analyzing a problem, people often approach it from what they know best—their own perspective (Cloven & Roloff, 1993a). After all, they observe and experience the event. A problem emerges when two people have different perspectives. When an individual engages in an action toward another, he or she often reports that something about the situation is causing his or her behavior. The person who is the target of the action often sees the actor as causing the behavior (Gioia & Sims, 1985). These different perspectives are especially problematic in conflict. For example, both members of a married couple may agree that one of them has not been especially affectionate of late. He or she has been disinterested in sex and hasn't even said "I love you" in a long time. However, they can disagree as to the cause. The unaffectionate spouse may attribute the problem to stress, fatigue, illness, or any number of external causes. However, their partner may see the same behavior as indicating a lack of love. In such cases, the dispute has escalated from a behavioral to an attributional conflict (Orvis, Kelley, & Butler, 1976). They agree as to the behavior, but disagree as to the cause.

Attributional conflict is difficult to resolve. It is hard to know exactly what is causing another's behavior. As a result, you might be suspicious of their explanation. Moreover, we tend to think of our own behavior as normal and assume that others are thinking exactly as we are (Ross, Greene, & House, 1977). Therefore, alternative explanations are rejected as cover-ups.

Hence, the second guideline: **Be open to alternative perspectives on a dispute.** To do so, one is often advised to consider the opposite of what one initially thinks (Lord, Lepper, & Preston, 1984). Lay out your initial perspective and then try to pick holes in the reasoning and assumptions. Ask the question, "Why might I be wrong?" In doing so, you may discover your perceptions are incorrect. Even if you conclude your initial thoughts are right, you can at least anticipate what the other person may say and be better able to respond.

Commitment

During the course of a conflict, individuals often become committed to pursuing a course of action. Psychologically, they are determined to carry out their course of action and when they communicate those intentions to others, they become locked in to it socially.

Commitment can be beneficial. Committed individuals try harder to achieve their goals than do those who are not committed. This added energy sometimes helps them find creative ways to achieve difficult goals (Huber & Neale, 1987; Roloff & Jordan, 1991). Moreover, communicating one's commitment signals one's sincerity and resolve to others. As a result, they know that you should not be taken lightly (Pruitt, 1981).

However, commitment can also have its drawbacks. If one makes a commitment to an action before getting all of the information, one may become prematurely committed to an unwise course of action (Walton & McKersie, 1965). When the commitment has been made public, one cannot easily back off without losing credibility. In others words, saying "take it or leave it" means just that. The final offer has been made and I will not accept any other one. If I do, then you have no reason to believe my statements in the future.

Commitment may also trap us into continued investment in a losing course of action (Bazerman & Neale, 1983). Despite significant losses, both labor and management will remain committed to a strike long after it has become apparent that it will not be successful. Governments spend millions and commit lives to wars that have little chance of victory. Often the only way to end involvement in counterproductive actions is to remove from power those who initially committed to them.

Commitment may be harmful if it extends to both goals and means of achieving goals. Dean Pruitt (1981) argues that negotiators are most successful when they are rigid with regard to their goals, but flexible as to how to achieve them. In a conflict, it is good to be stubborn about your goals. If you are not, you will give in too readily and the problem won't be settled. However, this must be coupled with an open mind as to the best way to achieve your objectives. If you come to a conflict with both a firm commitment to your goal and to a single solution, you will probably not reach an agreement.

Hence, the third guideline: **Be clear and committed to your goals but remain flexible as to the means of achieving them.**

Typically, there are several ways to meet your needs and you should generate as many alternatives as you can. That way, you avoid becoming committed to a single but potentially losing course of action. Also, you might find one that is acceptable to the person with whom you are in conflict. As a result, everyone wins.

Hidden Linkages

Often we treat an issue as though it is unrelated to any others. By doing so, we are unprepared for problems that arise from its links to others (Pruitt, 1981). There are five critical types of linkages that should be recognized. The first is a **resource linkage.** As Chair of my department, I often receive proposals for new programs. They are usually reasonable and articulate, but fail to address one critical question: Where will we find the resources (money, people, and effort) to implement them? Advocates can describe the reasons for doing something, but are unable or unwilling to consider the cost. A good plan is one that provides both a rationale for doing it and identifies resources for implementing it.

A second linkage **lies with the past.** Often an issue has a history. The issue has been discussed before and people have become committed to their respective positions on the issue. As such, there is pessimism about whether it can be successfully resolved. Therefore, one must find a way to recast the problem so that it is unaffected by the past.

The third linkage is **connected to the future.** Often issues can serve as a precedent for future action. When a student of mine asks for a delay on an assignment, I am concerned that I might have to give everyone a delay or that the student may come to me again in the future with the same request. To overcome resistance, individuals may have to clearly indicate that the current issue will have no bearing on future requests.

A fourth link is made to **values.** Sometimes in arguing for a position, individuals tie their positions to values. Although these linkages are meant to support the position, they may become problematic. If a person believes strongly that rewards should be divided equitably (each person should receive rewards in proportion to what he or she contributes), then he or she might resist a proposal that salaries should be based on equality or need. If the belief in equity is strong, a person may oppose such proposals, even if they would increase his or her own salary (Greenberg, 1978).

The final link is one **based on relationships.** Sometimes my support or resistance to a proposal is influenced by my relationship with the person who is advocating it, as well as how my friends feel about it. The specifics of the proposal are less important than who is for or against it.

Hence, the fourth guideline: **One must be aware of issue linkages, seek to remove ones that create resistance, and add those that will facilitate agreement.** Although this discussion has focused on problem linkages, they can be positive. By linking my proposal to something that another supports, I may be able to reach an agreement. One common technique for doing this is called logrolling (Pruitt, 1981). When logrolling, a person makes concessions on an issue that is less important in exchange for another person's concession on a more important issue. If my wife really wants us to attend the Chicago Symphony and I am indifferent, but I really want us to see the Rolling Stones in concert and she could care less, linking the two activities could avoid conflict. I go with her to Symphony Hall and she goes to Soldier Field with me to see the Stones.

Personalization

Personalization is probably the most destructive obstacle. When individuals perceive that they have been humiliated, they feel compelled to fight back (Brown, 1968). By retaliating, we punish them for hurting us and deter them from doing so again (Felson,

1978). Moreover, we restore our image of strength and capability in our eyes, as well as in those of others.

Although retaliation may be a natural response, it is clearly destructive. Verbal and physical aggression are often responded to in kind and each time the aggression tends to become more severe. These attacking cycles insure that the conflict will not be adequately managed (Putnam & Jones, 1982). Even if a weaker party is forced to submit, the initial problem has not been solved and a new one has been added. The original issue of the conflict becomes less important than restoring one's image. Thus, the weaker party becomes motivated to build its strength (Fagenson & Cooper, 1987) and the conflict escalates.

Hence, guideline five: **Be sensitive to the needs of others to appear strong and capable, but be less sensitive to their attacks on your own image.** This advice can be difficult to follow. It runs contrary to our nature. We must be respectful to individuals we don't like. When we must communicate negative information to another, we must do so in a manner that does not threaten their image. Negative feedback should be delivered so that it does not blame the person, is specific about the problem, and is considerate of their feelings (Baron, 1988). When others attack our image, we must stay focused on the real issue and not be distracted. We must not trade insults or threats. Avoiding destructive responses requires substantial self-control.

This advice does not mean that we should allow ourselves to be humiliated. We can appear strong without becoming aggressive. We can ignore insults and continue talking about the real problem. Stay focused and calm. If necessary, walk away from the dispute until tempers are back under control. Sometimes it is useful to bring in a neutral third party who can keep things under control (Folger, Poole, & Stutman, 1993). A trusted mediator can call for breaks during heated exchanges and keep individuals focused on the issue.

Relationships

Often people who are in conflict are involved in an ongoing relationship. This association can complicate managing conflict. On one hand, relational problems can make managing a dispute more difficult. For example, lack of trust is a major impediment to conflict management (Deutsch, 1973). When there is no trust, we become cautious. We are not entirely honest in our statements for fear that information might be used against us. Moreover, we are not inclined to believe what others say for fear that they are lying. Instead of looking for creative solutions to our problems, we focus on ones that appear to be safe.

Strangely, having a very positive relationship may also make conflict management difficult. When we are very much in love with someone, we may be too willing to forgive them (Hall & Taylor, 1976). To accommodate them, we sacrifice our own needs (Fry, Firestone, & Williams, 1983). Such an approach may temporarily avoid conflict but can eventually make us resentful.

Hence, the sixth guideline: **One should not let relationships cloud our approach to conflict management.** Certainly, you must be on guard if another is reputed to be untrustworthy, but you should not become so conservative that you overlook creative solutions to your problems. Find novel solutions and then build safeguards into them. Moreover, simply because you are close to someone does not mean that you should sacrifice your needs for them. The point is to find a solution that benefits all sides.

Unresponsiveness

As we noted earlier, conflict can turn into an escalating pattern of attacks. It can also turn into a cycle of destructive avoidance. Researchers have found such a negative pattern in some marriages. One spouse confronts the other with a demand for change and the partner responds by withdrawing from the conversation (Heavey, Layne, & Christensen, 1993). **Withdrawal** means not responding to the complaint in any fashion, looking away, refusing to discuss the matter, or psychologically disengaging from the conversation. This response typically infuriates the confronting spouse who increases the pressure. This frequently is met with more withdrawal and the conflict worsens.

The demand/withdrawal sequence could result from many factors. Some argue that individuals who are powerful maintain their control by not responding to the complaints of those who are less powerful. By not acknowledging a complaint, there is no pressure to change things (Sattel, 1983; Scanzoni, 1978). Others suggest that conflict can result in negative arousal and that to control these emotions, individuals psychologically distance themselves from the dispute (Gottman & Levenson, 1988). In effect, unresponsiveness is a way of exerting emotional self-control. Regardless, unresponsiveness is viewed negatively by a confrontative person (Alberts, 1989). They see it as signalling disinterest in their concerns and perhaps, as a sign that they don't matter as a human being. Hence, it is not surprising that demand/withdrawal cycles reduce marital satisfaction and the frustration that arises from them can even lead to violence (Scanzoni, 1978).

Hence, guideline seven: **Always acknowledge another person's complaints.** This does not mean that you have to agree or comply with him or her. You can disagree or present your view of the matter; just don't ignore him or her.

CONCLUSIONS

After reading this chapter, you should have reached several conclusions. First, although conflict is inevitable, it is does not always have to be destructive. Conflict can provide important benefits. Second, the degree to which conflict is constructive or destructive is related to how it is managed. By addressing problems that frequently occur during conflict, one can effectively manage disputes. Third, to be an effective conflict manager requires one to be sensitive to alternative perspectives and approaches while remaining committed to one's own needs. One must be able to persuasively present a position without dogmatically rejecting alternative viewpoints. Finally, effective conflict management is effortful. One must be creative and in self-control. In a sense, you must be able to rise above the heat and anger that often accompanies disputes. It is hard work.

To be honest, I would have trouble following my own guidelines with the thief who took Sparty. Even today, I would have much preferred to have smashed his face rather than to have respected it. Knowing about multiple perspectives in no way reduces my resentment toward those neighbors. Regardless, the self-control that I exerted prevented a potentially tragic escalation of that conflict. Not all conflicts can be resolved to one's satisfaction, but they can be managed so that they do not become worse.

REFERENCES

Alberts, J. K. (1989). A descriptive taxonomy of couples' complaint interactions. *The Southern Communication Journal, 54,* 125–143.

Barling, J., & Rosenbaum, A. (1986). Work stressors and wife abuse. *Journal of Applied Psychology, 71,* 346–348.

Baron, R. A. (1988). Negative effects of destructive criticism: Impact on conflict, self-efficacy, and task performance. *Journal of Applied Psychology, 73,* 199–207.

Baumeister, R. F., Stillwell, A., & Wotman, S. R. (1990). Victim and perpetrator accounts of interpersonal conflict: Autobiographical narratives about anger. *Journal of Personality and Social Psychology, 59,* 994–1005.

Baumeister, R. F., Wotman, S. R., & Stillwell, A. M. (1993). Unrequited love: On heartbreak, anger, guilt, scriptlessness, and humiliation. *Journal of Personality and Social Psychology, 64,* 377–394.

Baxter, L. A. (1984). Trajectories of relationship disengagement. *Journal of Social and Personal Relationships, 1,* 29–48.

Baxter, L. A. (1986). Gender differences in the heterosexual relationship rules embedded in break-up accounts. *Journal of Social and Personal Relationships, 3,* 289–306.

Baxter, L. A., & Wilmot, W. W. (1985). Taboo topics in close relationships. *Journal of Social and Personal Relationships, 2,* 253–269.

Bazerman, M. H., & Neale, M. A. (1983). Heuristics in negotiation: Limitations to effective dispute resolution. In M. H. Bazerman, & R. J. Lewicki (Eds.), *Negotiating in organizations* (pp. 51–67). Newbury Park, CA: Sage.

Benoit, W. L., & Benoit, P. J. (1987). Everyday argument practices of naive social actors. In J. W. Wenzel (Ed.), *Argument and critical practices: Proceedings of the fifth SCA/AFA conference on argumentation* (pp. 465–473). Annandale, VA: SCA.

Benoit, W. L., & Benoit, P. J. (1990). Aggravated and mitigated opening utterances. *Argumentation, 4,* 171–183.

Berkowitz, L. (1962). *Aggression: A social psychological analysis.* New York: McGraw-Hill.

Berkowitz, L. (1990). On the formation and regulation of anger and aggression: A cognitive-neoassociationistic analysis. *American Psychologist, 45,* 494–503.

Booth, A., & White, L. (1980). Thinking about divorce. *Journal of Marriage and the Family, 42,* 605–616.

Brown, B. R. (1968). The effects of need to maintain face on interpersonal bargaining. *Journal of Experimental Social Psychology, 4,* 107–122.

Cloven, D. H., & Roloff, M. E. (1991). Sense-making activities and interpersonal conflict: Communicative cures for the mulling blues. *Western Journal of Speech Communication, 55,* 134–158.

Cloven, D. H., & Roloff, M. E. (1993a). Sense-making activities and interpersonal conflict, II: The effects of communicative intentions on intrapersonal dialogue. *Western Journal of Communication, 57,* 309–329.

Cloven, D. H., & Roloff, M. E. (1993b). The chilling effect of aggressive potential on the expression of complaints in intimate relationships. *Communication Monographs, 60,* 199–219.

Coser, L. (1956). *The functions of social conflict.* New York: The Free Press.

Courtright, J. A., Millar, F. E., Rogers, L. E., & Bagarozzi, D. (1990). Interaction dynamics of relational negotiation: Reconciliation versus termination of distressed relationships. *Western Journal of Speech Communication, 54,* 429–453.

Deutsch, M. (1973). *The resolution of conflict: Constructive and destructive processes.* Cambridge, MA: Yale University Press.

Donohue, W. A. (1981). Development of a model of rule use in negotiation interaction. *Communication Monographs, 48,* 106–120.

Donohue, W. A., & Diez, M. E. (1985). Directive use in negotiation interaction. *Communication Monographs, 52,* 305–318.

Edwards, R., Honeycutt, J. M., & Zagacki, K. S. (1988). Imagined interaction as an element of social cognition. *Western Journal of Speech Communication, 52,* 23–45.

Fagenson, E. A., & Cooper, J. (1987). When push comes to power: A test of power restoration theory's explanation for aggressive conflict escalation. *Basic and Applied Social Psychology, 8,* 273–293.

Felson, R. B. (1978). Aggression as impression management. *Social Psychology, 41,* 205–213.

Felson, R. B. (1982). Impression management and the escalation of aggression and violence. *Social Psychology Quarterly, 45,* 245–254.

Felson, R. B. (1984). Patterns of aggressive social interaction. In A. Mummendey (Ed.), *Social psychology of aggression: From individual behavior to social interaction* (pp. 107–126). New York: Springer-Verlag.

Foa, U. G., & Foa, E. B. (1974). *Societal structures of the mind.* Springfield, IL: Charles C. Thomas.

Folger, J. P., Poole, M. S., & Stutman, R. K. (1993). *Working through conflict: Strategies for relationships, groups, and organizations* (2nd. ed.). New York: Harper Collins College Publishers.

Fry, W. R., Firstone, I. J., & Williams, D. L. (1983). Negotiation process and outcome of stranger dyads and dating couples: Do lovers lose? *Basic and Applied Social Psychology, 4,* 1–16.

Gelles, R. J. (1972). *The violent home: A study of physical aggression between husbands and wives.* Newbury Park, CA: Sage.

Gelles, R. J., & Straus, M. A. (1988). *Intimate violence.* New York: Simon and Schuster.

Gioia, D. A., Sims, Jr., H. P. (1985). Self-serving bias and actor-observer differences in organizations: An empirical analysis. *Journal of Applied Social Psychology, 15,* 547–563.

Gormly, J. (1974). A comparison of predictions from consistency and affect theories for arousal during interpersonal disagreement. *Journal of Personality and Social Psychology, 30,* 658–663.

Gottman, J. M. (1979). *Marital interaction: Experimental investigations.* New York: Academic Press.

Gottman, J. M., & Levenson, R. W. (1988). The social psychophysiology of marriage. In P. Noller, & M. A. Fitzpatrick (Eds.), *Perspectives on marital interaction* (pp. 182–200). Clevedon, England: Multilingual Matters.

Greenberg, J. (1978). Equity, equality, and the Protestant Ethic: Allocating rewards following fair and unfair competition. *Journal of Experimental Social Psychology, 14,* 217–226.

Hall, J. A., & Taylor, S. (1976). When love is blind: Maintaining idealized images of one's spouse. *Human Relations, 29,* 751–761.

Halverson, Jr., C. F., & Waldrop, M. F. (1970). Maternal behavior toward own and other preschool children: The problem of "ownness." *Child Development, 41,* 839–845.

Heavey, C. L., Layne, C., & Christensen, A. (1993). Gender and conflict structure in marital interaction: A replication and extension. *Journal of Consulting and Clinical Psychology, 61,* 16–27.

Hocker, J. L., & Wilmot, W. W. (1985). *Interpersonal conflict* (2nd ed.). Dubuque, IA: Wm. C. Brown.

Huber, V. L., & Neale, M. A. (1987). Effects of self- and competitor goals on performance in an interdependent bargaining task. *Journal of Applied Psychology, 72,* 197–203.

Janis, I. (1972). *Victims of groupthink.* Boston: Houghton Mifflin.

Kellermann, K. (1989). The negativity effect in interaction: It's all in your point of view. *Human Communication Research, 16,* 147–183.

Keltner, D., & Robinson, R. J. (1993). Imagined ideological differences in conflict escalation and resolution. *The International Journal of Conflict Resolution, 4,* 249–262.

Kirchler, E. (1988). Marital happiness and interaction in everyday surroundings: A time-sample diary approach for couples. *Journal of Social and Personal Relationships, 5,* 375–382.

Knapp, M. L., Stafford, L., & Daly, J. A. (1986). Regrettable messages: Things people wish they hadn't said. *Journal of Communication, 36,* 40–57.

Lakey, B., Tardiff, T. A., & Drew, J. B. (1994). Negative social interactions: Assessment and relations to social support, cognitions, and psychological distress. *Journal of Social and Clinical Psychology, 13,* 42–62.

Lord, C. G., Lepper, M. R., & Preston, E. (1984). Considering the opposite: A corrective strategy for social judgment. *Journal of Personality and Social Psychology, 47,* 1231–1243.

Luckenbill, D. F. (1977). Criminal homicide as a situated transaction. *Social Problems, 25,* 176–186.

Marshall, L. L., & Rose, P. (1987). Gender, stress and violence in the adult relationships of a sample of college students. *Journal of Social and Personal Relationships, 4,* 299–316.

McCorkle, S., & Mills, J. L. (1992). Rowboat in a hurricane: Metaphors of interpersonal conflict management. *Communication Reports, 5,* 57–64.

Newell, S. E., & Stutman, R. K. (1989/90). Negotiating confrontation: The problematic nature of initiation and response. *Research on Language and Social Interaction, 23,* 139–162.

Nezu, A., & D'Zurilla, T. J. (1981). Effects of problem definition and formulation on the generation of alternatives in the social problem-solving process. *Cognitive Therapy and Research, 5,* 265–271.

Orvis, B. R., Kelley, H. H., & Butler, D. (1976). Attributional conflicts in young couples. In J. H. Harvey, W. J. Ickes, & R. F. Kidd (Eds.), *New directions in attribution research* (vol 1: 353–386). Hillsdale, NJ: LEA.

Pruitt, D. G. (1981). *Negotiation behavior.* New York: Academic Press.

Putnam, L. L., & Jones, T. S. (1982). Reciprocity in negotiations: An analysis of bargaining interaction. *Communication Monographs, 49,* 171–191.

Rahim, M. A. (1986). *Managing conflict in organizations.* New York: Praeger.

Resick, P. A., Barr, P. K., Sweet, J. J., Kieffer, D. M., Ruby, N. L., & Spiegel, D. K. (1981). Perceived and actual discriminators of conflict from accord in marital communication. *The American Journal of Family Therapy, 9,* 58–68.

Roloff, M. E., & Cloven, D. H. (1990). The chilling effect in interpersonal relationships: The reluctance to speak one's mind. In D. D. Cahn (Ed.), *Intimates in conflict: A communication perspective* (pp. 49–76). Hillsdale, NJ: LEA.

Roloff, M. E., & Cloven, D. H. (1994). When partners transgress: Maintaining violated relationships. In D. J. Canary, & L. Stafford (Eds.), *Communication and relational maintenance* (pp. 23–44). New York: Academic Press.

Roloff, M. E., & Jordan, J. M. (1991). The influence of effort, experience, and persistence on the elements of bargaining plans. *Communication Research, 18,* 306–332.

Ross, L., Greene, D., & House, P. (1977). The "false consensus effect": An egocentric bias in social perception and attribution processes. *Journal of Experimental Social Psychology, 13,* 279–301.

Rusbult, C. E. (1987). Responses to dissatisfaction in close relationships: The exit-voice-loyalty-neglect model. In D. Perlman, & S. Duck (Eds.), *Intimate relationships: Development, dynamics and deterioration* (pp. 209–237). Newbury Park, CA: Sage.

Sadler, O., & Tesser, A. (1973). Some effects of salience and time upon interpersonal hostility and attraction during social isolation. *Sociometry, 36,* 99–112.

Sattel, J. W. (1983). Men, inexpressiveness, and power. In Thorne, B., Kramarae, C., & Henley, N. (Eds.), *Language, gender and society* (pp. 118–124). Rowley, MA: Newbury House.

Scanzoni, J. (1978). *Sex roles, women's work, and marital conflict.* Lexington, MA: Lexington Books.

Schlenker, B. R., & Darby, B. W. (1981). The use of apologies in social predicaments. *Social Psychology Quarterly, 44,* 271–278.

Schweiger, D. M., & Sandberg, W. R. (1989). The utilization of individual capabilities in group approaches to strategic decision-making. *Strategic Management Journal, 10,* 31–43.

Sillars, A. (1980). Attributions and communication in roommate conflicts. *Communication Monographs, 47,* 180–200.

Slugoski, B. R., Turnbull, W. (1988). Cruel to be kind and kind to be cruel: Sarcasm, banter and social relations. *Journal of Language and Social Psychology, 7,* 101–121.

Stamp, G. H., Vangelisti, A. L., & Daly, J. A. (1992). The creation of defensiveness in social interaction. *Communication Quarterly, 40,* 177–190.

Steinmetz, S. K. (1977). *The cycle of violence: Assertive, aggressive, and abusive family interaction.* New York: Praeger.

Stutman, R. K., & Newell, S. E. (1990). Rehearsing for confrontation. *Argumentation, 4,* 185–198.

Tedeschi, J. T., Gaes, G. G., & Rivera, A. N. (1977). Aggression and the use of coercive power. *Journal of Social Issues, 33,* 101–125.

Trapp, R., & Hoff, N. (1985). A model of serial argument in interpersonal relationships. *Journal of the American Forensic Association, 22,* 1–11.

Vuchinich, S. (1986). On attenuation in verbal family conflict. *Social Psychology Quarterly, 49,* 281–293.

Vuchinich, S. (1987). Starting and stopping spontaneous family conflicts. *Journal of Marriage and the Family, 49,* 591–601.

Walton, R. E., & McKersie, R. B. (1965). *A behavioral theory of labor negotiations.* New York: McGraw-Hill.

Wilson, S. R., Meischke, H., & Kim, M. (1991). A revised analysis of directives and face: Implications for argument and negotiation. In F. H. van Eemeren, R. Grootendors, J. A. Blair, & C. A. Willard (Eds.), *Proceedings of the second international conference on argumentation* (pp. 470–480). Amsterdam, The Netherlands: ISSA.

Wolf-Smith, J. H., & LaRossa, R. (1992). After he hits her. *Family Relations, 41,* 324–329.

Chapter Seven Case Study Quiz—Conflict

Instructions:

Please read the following case study carefully and select the best answers to the questions. This quiz is an individual assignment. Remember: sharing answers is a form of plagiarism.

A young intern at a Chicago hospital is paged to diagnose and treat a patient that has been brought to the hospital emergency room. Upon his arrival to the E.R. the intern in residency finds an unresponsive older male propped up in a bed surrounded by a group of what appears to be Buddhist monks, chanting and praying at his side. He learns that the old man is an elder and teacher at a Buddhist monastery who has been traveling the U.S. as an ambassador of goodwill. After a battery of extensive testing, the intern diagnoses his patient as suffering from a case of congestive heart failure, due to an abnormally functioning heart valve. Even though the case is severe, the problem can be corrected with a good chance of a full recovery if the patient has an emergency surgery to replace the defective valve. The monks listen intently as the intern explains the procedure and gives the monks their elder's prognosis. When he is finished, the intern prepares to take the elder to surgery with the signed consent of the necessary release form. However, the other monks politely refuse to sign the consent form as any invasive surgical procedure is against their religious beliefs. Try as he might, the frustrated doctor explains that there is a chance for full recovery with this routine operation, but the monks refuse to cooperate. Both parties acknowledge that without the operation the elder monk will die. In the end, the only thing that monks will permit is the administration of a morphine drip to ease the suffering elder's pain.

Student's Name _____

Section Number _____

Section Leader's Name _____

Chapter Seven Case Study Quiz—Conflict

1. Which of the five basic issues of conflict best describes the dispute between the doctor and the group of monks?
   a. Conflict from values
   b. Conflict from beliefs
   c. Conflict about resources
   d. Conflict over the nature of the relationship
   e. Conflict due to preferences and habits

2. Which origin of conflict best explains why there is a dispute between the doctor and the monks?
   a. Conflict is likely when people are interdependent
   b. Individuals are all raised in unique social environments
   c. Conflict results from tension
   d. Conflict results from our inability to forecast the impact of our behavior on others
   e. Conflict results from our commitment to our own world view

3. In this scenario, the doctor explains to the monks that if the elder does not have surgery, he will die. In terms of effective conflict management, we can say that the doctor best utilized _____?
   a. Singular perspective
   b. Commitment
   c. Personalization
   d. Directness
   e. Hidden Linkages

4. When the frustrated doctor repeatedly tries to explain that there is a chance for full recovery with routine operation to the other monks, we can say that he is in the _____ of conflict?
   a. Pre-confrontation stage
   b. Confrontation stage
   c. Post-confrontation stage
   d. Advocacy stage

5. If situations such as the one described happen to the doctor on a regular basis, which drawback of conflict might the doctor most likely suffer from?
    a. Conflict leads to physical aggression
    b. Conflict may destroy relationships
    c. Conflict affects psychological well-being
    d. Conflict makes individuals aware of problems

Chapter Eight

APPRECIATING CULTURAL DIFFERENCES

Mary Jiang Bresnahan and Timothy R. Levine
Michigan State University

Reflections on the Abduction of Legitimate and Sparty

Earlier in this book, we read about the mysterious disappearance of the unfortunate pooch, Legitimate, and the subsequent theft of his canine replacement, Sparty. Dr. Roloff described to us the confusion, and indeed anger, that he felt when he learned that he was a victim of a neighborhood code of silence. He wondered why the neighbors hadn't told him where his dog could be found, when they knew who did it, even though he had offered a big reward for the return of his beloved, abducted dog. He used this example of canine theft to build his own case for the manner in which conflicts originate, how they play themselves out, and then either linger indefinitely or find resolution. While we totally agree with Dr. Roloff's canine abduction conspiracy theory, with due respect to Dr. Roloff, Legitimate, and Sparty, we would like to suggest a **rival hypothesis** as an explanation for the illegitimate purloining of Legitimate. A rival hypothesis is simply an alternative explanation or theory to the explanation that has already been offered by someone. In this case, Dr. Roloff explained the loss of his dogs using conflict theory. We will explain the theft of the dogs using theories of intercultural communication.

In those days, Northwest Lansing was (and still is) a typical middle-class neighborhood inhabited mostly by hard-working, blue-collar families—no university intellectuals—that is until graduate student Roloff moved into the neighborhood. So not only was there an outsider in their midst, but an outsider with different goals, definitely suspect and not to be trusted. Added to this, the newcomer had a dog—not just your typical mongrel mutt but an expensive, out-of-the-ordinary dog. A typical Northwest Lansing family would consider spending several hundred dollars on a pedigreed dog wasteful. So from their **in-group** perspective, even Dr. Roloff's dog was an **out-group** member and definitely stood out as not one of them! Clearly, the neighbors, Dr. Roloff, and his dogs were caught up in a situation of intercultural paradox. This chapter will show how the situation was a paradox involving cultural differences.

We have already explained how Dr. Roloff and his dogs were seen as outsiders. A paradox is defined as a situation where the same event has two contradictory meanings and ways of playing themselves out. The key word in this definition is **contradictory.** It asks how a person or an event can have two different identities which seem to cancel each other out. To illustrate how Dr. Roloff's story describes a cross-cultural paradox, the reader should first consider that when Legitimate was illegitimately snatched by a known neighborhood insider, everybody clammed up and wouldn't squeal on the culprit. From our birdseye view as communication analysts, we are able to interpret this neighborhood concealment of the thief as an act of in-group loyalty and solidarity against the outsider. But their persistent concealment of the thief until the bitter end, when Dr. Roloff unwittingly stumbled onto the truth, made Dr. Roloff see red. It is not so much that Northwest Lansingites were against Dr. Roloff as much as they were for each other. The bottom line is that they were not willing to hand over the thief to Dr. Roloff because the thief was one of them. In-group loyalty was the primary value. Too bad for poor Legitimate! He became an untimely statistic, the victim of perceived intercultural differences.

The second piece of the paradox puzzle is this: Sparty's abduction was a different story. Remember an important detail. We are told by Dr. Roloff that someone from a **different neighborhood** took Legitimate's replacement. This is a significant clue for understanding why the neighborhood fully assisted Dr. Roloff in tracking down the second thief. In the previous doggie theft, Dr. Roloff was seen as an outsider, but in the second he was seen as an insider. How can this be? Sure, Dr. Roloff was working on his Ph.D., but he was **their** soon-to-be Ph.D., and Sparty was their pedigree! Besides, and more importantly, no one comes in from another neighborhood and steals from their neighborhood without severe consequences. It is the unwritten law of Northwest Lansing that in-group is protected against out-group, and now Dr. Roloff and Sparty were seen as part of the in-group. They had to be protected. In-group loyalty was the primary value. Thus, Sparty was saved because of the perception of intercultural similarity. Lucky for Sparty.

The paradox that Dr. Roloff described, and which we maintain as the source of his frustration and anger, is that Dr. Roloff recognized the essential contradiction of being seen as both out-group and in-group. Often intercultural/intergroup communication possesses this paradoxical quality and presents a challenge to people to be effective intercultural communicators. Learning to deal with this challenge of communicating with people who are different from you will be the primary focus of this chapter. The chapter begins by explaining the processes at work in situations of conflict and difference between in-groups and out-groups. Intercultural communication is like a bunch of dances all happening at the same time. Sometimes they are civil and neat, but other times, the dances are wild and passionate—even terrifying! Even if you or I as individuals choose not to dance, we become involuntary participants, either swept up in the choreography and staging of the dance of our group, or in the way of someone else's dance. Like Dr. Roloff, Legitimate, and Sparty, the dance takes us up and carries us away by events not of our own making and out of our control.

This loss of control can result in **cognitive dissonance and uncertainty apprehension.** Both of these concepts will be more fully developed in this chapter. Experience demonstrates that some people have a much easier time adapting across cultures than others. They seem to have a greater facility in coping with challenging differences and in dealing with the unknown. In order to better understand the process of cross-cultural adjustment, we examine some important group concepts including ethnocentrism, stereotyping, and the role of individual attributes in adjustment such as locus of control, tolerance for ambiguity, and intercultural communicative competence. We also explore some theories about communication and culture, notably that of Hofstede (1989), and towards the end of the chapter we ask you, the reader, to apply some of these theories and concepts to understanding problems like the paradox of poor Dr. Roloff, Legitimate, and Sparty.

Dr. Roloff's story illustrates that intercultural communication is not easy. Often intercultural encounters end up leaving participants mystified and confused. Some people take the safe path of avoidance. We would like to argue that the investment to try to understand someone from another culture or another neighborhood is well worth the effort with many unanticipated rewards and only a few losses along the way. We challenge our readers to become effective intercultural communicators, but in the final analysis you must challenge yourself!

Preview of the Chapter

We begin this chapter with our own **definition of how we understand culture.** Although many definitions are possible, we have formulated a definition which we believe captures the essential features which differentiate a group of people as a culture. We hope that readers will find our definition useful and compelling in order to understand the problems that we pose for your analysis at the end of this chapter. We know that several of you reading this book have already traveled and lived abroad. We call upon you to share your experiences with the rest of the class because your experiences are very valuable in helping others to understand the kind of adjustment that is required to be a successful communicator in somebody else's country and in using someone else's communication system. Your experience provides a litmus test for the examples that we suggest in this chapter.

Following the definition of culture, we provide you with an example of a cross-cultural dilemma, which will test your problem-solving resources. Fortunately, there is a happy ending to our story, but this is not always the case. Sometimes people's experience of another culture can be very negative and dis-affirming; this is unfortunate. We hope to teach you some survival skills that will equip you with a way to begin to deal with both pleasant and problematic cross-cultural experiences. In order to do this, we present a framework for identifying some critical areas of comparison between cultures. We also walk through the steps that are part of cross-cultural adjustment.

Finally, we return to the problem that was posed at the beginning of this chapter and we point out the areas of confusion where missteps have occurred. There is a summary at the chapter's end followed by four realistic intercultural problems, which we encourage you to try to solve in small groups. These cases ask undergraduates to apply their understanding of communicative processes explained in the chapter to situations involving group and cultural differences that a beginning college student would be likely to encounter.

Our generation (Dr. Levine's and mine) has done some good things, like focusing on the environment and limiting pollution in the ecosphere, but we've also made a mess of many international situations. The world is in the hands of your generation now. It's important that you commit yourselves to respecting other people's cultures and values even if you don't agree with them.

WHAT IS CULTURE?

The word "culture" is probably one of the more overworked words in the English language. Because of its conceptual appeal, it has been appropriated across many different contexts. In a single conversation you might hear mention of people from another culture along with reference to organizational culture, counterculture, yuppie culture, the culture of poverty, and cultural diversity. All of these usages share a unitary point of reference—**a group of people with**

a sense of belonging who are in it together for the distance. More typically, the word "culture" is used to mean a group of people:

1. who believe they share common characteristics
2. who other people on the outside see as having common characteristics
3. with a common destiny
4. across several generations.

These factors suggest that there are four tests for culture—

1. the test of membership
2. the test of looking from the outside in
3. the test of common goals
4. the test of time.

How Do These Tests Work?

You have often heard it said that perceptions are everything. Culture is very much based on people's belief that they share a common culture. Even if people are different, if they believe they are the same they will gravitate toward each other. Even if people are nearly identical in their life ways, if they think they are different, then they end up being different and disliking one another. For example, subgroups in the United States, even though they do not share the same ethnic and racial affiliations and values with each other, still think of themselves as American. In contrast, although citizens of Belfast and Dublin are nearly identical except for religion and political leanings, they think of themselves as being very different from each other. So, perceptions of similarity and difference are very important for group identity.

This example describes what the **test of membership** is all about. The second test of whether something is a culture is **how outsiders view it.** If the out-group sees an in-group as a unitary whole with a shared identity, then in all likelihood that group has enough in common to be thought of as a culture. We here in the United States recognize that there are many different subgroups and ethnicities within the boundaries of our nation. But for people looking in from the outside, they see us all as Americans. Indeed, when we are challenged by another country, we rise to the occasion. We all cringed with Nancy Kerrigan, our national hope for a gold medal in figure skating, as she cried in pain and rage after she was brutally attacked by Tanya Harding's hit man. At some point, it's every American child's dream to have her or his picture on a box of Wheaties. These examples show that from the outside looking in, we share a lot in common.

Common destiny comes from factors such as common history, language, background, aspirations, time concept, gender identity, ideas about marriage, inheritance, and the family—in short, common systems of meaning. These **shared systems of meaning** are the glue which holds a group of people together. On the basis of this common ground, we can work toward mutually beneficial goals. Instead of fighting with one another, we can all pull together in the same direction and get the work of living done in peace and harmony. On a personal basis, conflicting goals, if unresolved, can ruin a significant relationship with somebody whom you once loved. Looking around the world we see the full impact of conflicting goals with hundreds of trouble spots of intergroup conflict and violence. So, the **test of common goals** is a very important identifying criterion for saying that any group of people together constitute a culture.

The **test of generations** is also an important identifier for a common culture. Culture has to be transmitted in a real way, over a long time. This is not to say that culture never changes, for surely it does. The content of culture regularly undergoes transformation. It is the sense of belonging that is the steady, stable part being transmitted, rather than the physical and conceptual artifacts of culture, which are bound to change. Challenging the sense of belonging undermines the very essence of belonging. In real life, of course this disintegration of what formerly were unitary cultures regularly happens. History is replete with examples of a formerly powerless minority group overthrowing dominant elites.

An example which comes to mind is the American Revolution. The British elite lost their power of control over the American colonists as the goals of each group became more divergent. Our definition of culture is deceptively simple. Remember four key points—**a culture is a group of people who share common values, who are seen as sharing common values by others, who have common goals, and who stick together over several generations.**

WHY STUDY CULTURE?

Are there any benefits from learning about somebody else's worldview? Let's think this through with a real example of something that could happen to you when you start your career in a few years. Imagine at the last minute you are unexpectedly asked to replace a member of your company's marketing team in the Philippines who has suddenly taken ill and who has had to come home for emergency surgery. All of the team members received pre-departure cross-cultural training and orientation to Philippine culture and they learned some survival words and phrases in Tagalog, the language spoken in Manila. They have already been there for just over two months. You get your passport, your visa for the Philippines, your ticket, and your traveling orders and that's it—no time for any orientation.

So there you are in business class with your Fodor's guide to Manila tucked in your briefcase alongside the *Wall Street Journal* and the *Far East Economic Review* hoping you'll have time for some background reading during the long flight across the Pacific. You know nothing about the Philippines except you remember that the United States had some military bases there once where your dad spent some time when he was in the navy. That's it. You have very little time for Fodor's. You spend most of the twelve-hour flight getting up to speed on the accounts that you will be handling in the Philippines.

As you feel the plane begin to reduce altitude for its descent to Manila International Airport you catch your first glimpse of the Philippine archipelago from the air—precipitous peaks and languid lagoons, lush green vegetation veiled in a smokey mist against the deep blue Pacific. It is awesome to see land. For a second you know how Magellan must have felt when, after the long voyage across the Pacific, he spied land. You shake off your long fatigue and go to the cramped little restroom to splash water on your tired face. Back in your seat the flight attendant offers you a last cup of coffee before airport approach commences. You gratefully accept. Out of the humid mists of the jungle palms and mangrove, the endless expanse of congested, concrete Manila shocks your senses. The pilot announces landing is imminent and you vaguely remember reading a news story a few years back about Benigno Aquino being shot on the tarmac here at M.I.A. when he attempted to return home. You hope someone is here to pick you up. You can't wait to shower and put on fresh clothes. You think to yourself that it'll be good to sleep flat out on a real bed.

After making your way through customs and currency exchange you enter the arrival area. No one is there to meet you. You try calling but no one answers so you decide to take the long and perilous cab ride to Manila. As you walk out of the door of the air-conditioned international terminal the suffocating heat slaps you in the nostrils. You can hardly breathe for a second. Everything smells dank and moldy. You have no idea what a typical fare to Manila should cost in the local currency, so you try to ask a police officer standing there but he speaks no English. You flip open Fodor's and get a ballpark figure for the fare, and now you feel confident about hailing a cab. It's not air-conditioned so you take off your jacket and tie, open your collar, and roll up your shirtsleeves. The driver chain-smokes and listens to Tagalog radio as you mumble your hotel destination. The driver speaks little if any English. You wonder where your friends are and why they didn't pick you up. The wild ride begins. The shocks on this cab are shot and you bounce roughly as you take in the new landscape.

After riding by pleasant-looking suburbs, the city looms in the distance. It's much more high-rise and imposing than you imagined. You exit from the highway and make your way through unbelievably snarled traffic. At every red intersection vendors, who are mostly children, weave in and out among the vehicles offering fragrant flower leis, sticks of gum, cold bottles of Miranda orange, and single cigarette sticks for sale. You wonder to yourself, "It's a weekday. Shouldn't these kids be in school?" People are everywhere and it's blistering hot. Exhaust emissions from cars, trucks, and busses clog your nostrils, sting your eyes, and cover your skin with grime. For the first time you realize what the E.P.A. has really accomplished for the environment back home and you're wondering what you're doing here in this cab at all. Finally, weary, you arrive at your hotel and check in to air-conditioned, western splendor once more. You kick off your shoes, order up a cold beer, and call your company's office in Manila. The secretary tells you that no one came to meet you because everyone's up in Baguio City at an important meeting where you're supposed to join them. The only thing is that there's a typhoon up north and the company helicopter is grounded and can't come down to Manila to pick you up. You'll have to hire a car and drive up there. Your beer arrives. You drink it greedily. It tastes good. Hmm, San Miguel—St. Michael beer, you think. You lie back on the bed and think to yourself that you'll worry about the car tomorrow after you've had some serious sleep.

In the morning, refreshed with sleep, showered, and crisp in your clean clothes, you figure out how to rent a car. You learn quickly that rental cars as we know them here in the U.S. do not exist in the Philippines. There is no Avis or Hertz. Your next tactic is to head down to the hotel desk and see if they can't arrange for you to hire a car for the long trip up to Baguio City. You explain to the desk clerk exactly what you need and he says he'll try to find a ride for you. Finally you receive assurances that such an arrangement is possible and will be seen to. With business taken care of for the time being you decide to walk around the streets of downtown Hermita, the tourist neighborhood around the hotel. You notice lots of hostess bars, noodle houses, and restaurants. Numerous people approach you and say "Hi Joe" and ask for a handout. You stop at a handicraft shop and find a lovely embroidered blouse which, being a dutiful son, you decide to buy for your mother. Dad'll be a tougher problem—maybe some cigars. You decide to return to your hotel and see when your car will be ready. You are told the car and driver will be coming before lunch, so you return to your room and pack up your belongings and ask the desk to call when your car arrives. You turn on TV and are surprised to see an episode of *Friends* in English without dubbing or subtitles. There's another channel with locally produced programming all in Tagalog.

It gets to be 1:00 and still no car. Finally around 2:00 you go down to the desk and impatiently inquire as to what has become of your car. The desk clerk looks down and says he does not know. The car never arrives. You try calling the hotel in Baguio City where your colleagues are staying but the typhoon must have knocked out the phone lines. You cannot get through. You call your company's Manila office and no one answers, except for the infernal answering machine. What to do! You are aggravated by Manila. Everything here seems to happen at a snail's pace.

You remember that one of your company's Filipino clients visited the U.S. last year. You only met him briefly, and you struggle to remember his name. Let's see: it was Hernandez—Amado V. Hernandez. You remember it because he told you he was named after an important Filipino writer and labor leader. You look in the phone directory, and sure enough, there it is. You give him a call. The maid answers in Tagalog. She speaks no English at all. You try to explain that you need to speak to Mr. Hernandez, but to no avail. Just as you are about to hang up, a young man takes the phone and inquires in English what you need. He is the college age son of your client. Mr. Hernandez comes to the phone and remembers you. You explain your predicament. He invites you to stop by his house in New Manila and says his driver will be by in about 40 minutes to pick you up. You agree, but in your heart you think this will be a supreme waste of time. Later, on the way out of the hotel, you stop at the desk and again ask the clerk to keep trying to find you a car to Baguio. The clerk again looks down and mumbles another apology and promises to find something for you. You seem to have offended him, but right now you don't care.

Hernandez's driver speaks little English but he knows who you are. He introduces himself as Centes. You shake hands and he is a bit embarrassed. He opens the back door of a silver Mercedes; you hesitate for a minute and then ask if it would be all right if you ride along in the front seat. You feel really uncomfortable and awkward being chauffeured all alone by yourself in the back seat. He does not protest, but stares at his feet. To you sitting in the backseat seems like an unfriendly thing to do. So you get in the front seat anyway. The car is cool—almost cold—with the air conditioner pumping full throttle. You drive through the thick traffic out past the facade of concrete of the tourist district into the real Manila. You are struck by the busy congestion and you begin to notice the sharp contrast between your Mercedes and the tumble down busses chock-full with people. You get off the main thoroughfare and travel through the picturesque back streets. Centes is quiet and you respect his silence.

The Hernandez house is palatial, surrounded by a huge high wall with glass chards and barbwire embedded into the top. Just as you approach the property Centes picks up his walkie-talkie and says something in Tagalog as the large wrought iron gate is thrown open. The house and property is magnificent in a sort of outdated Miami Spanish style. Several dogs run up the drive alongside your vehicle. You assume they are guard dogs as well as family pets. The maid shows you into the sala. It is an opulent mahogany room decorated with oversize furniture and a grand piano on the far end. There is a faint scent of jasmine. A maid brings you a plate of elegant little rice cakes and asks if you would prefer kapey (coffee) or tsokolatey (hot chocolate). Even though she's speaking Tagalog, you guess what she's asking and respond "Kapey." You have never tasted anything like these little rice cakes. They are exquisite. Although you are very hungry you only eat two because you don't want to make a pig of yourself.

You hear footfalls and see an elegant, trim little man coming down a grand sweeping staircase like the one in Tara from *Gone with the Wind*. Mr. Hernandez shakes your hand and welcomes you warmly. You are surprised to see that he is almost your height. You remember him from his last stateside visit. You notice he is wearing a cool-looking, lightweight embroidered white shirt. He inquires about your trip and how your accommodations are at the hotel. You start to answer just as a lovely young woman breezes into the room and kisses Hernandez's hand and then presses it against her forehead while bowing low. He introduces you to his daughter. You are struck by her beauty. As she leaves, you inquire about his family and he tells you that he has five sons and the one daughter whom you just met; she is the youngest. You say something genuine, but awkward, like "What a nice family." You remember why you are here—to ask his advice about the Baguio problem; however, the timing seems wrong and you think you might offend, so instead you ask about the house and if it has been in the family for a long time. Hernandez tells you it was built by his father after World War II when the original family home in downtown Manila was destroyed by the bombing. "What bombing?" you say to yourself. Again you are embarrassed because you recognize how little you know about this country. Suddenly, Hernandez stands up and says he must leave for another meeting on the other side of town and that his driver will take you back downtown. You begin to mouth the words of your request but he interrupts and informs you that he has arranged for someone who owes him a favor to drive you up to Baguio City tomorrow morning at 8:00. Although you hardly know him and never expected this generosity, you are relieved. You pump his hand and genuinely say, "How can I ever repay you?" He says, "Oh, it is nothing." He also promises that when you return from Baguio, he will take you out to lunch and golfing at his club. You thank him profusely again and bid each other goodbye.

The next morning on your way out of the hotel you give the desk clerk a big tip and say, "Thank you for trying to help find me a car," and he grins broadly at you and says "Thank you, Sir." At 8:05 you are on your way to Baguio. This time when the tsuper (driver) opens the door for you, you sit in the back seat without protest. You are learning.

HOW TO BEGIN UNDERSTANDING CULTURE

The "Getting to Baguio" example illustrates some of the difficulties of adjusting to life in another culture, as well as suggests some stages that a person goes through in learning to become an effective communicator in a new situation. In this chapter, we walk you through the steps of cross-cultural adaptation from pre-departure to re-entry. We also provide a basic framework which will help you to begin to understand similarities and differences across cultures.

Processes of Adjustment

Most people experience **four stages of adjustment** when they go abroad and then return home. The initial excitement of a foreign sojourn is often tempered by uncertainty. The person either recovers from **culture shock** or becomes increasingly unhappy with the situation. At this point, the person either learns to cope or returns home. Learning continues for the person who is able to tough it out until a point of **intercultural communicative competence**—being able to function fully in the new culture—is finally reached. Most people are surprised to learn that returning home often poses adjustment problems too. Scholars have studied each of these four stages of adjustment.

The initial encounter often results in what is most commonly referred to as **culture shock.** Differences in self/group orientation, time orientation, and orientation to physical distance and perception of personal space, as well as reaction to accented speech, international differences, and differences in communication styles invalidate a person's ability to accurately make predictions about how others will behave. The invalidation of our cherished stereotypes for behavior results in what Festinger (1957) has called **cognitive dissonance.** What we already know from our previous cultural experience doesn't work in the new situation and we have nothing to substitute for it. This situation forces a person to regroup and to try to figure out a new alternative. This situation can be very threatening.

Culture shock can be partially alleviated by adopting several strategies. It helps to receive **pre-departure orientation,** whether in the form of a formal training program, or whether it's simply to talk to other people who have already been there and done it to find out what to expect and what contingencies are available to resolve unexpected problems. In addition to the comfort factor, there are also many great things about another culture that you might miss if you pass up other's recommendations, which are often invaluable. Pragmatically speaking, sometimes this kind of preliminary, pre-departure fact-finding is not possible, as in an unexpected work assignment or the opportunity to travel at the last minute. Then we have to wing it as best we can and be receptive to learning because we will make many mistakes as we go. The important thing is to be able to learn from our mistakes. This leads into the next stage of cross-cultural adjustment.

Beginning to adjust to differences suggests that we have reached the point where we are able to stand back and assess how we might change our behavior to conform in the direction of our **host culture.** When people in the new culture communicate with us, they are also simplifying and changing in our direction, even if we don't realize it. They are **accommodating** their communication style to help us learn how to behave in their culture. This stage signals that we have reached a point where we are capable of self-reflective analysis and also that we have a willingness to change to the local idiom. We may still get it wrong but at least we recognize that there are differences and that what we have been doing up to this point isn't working. So we try, try, and try again until we get it right. This is what being an effective cross-cultural adaptor is all about—being respectful towards the target culture, being tolerant for the ambiguity that we are experiencing, and being aware of our own ethnocentrism.

The formal name for the theory of mutual gravitation toward the other is **Communication Accommodation Theory** (Just remember **CAT**!) as formulated by Giles (Gallois, Franklyn-Stokes, Giles, & Coupland, 1988). When we try to change our communication style in the direction of someone else's communication style, we are said to be engaging in **convergence**—making ourselves more like the other. Sometimes this backfires and one of the parties draws away and shows that he or she wants to be different and that they want to preserve the difference. This movement away from the communication style of the other is called **divergence.** For example, you yourself may criticize national politicians, but when you are abroad and someone makes an anti-American remark you rise to the defense of your country. This is an example of divergent behavior. Or maybe someone from England criticizes the way Americans talk, so you exaggerate your East Lansing accent to show him or her that it's something to be proud of. In divergent behavior, a person wants to emphasize that she or he is different from the target culture in order to reaffirm solidarity with the home culture. Although it is divisive, divergence should not be thought of as a negative practice.

Becoming an Effective Intercultural Communicator

It helps to read travel guides and to study language, history, literature, and customs of another country, and to learn theories of cross-cultural communication; however, these strategies will not cover every situation that you find yourself in when your live in another culture. **Tolerance for ambiguity** is very important when you are living abroad. You can learn to develop greater tolerance for ambiguity by starting to reserve judgments about your experience. You can begin to do this by sharpening your analytic skills so that you can recognize problems as they are happening. Reading a book such as this, is one good way to begin to do this. Once you have acquired some analytic skills, tolerance for ambiguity will kick in. You must be willing to think about your own behavior and what changes you *can* make, as well as what changes you are *willing* to make.

If eating dog is part of the traditional celebration in the country you are visiting, you don't have to eat it; but even though you are a staunch animal rights advocate in your own country, you should try to respect the custom in the host country no matter how much it repels you. You might think this to be an extreme example, but it illustrates a real test of a person's tolerance for ambiguity. Intercultural encounters regularly provide these tests of tolerance. Eventually, if you persist, you'll discover the formula that is right for you to become a competent, effective intercultural communicator. You will still make mistakes in other contexts, but at least, you're making progress. Eventually, you will figure out that you need to sit in the back seat when you're being driven to Baguio City because that's the way it's done in the Philippines. You'll learn that if dog is being served at a wedding, you don't have to eat it but you shouldn't lecture the host on cruelty to animals. Your values, while respected, don't really count here. The recognition of one's own **ethnocentrism** is a hard thing to realize, but it is an indicator of progress in adaptation.

Returning Home: Adjusting to Cultural Re-entry Shock

Up until recently, **cultural re-entry shock** was a neglected area of research investigation. Often cross-cultural sojourners are profoundly affected by their foreign experiences—so much so that when they return home, they see their home country and culture as a foreign culture where they no longer fit. This feeling of being ill at ease is often exaggerated because the people back home either fail to recognize that there has been any change in you, or they see the change and wish that the old person was back. They don't really know the new person any more and think that she or he has changed and not for the better. And so the sojourner ends up with feet planted in two different cultures no longer a part of either. We are learning that it is very important that people have an opportunity to come to terms with their cross-cultural experiences and that their experiences receive validation from sharing it with others (see Austin, 1987 and Schmidt, 1986 for more information on cultural re-entry adjustment). Not to do so is to waste a valuable resource and to assure maladjustment.

In addition to these steps that are involved in the process of cross-cultural adaptation and adjustment, there are also strategic identifiable categories where we can begin to make comparisons across cultures. These categories are "strategic" because experience from anthropological and social comparison demonstrates that they are likely to be places where cultural differences will be realized. The next part of this chapter will present a framework, which is composed of five factors including **group orientation, power orientation, uncertainty orientation, interaction orientation, and time orientation.** There are many other parts of culture that might be examined but we have intentionally selected these as being important things to try to understand about another culture. We also believe that these factors are central for acquiring some beginning level of communicative competence in the new culture.

Group Orientation

Edward T. Hall developed a theory of cultural context to systematically categorize differences that he observed across cultures. He described a continuum across cultures with two opposing anchoring points of **high context culture** and **low context culture.** What is involved in these distinctions? High context culture suggests that there is a densely layered support network of people that shores up everyone else—united we stand, divided we fall. It has also been called the "We" identity. The fate of the individual is closely linked to the good of the group. This means that individuals will often suppress their own desires in order to be able to conform to the good of the group. Not to do so would have high social costs attached to it. This is not to say that people in high context cultures have no sense of individuality, for surely they do—only that the primary goal in high context cultures is for the good of the group. High context cultures are characterized by the extended family. The obligation structure, even between distant relatives, is much more articulated. It would not be unusual for a better off relative to sponsor the schooling and provide a place to live for several distant poorer relatives from rural areas. Consensus is the preferred norm, while conflict and criticism are avoided. Japan, China, and India exemplify high-context cultures.

In a low-context culture the needs of the individual are seen as separate from the group and if forced to choose, individual needs come first. Low-context culture has also been called "I" identity. Because groups change so much in low-context societies, allegiance to the group is not as important as allegiance to self. One might bargain fiercely for one's family, but the rest of the group can easily be sacrificed because they will, in all likelihood, be moving on to a new position before long; loyalty is only to oneself and a very select group. Most people expect this to be the case and consider the overly altruistic, self-sacrificing person as a bit foolhardy, if not just outright foolish. This is not to say that there is no sense of community, for surely there is—only that individuality is the primary value in low context cultures. Debate and discussion, which challenge the norms, are welcome and regarded as healthy, even by conservatives. England, Australia, Germany, and the United States are examples of low context cultures.

Dr. Roloff's mixed experience of living in a neighborhood in Northwest Lansing illustrates some important dynamics of cultural context. The neighborhood was high-context and they placed a primary value on group loyalty. Some societies place more overall influence on loyalty to the group, while others place emphasis on the individual. At first glance this seems pretty complex. How can you tell which is which? Let's say you work very hard—harder than anyone else at your place of work—and you bring in more profits for your company, too. When raise time comes along, if you expect to receive a bigger raise than your co-workers, consider yourself to be part of a low-context culture. If everyone got the same amount you would scream "Rip-off!" and stop working so hard, or even become demoralized because your laudable efforts received no special reward. If you would say nothing if everyone received the identical raise, then you are exhibiting traits of high-context culture, sacrificing your own good for the better good of the group. This way everyone gets the same amount and no one feels bad, overly competitive, or bent on engaging in strategies of self-promotion at the expense of everyone else. If you got a big bundle of cash compared to everyone else you would be extremely embarrassed because you had been singled out for praise, and this would compromise any future relation with the group. You might even refuse to accept the big bundle of cash and ask only for the same amount as everyone else so that you wouldn't stick out like a sore thumb.

Closely related to low-context and high-context, **individualism** and **collectivism** are broadly studied social constructs which address the concept of the self with respect to others. The relationship and obligation that we have to other people is referred to as collectivism. Triandis and his associates (1988) argue that individualism results from several factors, including cultural complexity, cultural heterogeneity, affluence, social mobility, and geographic mobility. As the number of groups which exist in any given society expand, so, too, do the number of choices. Thus, people who formerly were part of the same group, tend to gravitate away from one another. The more ethnic and racial groups that comprise a society, the more people are likely to be exposed to divergent values. They may decide to adopt these new values, or at the very least, question their own values and those of their group. Affluence results in greater freedom and a greater range of choices. With more spare time, people have a chance to think about more than just survival of their families. They are free to experience many new things. Social systems, which permit movement upward, also encourage greater individualism. Finally, geographic dispersement of families forces people to rely upon themselves.

Ting-Toomey (1988) suggests that people in individualistic cultures use direct, dominating, goal-oriented **conflict styles,** while members of collective cultures tend to prefer **conflict avoidance.** If conflict occurs in collectivist cultures, then showing respect to the conflictant is preferred. Leung and Lind (1986) similarly found that North Americans preferred competitive, adversarial procedures, while collectivist cultures advocated more passive, indirect, face-sensitive conflict resolution strategies that avoid threatening one's face or public identity. Trubisky, Ting-Toomey and Lin (1991, p. 68) observed that: "On a comparative basis, members of individualist cultures tend to stress the value of straight talk and tend to verbalize overtly their individual wants and needs, while members of collectivist cultures tend to stress the values of contemplative talk and discretion in voicing one's opinions and feelings."

Power Orientation

Power distance is a relational indicator, which focuses on how powerless people deal with their status of inequality. This inequality can be based on a number of factors, including physical and mental characteristics, gender norms, social status and prestige, wealth, power, and law. Hofstede (1989) developed his power distance index by systematically asking three questions of thousands of people in forty countries: Do you fear disagreement with people who have power over you? Do you think the people who have power over you make decisions without consulting you? Do you want them to make decisions without consulting you? **Low power distance** countries value independence, loose supervision, consultative management, friendly disagreement, positive value of wealth and reward, and legitimate and expert power. **High power distance** countries value conformity; close supervision; autocratic, paternalistic managers; conflict avoidance; negative association with wealth; prefer coercive referent power; with more centralization and broader acceptance of authority. Predictably, Hofstede found that Euro-American countries tended to be low in power distance, while equatorial countries tended to be higher in power distance.

Uncertainty Orientation

Life is filled with uncertainty. There's a lot we don't know or don't understand. People are very complex creatures and even when we think that we know what they are about, they may surprise us with their behavior. New situations often create uncertainty and anxiety. We just don't know what to expect or how to behave. Often, our predictions are not supported and we feel like we are at a real disadvantage. This concept of uncertainty reduction was originally developed by Berger and Calabrese (1975) to describe monocultural initial interaction. Based on our first impressions of someone, we look for traits to support our impressions and we generalize the attributions we have made about the other to the entire person (**implicit personality theory**). If we discover that our predictions are inaccurate we experience cognitive dissonance. Gudykunst, Kim & Hammer in the early 1980s extended this theory to the study of intercultural communication. After all, the situations in which our predictions are most likely to be inaccurate are when we communicate with people from other cultures. They argue that cross-cultural communication is characterized by uncertainty.

Uncertainty is a well-documented communication construct, which examines how people deal with situations of interactional ambiguity. **High uncertainty avoidance** suggests intolerance for ambiguity, doing everything possible to prevent uncertainty. Other people are not particularly bothered by uncertainty. They consider it a way of life. Countries have been characterized by their tolerance for uncertainty and their need to have rules. In high uncertainty avoidance countries, change is seen as threatening, there is less achievement motivation, fear of failure discourages risk-taking, there are many rules that are observed, conflict is seen as undesirable, and competition is discouraged. **Low uncertainty avoidance** countries welcome change, have high personal motivation to achieve, encourage greater risk-taking, are highly pragmatic, see conflict as positive and feature high tolerance for ambiguity (Hofstede 1989, p.132–133).

Interactive Orientation

Individualist cultures are those which place value on direct or instrumental communication styles. Instrumental communication style is sender-oriented, emphasizes assertiveness, self-reliance, self-actualization, goals, and is concerned most with **negative face.** Negative face emphasizes your own autonomy, rights, and obligations, while **positive face** focuses on maintenance of social identity. Thus, it is generally seen as better to come right out and say what is on your mind rather than going through contortions of indirection, hint, and suggestion for people in individualist cultures.

The counterpart for direct style is indirect, collaborative communication style. Collaborative style includes behaviors that are nurturing, affiliative, and helpful, rather than competitive, compassionate, and conformative. Expressive tasks are preferred in the cooperative mode. Collectivist cultures do not necessarily value ambition, competition, and individual achievement in the same way that individualist cultures value such traits. Strong goal orientation and desire for material rewards may not be the primary value of communication.

Time Orientation

I (Professor Bresnahan) remember one of my college professors who had traveled extensively, and who had lived for several years in Burma and Indonesia, said that when you travel to Burma and Indonesia everything is the opposite of your expectations. I didn't believe this until I had a chance to go there myself and found it to be true. It's a good rule of thumb to expect that your predictions may be off the mark by as much as 180 degrees. This is particularly a problem when low-context and high-context individuals go to each other's cultures. Low-context culture is described as **monochronic** in its time orientation. This means that deadlines and appointments count. Think about it. If you or I go to the dentist and we are made to wait for an hour, we complain to the receptionist about the value of our time or the price of the baby sitter. We don't like to be kept waiting. Members of low-context cultures place a high value on efficiency. We like to get to the point and then relax later after the important business is done.

It's just the opposite in a **polychronic** culture. The multi-course banquet and socialization come before contracts are signed. This exchange provides an opportunity to demonstrate your level of commitment to each other, which is what the contract is all about. The actual contract itself is just a footnote to the relationship that has been agreed to in principle. Appointments and schedules are approximate. You call upon someone when you have a problem. Things get done slowly, but they do achieve closure. The pace of life is a little less hectic and maybe not quite as stressful. A person does what he or she realistically can and then turns it over to fate. It is easy for the reader to see how these two contrasting systems tend to clash.

SELF-CONSTRUALS—WHAT ARE THEY AND WHY DO WE NEED THEM?

Earlier we talked about cultural-level individualism and low-context that we contrasted with cultural-level collectivism and high-context, but there is no way for scholars to measure culture directly. All we can do is to observe people as individuals or in small groups. In response to this methodological problem, Markus and Kitayama (1991 & 1998) suggest that culture is translated to knowledge at the individual level based on a concept that they call personal self-construal. They identify two types of self-construals (independent and interdependent), and argue for the systematic influence of self-construals on how we internalize our culture. **Independent self-construal** encourages people to stress their uniqueness, autonomy, and to stand up for their own beliefs, while **interdependent self-construal** focuses on the importance of fitting in and is based on relationships with others (Cross & Madson, 1997). This is not to say that people who are independent do not value relationships with others or that people who prefer interdependence do not have a concept of their selfhood.

Problems with Self-Construal Measurement

To this point, a growing number of studies have measured culture at the individual level using the self-construal construct. The concern over the validity of self-construal was originally articulated by Matsumoto (1999). More recently, Levine et al. (2001) provided evidence from meta-analysis, priming, and measurement studies that there are major conceptual and construct validity problems with widely used self-report, self-construal measures (e.g. scales by Gudykunst et al., 1996; Kim & Leung, 1997; Singelis, 1994). Their analysis demonstrated that effect sizes are either very small, widely variant across studies in the same culture using the same measures, or are in the wrong direction from predictions. While self-construal was originally identified as consisting of two factors, Levine et al. (2000) suggested that self-construal appears to be multidimensional. Recent work by Cross, Bacon and Morris (2000) has similarly suggested that interdependence consists of at least two factors—cultural and relational interdependence.

The New Wave—Indigenous Theories

Kim, Park, and Park (2000) identify three approaches to the development of cross-cultural theory: **the universalist approach, the integrationist approach, and the indigenous approach.** The goal of the **universalist approach** is to discover universal nomothetic "laws" which govern and explain human behavior (regardless of culture). Behavioral scientists equivalently want to amass a periodic table of laws for human behavior. The **integrationist approach** attempts to test theories of behavior using local knowledge to arrive at verifiable reality. With both of these approaches if cross-cultural data is not consistent with "North American" theories of behavior, it's explained as a problem in translation, data collection, or methodology (all of which it may be), but rarely as falsification of the theory.

Indigenous theory is rooted in the culture under investigation. It is based on the belief that reliance on theories of communication which were developed in the west, specifically the United States can distort understanding of other cultures. A major difference in indigenous theory is that an inside investigator looks at behavior through the eyes of its native people. Much of the meaning of behavior cannot be directly discerned but must be inferred. Who is better to infer what behavior means than an insider from that culture?

Critics of indigenous perspectives ask whether it is reasonable to expect that every group will have its own theory of the mind. Are there any generalizations that apply widely to human behavior? Isn't it reasonable to assume there are many such generalizations and aren't these primary ones that behavioral scientists want to capture?

APPLYING THIS FRAMEWORK

Let's apply this analytic framework to the Baguio City problem and see what we get. To begin with, going "cold turkey" into another culture is always a bad idea because you place yourself at a real disadvantage. In this case it couldn't be avoided. Our visitor to Manila from East Lansing got off on the wrong foot with the desk clerk. It is expected that one give a tip in advance for such special services, as well as a tip once the service happens. The visitor should have slipped a couple of hundred pesos in an envelope and handed it inconspicuously to the desk clerk as he made his request to find someone to drive him to Baguio City. Although we generally don't think that tipping is necessary in the case of a car rental, the situation is very different in Manila. This would have provided a special incentive to the desk clerk to make every effort to find someone who could help. As it was, the desk clerk felt no special obligation to follow up on finding a ride for the foreigner. The American visitor should have realized that everything happens a bit more slowly in the Philippines. The urgency of his situation is just a bit less urgent in Manila. If he waited, eventually the desk clerk would have been able to find him a car to Baguio. Also, the more demanding foreigners, especially Americans, become, the more they are ignored by Filipinos. That's just how it is. There are historical reasons for this. So, as the visitor became more aggravated and demanding, he was roundly ignored by the hotel staff. This was apparent from the desk clerk's verbal and nonverbal behaviors.

The situation with the driver, Centes, was another matter. Centes knew that he would be criticized by the Hernandez staff when he arrived home with an important foreign visitor sitting in the front seat. He worried that perhaps this would cause him to fall out of Hernandez's favor and he needed his job to support his large family including his parents. In fact, working as Mr. Hernandez's personal driver was the best job he had ever had. Plus he felt very proud driving the silver Mercedes. It gave him real status back in the barrio. Before this job he was nothing. So Centes worried about being replaced, even though Hernandez had never even suggested this as a possibility. Of course, Centes can't say anything to the visitor, but he deeply resented being placed in this awkward position. He plans to give the Mercedes an extra special polish this weekend to try to convince Mr. Hernandez that he is a loyal, sensible, and grateful employee. That Amerikano doesn't know!

The cook at Hernandez' house was just about to lie down when the foreign visitor arrived. She ran around the kitchen to prepare a gracious merienda snack. She felt tired and dizzy as she stood over the coffee grinder preparing the rich Batangas beans for the coffee pot. After the guest had left she noticed that he only ate two of the special ricecakes that she had spent hours making. They were the hardest to make, but they were Mr. Hernandez's favorite from his province and he had been so kind to her and her children. Her daughter was going to business school because of the patronage of Mr. Hernandez. She blessed him under her breath. He had been so good to them. What a saint Mr. Hernandez was! Ingrate American, he only ate two of my prize rice cakes. He must not have liked them, she thought!

Larissa Hernandez is a high school student at Maryknoll. This is the best, most expensive, private school in Manila. Her father would do anything for her, as she is his favorite and, knows it. Everybody in the family calls her "Baby!" She was very glad her father introduced her as "Larissa" to the young stranger. He was nice, she thought. He must have just graduated from college stateside. He looks pretty young. Larissa thought what a good and generous person her dad was. He was constantly helping relatives and people in trouble like this stranger. Right now there were five relatives from the provinces living in their New Manila home helping in the family optical business in return for tuition for their schooling. Without this help they couldn't get any schooling. And there had been numerous others over the years since she was a little girl. She thought, "How right when I come into a room I kiss my father's hand and show him respect. Magmano (the showing of respect) is a good custom. I think I'll go to the kitchen and see whether Beatrice has any of her delicious rice cakes and maybe I can ask her to make me some tsokolate! I'm so hungry after school."

Hernandez thought to himself, "These helpless Americans. They're always getting themselves into trouble over here." He could hardly remember meeting this visitor back in the states. "Oh well, might as well do something to help him." He called around and found a friend who needed to make a delivery to Baguio City and who was sending his chauffeur to do it:

"Would you mind doing me a favor?" Hernandez asked.

"Of course not, Mang Amando," his friend said, "Anything for you."

"Well, there's this American who needs a ride up to Baguio."

Hernandez's friend replied, "Sayang pala—is that so! How do you know him?"

"I do business with his company from time to time," Hernandez explained.

"Of course then," his friend said.

Hernandez then explained what happened during the American's visit: "He rode here in the front seat. Poor Centes. I'll have to tell him that I understand how it is with foreigners.

He's probably worried that I'm embarrassed. Beatrice must be upset because the American ate only two of her extra special rice cakes which she makes for me. I'll have to speak to her, too. I know how hard she works to please me. I'll have to tell her how delicious they were this time and that he just didn't know what he was missing. Larissa seemed to like this young man, he thought. He sighed deeply. Sometimes it's hard to be in charge of so much with so many dependent on you. I'll call the foreigner when he gets back and introduce him around at my club. He looks like an athletic chap. Perhaps he will finally give me a challenge on my great golf game. I'll call Baguio tomorrow and see if he got there safely. Besides, I have some business with his boss."

The hotel clerk, Centes, Beatrice, Larissa, Mr. Hernandez—everyone who comes into contact with the outsider tries to accommodate. Even so, this analysis shows the ways in which these interactions are fraught with miscommunication.

Strategies for Cross-Cultural Communication

So, is there anything that we can do to better prepare ourselves not to end up being misunderstood like the example of the hapless guy from East Lansing? Are there any recommendations that can be derived from all that we have discussed in this chapter? We think there are several which immediately come to mind.

1. **As much as possible, prepare before you go.** Read as much as you can about your destination. If pre-departure training is available, take it, and be sure to talk with people who have already been there. Their recommendations will be very helpful. The more you are able to learn about your destination, the more confident you will be and you will likely experience a lower level of uncertainty. This knowledge should facilitate your cross-cultural adjustment period. If you can, be sure to study the language spoken in the destination. Even a faltering knowledge will be better than nothing.

2. **As much as possible, reserve making judgments about the way people behave in your destination country.** Some values they hold dear may be ones that you despise, but if you write them off you will become miserable. It's important to keep an open mind and to wait and see down the road.

3. **Be respectful of the other culture.** Even if you disagree with a custom, you don't have to proclaim your disagreement. As Edith Bunker would advise—Stifle! Even though they're not your customs, they are customs deserving of respect. It's important to find out what respectful behavior means in the distant culture. Don't assume that you already know.

4. **Find a trusted, insider friend who can advise you and take you under his or her wing.** This eliminates much of the trial and error. Our visitor to Manila from East Lansing might still be looking for a car without Mr. Hernandez. Cultural insiders can provide a very rich perspective on their culture and if you are at all curious, they will be pleased to educate you.

5. **Be adventurous but not at the peril of your own safety.** Remember, most big cities in every country are very dangerous. This is especially true if you are a clearly distinguishable foreigner. Be vigilant about your own safety and don't be afraid to ask about trouble spots and crime. Be smart and enjoy your time abroad!

CONCLUSIONS

This chapter began with a definition of culture and suggested four tests for saying when a collectivity could be considered a culture. Following this, a framing example for this chapter was presented—a real-life problem that the reader might be likely to encounter. The steps that are involved in cross-cultural adaptation were examined. A five-point analytic framework for cross-cultural comparison was then presented. Self-construals and indigenous theories were then discussed. Finally, the reader was guided through the original problem, this time with an explanation of some of the cultural miscommunication factors in play. In the final section of this chapter, we present you with four problems and we ask you to use what you have learned to devise solutions for these culturally sensitive situations.

REFERENCES

Austin, C. N. (1987). *Readings in cross-cultural re-entry.* Abilene, TX: ACU Press.

Berger, C. R., & Calabrese, R. J. (1975). Some explorations in initial interaction and beyond: Toward a developmental theory of interpersonal communication. *Human Communication Research, 1,* 99–112.

Bond, M., & Forgas, J. (1984). Linking person perception to behavior intention across cultures. *Journal of Cross-Cultural Psychology, 15,* 337–353.

Cross, S. E., Bacon, P. L., & Morris, M. L. (2000). The relational-interdependent self-construal and relationships. *Journal of Personality and Social Psychology, 78,* 791–808.

Festinger, L. (1957). *A theory of cognitive dissonance.* Evanston, IL: Row, Peterson.

Gallois, C., Franklyn-Stokes, A., Giles, H., & Coupland, N. (1988). Communication accommodation in intercultural encounters. In Y. Y. Kim & G. B. Gudykunst (Eds.), *Theories of intercultural communication* (pp. 157–185). Newbury Park, CA: Sage.

Gudykunst, W. B., Matsumoto, Y., Ting-Toomey, S., Nishida, T., Kim, K., & Heyman, S. (1996). The influence of cultural individualism-collectivism, self-construals, and individual values on communication styles across cultures. *Human Communication Research, 22,* 510–543.

Ho, D.Y.F.(1998). Indigenous psychologies: Asian perspectives. *Journal of Cross-Cultural Psychology, 29,* 88–103.

Hofstede, G. (1989). *Culture's consequences: International differences in work-related values.* Newbury Park: Sage.

Hui, C. H., & Villareal, M. J. (1989). Individualism-collectivism and psychological needs: Their relationships in two cultures. *Journal of Cross-Cultural Psychology, 20,* 310–323.

Kim, M. S., & Leung, T. (1997). *A revised version of self-construal.* Manuscript, University of Hawaii.

Kim, U., Park, Y. S., & Park, D. (2000). The challenge of cross-cultural psychology. *Journal of Cross-Cultural Psychology, 31,* 63–75.

Lapinski, M. K., & Levine, T. R. (2000). Culture and information manipulation theory: The effects of self construal and locus of benefit on information manipulation. *Communication Studies, 51,* 55–73.

Leung, K., & Lind, E. A. (1986). Procedure and culture: Effects of culture, gender, and investigator status on procedural preferences. *Journal of Personality and Social Psychology, 50,* 1134–1140.

Levine, T. R., Bresnahan, M. J., Park, H. S., Lapinski, M. K., & Wittenbaum, G. M. (2001). *Self-construal scales lack validity.* Paper presented at the annual meeting of the International Communication Association, May 2001, Washington, D.C.

Matsumodo, D. (1999). Culture and self: An empirical assessment of Markus and Kitayama's theory of independent and interdependent self-construals. *Asian Journal of Social Psychology, 2,* 289–310.

Sanders, J. A., & Wiseman, R. L. (1991). *Uncertainty reduction among ethnicities in the United States.* Paper presented at the 1991 meeting of the International Communication Association, Chicago.

Singelis, T. M. (1994). The measurement of independent and interdependent self-construals. *Personality and Social Psychology Bulletin, 20,* 580–591.

Ting-Toomey, S. (1985). Toward a theory of conflict and culture. In Gudykunst, Stewart & Ting-Toomey (Eds.), *Communication, culture and organizational processes* (pp. 71–86). Newbury Park, CA: Sage.

Triandis, H. C., Bontempo, R., Villareal, J. Asai, M., & Lucca, N. (1988). Individualism and collectivism: Cross-cultural perspectives on self-in-group relationships. *Journal of Personality and Social Psychology, 54,* 323–338.

Triandis, H. C., Leung, K., Villareal, M. J., & Clark, F. L. (1985). Allocentric vs. idiocentric tendencies: Convergent and discriminant validation. *Journal of Research in Personality, 19,* 349–415.

Trubisky, P. Ting-Toomey, S., & Lin, S. (1991). The influence of individualism- collectivism and self-monitoring on conflict styles. *International Journal of Intercultural Relations, 15,* 65–83.

APPLICATIONS

Problem 1

You just got a job working with the overseas study office. Your first assignment is to conduct a workshop for 20 American students who are returning from a year of study in China. Why is this workshop important? What would you hope to accomplish in this workshop?

Problem 2

Your department has asked you to be an undergraduate teaching assistant in a section of a course in your major taught by an international teaching assistant who is having a hard time being understood and dealing with student questions. Many of the undergraduates respond to his difficulty by being rude, disorderly, and inattentive. What would you do to help the ITA?

Problem 3

A bulletin board in your dorm lists meetings and activities for minority groups including African-Americans, Hispanic Americans, Asian Americans, and Native-Americans. Someone anonymously posts a sign on the bulletin board, which reads "Equal time for White Americans!" Why is this a problem for everyone living in your dorm?

Problem 4

You are the manager of customer relations at a large pharmaceutical company that also makes pacemakers. You have been very fortunate to hire three foreign-born cardiac surgeons who still haven't got their U.S. licenses to practice medicine in the U.S. They are handling customer service on the phone. They have all done pacemaker implantation and are very well acquainted with some of the things that could go wrong. You feel lucky to have hired such well-qualified people for such a low price. Although they are extremely well informed, the problem is their accents. Most of your pacemakers customers are older. When they call your company with a problem, many have experienced difficulty understanding the accented English of the doctors. There have been many complaints. Your boss asks you to find a solution for this problem. What would you do?

QUESTIONS FOR THOUGHT AND DISCUSSION

1. What rival hypothesis do the authors offer to explain the theft of Dr. Roloff's dogs? Have you ever found yourself in a situation like the one that Dr. Roloff found himself in, where people were reluctant to help you though they had the information?

2. How can culture be described as a dance? What other metaphors do you think would be appropriate for describing culture?

3. How can intercultural communication contribute to cognitive dissonance and uncertainty apprehension?

4. What four features of culture are identified by the authors? Can you explain how each of these features contribute to their definition of culture? What four tests are suggested to identify a group of people as a culture?

5. What four stages of cross-cultural adjustment are identified by the authors? Have you ever experienced any of these?

6. What are some ways in which you can accommodate your communication style when you talk to a person from another country?

7. How is convergence different from divergence? What positive meanings does divergence convey?

8. Why is tolerance for ambiguity important in cross-cultural adaptation? Can you provide any personal examples of how this works?

9. What is cultural re-entry shock? How is it different from what is meant by culture shock?

10. What is meant by cultural context? How is high-context different from low-context and what are the implications of these differences?

11. Who would be more likely to believe that silence is golden—an individualist or a collectivist—and why might this be the case?

12. What three indicators did Hofstede use to determine perceptions of power distance?

13. Does your family use low or high power distance? Why?

14. Are you personally more monochromic or polychronic? Have you ever visited another country and observed time differences? Can you describe some of these differences? How did they make you feel?

15. What are some problems which affect self-construal measurement? Why is this an important issue for research?

16. What three approaches to cross-cultural theory are identified by Kim et al.?

17. What kinds of pre-departure preparation help in cross-cultural adaptation?

Chapter Eight Case Study Quiz—Culture

Instructions:
Please read the following case study carefully and select the best answer to the questions. This quiz is an individual assignment. Remember: sharing answers is a form of plagiarism.

Twenty-Five year old Maria arrived in Raleigh, North Carolina to attend the University of North Carolina after living in Mexico her entire life. She speaks Spanish and English, but has trouble understanding some English translations. Her parents were unhappy that Maria decided to attend a university so far away from home, in a culture different then their own and because it seemed as if Maria was separating herself from her family. In Raleigh, Maria found herself challenged in different areas including her class work, making friends, getting to know the southern culture, and improving her English. During the first three months in Raleigh, Maria became depressed and her family back in Mexico believed a trip home would lift her spirits. Her family also secretly hoped she would stay in Mexico, but Maria went back to school. After returning to Raleigh after winter break, it was clear Maria's depression had not improved so she made an appointment to meet a doctor. The American, English-speaking doctor carefully examined Maria and tentatively diagnosed her as bipolar. To relieve the symptoms of the bipolar disorder, the doctor prescribed Lithium to Maria. The doctor did not clarify the prescription as they assumed Maria would understand the directions because she spoke English. The prescription was labeled "ONCE," indicating that Maria should take the Lithium once a day. However, Maria received her prescription and read "ONCE" on the bottle. In Spanish, "ONCE" means "eleven." Maria ended up taking ten times the amount of Lithium prescribed by the doctor! After becoming sick due to dosage she had been taking, she returned to the doctor who discovered the mistake. Sick and embarrassed, Maria decided to take the rest of the semester off and returned home to stay with her family. Upon returning to Mexico, Maria discovered she missed her freedom of living on her own in Raleigh and found it difficult to reconnect with her Mexican friends. Her medical condition continued to worsen, as she did not feel comfortable in either North Carolina or Mexico.

Student's Name _____

Section Number _____

Section Leader's Name _____

Chapter Eight Case Study Quiz—Culture

1. According to what test of culture explains why the American doctor did not clarify the "ONCE a day" dosage of the Lithium prescription?
    a. Test of membership
    b. Test of looking from the outside in
    c. Test of common goals
    d. Test of time

2. Maria's parents did not want her attending school in America. Which of the following concepts would reflect WHY they did not want Maria to leave home?
    a. America has low power distance
    b. America would cause divergence in Maria
    c. America has high power distance
    d. America would cause interdependent self-construal in Maria

3. During which following event did it become clear that Maria did not experience intercultural communicative competence in America?
    a. Maria returned to Mexico permanently
    b. Maria was challenged by her class work and making friends
    c. Maria did not inquire about her prescription and misunderstood the translation of the dosage
    d. Maria became depressed

4. What strategy could Maria have employed to create a more positive experience traveling outside of Mexico?
    a. Been respectful of American culture
    b. Prepared for the trip prior to departing
    c. Found a trusted friend to advise her
    d. Reserved making judgments about America

5. What stage of cultural adaptation did Maria NOT experience?
    a. Frustration
    b. Readjustment
    c. Honeymoon
    d. Resolution

Case Study **183**

Chapter Nine

PERSUASION

Deborah A. Cai and Edward L. Fink
University of Maryland

On a hot, sultry summer afternoon, twelve jurors are sent into a small room to determine the fate of a young man accused of murdering his father. In the center of the room is a long table with twelve chairs positioned around it. There's no air-conditioning, and the one and only fan doesn't even work. Each of the twelve people has somewhere he or she would rather be than in this hot room.

Once settled in their chairs, the jurors are asked to state their initial verdict. One by one, they each speak. For eleven of the jurors, the verdict is clear: guilty. One lone man (call him Juror A) supports a verdict of not guilty, much to the dismay of the other eleven. "Why?" they ask. They argue with him. If he would only agree with the rest of them they could all go home and have this whole thing over with. Several have jobs they would like to get back to, one is retired and would just like to go home, and another could still make it to a baseball game for which he has tickets. Why would one man keep the rest of them from getting out of there? They have all heard the same arguments, the evidence was there, and the overwhelming majority all agreed that the young man was guilty. Why would Juror A stand alone and keep the rest from having this job done and over with?

Juror A speaks. He explains that it's not simple to send a young man to the electric chair. Maybe the young man is guilty, but at least some discussion should go into the decision. And he's just not sure about the evidence.

"Come on!" the others say. But Juror A holds firm. Then, as he begins to present the questions that he has about the evidence, about motive, and about the justice of the trial, one by one the jurors begin to change their minds and turn away from their initial view. One turns simply because Juror A stood firm and with conviction, so the juror felt the lone man deserved some support. Another turns based on logical arguments about the case. Another seems to turn because Juror A is kind to him, showing the juror respect for his opinions even while the remaining jurors begin to belittle him, perhaps because the heat is causing their tempers to flare. Another juror turns because he begins to identify with the defendant and is thus able to see flaws in the prosecution's arguments. And another turns because so many have turned, that it's simply expedient to vote "not guilty"; it will make this whole thing end sooner if she goes along with the new majority.

Some of the jurors' opinions are fairly easy to sway; others hold firmly to their initial conviction that the defendant is guilty; they are very difficult to persuade. But in the end, all twelve finally agree. There is not enough evidence to convict the young man. Every one of the twelve jurors votes "not guilty."

This vignette is based on the movie *Twelve Angry Men* (Rose, Fonda, & Lumet, 1990; original film, 1957), starring Henry Fonda as the lone man—our Juror A—who eventually sways the verdict of the remaining eleven jurors. It is a classic black-and-white film, which provides an excellent and still up-to-date look at the processes of persuasion.

DEFINING PERSUASION

Persuasion is communication that is intentionally aimed at changing the attitudes, beliefs, or behaviors of another person or persons. There are several features of this definition that help us to understand what persuasion is and what it is not.

1. **Persuasion is social, involving two or more people or parties.** It is the attempt by one person or party to bring about change in another person or group of people. In *Twelve Angry Men*, the lone man and the other eleven jurors are each trying to change the others' opinions.

2. **Persuasion is intentional.** For persuasion to occur, there needs to be intent on the part of the sender to bring about change on the part of the receiver. Intent means that the sender has, as a purpose, the modification of the others' attitudes, behaviors, or beliefs. The lone juror (Juror A) wanted the other jurors to simply think about their decisions, which would be a change in their behavior. The eleven other jurors wanted to have the lone juror (Juror A) switch his verdict completely, a change in belief (if he were convinced the guilty verdict were correct), or perhaps a change in behavior unaccompanied by a change in belief. The desire on each party's part to bring about change was intentional, not accidental.

   When there is no intent to persuade on the part of the sender but change occurs in the receiver, then the receiver is unintentionally influenced, but not persuaded. For example, if you really admire your professor's teaching style and personality, and therefore decide to go on to graduate school and become a professor, then you have been influenced by that professor. But if the professor sits you down and tells you all the many reasons why you would do well to become a professor, with the intent to convince you to at least consider going to graduate school, that communication is an example of persuasion.

3. **Persuasion involves some amount of choice and interpretation on the part of the persuader.** When persuasion occurs, the receiver can choose, at least to some degree, whether to conform to the persuasive message or not. In *Twelve Angry Men*, the lone juror chose not to go along with the other eleven, even when they argued with him. In the end, the eleven jurors all changed their votes about the verdict from guilty to not guilty. Although there were very different reasons for each one changing, they did so of their own volition.

   Sometimes the amount of choice may not be very obvious. Coercion occurs when a person is placed under great duress to behave in a certain way. For example, during "Desert Storm," the war against Iraq, some captured pilots issued statements against the U.S. military action. However, these statements were not taken seriously by the U.S. government because it was clear that the pilots were threatened with harm if they did not do as they were told. Note, however, that in these cases the pilots had to interpret the threat as real, and weigh the costs of complying against the costs of not doing so. Thus, coercion is an example of behavioral change under extreme circumstances, but it nonetheless involves persuasion.

4. **Persuasion is an attempt to form, reinforce, or convert (change) a receiver's attitudes, beliefs, and/or behaviors.** Although persuasion is often thought of as trying to change the mind of the receiver, there are actually three possible goals for persuasion. **Conversion,** or the changing of a receiver's current attitude, belief, or behavior to another, is only one of the three possible goals. Commercials that try to get you to switch from one long distance company to another are examples of conversion attempts. A second goal of persuasion is to **reinforce,** or to strengthen an existing attitude, belief, or behavior. AT&T commercials often target current customers, telling them how glad they should be that they have remained loyal to AT&T because so many people are switching back. This type of advertisement is aimed at reinforcing current customers to continue using AT&T, and to resist switching.

A third goal of persuasion is to **form or shape** an attitude, belief, or behavior that a receiver has not previously had. Children often do not have opinions of their own about smoking or drugs. As a result, parents and teachers may spend a lot of time trying to shape children's views about these topics. If children do not currently hold beliefs about smoking or drugs, the persuasion attempt creates and shapes new beliefs.

Now that we have a definition of persuasion and understand the components of the definition, we can look at how attitudes, beliefs, and behaviors are modified through persuasion.

RELATIONSHIPS AMONG ATTITUDES, BELIEFS, AND BEHAVIORS

Attitudes are a person's general affective response, or feelings, about an object, person, idea, or action. In *Twelve Angry Men,* Juror A did not initially hold strong attitudes about the defendant, but he disliked the process that simply characterized the young man as guilty. He wanted to modify the attitudes of the other jurors by making them feel bad about acting without due care.

Beliefs are a person's estimates of probability that an object, person, idea, or action, possesses a particular attribute, or that a claim about an object, person, idea, or action is true or false. For example, most of the jurors initially claimed that the defendant was guilty. Juror A's belief was not very certain about the defendant—maybe he was guilty, maybe he was not; his purpose was to modify the certainty of belief of the remaining jurors.

Behaviors are actions that people do or perform that can be interpreted by one's self and/or by others as revealing something about the person who is behaving. The behavior in question in *Twelve Angry Men* was the vote indicating the juror's sense of the defendant's guilt or innocence. Such a vote is viewed as revealing the underlying belief each person has about the accused. Eleven jurors voted guilty although Juror A voted not guilty. If the eleven jurors could change the behavior of Juror A, they could all go home. But if the lone juror could modify the behavior of the remaining eleven by getting them to wait before voting and to consider carefully the evidence one more time, he would feel justice was done.

What is the relationship between attitudes, beliefs, and behaviors? For example, do attitudes affect behaviors or do behaviors affect attitudes? How attitudes, beliefs, and behaviors affect each other forms the basis of much research concerning persuasion.

It makes a lot of sense to say that attitudes and beliefs cause behavior: We try to avoid people we don't like; we don't buy products that we believe are inferior. These show examples of how our attitudes and beliefs can affect our behavior.

On the other hand, sometimes our actions cause us to change our beliefs and attitudes. We were required to take a communication course, though perhaps we didn't like the idea and thought the course wouldn't do us much good. Now we find (it is hoped) that the subject is enjoyable (attitude change), and that we think it will eventually help us do well in our career (belief change).

Do all behaviors affect our attitudes and beliefs? To answer this question, we need to know what the relevant attitudes and beliefs are. For example, when Mark Twain's Tom Sawyer (in the novel of the same name; Twain, 1959) was whitewashing the fence, he obviously found the task to be a chore. When he recruited other boys to do it for him, they became convinced that the chore was enjoyable. Part of their attitude was the result of being persuaded by Tom Sawyer, but part of it was probably the result of their having to justify their own behavior: They saw themselves voluntarily engaging in an otherwise onerous task, and came to believe that the task must be fun.

Did Tom Sawyer experience any attitude or belief change as a result of his behavior? Perhaps he became convinced that he was a good persuader (an example of belief change), and that he liked tricking others (an attitude change).

When we view our behavior as not revealing the "real" us, then behaviors should play a limited role in affecting our attitudes and beliefs. When we view our behaviors as indicating something about ourselves, then behaviors should cause change or formation of attitudes and beliefs.

Consistency theories are based on the assumption that people want their attitudes to be consistent with their behaviors. These theories posit that when people are aware that their attitudes and behaviors are inconsistent, they feel uncomfortable and try to restore consistency by changing either the behavior or the attitude.

Balance Theory

Balance theory (Heider, 1958) proposes that people strive to maintain balance in their attitudes toward other people and objects. Simply stated, balance theory suggests that we tend to agree with people we like and disagree with people we dislike. We have attitudes toward people with whom we have contact, such as friends, professors, parents, and even political figures we are aware of through the mass media. To varying degrees we like (or dislike) these people. Similarly, we have attitudes toward objects. Heider suggests that we have a need to maintain balance between attitudes toward people and objects. Balance is a stress-free state of mind, whereas being unbalanced is stressful.

Balance comes about when we perceive that people we like, like what we like, and people we dislike, dislike what we like or like what we dislike. For example, say you have a very good friend who really likes watching *NYPD Blue,* but you really can't stand

TABLE 9.1 Illustration of Balanced vs. Imbalanced Relationships

	Self to Other	Self to NYPD Blue	Other to NYPD Blue	Relationship
1	+	+	+	Balanced
2	+	+	—	Imbalanced
3	+	—	+	Imbalanced
4	+	—	—	Balanced
5	—	+	+	Imbalanced
6	—	+	—	Balanced
7	—	—	+	Balanced
8	—	—	—	Imbalanced

+ = Like   — = Dislike

watching that show. Heider's balance theory would say that you would be in a state of imbalance—you like your friend, your friend likes *NYPD Blue*, but you do not like *NYPD Blue*. You have some choices that you can make to restore balance. For example, you could end your friendship, figuring if this person has such bad taste in television shows you couldn't possibly be friends. You could learn to like *NYPD Blue*; after all, your friend likes it so there must be something good about it. You could try to persuade your friend as to why *NYPD Blue* is not a good show and eventually get your friend to agree that it's not that good. In any case, balance theory would suggest that you have a need for balance in your attitudes relating you, the object, and the other person; otherwise, you will feel discomfort.

As another example, say that you can't stand the person who lives next door to you, but you find out that this person is a staunch supporter of the same politician for whom you volunteer every week. You think this politician is really great, too. Balance theory says that you will experience some discomfort from this situation—you really dislike your neighbor, you really like the politician, but your neighbor really likes this politician also. You need to resolve this imbalance. One possible solution is to decide your neighbor isn't so bad; after all, this person has good enough judgment to have the right political views. On the other hand, you could decide that you don't like the politician anymore; if dingbats like your neighbor like him, then he must not be so great. Or perhaps you could try to deny your neighbor's attitude toward the politician and figure that your neighbor is just too stupid to know that he's really for the other party. In any case, balance theory suggests that you need to restore a stress-free state between you, your perception of your neighbor, and the attitudes you and your neighbor hold toward the politician.

In *Twelve Angry Men*, one juror (call him Juror B) initially votes guilty, but he is demeaned by his fellow jurors. Only two people in the room treat him with any respect—Juror A and another juror who is the first juror to change positions. According to Heider's balance theory, Juror B comes to like, or feel liked by, the lone juror (Juror A). The lone juror's initial verdict is not guilty, whereas Juror B's initial verdict is guilty. This situation should cause Juror B to experience psychological imbalance. This imbalance is also present in his relations with the other jurors. Juror B dislikes the other jurors, but they hold to a guilty verdict just as he does. The easiest way to restore balance in both of these cases is for Juror B to switch his verdict to not guilty. By doing so, he restores balance in two ways: He agrees with those he likes, and disagrees with those he dislikes.

Cognitive Dissonance

The theory of **cognitive dissonance** (Festinger, 1957) relates to Heider's balance theory in that it proposes that people want to reduce inconsistency; however, the theory of cognitive dissonance has broader application than balance theory. The theory of cognitive dissonance deals with cognitions that we have. Cognitions are beliefs, opinions, attitudes, or knowledge that we have about a person, place, object, or issue. Festinger suggested that cognitions can be related in three ways: they can be irrelevant to each other, consonant, or dissonant.

Irrelevant cognitions are two thoughts (in the form of grammatical clauses) that are unrelated. For example, "I have a really great dog!" and "I am worried about the test I have to take tomorrow" are, for all practical purposes, unrelated to each other. **Consonant cognitions** are two thoughts or opinions that are consistent with each other. For example, "I stayed up too late last night," and "I'm too tired to study for my test tomorrow!" are consonant because one is consistent with or follows from the other. Dissonant cognitions, however, are two cognitions that are inconsistent with each other. For example, "I oppose cruelty to animals" and "I love to go hunting" are views that seem inconsistent with each other.

Dissonance creates psychological tension and motivates individuals to reduce the dissonance. For example, in *Twelve Angry Men,* one of the jurors (Juror C) says pridefully that he is a very fair and reasonable man. Yet, near the end of the story, even though much of the original evidence against the defendant has been shown to be inaccurate or insufficient, Juror C still holds to his original verdict. Another juror then points out to Juror C that if he were truly fair and reasonable, he would accept the new evidence and change his verdict. In this case, it has been made clear that Juror C is inconsistent: Juror C says he is fair and reasonable, yet he rejects the more reasonable evidence.

Once someone experiences dissonance, the tension brought about by the dissonance should motivate the person to reduce it. There are several ways by which this can be done. One way of managing dissonance is through **selective exposure,** that is, by avoiding information that may increase dissonance. Juror C could have walked away while the others pointed out flaws in the existing evidence. He thus could have simply avoided additional information that would cause him to feel that he was being unreasonable. Another way to reduce dissonance would be to justify holding on to one's original position. In this case, Juror C would have to think of sufficient reasons for not changing his verdict. Although Festinger's theory does not predict exactly how a person will reduce dissonance, the theory does predict that dissonance will be reduced in the easiest possible way. In the case of Juror C, the easiest way to reduce dissonance is for him was to simply change his verdict, which is just what he is portrayed as doing in the film.

Both balance theory and the theory of cognitive dissonance show us how our behavior can influence our beliefs and attitudes.

PERSUASION WITHOUT THOUGHT

Often we are not aware of what it is that makes something persuasive. In fact, as receivers of a great many persuasive messages, we often are cognitively "lazy" and are persuaded by information unrelated to the quality of evidence or arguments found in a message. Have we ever been influenced by:

- A beautiful woman in a tight dress in a commercial for a car?
- A picture of a sunset over a quiet ocean behind a bottle of wine, in an advertisement for the wine?
- Canned laughter in a situation comedy?

These images and sounds are often more persuasive than any verbal message because we may be less likely to fully process the nonverbal message; we may mindlessly respond to these not-so-relevant cues, without having been motivated to consider the message critically. In this section we will focus on influences of which we may be unaware.

Source Effects

Sometimes the source of a message may affect our acceptance of a message in ways of which we are unaware. What makes a speaker or a source persuasive? There are many things about a source that can make the source even more persuasive than we may realize. For example, if we were to rank George W. Bush, Oprah Winfrey, Tiger Woods, Christopher Reeves, and Reese Witherspoon according to how persuasive they are, we would each probably rank them in different orders based on different criteria.

The extent to which a source is generally perceived to be persuasive is the source's **credibility.** Credibility is based on the receiver's perceptions of how believable the source is; it is not an intrinsic property of the communicator. Because credibility is based on perceptions of believability, a source may be viewed as highly credible by one person, yet not at all credible by another. Sources commonly viewed as credible are more persuasive than sources who are commonly seen as having low credibility.

In persuasion research, credibility is generally considered to consist of three components. The first component is the **competence** of the source. Does the source know what he or she is talking about? Does the source have the credentials to be promoting a position? Is the source in a position to know the truth and to know what is right and correct? Does the source seem knowledgeable and able to discuss the message position well?

The second component is the **trustworthiness** of the source. Is the source sincere or does the source personally benefit from advocating the position in the source's message? Is the source known to be generally honest? Is the source of good character?

The third component is the **likeability** of the source. Is the source someone you can relate to? Is the source similar to you?

Around 500 B.C., Aristotle described these three components of speaker credibility. In his terms, **logos** has to do with the competence or expertise of the source. At least initially after a persuasive message or speech, the greater the perceived expertise of a source, the greater the amount of attitude change.

Aristotle also recognized that the **ethos** (trustworthiness) of the source is important for the source to be persuasive. Generally, receivers tend to discount messages from sources who are not trustworthy.

The third component is **pathos,** or dynamism. The more dynamic, or appealing, a source is, the more attention the source gains. This attention is one reason why supermodels and famous movie stars are so popular in advertising.

Based on competence and trustworthiness, Eagly, Wood, and Chaiken (1978) proposed two types of bias that impede source credibility. A **knowledge bias** occurs when a receiver believes that the source's knowledge about the subject doesn't reflect the true state of affairs. In other words, the source is believed to have limited knowledge that would result in a biased description or message. For example, suppose a friend of yours, not known for great knowledge about cars, recommends that you buy a Swedish car. If you know that your friend generally likes Swedish things, and has really very little information about cars, you are likely to believe that your friend's recommendation is biased, because it may reflect more about your friend's favorability toward Swedish things than about any car sense. On the other hand, you wouldn't think that your friend is purposely trying to deceive you with this recommendation.

A second type of bias is a **reporting bias.** This bias occurs when you consider the source to be less than trustworthy. For example, if a car salesperson who happens to sell Volvos and Saabs recommends that you buy a Swedish car, you may believe that message is biased, because the source has a stake in the outcome: The recommendation may reflect more about earning a commission than about what is the best car for you.

If a receiver believes that there are knowledge or reporting biases in the messages provided by the message source, then the receiver is not likely to adopt the position advocated by the source.

Mere Exposure

Robert Zajonc (1980) discussed another way in which information may affect us without our being aware of it. The mere exposure hypothesis is the idea that the more we are exposed to a stimulus, the more we wind up liking the stimulus. Recent research regarding the mere exposure hypothesis has examined the impact of stimuli presented in ways such that the perceiver is unable to report perceiving the stimuli. For example, imagine being shown a picture of a face for a few milliseconds (thousandths of a second). Under these circumstances, you would be unable to report having seen the picture. Nevertheless, if you are subsequently asked to rate how much you like the picture, the evidence is that you rate it higher (like it more) than if you were not exposed to it previously.

What does this mean for persuasion? Our liking for many things in our environment has been affected by our exposure to them over prolonged periods of time. Over our lives we see, hear, taste, smell, and touch many different stimuli. However much we believe that we control our feelings, it seems that there are forces that affect our responses that we do not control. As a consequence, changing someone's attitude requires understanding that there may be a non-conscious basis for them.

Learning and Reinforcement

Attitudes and behaviors are shaped by conditioning processes. There are three kinds of conditioning that have been studied for their effects on learning and persuasion. The first, **instrumental (or operant) learning,** takes place when our actions bring about a change—positive or negative—in our environment. If we study and then get a good grade, we may learn to study: The positive outcome (the good grade) reinforces the behavior (studying). Similarly, negative outcomes cause us to lessen the behavior that is associated with it. If every time we ask for a date we're turned down, we may stop asking for dates. Instrumental learning may be used to mold behavior by providing positive reinforcements for behaviors that we like in others, and negative reinforcements for those that we do not like. However, negative reinforcement is a little more complicated, because, if the recipient of negative reinforcement is not required to remain in the situation, the recipient may leave rather than reduce or eliminate the behavior that is negatively reinforced.

Instrumental Learning:
Behavior——> Outcome——> Future behavior

A second type of learning is called **observational learning.** We can be affected by observing the behavior of others (behavioral models), and seeing how this behavior is positively or negatively reinforced. Observational learning helps explain how children can learn to act violently by seeing models of violence in the movies or on television. For example, many television shows depict people who are liked, praised, and benefited from engaging in violent acts. A child seeing this behavior may come to engage in violent behavior. Research by Albert Bandura (1977) provides evidence for the effectiveness of observational learning.

Observational Learning:
Model's behavior——> Model's outcome——> Own future behavior

A third type of learning is **classical conditioning.** If a neutral stimulus (e.g., a word) becomes associated with a positive stimulus (e.g., a pleasant smell), we learn to respond positively to the (previously) neutral stimulus. This idea was demonstrated with dogs by Pavlov (1927) and others (e.g., Staats & Staats, 1958) have demonstrated this type of reinforcement with people. The implications for persuasion here are straightforward: Advertisers regularly associate their products (neutral stimuli) with fun, sex, good food, etc., so that we consider their products positively.

Classical Conditioning:
X (neutral stimulus) + Positive [negative] stimulus——> X (positive [negative] stimulus)

INFLUENCE IN GROUPS

Within groups, the pressure to conform can be quite great. As discussed in the chapter on socialization, we all need to be a part of groups and need to feel accepted by others. At times, however, the need to be accepted can result in taking on the attitudes, beliefs, and behaviors of the group members without considering whether doing so is a good idea.

In a classic study on **group conformity** by Solomon Asch (1956), participants were presented with three lines and asked to judge which of the lines matched a fourth line in length. The study was conducted in a group setting, where all but one of the participants were confederates, or people working for the experimenter. The only real participant was the last person to answer. One by one, the members of the group answered that the same wrong line matched the fourth line. Results showed that most of the participants were influenced by the group and conformed to the majority opinion. Only about one-fourth of the participants were not so obviously influenced by the group.

Contagion is another form of group influence that has a potentially powerful effect. Group contagion occurs when individuals behave within a group in a way that would be unlikely if they were not in the group. For example, people are unlikely to stand up in the middle of an auditorium, throw their arms up in the air, and sit back down on their own initiative. But when the "wave" comes around the football stadium, people conform. Within a group, individuals become uninhibited and follow the lead of others. Contagion can cause harmless behavior like the wave, as well as violent behavior such as we saw in the rioting following the Rodney King verdict or some Italian soccer matches.

Consider the consequences of group conformity as found in *Twelve Angry Men*. If Juror A had gone along with the group, the defendant would have gone to the electric chair. In the end, all of the jurors rethought their positions and changed their minds. Most of them based their change of mind on new evidence, as well as on the realization that the initial information was inadequate for making a decision. The fact that Juror A chose not to conform saved an innocent life.

PERSUASIVE MESSAGES

Much of what we think about persuasion has to do with persuasive messages and what makes them effective. This section will look at some of the attributes of persuasive messages: What makes different messages more or less persuasive?

Aristotle's Appeals of Reason

Aristotle proposed three types of reasoning that can be used to persuade. The first type is to **reason from cause.** This type of reasoning attributes a given effect to some particular cause in an attempt to persuade. For example, we might argue that there is an increase in speeding on the highways because of having lifted the 55-mile-per-hour speed limit. The cause in this case would be lifting the previous limit, and the effect is an increase in speeding. The caution about this type of reasoning is that our sense of causal direction may be uncertain or wrong. For instance, at the turn of the century Americans were concerned that the intelligence of recent immigrants was lower than the intelligence of immigrants who had already been in the United States for longer periods of time. Many Americans concluded that the more recent the immigration, the more stupid the immigrants. With this evidence they campaigned to end immigration. However, we now know that the reasoning here was faulty: It wasn't that newer immigrants were less intelligent; rather, older immigrants were here longer, and therefore learned the American language and American culture, and thus were able to do better on intelligence tests. Nevertheless, some might say that, although the causal analysis was faulty, the messages about immigration were successful. Reasoning from cause may be effective, even when the causal analysis is wrong.

Another type of reasoning is **reasoning from sign.** This type of reasoning takes one event as evidence of another event, without explaining how the evidence and conclusion are related. In other words, if you look out and see that it is snowing, you may argue that it is winter. You need not explain why snow is necessarily evidence of winter. Another example is proposing that someone important must have died because the U.S. flag is flown at half mast. The flag is the evidence; the conclusion is that someone important died, but it is not necessary to explain how the federal codes that dictate that the flag's position is related to this conclusion.

The third type of reasoning is **reasoning from analogy.** This type of reasoning claims that two things are so alike that what is true for one is true for the other. For example, some Americans argued against the Gulf War, saying it would be like the war in Vietnam; others argued for the war in Vietnam, saying not fighting would be like giving in to Hitler at Munich. In both of these cases, we try to persuade others about a new situation by using an analogy to an old one.

The fourth type of reasoning is **reasoning from generalization,** better known as inductive reasoning. This type of reasoning uses a sample to draw conclusions for a population that the sample is from. This type of reasoning is frequently seen in advertising, such as in the commercial for Trident gum that suggests that "four out of five dentists prefer Trident for their patients who chew gum." The conclusion proposed is that because four out of five dentists prefer it, then your dentist would probably also recommend this gum, so it's good for you also. Certainly not every dentist in the country was surveyed, but a sample was used to represent the whole dental community. When the sample is constructed scientifically, our conclusions, at least about the questions studied, may be valid for the population, but when the sample is drawn by the advertiser, we may be suspicious of the conclusions—we may suspect a reporting bias.

Although not discussed by Aristotle as a type of reasoning, we can include **deductive reasoning** as an important type of reasoning by which good arguments can be made. Deductive reasoning uses **syllogisms,** which show how we can reason from the general to the specific. Syllogisms follow a logical sequence like this one:

1. All students at Michigan State University are brilliant.

2. You are a student at Michigan State.

3. Therefore, you are brilliant.

In this example, deductive reasoning begins with a generalization about the students at a particular university (1). Then a specific case is pointed out (2), and the syllogistic argument is made that if I am a student within the given category, I therefore fit within the generalized group (3). Of course, it is important to be sure the generalization is correct and that the specific case fits the general category; otherwise, the argument will be misleading.

Emotional Appeals

Emotional appeals are often used in persuasive messages to arouse feelings of pride, love, pity, nostalgia, concern, anger, or fear. Organizations such as World Vision International have used commercials that show pictures of children from developing countries who are small and have big brown eyes. These pictures elicit emotional responses like compassion, and motivate people to raise funds for the children and provide support for the organization. Alumni organizations send out brochures reminding former students of the great times they had in their college days so as to bring about feelings of nostalgia and to promote greater willingness to give money to their alma mater.

Fear appeals are widely used in advertising, especially for health-related messages. You can probably think of many fear appeals you have seen, warning against dangers such as death from drinking and driving, unsafe sex, cancer from smoking, or a brain fried by drugs. A fear appeal is a particular type of emotional appeal that links negative consequences with a failure to accept the message's recommendation. An effective fear appeal has several important elements:

1. **The fear appeal establishes a threat.** For example, the "Crash Dummies" TV spots demonstrate the threat of what will happen to our bodies if we don't wear seatbelts.

2. **The fear appeal shows that the threat is real for the receiver.** For the fear appeal to be effective, the receiver has to see that the threat could actually happen and that he or she is vulnerable. For example, when Magic Johnson announced that he was infected with HIV, he pointed out that he originally thought that he wasn't vulnerable. Part of his campaign in talking with young people has been to let them know that the threat of HIV is very real for people who are not practicing abstinence or are not using proper protection.

3. **The fear appeal should show that the proposed action will stop or reduce the threat.** In the well-known commercial of the egg and the frying pan, in which the narrator says, "This is your brain; this is your brain on drugs; any questions?" the implied conclusion is that you should not use drugs; not using drugs will eliminate the threat, or, in other words, your brain will not be fried.

4. **The fear appeal should show that the proposed action is easy.** The "Just Say NO!" campaign of the 1980s is a good example of a proposal that was made to sound easy. The message was that it was not difficult to resist drugs—just say "no." For a fear appeal to be effective, the proposal should seem as though it wouldn't take a lot of effort to comply; otherwise, the receiver is not likely to even try to engage in the advocated behavior.

5. **The fear appeal should show that the proposed action is doable.** Cars used to be made without seatbelts. To tell someone to buckle up and that it's easy to do so is great, but if there are no seatbelts in the car the proposal is not very doable. An effective fear appeal should show the steps necessary to comply in a way that makes each step seem capable of being performed.

Motivational Appeals

Similar to emotional appeals are appeals based on human needs and the motivation to satisfy those needs. Humans have certain needs that must be fulfilled in order to live. Needs may be based on human biology, or may be primarily social in origin. Biologically based needs include drives to avoid hunger, thirst, and pain, and to have sex. Socially based needs include the needs for friendship, love, loyalty, and competition.

Abraham Maslow (1970) proposed that human needs can fit into five interrelated categories and that the categories of needs must be met in a way that the lower categories are fulfilled first. As lower categories are met, then the higher needs become more important. The five categories are as follows:

1. **Physiological needs.** These include the need for food, water, and air. These are essential needs for every human, without which survival is simply not possible.

2. **Safety needs.** Once the physiological needs are met, humans need protection from harm. Maslow also included in this category the need for structure and order in life, as well as the need for both physical and emotional security.

3. **Belongingness and love.** When physiological and safety needs have been met, then individuals are likely to have an increasing need for socialization and inclusion with people and groups, and the need to form bonds with others for reasons other than meeting physiological or safety needs.

4. **Self-esteem.** Self-esteem is how much we like ourselves. Typically it is accompanied by the knowledge that we are competent and have positive value. The need to achieve and to enhance our status and reputation becomes more important as the basic needs of food and water, safety, and love are met.

5. **Self-actualization.** Self-actualization is a person's desire to realize his or her own potential as a human being. For each person this may involve different things, such as the need to make some type of lasting contribution to the world or the need to reach the summit of Mount Everest. Motivational seminars appeal to this need and encourage audiences to "be all that you can be."

Taking into account the particular needs of our message receivers (our audience) helps us tailor effective persuasive messages for them. Politicians frequently make appeals based on these needs to persuade the public to agree with their positions. For example, politicians favoring the school lunch program argue that reductions in the program would take food from the mouths of children. Cuts or increases in welfare and education programs often are opposed or promoted based on arguments that build or reduce self-esteem in their audience, or in the ability to achieve self-actualization on the part of the beneficiaries.

Message Composition

When trying to persuade a friend to go to a party or a professor to give an extension on a paper assignment, we often don't give much thought to the way the message is composed. Chapter Three on social knowledge acquisition provides a good discussion about compliance-gaining and the messages we use to persuade others to do things like keep a promise or do a favor. But there are specific elements of a message that are important to consider when trying to design an effective persuasive message. Evaluation of the audience at whom the message is aimed will help to determine how the message should be constructed.

One-sided versus two-sided messages. A one-sided message presents only those arguments that favor the recommendation that the persuader is making. This type of message is best used when the audience is already in favor of the proposal. It is also better to use one-sided messages when the audience is not well informed about the issue. For example, Governor John Engler is a Republican. Western Michigan is typically a Republican region. Because western Michiganders are likely to be in favor of many of Governor Engler's positions, he can be very effective with this audience with one-sided messages. Thus, when talking about the need for cuts in taxes and social programs, he will likely present only the arguments in favor of his views.

A two-sided message presents arguments in favor of the recommendation made by the persuader; in addition, it presents and refutes or disparages arguments that oppose the recommendation. Two-sided messages are best to use when the audience is well-informed about the issues being addressed or when the audience initially opposes the position being advocated. In these cases, in addition to presenting the advocated position, the persuader will want to counter the possible negative positions by refuting them. For example, eastern Michigan is typically a Democratic region, so Governor Engler is likely to encounter opposition to his positions on issues such as cuts in taxes and social programs. Therefore, when Governor Engler addresses audiences on the eastern side of the state, he should give his arguments for the proposals he is making, as well as refute the positions with which he disagrees that may be held by members of the audience. In this way, he would support the pros and counter any cons regarding his positions.

Explicit versus implicit conclusions. A good persuasive message will suggest one or more beliefs or attitudes that the audience should agree with or behaviors that the audience should adopt or avoid. The proposed conclusion can be either *explicit*, laying out clearly what the recommendation is that should be adopted or held, or it can be *implicit*, leaving the audience to draw its own conclusions based on the evidence provided by the persuader.

In the commercial against drug use with the egg and the frying pan, the conclusion is implicit. Based on the evidence given—the egg frying represents your brain—you are to conclude that it may be foolish to use drugs because you don't want anything like that to happen to your brain. Implicit conclusions are most effective when the audience is able and motivated to process the message. The egg and frying pan commercial is short and easy to figure out, so it is not difficult for the audience to come to its own conclusions about the message; this is the conclusion advocated by the message source.

On the other hand, a message attempting to persuade you to vote a particular way on a technical proposal related to deregulation of insurance companies may be more difficult to process. Thus, it would be more difficult for the audience to draw its own conclusions, particularly if new and unfamiliar evidence is presented. In this case, the persuader would do well to provide an explicit recommendation. If the audience is not likely to generate its own conclusions, or may be unable to process the message clearly, it is best to provide an explicit conclusion if we want our message to be persuasive.

Primacy versus recency. In situations like the presidential debates, two persuaders have the opportunity to present opposing viewpoints. In cases like these, is it better to go first or second? The answer depends on the topic being debated.

For certain topics, the audience will remember what they hear first. This idea is called a **primacy effect**. When a topic is controversial, it is better to present your arguments first because the audience is more likely to recall the first arguments it hears. Similarly, when the topic is more interesting, or when your arguments are stronger than your opponent's, or when the audience is quite familiar with the topic, a primacy effect is likely. Thus, it is best to present your arguments first in these situations.

In contrast, when the topic being debated is not controversial, is uninteresting, or is unfamiliar, then a **recency effect** is likely to occur; that is, the audience is likely to remember what it heard last. In addition, if there is a long delay between the messages from first persuader and those of the second persuader, the audience is more likely to recall what it heard last.

CONCLUSIONS ABOUT MESSAGES

Whatever the topic, a persuasive message should be carefully planned and prepared. Clear, understandable arguments are necessary for any persuasive campaign. Although there is some debate over just how many arguments a persuader should include, remember that it is always better to use a few strong arguments than a great many weak ones.

Good persuasive evidence is evidence that is clearly relevant to the topic and comes from an especially credible source. In other words, citing the *National Enquirer* is probably not recommended!

The use of good evidence is more likely to produce attitude change than using no evidence, but the use of irrelevant evidence is likely to backfire. Use of strong and recent evidence also boosts the credibility of the persuader. Thus, if you are addressing an audience that doesn't know you well, the evidence you choose to support your claims will help to boost your credibility and thus help you to be more persuasive. This idea is good to keep in mind when writing research papers as well: The use of strong supportive evidence from credible sources, such as well known researchers published in reputable journals, will make your paper more believable and seem better researched. A good research paper should "persuade" your professor that you know what you're talking about!

LEARNING TO PERSUADE

When we understand the process by which persuasion occurs we can begin to become more effective producers of persuasive messages, and we can also become more critical consumers of persuasive messages. There are several things that you can start doing to improve your persuasive skills and to learn to be an effective persuader.

Boost Your Credibility

Credibility is an invaluable attribute of a persuasive person. To become a better persuader, work on bolstering your credibility, remembering that credibility comprises competence, trustworthiness, liking, and dynamism.

Competence: Know the topic about which you are trying to persuade. There are no shortcuts to competence. Researching the topic or issue and studying it carefully will make you a prepared speaker and give you the confidence and knowledge with which to address your audience. Consider the topic about which you are trying to persuade and determine what is necessary to become competent in that area.

Trustworthiness: An African proverb says that it takes a thousand actions to build trust and only one to break it. Trustworthiness, like credibility, is something that must be worked at. It cannot be acquired just before you want to engage in persuasion. To become a persuasive person you must work at building trust with the people who will be the targets of your persuasive attempts.

Dynamism: Dynamism can be learned. Few people are born with a natural dynamism that others see radiating from them. Similarly, few people have a natural ability to write well. These are skills that can be learned and can always be improved. Learning to speak effectively and comfortably in front of groups and learning to communicate clearly in your writing will improve your effectiveness as a persuader.

Analyze Your Audience

A good persuader gives careful consideration to the audience or receiver of the persuasive message. Knowing your audience takes careful preparation beyond preparing for the specific topic or issue. You will want to know the number of people you may need to persuade at one time; are you addressing one individual or a group of ten or of one hundred? Furthermore, you will want to know demographic information about the audience: Is the audience well-educated? Rich or poor? Young, middle-aged, elderly, or mixed? Interested or ambivalent toward the topic? How might these and other audience attributes affect their responses to your message?

Is the audience informed about the topic on which you are speaking? Is the audience apathetic to your point of view? Perhaps the audience is critical of your perspective or even hostile to your recommendation. Or maybe the audience is well informed and in agreement.

If your audience is uninformed about the topic, you will need to provide sufficient information to educate them about the issue so that your message can be processed. If the audience is apathetic to your point of view, you will need to create a sense of excitement about the issue and your perspectives on it. If the audience is critical or hostile, you may want to create doubts in the audience about its position, or you may need to consider how you can get the audience to be more receptive, so that your position can be heard. And for a well-informed audience that agrees with you, you will need to be well-prepared to reinforce its position with evidence that will be deemed credible.

Careful consideration of the attitudes currently held by the audience will help you to tailor your message appropriately. A good persuader, whether addressing one person or a thousand, will know about his or her audience and adapt the persuasive message according to the attributes of the audience. One way of planning a persuasive campaign is by interviewing a variety of people who are similar to the recipients of your persuasive message. You might want to ask them:

- What are the words, ideas, or concepts that come to mind when you think about [your topic]?

- Why do you think some people are for [your position]? And why do you think some people are against [your position]?

- Who do you think is for [your position]? Who do you think is against [your position]?

You may then probe further, trying to understand how your topic and the position that you are advocating are related to other issues, and how different positions and related issues are tied to different social groups. This knowledge is tremendously important if you are to wage an effective campaign. Woelfel and Fink (1980) describe some sophisticated methods that rely on this kind of audience analysis in order to create effective persuasion campaigns.

Interpreting Persuasion Attempts and Practices

Throughout this chapter we have taken the position of the sender or source of messages. Another perspective is that of the receiver. You should now be able to understand how others try to get you to adopt their attitudes and beliefs, as well as to change your behavior.

We are all exposed to many persuasive messages every day. Some of them come from sources that we do not know personally, and they try to get us to buy a particular product or vote for a particular candidate. Some of them come from friends or family members: We are told to clean up our room, study harder, try a new outfit, smoke or drink, have sex, or miss class. We have provided some ideas that should help you evaluate the messages that you receive. For example:

- Is the message made to seem consistent with liked others? Is the position advocated tied to ideas that you like?
- Who is the source of the message? How trustworthy and knowledgeable is this person?
- Are the ideas associated with rewards or punishments gotten in the past? Does this affect your consideration of the message?
- Are others pressuring you to conform? What are the rewards for conforming, and what are the costs?
- What do people say when they attempt to persuade? Are their arguments one-sided? If so, what is the opposing view? If not, has the opposing side been characterized appropriately?

Once you know something about persuasion, you have a tool that can be used honestly or deceptively. As we have discussed, one component of source credibility is trustworthiness. Anyone known for being deceptive will, in the long run, lose trustworthiness and, therefore, effectiveness as a source. Although there are certainly moral and religious reasons for being honest, there is also a very practical one: We don't believe those who have deceived us. In the long run, we should expect deceptive practices to fail.

REFERENCES

Asch, S. (1956). Studies of independence and conformity: 1. A minority of one against a unanimous majority. *Psychological Monographs, 70* (416).

Bandura, A. (1977). *Social learning theory.* Englewood Cliffs, NJ: Prentice-Hall.

Eagly, A. H., Wood, W., & Chaiken, S. (1978). Causal inferences about communicators and their effect on opinion change. *Journal of Personality and Social Psychology, 36,* 424–435.

Festinger, L. (1957). *A theory of cognitive dissonance.* Stanford, CA: Stanford University Press.

Heider, F. (1958). *The psychology of interpersonal relations.* New York: John Wiley & Sons.

Maslow, A. H. (1970). *Motivation and personality.* New York: Harper & Row.

Pavlov, I. P. (1927). *Conditioned reflexes.* London: Oxford University Press.

Rose, R. (Story & screenplay, & Producer), Fonda, H. (Producer), & Lumet, S. (Director). (1990). *Twelve angry men.* [Videocassette release of the original 1957 motion picture by United Artists]. (Available from United Artists).

Staats, A.W., & Staats, C. K. (1958). Attitudes established by classical conditioning. *Journal of Abnormal and Social Psychology, 57,* 37–40.

Twain, M. (1959). *Tom Sawyer.* London: Collins.

Woelfel, J., & Fink, E. L. (1980). *The measurement of communication processes: Galileo theory and method.* New York: Academic Press.

Zajonc, R. B. (1980). Feeling and thinking: Preferences need no inferences. *American Psychologist, 39,* 151–175.

Chapter Nine Case Study Quiz—Persuasion

Instructions:
Please read the following case study carefully and select the best answers to the questions. This quiz is an individual assignment. Remember: sharing answers is a form of plagiarism.

Millions of people have been offered the opportunity to participate in the Publisher's Clearing House (PCH) sweepstakes in which their lives will change by winning the BIG jackpot of money. Further, there are many customers who believe ordering merchandise will increase the likelihood of winning the BIG prize. When reviewing the practices of the PCH, there are many heuristics used in direct mailing to convince the customers that they will be the BIG winner. Such strategies include sending customers these types of letters: the "Dear Friend" theme, the "Help Needed" theme, and the "President's Club" theme. In the "Dear Friend" theme, customers receive letters from the PCH that attempt to create a personal friendship between the customer and the PCH. Because the PCH likes the customer, the customer will purchase more. The second theme is labeled the "Help Needed" theme and it refers to how the PCH attempts to let customers know that the PCH is in trouble, but it is them (the customer) who can help the PCH! Customers feel a social obligation to help the PCH by purchasing more merchandise. And finally, the "President's Club" theme lets customers believe that they have been selected because of their outstanding record as a customer and because of this, these customers will have more of a chance to win the BIG prize if they buy more. Many customers have filed complaints against the PCH because of their misleading tactics.

Student's Name _____

Section Number _____

Section Leader's Name _____

Chapter Nine Case Study Quiz—Persuasion

1. Sally has started to receive letters in the mail from the PCH. Never having been interested before, she found herself reading the letters. By the time she has received the fourth letter from PCH, she is ready to join, purchase merchandise, and increase her odds of winning the BIG prize. Sally's actions can be explained by which influence?
   a. Learning and reinforcement
   b. Cognitive dissonance
   c. Mere exposure
   d. Classical conditioning

2. Mark has received a PCH letter with a "President's Club" themed tactic. The letter stated that he could be one of the top customers and that all the TOP customers win the BIG prize. Mark reasons that if he is a top customer and all top customers win the BIG prize, then he will win the BIG prize. What kind of reasoning did Mark use?
   a. Reasoning from analogy
   b. Reasoning from sign
   c. Reasoning from generalization
   d. Deductive reasoning

3. Jareel has seen the PCH television commercials in which normal people just like him have won a lot of money. They won the money because they increased how much merchandise they ordered. Jareel is now striving to purchase more merchandise so he can win the money too. This is what kind of learning?
   a. Observational learning
   b. Instrumental learning
   c. Classic Conditioning
   d. Participatory learning

4. Ultimately, the PCH is persuading their customers to purchase more merchandise. What is being influenced?
   a. Attitudes
   b. Beliefs
   c. Behavior
   d. Values

Case Study   **205**

5. PCH wants customers to think that they will win lots of money and that ordering more merchandise will increase their chances. These are:
   a. Irrelevant cognitions
   b. Consonant cognitions
   c. Dissonant cognitions

Chapter Ten

COORDINATION AND ORGANIZATIONAL COMMUNICATION STRUCTURE

J. David Johnson
University of Kentucky

William A. Donohue
Michigan State University

The maturing of the Internet has precipitated an exciting revolution in ideas about how effective organizations work. Old ideas about how businesses and organizations should be structured are being retired daily, and new approaches are taking their place. The high-tech businesses on the front end of these changes are now throwing out their organizational charts as old-thinking relics. These formal, hierarchical relationships are often obsolete hours after they are written. Organizations function today in a much more rapidly changing environment and they must build structures that help them adapt. It is vital that you understand how these new organizations are taking shape since you will likely go to work in one of them.

Our goal in this chapter is to describe these changes in organizational structure and place them in the context of more traditional and familiar structures that dominated organizations before the Internet. However, it is important to realize that this revolution in structure is not necessarily embraced by all organizations. Technology-based firms are leading the charge, but others are following as they see the enormous performance potential of building organizations founded on the need for communication rather than on command and control.

The New Corporation

Perhaps it is best to begin our explorations by describing how one organization revolutionized its corporate structure almost overnight, with incredible results. In a recent article in the magazine *Strategy and Business,* Lawrence Fisher (2001) examined the economic miracle at Nortel Networks, a Canadian Telecommunications firm producing hardware such as raw semiconductor components, circuit boards, and other finished products for computers. The title of his article is, "From Vertical to Virtual." In the article, Fisher explored the strategies Nortel used to move from a traditional computer hardware-manufacturing firm to a highly integrated virtual organization capable of rapidly expanding into the highly prosperous fiber optic cable market. Fiber optic cable uses light to transmit data that greatly expands the amount of data that can be carried from computer to computer.

The results of their transformation were amazing. From 1999 to 2000 profits expanded 125%. Nortel dramatically increased its percentage of this highly profitable fiber optic market, and is poised to be the largest supplier of this cable in the world. How did they do it?

How did they explode from a sleepy manufacturer of computer equipment with small profit growth to a giant in the fiber optic cable market in just a few short years?

The answer is that they changed the way they communicate. Nortel changed from a company of five manufacturing units that were vertically integrated (people only talked to others in their own units) to a company with horizontally integrated teams that restructured quickly to respond to customer needs. That is, Nortel changed their entire organizational structure and their fundamental relationship with customers. To really understand these rapid and difficult shifts, it is important to step back and describe several concepts about organizations and how they communicate.

UNDERSTANDING ORGANIZATIONS

Basic Management Models

There are essentially four ways in which organizations or companies can be organized. These four models differ in terms of power and communication.

Holding Company Model. In this first model, a group of people buys several companies and simply holds on to them as investments. There is very little communication with the leaders of the firms, and the firms in the holding company don't interact a great deal. It is a hands-off, laissez-faire type of leadership.

Strategy and Oversight Model. In this second model, the company forms what are called Strategic Business Units, or teams, that are highly flexible and focused on satisfying customer needs. The leaders provide strategic direction for the team by hiring and training talented people, and turning the teams loose to make customer-focused decisions. Managers are largely consultants to the teams. Communication between teams and customers is vital to the success of this model.

Active Leader Involvement Model. For this third model, the company managers become more actively involved in directing the team members. The team members look to company managers to make the important decisions allowing managers and team members to share power. Unlike model two, in which teams are primarily accountable for their own success, managers and teams share the accountability for results.

Command and Control Model. In this fourth model the team members report to the managers who make most of the decisions. Traditionally, managers form teams or strategic business units of some kind, and create a fairly static (little change happens) organization with primarily top-down communication. The team members have very little power and are not accountable for their success or failure. This top-down style is called a vertically-integrated organization in which communication is up and down and not horizontal or between business units.

Nortel changed from a Command and Control corporation with vertically integrated units to a Strategy and Oversight model in about two years. The Command and Control model is often used in vertically integrated organizations. In such structures, there is a static organizational chart with many layers of management. Few people at the lower levels of management make decisions and provide much input to people at upper levels. Sometimes this model is useful in crisis situations when people must be told what to do and command must be centralized; however, this model is not very useful for creatively responding to customer needs because it limits communication.

FIGURE 10.1 The Command and Control Model

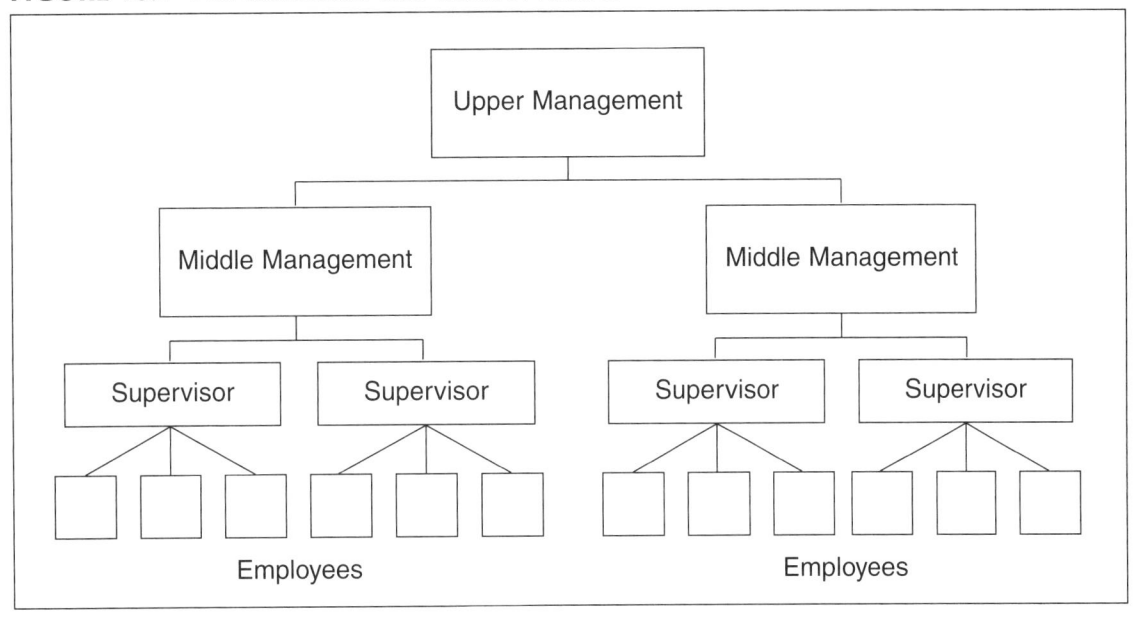

In a Strategy and Oversight model, individuals form teams that are horizontally integrated across the business units. In other words, people are not so concerned about their unit or divisional identity. They work in teams to respond to customer problems or important business opportunities. Decision-making is pushed down to the teams who work closely with the customers. It is not concentrated at the top as in the Command and Control model. When rapid customer response is needed to take advantage of a new opportunity, people must change the way they communicate.

FIGURE 10.2 The Strategy and Oversight Model

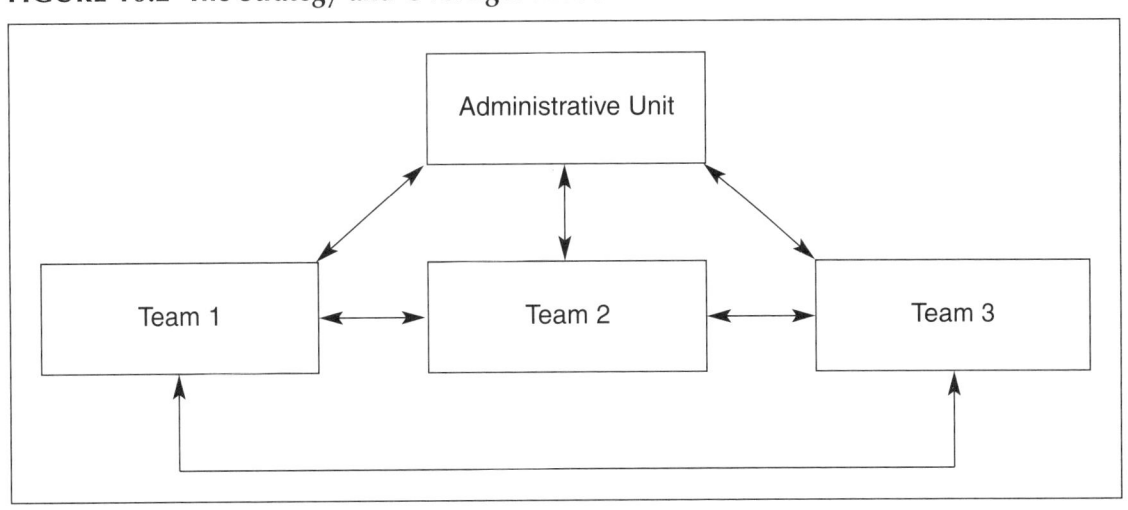

Coordination and Organizational Communication Structure

Nortel accomplished this transformation by selling off most of their manufacturing facilities to key suppliers, and then creating a company Intranet linking suppliers with customers. Then, business teams formed around customer groups (computer component customers, fiber optic customers, etc.) to insure that customer needs were getting met. Put another way, the primary technology that allows a company to restructure the way it communicates is the Internet. Using the web, customers can order more quickly, Nortel can monitor customer needs, and teams can communicate quickly and efficiently with one another from anywhere in the world. Without the web, these communication changes would not be possible. In a very real sense, the web has opened up a huge opportunity to rethink how we function as businesses and organizations.

Think about this transformation from a company culture standpoint. It is quite remarkable. Nortel knew that growing meant changing the management model they had for years, and altering internal relationships between managers and employees and external relationships between Nortel and its customers. The company had constructed a culture around one business model and totally restructured that culture to accommodate the new model. But again, the key to the change was communication. So, to better understand the role communication played in reshaping the organization, let's take a closer look at some key concepts associated with the Nortel shift in communication strategy.

Communication Structure

Communication structure refers to a stable, relatively enduring set of communication patterns between elements (people, computers, etc.) of an organization. Traditionally, researchers have focused on patterns of information exchange between individuals and the manner in which those patterns shape their relationships. For example, the Internet allows managers and team members to communicate directly with one another on a routine basis. This direct communication changes the relationship between the parties so that everyone has nearly equal status, particularly under the Strategy and Oversight model. Before web applications and e-mail, employees were forbidden to talk to managers several layers over them. They had to go through supervisors and others to communicate. And, customers had the same problem.

Downward Communication. Early research studying communication structure in organizations concentrated on the organizational chart. These approaches primarily focused on the flow of messages within the formal authority structure of the organization. The formal authority between the boss and worker was the primary relationship examined in this research. Most of this research examined the concept of **downward communication** that originates from upper levels of management, and is targeted for lower level personnel. This type of communication is meant to control the organization and the operations of its personnel. Typically, downward communication messages, since they are official, are very formal and usually they are in writing.

Perhaps the most common form of downward communication content deals with job instructions. These are usually very direct messages that instruct an employee to perform a specific operation at a particular place. Other types of downward communication messages deal with providing employees with job rationale information designed to put their jobs in the context of other work and to tell employees why it is important to do particular things. Somewhat related to job rationale is the indoctrination to the goals of the organization, which is intimately related to organizational socialization, a topic of growing concern.

Probably the biggest failure in downward communication content lies in feedback about job performance. Often organizations fail to adopt systematic means of providing members with feedback such as appraisal interviews about job performance. Employees want to know how well they are doing and where they need to improve, but many elite organizations operate under the guidelines that no news is good news. According to several studies, excellent companies have the opposite philosophy. They believe that positive employee recognition is the best motivator. We know from many studies that feedback is essential to improve performance and commitment to the organization. If people have no idea how well they are progressing, they lose interest in the organization, and become isolated in their own interests.

Upward Communication. The second kind of communication pattern of interest is **upward communication** (communication from workers to bosses). Upward communication in Command and Control organizations tends to be formal, in writing, and flows along the formal chain of command represented by the organizational chart. Without adequate upward communication from workers management cannot react quickly enough to change to prevent major problems from developing for the organization. Upward communication is often very difficult in these formal Command and Control organizations because there are many layers of management between people at the bottom and people at the top. Also, these layers cause status problems. People at the top often think they don't have to listen to people at the bottom; so upward communication is not often valued in traditional organizations.

However, in more team-based organizations, upward communication is essential. These organizations have only a few layers of people who respect one another's opinions; so information tends to flow more freely. One of the most significant changes Nortel experienced when it changed organizational structure was a huge increase in upward communication. Suddenly, people were talking to each other and they used the Internet as the tool to make this communication possible.

Horizontal Communication. The third kind of pattern is termed **horizontal communication.** It occurs at the same level or sideways along the organizational chart. This type of communication is informal, face-to-face, and personal. Since it is much faster and more attuned to the personal needs of communicators, horizontal communication also tends to be used more to coordinate activities. For example, two workers may decide between them how they are going to tackle a particular project, what tasks each will perform, when the tasks will be performed, and how to keep each other posted as to their problems and progress. This type of communication is very common in a team-based business style. Individuals figure out who they need to talk to and simply contact those individuals.

What's exciting about the revolution in organizational structure is the great increase in horizontal communication. What Nortel tried to achieve was the integration of suppliers, Nortel team members, and customers in a large horizontal communication network. For example, by linking customers and suppliers directly, Nortel can now insure that customers' needs are handled quickly and effectively. A customer can simply access the supplier's website and track an order without having to call anyone or waste time figuring out who to call. The Nortel team member can be notified immediately via e-mail that a request has been made and the Nortel people can follow-up to determine if the customer's request was handled properly. Customers, suppliers, and Nortel team members can also design a new computer part in an on-line conference. This process insures that the right part is created at the right time for the customer. Each person can provide his or her input, cutting out hundreds of hours of wasted time in product development.

NETWORK ANALYSIS

The key to understanding downward, upward, and horizontal communication structures is **network analysis.** This approach is used by almost every social science (anthropology, history, management, political science, sociology, and communication, to name a few) to study **who communicates with whom, about what, and how often.** In other words, organizations often need a visual map of their communication patterns to see if those patterns are appropriate for what they are trying to accomplish. Network analysis has been the primary means of studying communication structure in organizations over the last two decades. It has enabled communication researchers to get a comprehensive look at emergent communication networks, which include both formal and informal relationships. One of the primary benefits of network analysis is that it frees us from viewing communication exclusively in terms of the formal organizational chart. Now we can begin to explore the processes by which people naturally communicate with one another.

For example, when Nortel first decided to switch their organizational structure, their network analysis (had they conducted one) would have revealed that most people communicate downward with people in their own units mostly about business issues. There was very little horizontal communication between units, and very little upward communication even within units. However, after the restructuring they would have noticed that several team members are linkers (individuals who link units) who exhibit a great deal of horizontal integration, and more communication outside the walls of the traditional company. The map would look much bigger with a lot more horizontal lines.

Communication Links

What really determines the usefulness of any network analysis is how we define the relationships, or links, between individuals. Several communication properties can be used to define the nature of a linkage. For example, **content** refers to the substance of the messages individuals exchange. When individuals exchange task information, such as how to do the job, or problems about the job, then they are exchanging **production-related information. Innovation messages** focus on new ideas. The final kind of conversation deals with **social functions.** Specifically, talk about personal or relational matters falls into this category.

When Nortel changed its communication structure from Command and Control to Oversight and Strategy, they not only increased horizontal communication, they also dramatically increased innovation messages. People started talking about new ways to link suppliers, customers, and Nortel team members. In a sense, this change brought about a renaissance to the company regarding new ways of adapting to change. Reliance on downward communication tends to stifle innovative talk as individuals simply go about doing their jobs without much thought about improving it.

Communication links also seek to understand the channels of communication, or the means by which messages are delivered. These channels might include written, face-to-face, telephone, or telecommunication networks. Certain channels are used for

212 Chapter Ten

various kinds of communications. For example, we tend to prefer face-to-face communication when communicating about relational matters. The broader bandwidth of face-to-face communication (we can send more information since we can involve all five senses in the communication process) allows more information about trust and affection to enter the interaction. When relational messages are not critical narrow channels (little information flow) can be used, such as the phone or electronic mail.

Reciprocity refers to whether or not both parties to a relationship characterize it in the same way. For example, often a supervisor will not be as aware of relationships with workers as they are of the relationships with their bosses. So when asked with whom they communicate they will forget about a worker, but the worker will remember their relationship with the boss. This linkage will therefore be unreciprocated because the worker believes it exists, but the manager does not. Another important general property of a link is strength. While typically the frequency of communication is used to indicate the strength of a link, many other properties, such as the duration of the contact and its importance, could also be used.

The manner in which these various properties are combined can determine the real value of any single network analysis. For example, when companies like Nortel are changing their organizational structure to respond better to customer needs, they need a way to monitor changes in communication patterns. Are they seeing more horizontal communication that expands beyond individual units? Are more individuals exchanging innovation messages when they communicate? Are links more likely to be reciprocated now that communication has opened up between individuals? Without this kind of diagnostic effort, it is impossible to determine if the organization is moving information at a level required to do the job.

Communication Roles

Not only is it important to understand how individuals are linked in networks, it is essential to understand the roles they play in those communication networks. An individual's **communication role** is determined by the overall pattern of their communication linkages. Some individuals, labeled **non-participants,** have relatively few communication contacts with others. **Participants,** on the other hand, form intense patterns that represent communication groups and linkages between these groups. Several research studies have found key differences between these two groups of individuals, with participants being more outgoing, influential, and satisfied, and non-participants deliberately withholding information and having lower satisfaction with communication.

The most important communication role is that of a **liaison.** The liaison links two or more communication groups, while not being a member of any one group. This strategic positioning of liaisons has earned them the label of linking pins. These individuals bridge relations between units, or between customers and suppliers, for example. They are generally very skilled as communicators, friendly, and attentive. Liaisons tend to promote more positive working climates and are often responsible for the successful coordination of organizational functions and cohesion.

The role of the liaison is closely tied to the concepts of integration and differentiation. That is, as the organization divides into more and more groups, greater efforts have to be made at pulling these groups together through integrating mechanisms. These integrating mechanisms are crucial to organizational survival, since without them, the organization would be a collection of groups, each going off in its own direction. Typically, liaisons are the most efficient personal integrating mechanism because of their strategic positioning. Due to their centrality and their direct linkages with others, liaisons reduce the probability of message distortion, reduce information load, and increase the timeliness of communication.

Unfortunately, however, liaisons are relatively difficult to find in organizations, a fact which is reflected in the generally low level of communication between diverse groups in organizations. Before Nortel initiated its organizational shift there were probably very few liaisons in the company who successfully bridged production units. Once they made the switch to a different kind of organization the number of liaisons ballooned rapidly. Soon there were many liaisons who bridged teams. These connectors kept communication flowing between suppliers, Nortel team members and managers, and customers. Often a change in organizational structure is required to activate the need for more liaisons.

Inside organizations, why do some people emerge as liaisons and others do not? Several factors explain this emergence. First, liaisons tend to develop more open communication relationships with others. People like to talk to them. Second, they initiate conversations more, opening up communication between diverse groups. Third, liaisons exhibit considerable skill in processing information. They think quickly and creatively. In fact, many of the characteristics of a liaison (i.e., openness, trust, sensitivity to others, and getting a wide array of input) have also been used to specify the characteristics of democratic managers, and more generally, of open communication climates. The greater the numbers of managers who are also liaisons, the greater the likelihood that a modern organization can achieve the unity of effort necessary for diverse groups to collaborate towards the achievement of common organizational goals.

While relational and cognitive factors are essential to a liaison's role performance and emergence, **motivational factors** determine whether or not an individual will aspire to such a role and perform effectively within it. The emergent nature of network linkages is, in part, a picture of the more voluntary and spontaneous choices that organizational members make in their communication relationships.

CULTURAL APPROACHES

Communication structures always function within a communication culture. Interest in organizational cultures has increased dramatically in recent years within the field of communication. This interest arises partly out of the realization that meanings are created through the social communication people have with each other; they are emergent properties of this communication. Communication thereby constructs the realities of the organization (the culture) and, in turn, organizational culture shapes how members communicate. Accordingly, organizational culture consists of the framework of beliefs, values, and patterned behaviors that organizational members create, maintain, and modify through their communicative interactions. Culture enables organizational members to understand their work environment, especially the attitudinal and behavioral expectancies.

In fact, another way to think about the shift at Nortel focuses on this issue of culture. Not only did they need to change their communication structure, but they needed to change their organizational culture, or values about customers, communication, suppliers, and relationships. Culture is a difficult element to change because people become comfortable within a culture and often resist change; however, Nortel employees were ready for a change. They wanted to essentially open up the company and create a more highly integrated firm capable of taking advantage of significant business opportunities. That could not have happened without a significant cultural change. Let's explore the dimensions of culture that are important to understand when addressing the issue of cultural change.

Rules

Many of the deeper elements of cultural value systems become embedded and reflected in the rules governing organizational members' behaviors. The notion of rule has always been central to theorizing about organizations. In fact, the earliest thinking about bureaucracy noted the importance of rules for determining the actions of organizational members. For our purposes **we define rules as clear guidelines for action.** They are prescriptive in the sense that if they are not followed, then the organization may punish the violator in some manner.

For example, the old Nortel probably enforced rules that prohibited employees from talking to anyone higher than their immediate boss. Going over the boss' head is frequently punished in many Command and Control organizations. In fact, this very rule is responsible for many organizational disasters. People see something, but are afraid to say anything, or don't feel it's their job to say anything. Rules function to regulate, evaluate, justify, correct, and predict behavior. Rules are particularly important for determining the nature of communicative relationships in organizations. They determine what people can talk about, whom they can talk to, and when they can communicate. When Nortel changed their structure they also changed rules about communication. It soon became acceptable to talk to people in other units, to include suppliers in designing products, and to broaden the involvement of customers. The shift to teams also required a shift in communication rules. After the structural changes, people were expected to communicate more horizontally and to provide more innovative communication. The rules for communicating changed, and as a result, the culture changed. Therefore, rules are critical elements of the cultural approach to examining communication structure in organizations.

The first distinction that must be made concerning rules is whether the rule is formally or informally proscribed. **Formal rules** are official and written. For example, companies often state officially that their managers have open door policies. They expect their managers to be available to employees, so that employees can come in and talk to them about anything that is of concern to them. However, employees soon find that managers are very busy. If the employee is seen as constantly bothering the boss over trivial problems, then the boss may form a negative evaluation that the employee needs too much direction. This evaluation, if included in formal appraisals of the employee, could be extremely damaging. This is but one example where an understanding of **informal rules,** which are not written down but may still contain clear expectations concerning the behavior of organizational members, is more critical to an employee's advancement than an understanding of formal organizational policies. You can understand the potential for confusion when rules change dramatically. Some people like to hold on to the old rules, and others want change.

Rites and Rituals

One specific element of culture, which has a number of potential implications for organizational communication structure, is the study of **rites and rituals.** Rites and rituals provide a good focus for cultural studies, since they consolidate several cultural forms stories, sagas, symbols, language, etc. which have implications for communicative processes within organizations. Thus rituals themselves, in addition to being reflections of culture are also elements of organizational communication culture.

Rites and rituals have been defined in various ways. For example, researchers describe rites and rituals as those behaviors which members regularly or occasionally participate in. These could be semi-annual reviews, weekly staff meetings, or daily coffee breaks. These behaviors are programmatic and routinized activities of everyday life that enable the organization to accomplish its goals. Others define rites as relatively elaborate, dramatic, planned sets of activities that consolidate various forms of cultural expressions into one event, which is carried out through social interactions, usually for the benefit of an audience. Rites and rituals, then, represent organizational events that members participate in, and which are relatively elaborate, since they contain multiple forms of cultural expressions.

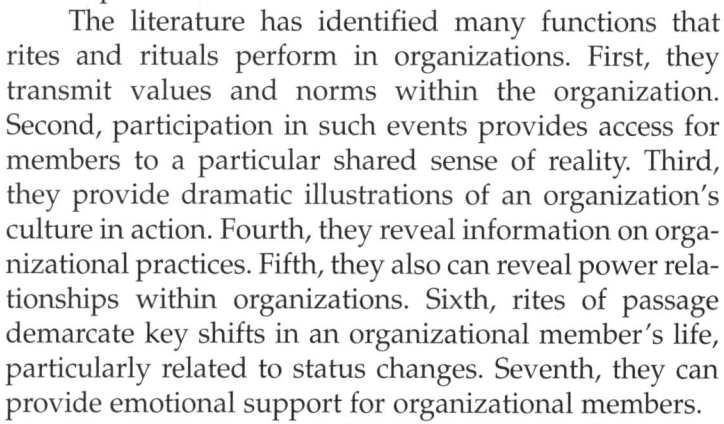

The literature has identified many functions that rites and rituals perform in organizations. First, they transmit values and norms within the organization. Second, participation in such events provides access for members to a particular shared sense of reality. Third, they provide dramatic illustrations of an organization's culture in action. Fourth, they reveal information on organizational practices. Fifth, they also can reveal power relationships within organizations. Sixth, rites of passage demarcate key shifts in an organizational member's life, particularly related to status changes. Seventh, they can provide emotional support for organizational members.

Researchers conducted a study of rites and rituals in a high technology organization (like Nortel) that points to the relationship between rites and rituals and other approaches to organizational communication structure. This study suggested that one's position within the organization has important cultural implications. Specifically, explicit differences between boundary spanners and non-boundary spanning personnel exist in terms of the rites and rituals they engaged in. **Boundary spanners** are people who have direct communication contacts with people who work for other organizations. The boundary spanners in this study, system engineers, identified themselves as those personnel who bring in the money. They see their function as central to the success of the company by having a direct effect on incoming revenue. As such, they were the main product of this organization that uses system engineers to implement computer software systems for their clients. **Non-boundary spanners** (i.e., managing and marketing support, accounting, human resources) view themselves as serving a support function. They are involved in the acquisition and maintenance of client accounts.

These differences in function were reflected in the rites and rituals members of these groups engaged in. When prompted for subjective judgments of the value of organizational events, non-boundary spanners liked meetings, but not social events. In contrast, the engineers, who were the boundary spanners, liked the social events and not the meetings. When the engineers were asked which activities they looked forward to the most, they responded by citing beer blasts, Christmas parties, picnics, and ski trips as their most favorites. The boundary spanners liked the rituals while non-boundary spanners did not. These rites and rituals seemed to act as a communicative tool to maintain a sense of organizational togetherness among the systems engineers because they were not as thoroughly integrated into the organization as the non-boundary spanners.

Strengths and Weaknesses of the Cultural Approach

In this section we have illustrated how two aspects of culture, rules and rites and rituals, related to organizational communication structure. Structure and culture are thus intimately related to each other. When managers change structure, they must expect a change in culture, as well. Or, if a new person comes into an organization and successfully changes culture, then structural changes are likely to result. So, the key advantage of the organizational culture approach lies in its usefulness in explaining the underlying factors manifested in particular communication structures. One of the key factors behind management's interest in organizational culture in recent years lies in its use as a tool to increase the predictability of organizational member behavior. A strong organizational culture makes behavior more uniform and more in accordance with managers' interests. Thus, cultural approaches are centrally concerned with predictability. In this connection cultural approaches also serve to promote the temporal stability of behaviors. In fact, most organizational socialization efforts are aimed at passing on and continuing the existing cultural behavior patterns of an organization to new members.

Similarly, cultural approaches, especially those related to rules, promote an in-depth understanding of communication relationships, contribute greatly to our understanding of how they form, and what the substance of them is likely to be. The only major drawback of the cultural approach may come in what it reveals about patterns of interaction. Except at the level of individual interactions, cultural approaches have not been concerned with developing techniques for systematically describing communication patterns. Thus, no technique is currently available for describing the overall pattern of culturally-related communication behaviors at the level of the whole organization. Certainly no technique is available that has the mathematical and computer sophistication of the network analysis and gradient approaches.

COORDINATION: THE PROCESS OF ORGANIZING

The final issue that is important to understand about why Nortel's structural shift was so successful deals with the issue of coordination. At the end of the day what Nortel really accomplished through their use of web-based communication tools is enhanced coordination among its key employees, suppliers, and customers. What is coordination, and what factors encourage or discourage people to coordinate? Coordination is really the essence of organizational communication. So, it bears closer scrutiny now that the groundwork for understanding organizations has been laid.

What Is Coordination?

Coordination is the process of creating interdependence. As people evolve into a team, or need each other to perform some task, they must coordinate with one another. Why is coordination important? Coordination allows information to flow unhindered throughout the organization; information is the essential tool individuals need for effective decision-making and responding to change.

Coordination hinges on the ability to exchange resources and sentiment to achieve organizational goals. Let's look at these two commodities more closely. Resource exchange involves sharing both information and other, more tangible resources such as personnel, money, inventory, and so forth. When people give these items to one another, it demonstrates that they are serious about working together. Oddly enough, information is not often perceived as adequate for building interdependence. Perhaps members believe that information is cheap, and is really not tangible. Nevertheless, until other, more tangible resources are shared, people tend not to feel that they are fully coordinating with one another.

Sentiment is really the desire or motivation to coordinate. For example, before Nortel could make a structural shift that required different kinds of coordination they had to determine the level of interest employees had in teaming up with members of other units in the company. Fortunately, their sentiment toward coordination was decidedly positive. People knew they needed to coordinate to grow. If they lack this motivation, individuals tend not to share information and other resources. This impedes information flow and discourages quality decision-making. So, there must be some compelling reason driving the coordination. In Nortel's case it was the need to enter and perhaps dominate the fiber-optic market. There were some very specific, tangible rewards available to units that could coordinate. If management had not made the case for the potential rewards then the sentiment to coordination would be lost. Whatever the driving force, sentiment is a key to coordination.

This is the point at which network issues come into focus. Managers continuously struggle with the issue of coordination, and how to develop it more fully. Basically, the manager's goal is to create a production network of individuals where none existed before. How does the manager accomplish this objective? The most straightforward approach is to build the production network on top of some other network in which these same individuals are already coordinating.

This approach requires managers to turn to the social maintenance network. This network exists because individuals have naturally come together and built relationships out of mutual trust and common interests. Why not use this network, and perhaps expand or shape it a bit to do additional tasks? In fact, this is a highly effective strategy. Social networks are very solid, and can often support production talk.

Leadership

One of the most important elements affecting coordination is leadership. Effective leadership is essential for coordination. Effective leaders demonstrate the following characteristics, according to a recent book by Kouzes and Pozner (1995):

- **Leaders challenge the process.** They are always on guard to make things simpler, keep on the task, and keep things focused and moving ahead.

- **Leaders inspire a shared vision.** Leaders are constantly looking to the future to help reduce others' uncertainties about the future. How can we shape ourselves for the challenges ahead?

- **Leaders enable others to act.** Listening to people to help and empower them to make decisions on their own. Leaders don't push; they pull people along. They provide them with the skills to be independent thinkers, creatively contributing to the organization.

- **Leaders model the way.** They act with credibility. Demonstrate your knowledge, show that you are trustworthy, and create a dynamic atmosphere. People want to follow someone who is credible.

- **Leaders encourage the heart.** This is the motivational aspect of leadership. Encouraging the heart means helping people become committed to the organization's success. People need to buy into the vision and work creatively to accomplish that vision.

Of course, everyone can demonstrate leadership skills. Different situations call for individuals to step in and become leaders. For example, a team member will need to use leadership skills in encouraging other members of the team to perform their best. Or, that member may see something about the team's structure that needs changing and make suggestions to improve that structure. Leadership is all about positive change. Certainly the management at Nortel recognized the need for change and initiated events to make that change happen. But, those supporting the change also needed leadership skills to implement the major shift in direction.

A key point in this discussion about change is that leadership is generally earned rather than given to people. For example, liaisons in many organizations are viewed by their peers as leaders regardless of their formal title. Others look to them for information, direction, and resources. In changing their structure, Nortel needed to find these individuals and work with them to help shape the culture and increase the sentiment for coordination. You will ultimately be judged by the extent to which you are willing to adopt and use leader-like behaviors. Using them means you are a force for positive change in the organization.

Certainly, there are several barriers that can stand in a leader's way. For example, many studies have found that most employees trust their immediate supervisor, but mistrust middle and upper management people. Thus, individuals are unlikely to want to coordinate with other units in the organization if their supervisors are not involved. Trust adds a great deal to coordination since individuals tend to coordinate with people with whom they have solid interpersonal relationships. Clearly defined leadership roles with strong interpersonal ties facilitate coordination. It is rare to find a great deal of coordination when leadership is ambiguous or absent, and trust is low. After all, coordination rarely goes smoothly. When barriers emerge, leaders must take charge to move barriers aside and press on.

Building Effective Coordination in Organizations

The first step in building effective coordination in organizations is to have leadership in place that will inspire people to coordinate. We mention this point over and over again because without leadership individuals will not coordinate effectively. Moreover, organizations must also commit to creating a unit in charge of coordination. The unit must monitor how successfully groups work together to make sure that the sentiment and the resource exchange remains high. This coordinating agency also has the responsibility of managing conflicts between groups that inevitably arise because one group might feel used by another group.

Voluntary coordination driven by strong sentiment works best. If people see that coordination is in their best interests, they will work together more productively. Individuals often adopt this position spontaneously in the face of disaster. When a tornado hits, an earthquake erupts, or a war breaks out, individuals suddenly bind together to fight a common enemy. They feel an urgent need to coordinate to respond to the crisis. Oftentimes when the crisis goes away, the coordination disappears as sentiment evaporates. Keeping it from disappearing is accomplished by encouraging the group to interact socially, and giving them challenges that require coordination.

CONCLUSIONS

What lessons might we learn from Nortel's total organizational restructuring? Perhaps the most important lesson is that restructuring is possible when organizations commit to changing the way in which they communicate. This is a very significant commitment because organizations typically develop communication habits that are hard to break. Nortel had evolved into a very traditional, vertically-integrated firm; but Nortel sold the idea that the fiber-optic market had great potential, creating the sentiment or motivation for individuals to change. Then, they used the Internet to implement their communication changes in combination with some very significant business moves, and dramatically improved their productivity. Let's review those steps briefly.

- Nortel recognized a great potential in the fiber-optic market, creating the sentiment for change.
- Nortel developed a plan to change from a Command and Control organization to a Strategy and Oversight organization.
- The company restructured their communication patterns with management, team members, suppliers, and customers using the Internet.

It is important to note that not all companies will recognize the need for change. Many remain very comfortable with the old way of doing business. These patterns are not necessarily counterproductive since many of these organizations get along just fine. However, the Internet has made it possible to make dramatic shifts in organizational structure almost overnight. Companies can suddenly reshape themselves, almost on demand, to meet lightning-quick changes in customer needs. What better strategy than to continuously remold the company to take advantage of business opportunities? You may someday find yourself working for one of these organizations. It will demand your creativity, leadership, technical knowledge, and most importantly, communication skills.

REFERENCES

Fisher, L. M. (2001). From vertical to virtual: How Nortel's supplier alliances extend the enterprise. *Strategy & Business, 22*, 152–161.

Kouzes, J. M., & Posner, B. Z. (1995). *The leadership challenge.* San Francisco: Jossey-Bass Publishers.

Chapter Ten Case Study Quiz—Coordination

Instructions:

Please read the following case study carefully and select the best answers to the questions. This quiz is an individual assignment. Remember: sharing answers is a form of plagiarism.

Human Communication (COM 100) is a large course that serves 600-750 students depending on the semester. Because of the size of the course, there are several key people who ensure that the class operates smoothly on a daily basis. Professor Donohue conducts lectures and relays the expectations and the responsibilities to the course coordinator. The course coordinator reports to Dr. Donohue and also conducts training and information exchange with the Graduate Teaching Assistants (TAs) and Undergraduate Section Leaders (SLs). The course coordinator meets with the TAs each week where updates on the class are made. In turn, the TAs notify the SLs of such information as well as they make appropriate announcements to the students in class or via email. At times, students have questions about the requirements of the class as well as questions about the grades they have received. Due to this, certain procedures are set up to create ease for students addressing such concerns. Generally, students first discuss class issues with their SL because they feel more comfortable talking to someone they view as a peer. However, questions about grades must be directed to TAs because they are responsible for the grades. If issues cannot be resolved with TAs, then students may approach the course coordinator and/or Dr. Donohue. Such procedures are set up so that all students can be heard and that each student's circumstances are considered in the same fashion.

Student's Name _____

Section Number _____

Section Leader's Name _____

Chapter Ten Case Study Quiz—Coordination

1. _____ is what takes place when students speak with their TA about their grade and _____ takes place when the TA makes an announcement about an assignment in recitation.
   a. Horizontal communication; downward communication
   b. Downward communication; upward communication
   c. Upward communication; downward communication
   d. Upward communication; horizontal communication

2. What basic management model BEST mirrors the structure of COM 100?
   a. Holding Company Model
   b. Strategy and Oversight Model
   c. Active Leader Involvement Model
   d. Command and Control Model

3. The Course Coordinator reports to the Professor and also communicates with TAs, but is neither an instructor nor a TA. Their communication role would be labeled as a(n):
   a. Participant
   b. Non-participant
   c. Liaison
   d. Manager

4. When the Course Coordinator gives the TAs information on specific details for grading a class assignment, the Coordinator is relaying what kind of information?
   a. Participatory information
   b. Production-related information
   c. Innovation information
   d. Social function information

5. Sometimes students have questions about their grades. There is a written procedure in the syllabus that indicates how students should go about asking such grade questions. What type of rule?
   a. Informal rule
   b. Formal rule
   c. Cultural rule
   d. Ritual rule

Case Study

Chapter Eleven

COMMUNICATION AND THE DECISION-MAKING PROCESS

Abran J. Salazar
University of Rhode Island

Kim Witte
Michigan State University

What follows is a gruesome tale. It is not for the faint of heart or the weak of constitution. So if you are faint of heart (if, for example, you found yourself crying at the movie, *Crouching Tiger, Hidden Dragon*) you might want to skip to the next section of this chapter.

In March of 1995, Maguntu Sebele came home from a day's work to find his 19-year old daughter deathly ill. She had been very weak for the past three days, and had lain most of the past two days in bed with stomach cramps, red and white splotches on her skin, and was now convulsing. Over the course of the last few days, Maguntu had watched his daughter turn from a young, beautiful, vibrant, and athletic woman, to someone whom he now had trouble recognizing as his own flesh and blood. He went over to her bed and stroked her hair and arms. She was too weak to speak, and returned his gentle touch by coolly looking back at him. In a few hours, Maguntu's daughter was dead. It was not the most pleasant of deaths. It was, in her father's eyes, exceedingly long and excruciating.

At sunrise, as was the tradition in Maguntu's village, the decision was made to prepare the body for burial. Despite the condition of the body, it was decided to proceed with the customary procedures for preparing the body according to the traditions of his family, his village, and his religion.

This entailed enacting an ancient ritual that had been established long before he had been born. The ritual involves extensive contact with the body and eventually involves removal of internal organs. This was especially unfortunate for the persons intimately involved with the preparation of the body. For the Ebola virus, the cause of Maguntu's daughter's death, is transmitted by contact with body fluids, especially blood. It is fatal in ninety percent of cases.

In March of 1995, the virus took over one hundred lives. The city of Kikwit, Zaire (now known as the Democratic Republic of Congo), the town which had been the center of the epidemic, lacks two elements that would have made containment of the outbreak much easier: adequate health facilities and communications systems. Hospital personnel reused blood-soaked bedding. Individuals were sent on bicycle treks to spread information regarding the virus and to identify possible victims. How different the decision to proceed with the ritual of removing the internal organs by hand would have been if the people involved had only known that Maguntu's daughter suffered from a disease that was spread by body fluid to skin (or other organ) contact.

The point here is that we all make decisions, whether as individuals or groups, that have a profound effect not only on us, but also on those around us. Our decisions, many times, do not take place in a vacuum. They do impact other people; some to a greater degree than others. We all make decisions, whether as individuals or groups, subject to the knowledge that is possessed, and rules of the traditions that have been established and to which we have been exposed. That is, we make decisions in some kind of context. A context that lays down the rules we will follow and the types of resources that are available to us in making a decision.

Sometimes these decisions work to our (and others') benefit. Sometimes these work to our (and others') detriment, as was the case with the Ebola virus epidemic in Zaire, especially if contrasting information is not brought to light. Maguntu was following the traditions of his ancestors in preparing the body for burial. He was not aware of information regarding the Ebola virus. He did not have access to such information. His decision to prepare the body in the traditional manner may have been different had he been exposed to such information.

Often, we are used to proceeding in particular ways when we go about making decisions. Unless new information is brought to light, it will not be considered and accorded weight in the decision-making process. However, when new information does have an impact on the decisions we make, this contrasting information is brought to bear on decisions through communication by interacting with others in a group context and sharing that information with others.

Everyone, at one time or another, will be part of a group. This is one of the inevitabilities of being human—of being a social animal. As a result, we will participate in group meetings and communicate with other group members. Our communication in groups may serve any one or more of a number of primary purposes. If we are involved in a decision-making group, we communicate with others to let them know which alternative we prefer. In support groups, we let others know about problems, past and present, that we may have dealt with both successfully and unsuccessfully. We may present information to a meeting of the board of directors of a particular organization. We may voice our opinion to other family members about which video we prefer to watch on a Saturday night.

Regardless of the primary purpose of our communication in small groups, one thing is certain: it will occur. It is inevitable that you will be involved in group discussions. From informal interactions with friends, discussing ideas with classmates for an upcoming class project, to interaction at the family dinner table, you will be involved in groups.

At times you may walk away satisfied from a group meeting or discussion. At other times, you may feel very dissatisfied with what took place in the group meeting. Although there may be various reasons why we may feel either satisfied or dissatisfied with group meetings, this chapter will focus on one: group discussion. It will focus on the communication that occurs in groups—particularly decision-making groups. The goal of this chapter is to examine how communication may lead to satisfactory and unsatisfactory outcomes regarding decision-making in groups.

The goal of this chapter is an important one because increasingly, we will be called on to take part in discussions with people whom we might not have (at least not very frequently) a few years ago. Group discussions among members of different ages, ethnicities, and gender will become more commonplace. There are a number of reasons for this.

Chief among these reasons is the trend toward participatory decision-making in the workplace. This trend will result in more and more group meetings, and thus greater opportunity for us to engage in group discussion. Second is the increasingly diverse workplace which contains increasing numbers of older persons, ethnic minorities, and women. Greater diversity in the workforce will provide greater opportunity for us to interact with a wider variety of people.

Whenever groups are comprised of different people, their differences, whether real or perceived, may affect the ways in which we communicate. Sometimes, problems in the communication process may arise from such heterogeneity. These problems may in turn have an effect on how satisfied we are with the group experience, and the effectiveness of the decisions we make in the group context. Understanding the possible problems one might face as a result of communicating in such heterogeneous groups becomes very important. The study of communication, then, becomes very important.

But the study of communication, as it occurs in small groups, is important for another reason. Communication is an important defining characteristic of groups. In fact, some scholars have claimed that the communication that occurs in small groups is so vital that without it, one would be hard-pressed to identify the existence of a small group. That is, these scholars would say that a group is not a group unless its members participate in discussion and communicate with one another.

This chapter focuses on the communication that occurs in small groups. Its purpose is to get you acquainted with one particular function of that communication. Many times communication in small groups serves a decision-making and problem-solving function. It is a function that pervades many groups, even if their primary purpose is not to make a decision or to solve a problem. In this chapter, we will explore that decision-making and problem-solving process, examine some of the common pitfalls associated with it, and how groups may avoid those pitfalls in hopes of reaching the best decision possible.

GROUP DECISION-MAKING AND PROBLEM-SOLVING

Group decision-making is a term that we will use to refer to the process of picking a solution out of a set of alternatives. Decision-making is actually part of the problem-solving process, because in the course of solving problems, groups make decisions all the time. Typically, when engaging in decision-making, group members develop this set of alternatives themselves. However, sometimes group members have the job of picking one out of a pre-determined set of alternatives. These alternatives may have been developed by another group or individual. In either case, the process of selecting an alternative, out of those possible, is the process we will call decision-making.

Problem-solving, on the other hand, refers to "seeking a solution to a problem caused by an obstacle" (Beebe & Masterson, 1994, p.165). Problem-solving entails managing the obstacles that groups face as they travel down the path toward making a decision. These obstacles may be relational, as when group members engage in conflict that is spurred by differences in personality. Obstacles may also be task-oriented, as when members disagree over substantive issues directly related to the task. In the course of managing and dealing with these obstacles, decisions are made. These decisions ultimately have an effect on which alternatives are considered and the one that is eventually selected by the group.

To the extent that a group is able to manage problems and obstacles effectively, it should make a good decision. To the extent that it cannot manage these problems and obstacles effectively, it will probably make a bad decision. Perhaps we can all readily identify instances when a group in which we participated did not perform as effectively as we believed it should. In fact, at times groups perform so poorly and are so ineffective that some scholars have claimed that they are often not needed to make decisions—that individuals will typically outperform groups.

Indeed, a research tradition in social psychology emphasizes the adverse effects of group decision-making; it asserts that the communication that occurs in groups, or the mere organizing of people together for making a decision or solving a problem, often has a negative effect on performance. We begin by exploring this issue. We first examine whether groups are necessary for effective decision-making and problem-solving.

DO GROUPS MAKE BETTER DECISIONS THAN INDIVIDUALS?

A question that has always intrigued small group decision-making scholars concerns whether individuals or groups are better at making decisions. That question is still far from being definitively answered. However, we have gained a better understanding of the issues involved in coming up with an answer. The earliest studies seeking to answer that question met with contradictory results. Some studies determined that individuals were better while others concluded that groups were superior to individuals.

In 1913, Max Ringelmann published an article in which he sought to determine, for additive tasks, whether groups always lived up to their expectations. An **additive task** is one in which individual efforts are basically summed to yield group outputs.

He wondered if, for example, in games such as the tug-o-war, every individual on a five-member team could maximally exert fifty pounds of "pull" on the rope, whether all members pulling together would be able to exert 250 pounds of pull. Or, when lifting heavy objects, if each individual on a five-member team could, at their maximum, lift a fifty-pound weight, whether all members working together would be able to lift a 250-pound weight.

What Ringelmann found was that this was not the case. Invariably, as more members were added to the team, individual effort declined. Thus, while one member is able to lift 50 pounds, adding another member does not guarantee that both lifting together will lift 100 pounds. Indeed, the number is less than that. Ringelmann found that with each additional member added, actual productivity increasingly did not meet the group's potential productivity. That is, members worked at increasingly lower percentages of maximum efficiency as more individuals were added to the group. This phenomenon became known as the **Ringelmann Effect.**

Ringelmann theorized that there were a couple of reasons for these findings. First, he claimed, **groups often suffer from poor performance due to poor coordination of effort.** As a case in point, take the tug-o-war game. In instances in which members fail to

228   Chapter Eleven

pull together at the same time on a rope, for example, the group will perform at a lower level than it should, or has the potential of performing. One person, for example, might consistently pull when all other members are concentrating more on getting a firm foothold, or a better grip on the rope. Thus, all members are not exerting maximum effort at the same time. In short, they are not coordinating their effort in the best possible manner. As a result, the group does not perform at a level that would be expected if we had knowledge of the individual members' abilities.

A second reason for why groups' actual productivity may not equal their potential has to do with a concept called **diffusion of responsibility.** If you have been a member of a group that has been assigned a class project, you have probably seen diffusion of responsibility at work. Almost without fail, you will run across members who, despite your best efforts to prod them, do not want to do their share of the work.

Although there may be various reasons as to why this is the case, Ringelmann focused on one. He claimed that in cases where individuals are given the opportunity to slough off work on someone else, they probably will. In other words, a particular member or members may not work as hard on their parts of the group assignment if they perceive that others in the group will "cover" for them.

So for example, the responsibility that one person may have for doing some library research on a particular issue to be covered in the group project, may be diffused among other group members. As a result, some group members may be straddled with work that was not their responsibility to begin with. This being the case, group members cannot devote their maximum energies to covering all bases doing the work they were assigned, as well as the work which was assigned to others. Group performance invariably suffers.

Thus, on the basis of Ringelmann's research, we are given the impression that groups are not very good contexts in which one would want to work. There are a variety of factors that can, and often do, interfere with a group's ability to perform at a level that is in line with, or surpasses, the talents of its individual members. However, another researcher, working some twenty years after Ringelmann, found that this is not always necessarily the case. That researcher was Marjorie Shaw.

Shaw (1934) had groups and individuals work on what have been termed **intellective tasks** by Joseph McGrath (1984). All intellective tasks possess a correct answer. That answer may also be demonstrated to be the correct one on the basis of culturally accepted standards of coherence and rules of logic.

Some intellective tasks, however, possess answers that are more difficult to demonstrate as being correct, than others. McGrath (1984) has distinguished between three types of intellective tasks along a dimension of demonstrability. With the first type of intellective task he has identified, **eureka tasks,** once the answer is demonstrated to be correct, it will immediately be recognized as the superior choice by all group members (a person will often say to him or herself, "Eureka!! This is the correct answer!" Or not.).

If a group member were to show you, for example, what the correct answer is to one of these tasks, you will in all likelihood agree that it is the correct answer. Even group members who might not have picked or come up with that answer on their own, will immediately know it is correct once it is demonstrated to them.

Take for example, the following task, which has been termed the "Tower of Hanoi." It is a eureka task because it does have a demonstrably correct answer which will be immediately adopted by others once it is made known to them.

> **Your task is to move all the rings on pole "A" to pole "B." You must move one ring at a time, and in no instance is a larger ring to be placed on top of a smaller ring. Keep a record of all moves.**

The fewest number of moves in which one should be able to accomplish this particular task is seven. Individuals working alone are usually able to reach the correct answer. Some, however, are not. Working with this type of task, Shaw (1934) found that groups typically did outperform individuals. That is, in Shaw's study, groups generally made fewer errors and were quicker to arrive at a correct answer than were individuals.

However, a criticism against Shaw's study has been advanced. Kanekar (1987) claimed that Shaw's study was not a fair test of the groups versus individuals question. This is because of a design flaw in Shaw's study. For example, Shaw basically compared a five-member group against one individual. Thus, Kanekar argued, the probability of the group possessing one person with the correct answer was greater than the probability that the one person, to whom the group's performance was compared, had the correct answer. So of course we would expect groups to do better, but not because of the fact that people communicated and interacted with one another. Groups performed better because the odds were unfairly stacked in their favor.

Using a modified design (for example, comparing a five-member group against five noninteracting individuals—what has been called a statisized group), no differences in group versus individual performance were found. In fact, Laughlin and Ellis (1986) found that when individuals who do not possess the correct answer are placed in a group with at least one member with the correct answer, they adopt the correct answer once it is demonstrated to be correct by the member or members with the correct answer.

A second type of intellective task, the **demonstrable task** (McGrath, 1984; Salazar, 1991, 1996), also has a correct answer which may be demonstrated to be correct. However, that answer is also a little more difficult to demonstrate as being correct than the answer for a eureka task. In a group, there may be some debate as to whether one or another answer is the correct one. Take the "Horse Trading Problem" as an example. It goes like this:

> **A man was in the horse trading business. He bought a horse for $60 and sold it for $70. Then he bought the horse again for $80, and sold it one more time for $90. How much money did the man make in the horse-selling business? ($0, $10, $20, $30)**

Do you think you obtained the correct answer? Again, as with the Tower of Hanoi problem, some individuals are able to obtain the correct answer to the Horse Trader Problem. That number, from our experiences in having students work on the problem, is less than the number who come up with the correct answer to the Tower of Hanoi. When students figure out the answer to the problem as individuals, and then are placed in a group to try to come up with a group answer, there is often some debate about whether particular answers are correct.

Typically, however, if a group contains at least two members who have arrived at the correct answer as individuals, all other group members will adopt that answer. Eventually, it becomes the group's answer. (Incidentally, the correct answer to the Horse Trader Problem is twenty dollars.)

Yet a third type of intellective task exists. These also have a correct answer, but, unlike eureka and demonstrable tasks, they depend on expert judgment or consensus to determine the correct answer. These types of intellective tasks we may label **expert judgment tasks** (McGrath, 1984; Salazar, 1991, 1996). For these tasks, an answer is correct because experts have actually solved the problem presented by the task. They have considered alternatives, and provided reasons for why an answer is the correct one. An example of this task is Hall and Watson's (1970) NASA Moon Problem.

FIGURE 11.1 NASA Moon Survival Problem

Consider yourself a member of a spaceship crew of three. Your spacecraft was originally scheduled to rendezvous with a mother ship on the lighted surface of the moon. Due to an entry failure, however, it was necessary for you and your crew to crash-land some two hundred miles from the mothership. In landing, much of the equipment was damaged beyond use and each member of the crew was injured. Ten items of equipment were left intact and undamaged during the crash-landing. Because it is necessary for you to reach the mothership as quickly as possible if you are to survive, only some of the undamaged equipment may be taken on the 200-mile trek which lies ahead. You have been given a sheet which lists the fifteen items of equipment that are still in serviceable condition.

Your task is to rank the items on the basis of their *utility* and *importance* in ensuring your survival on the journey to the mothership. Consider at all times what you know about moon conditions in making your selections.

_____ Food concentrate
_____ Two .45 caliber pistols
_____ 2-100 lb. tanks of oxygen
_____ Signal flares
_____ First-aid kit also containing injection needles
_____ One case dehydrated Pet Milk
_____ Parachute silk
_____ 5 gallons of water
_____ Magnetic compass
_____ Solar-powered FM receiver-transmitter
_____ Fifty feet of nylon rope
_____ Stellar map of moon's constellation
_____ Life raft
_____ Portable heating unit
_____ Box of matches

The expert's rankings for each individual item is presented in parentheses. Members of the Crew Equipment Research Unit at NASA ranked the items according to survival value. How close did you come to approximating the experts' choices? For this task, there is a way to find out: we obtain what is called a deviation score. Begin first by placing your ranking next to the experts'. Then, for each item, obtain an absolute difference score. That is, take the absolute value of the difference between your ranking and the experts' ranking. So, for example, if your ranking of the stellar map was 8, the absolute difference between your ranking and the experts' would be 5. Do this for each of the items. Add the difference scores. The sum is your deviation score. The lower your deviation score, the better you did in approximating the experts. Compare your score with those of your classmates. How did you do?

Note that rarely will an individual's rankings match the experts'. Typically, after having completed the task as individuals, people are placed into groups and then asked to come to a consensus decision about how to best rank the items. This is done without prior knowledge of how well each individual did in comparison to the experts. When consensus has been reached by group members about how the items should be ranked, these group rankings, at times, are better than the best group member's individual rankings. That is, the group manages to obtain a deviation score which is lower (they more closely approximate the experts' rankings) than that obtained by the best performing individual member. When this occurs, an assembly effect bonus (Collins & Guetzkow, 1967) has occurred. That is, group members, communicating with one another, have been able to achieve something that exceeded the performance of the group's best individual member. The group has exceeded its potential productivity. Communication has had a positive synergistic effect (Salazar, 1995, 1996, 1997).

At other times however, a group performs at a level lower than its best member. In this case, group members communicating with one another have detracted, in one way or another, from the group's potential performance—a process loss has occurred (Steiner, 1972). The group has not performed in a manner consistent with its capabilities. Somewhere along the way to making a decision, members communicated in a way such that the group was unable to make the best use of the resources available to it. In such instances, communication may be said to have had a negative synergistic effect on group decision-making quality (Salazar, 1995, 1996, 1997).

Each of these tasks has an answer that may be demonstrated to be the correct one. Some answers are more easily demonstrated to be correct than others. In fact, we might place these tasks on a continuum denoting the ease with which the answer may be demonstrated to be correct. The task with the easiest to demonstrate answer, the Tower of Hanoi, falls at one end of the continuum, and the task with the most difficult answer, the NASA Moon Problem, falls at the other end.

With each of the first two tasks we have examined (the Tower of Hanoi, and the Horse Trader Problem), a group is likely to obtain the correct answer if it has one or two members who know the correct answer prior to discussion. In these two cases, it probably would not have made a difference if people had been placed in a group or not. The communication that would have occurred in the group would not have played a positive or a negative role. That is, we could have predicted, without group members ever interacting with one another, whether a group would have come up with the correct answer. That prediction is a function of whether or not the group possesses members with the correct answer.

On the other hand, the communication that takes place in a group may play a much more important role when group members work on a task whose answer is not so easily demonstrable (Salazar, 1997). Although communication may serve to yield a process loss, it has still played a more important role, though it is one we would not like to see happen. In cases where an assembly bonus has occurred, communication has had a positive and beneficial effect. The key to effective group performance, then, is to identify those conditions and communication characteristics that lead to an assembly effect bonus (positive synergy) and a process loss (negative synergy). Groups may then be instructed in what sorts of processes lead to beneficial outcomes.

Groups, then, and particularly the quality of the communication that takes place in groups, may become more important as the demonstrability of the task's answer decreases (Salazar, 1995). The less demonstrable the task, the more important quality group communication becomes. Thus, tasks that are characterized by high degrees of ambiguity and uncertainty thus are perhaps best tackled by a group, rather than by individuals (Salazar, 1996).

THE ANATOMY OF A DECISION: GROUP DECISION DEVELOPMENT

For the most part, groups do not approach decision-making in a haphazard way. It may seem that way at times, but there is generally a process that groups go through in reaching a decision. A number of communication scholars, as well as scholars in other disciplines, have attempted to identify the patterns of communication that typify that process. Among these attempts is that of Fisher (1970).

Fisher claimed that groups progress through various phases of communicative activity on their way to reaching a decision from the time members first encounter each other, to the time that a decision is actually made. He discovered four such phases: **orientation, conflict, emergence, and reinforcement.** These phases unfold sequentially in time. They thus compose a particular unitary sequence that groups follow. More will be said about unitary sequences later.

The **orientation phase** occurs in the initial part of the group meeting. During the orientation stage, a group's members try to get to know each other. They may ask each other for their names if they have never met before, or group members may introduce themselves. Other questions are asked that reduce some of the uncertainty they may have regarding other group members. Further, in the orientation stage, group members are very agreeable toward one another in an effort to avoid creating an undesirable group atmosphere. The emphasis at this stage is on getting to know one another, and being nice to others. An attempt is made to not stir the waters or lay a bad foundation from which to initiate discussion on the issue/problem confronting the group. Group members may also tentatively advance claims in this stage of the decision-making process.

After the orientation phase, groups progress to the **conflict phase.** In the conflict phase, group members are no longer tentative, and they openly disagree with one another about positions taken. At this point, where particular individuals stand on issues becomes rather clear. As a result, individuals with similar opinions or stances on issues may form coalitions in an effort to strengthen their respective positions.

Once groups have progressed through the orientation and conflict phases, they then move to the **emergence phase.** During the emergence phase, conflict declines. By this point, differences have pretty much been ironed out, disagreements have been raised and refuted, or individuals may sometimes remain quiet if they do have a disagreement. Coalitions disband and ambiguity is present, but at this stage ambiguity functions as a means to indicate disagreement. It is a way of disagreeing with someone's ideas or comments without being disagreeable.

When groups finally reach the **reinforcement phase,** group members have reached a consensus on decisions. All members, either truthfully or ostensibly, agree on a given course of action. At this point, group members also reinforce each other and show signs of unity. Congratulations on a job well done abound.

Other unitary sequence models of decision development have been proposed. Tuckman (1965) for example, discovered a series of phases which he labeled **forming, storming, norming, and performing.** Whatever the unitary sequence model examined, all models make the assumption that groups make decisions in a straightforward and linear manner. That is, in coming up with a decision, groups progress through each of the stages or phases, in order. It is assumed that once groups have progressed through a particular phase, there is no return to previous stages.

Marshall Scott Poole, however, disagrees with the assumptions of the unitary sequence models. He and his colleagues have claimed that sometimes groups do not progress through stages in a straightforward manner; there may be a lot of jumping around, from stage to stage, that groups do as they make a decision. He relies on a theory called **Structuration Theory** to provide an explanation for why groups do not always follow the assumptions of unitary sequence models of group decision-making.

Structuration Theory was originally developed by a sociologist named Anthony Giddens. Giddens' goal in proposing this theory was, among other things, to outline a framework for understanding how and why human action or behavior becomes patterned or structured. The theory has been subsequently applied to the small group setting by Marshall Poole, David Seibold, and Robert McPhee (1985, 1986, 1996). The discussion that follows is a description of structuration theory as it has been applied to the small group setting, particularly as it concerns decision development.

At its crux, Structuration Theory accounts for the patterning of human behavior and social practices in terms of structures. **Social practices** are "naturally bounded activities, recognized as coherent wholes" by individuals (Poole, Seibold, & McPhee, 1986, p. 244). Social practices include such patterned human activity as weddings, making decisions, football games, etc. **Structures** are made up of rules and resources. Rules define how something ought to be done in particular situations. Also, rules help us determine how certain communicative behaviors are to be interpreted. A resource is a means of exerting influence over others. Rules and resources are typically not seen, but we can infer that they exist by observing other people's behavior.

People draw on structures to perform particular behaviors. These behaviors constitute social practices. **Social systems,** on the other hand, are "reproduced relations between actors or collectivities, [which] are organized as regular social practices" (Giddens, 1979, p.66). Examples of social systems include status hierarchies in organizations, groups, class, and gender. The production and reproduction of social systems through the application of structures in interaction is referred to as the process of **structuration.** It is important to note, that at the same time that structures enable individuals to perform behaviors, they also constrain individuals in the range of behaviors that they perform.

An important concept in the theory of structuration is the **duality of structure.** As stated previously, structures enable the production of action (behavior) in groups. They serve as "recipes" for how something is done. As such, they are the means or the medium for the production of action. At the same time, however, structures are also the products of interaction. That is, they have no existence apart from being produced in group members' interaction with one another. The duality of structure, then, refers to structures being both the medium and the outcome of interaction. Take for example, money being used as a resource. Money, as a resource, enables one person to influence another. Yet, at the same time that it is used as a means of influence, the use of money in such a manner is legitimated or reinforced.

Decision-making may be conceived of as a social practice. As such, there are various structures that underlie its production and reproduction. Marshall Poole has used structuration theory to help us understand how groups structure their communication as they make a decision. His work has described how decisions develop in group contexts.

Poole claims that sometimes groups do not progress through phases in a simple and linear manner. That is, groups do not always follow a unitary sequence of phases as they make a decision. There may be **multiple sequences** that describe a group's progression on its way to making a decision. Sometimes groups double back to an earlier stage, or may skip stages altogether. The sequence or path that a group does take is dependent on various factors. Initially, Poole claims that group members enter a decision-making situation with some sort of idea about how to proceed in crafting a solution. This idea may derive from a cultural norm which is generally understood by members.

So, for example, when making a decision, group members generally recognize that the best way to make a decision is to proceed in the following manner: **recognition that a problem exists, defining the problem, marshaling a range of solutions, specifying criteria for a good solution, and planning how to implement the solution eventually picked** (Poole & Roth, 1989a). This series of steps implies a unitary sequence of phases. This set of procedures, however, may be task-dependent; the general idea that we have about the procedure to be followed in solving a decision-making task may not be the same idea that we would have about solving a bargaining task. As such, the task defines the particular structures (rules and resources) available to individuals in carrying out their decision-making behavior.

When groups do proceed in accordance with the norm, phases tend to emerge. There tend to emerge distinct time-periods of patterned communicative behavior that follow a unitary sequence. However, various other factors exist which also shape the general path a group will follow; Poole calls these **contingencies.** These contingencies may cause the group to deviate substantially from the ideal unitary sequence or the cultural norm. These contingencies are the nature of the task (whether it primarily involves a discussion of values, which course of action should be taken, or whether the task is a novel one to most group members, etc.) and group structure (the degree to which group members like one another, the size of the group, etc.) (Poole & Roth, 1989b). So while the cultural norm informs us at a general level about how we should go about making a decision, contingency factors ultimately shape and define what that path will ultimately look like.

Examining a pool of 47 decisions made by 29 groups, Poole and Roth discovered that groups do not always follow a unitary sequence. The researchers found that only eleven of the decisions followed a **unitary sequence path.** These groups initiated discussion by focusing on the analysis of the problem, and progressed to solution activity. Twenty-two of the decisions had **complex cyclic paths,** in which groups cycled back and forth between discussion of the problem and discussion of solutions. Fourteen of the decisions exhibited **solution oriented paths,** in which groups primarily focused discussion on solutions.

Some of the contingencies identified by the researchers seemed to affect the decision-path that would be taken by groups. Groups that followed a unitary sequence path also tended to be larger, power was shared among members, and they worked on a factual problem for which goals were unclear and group members were not supplied a list of solutions from which to choose. Further, these groups tended to be low in cohesiveness, unless the group was also large. Groups that tended to follow a solution-oriented path were small cohesive groups with a centralized power structure, clear goals, and solutions from which to choose.

So, in general, the path that is ultimately taken by the group in coming up with a solution is dependent on various factors. It is no longer taken as truth that group decisions develop in a straightforward and linear manner, as implied by unitary sequence models.

GROUP COMMUNICATION AND EFFECTIVE DECISION-MAKING

As group decisions develop, there are a variety of communication-related factors that may enhance or inhibit effective decision-making. These may range from having one person dominate discussion, members not being willing to provide input because they fear being evaluated by others, and having a leader who exerts his or her will on the group.

Randy Hirokawa and his colleagues have identified specific communication related problems that may arise during decision-making. They have also identified those communication related aspects which seem to promote effective decision-making. Randy Hirokawa and Roger Pace (1983) conducted a study in which they attempted to identify the communication patterns associated with effective and ineffective group decision-making. In general, they concluded that effective decision-making groups were characterized by four recurring themes of communicative activity.

First, **effective groups rigorously examined and evaluated validity of opinions and assumptions.** That is, information advanced by group members, and claims concerning that information, were closely scrutinized in effective groups, while receiving cursory treatment in ineffective groups. Although group members may not always have access to all the pertinent information needed to make a good decision, they will greatly enhance their chances of arriving at a high-quality decision if they carefully look over and scrutinize the information they do possess and use. Making unwarranted leaps in logic, without checking to see if they are unwarranted, will no doubt result in poor decisions.

Second, **effective groups more rigorously evaluated suggested courses of action, and rigorously tested them in light of pre-established criteria.** Courses of action represent the possible solutions suggested by group members. Pre-established criteria refers to standards that group members establish about how to go about evaluating those suggestions. In short, these criteria act as minimal hurdles that solutions must pass over in order to even be considered as part of the final pool from which the group will choose one alternative.

Implicit in this characteristic of successful groups is the assumption that at some point in the discussion, group members have established criteria by which to judge alternatives, or that criteria has been provided to them. Effective groups, according to Hirokawa and Pace (1983), methodically examined the alternatives that had been advanced by determining whether they met these standards. In ineffective groups, members rarely discuss the consequences of proposed solutions or compare alternatives against criteria in a superficial way, almost as if they are merely "going through the motions." In the Hirokawa and Pace study, members of ineffective groups also tended to give short, "yes" or "no" answers without elaboration.

Third, **effective groups based their final choice on facts, assumptions, and inferences that seemed to be reasonable and accurate.** That is, an outside observer would normally judge the assumptions and inferences made to be reasonable. Ineffective groups, on the other hand, based their final decision on facts, assumptions, and inferences that appeared to be highly questionable.

Although the assumptions and inferences made by ineffective groups may seem reasonable to group members, they may not seem that way to someone observing from the outside. At some point in the discussion, members may have made inferential errors that set the stage for other inferences to be made. Of course those inferences may seem unreasonable to an outside observer, but may seem very reasonable to group members. Clearly, assumptions made on the basis of invalid inferences have little chance of being correct. Group decision-making suffers as a result.

Fourth, **in effective groups, influential members asked appropriate questions, pointed out important information, challenged and persuaded the group to reject unwarranted assumptions, and kept the group from digressing to irrelevant topics.** For group members in ineffective groups, influential members introduced and persuaded the group to accept unwarranted or erroneous assumptions and arguments, and led the group to irrelevant discussions.

In addition to the preceding communication behaviors that seem to promote effective decision-making, a few others should also be mentioned. First, **group members should define and determine the extent of the problem situation** (Hirokawa & Rost, 1992). Proper analysis and definition of the problem area should help the group in determining whether a given alternative will successfully deal with the problem. Identification of the extent of the problem, that is, its social and economic impact should give group members a good idea of the seriousness of the problem, and may also establish a timeframe within which to work.

Second, **the alternatives under consideration by the group should be considered in light of their negative and positive consequences.** That is, group members should determine, for each alternative, the possible benefits, as well as the possible disadvantages. Such analysis seems to promote effective decision-making (Hirokawa & Rost, 1992).

Following these suggestions may help group members make good decisions, but it may not help groups make the best use of the resources (skills and abilities) brought to them by other group members. That is, these suggestions may not be a sufficient precondition for achieving a process gain (Salazar, 1996), but carrying out these suggestions may be a sufficient precondition (in most cases) for avoiding a process loss.

Third, **because task-oriented obstacles are important, group members should not be afraid to introduce them if discussion has proceeded without them** (Salazar, 1995; in press). Such obstacles would include introducing questions about various alternatives, injecting diverse viewpoints (Sauser, 1988), playing the devil's advocate by trying to find fault in each proposed alternative (Sauser, 1988; Schweiger & Steinberg, 1989), and openly disagreeing and promoting constructive conflict. Constructive conflict entails disagreeing over issues and task related matters, and not over personalities. Every effort should be made to divorce people from ideas.

Fourth, **disagreeing, questioning, and playing the devil's advocate may not be enough.** Members should also strive to resolve disagreements, answer questions, and settle constructive conflicts. Every effort should be made to avoid glossing over questions, disagreements, and conflicts. The emphasis should be placed on resolution through critical examination, rather than consensus through superficial appeal.

Fifth, **everyone should be encouraged to participate, and be provided the opportunity to communicate** (Salazar et al., 1994). Members who remain silent almost always have something to say, but, for some reason or another, decline to say it. All members should be asked for input and be assured that the group is interested in hearing what they have to say. Many times, piggybacking off of others' ideas is a useful exercise, and ideas generated by such an activity go unreported; consequently, the group is left to work with previously established (however erroneous) assumptions, ideas, or conceptions. Encouraging others to participate increases the probability that such ideas will be shared with the group.

These latter two suggestions are particularly important when one considers the phenomenon know as the **Abilene Paradox**. The Abilene Paradox starts out as a family discussion about where to spend this year's vacation. Several alternatives are considered and rejected, until someone mentions Abilene, Kansas. The suggestion receives mild support from others. However, some group members might actually disagree with the choice—even the person who raised the option. All family members go to Abilene and have a lousy time, only to realize when they get back home that no one wanted to go to Abilene in the first place. Encouraging disagreements and encouraging participation may avert the Abilene paradox.

Finally, **groups ought to be kept relatively small.** As group size increases, the opportunity that group members have to communicate with one another, especially under time constraints, diminishes. Smaller group sizes better facilitate member input. These are only a few of the suggestions for increasing the probability of making effective decisions.

CONCLUSIONS

We are all likely to spend a significant amount of time and energy participating in groups to make decisions—particularly after we enter the workforce. This chapter details the importance of communication in group decision-making tasks, examines the quality of decisions made by groups as compared to individuals, analyzes the patterns of communication leading to decisions (i.e., unitary sequences versus Structuration Theory approaches), and identifies the characteristics leading to effective (versus ineffective) decision-making in groups.

We hope you can take the information presented in this chapter and apply it to areas of your life where you interact with other people in groups to make decisions. Sometimes difficult decisions must be made in groups, as in the Ebola virus case described in the beginning of this chapter. Other times, decisions may be relatively easy, like what movie to see or where to eat dinner. All in all, it appears that "effective" or "good" decisions are made when concrete problems and action steps are identified, some sort of standard or criteria is set to compare proposed solutions against, and all group members have the opportunity to air their views and examine alternative solutions against these set standards or criteria. This chapter equips you with a basic knowledge about how to make good and effective decisions.

REFERENCES

Beebe, S. A., & Masterson, J. T. (1994). *Communicating in small groups: Principles and practices* (4th ed.). NY: Harper Collins.

Collins, B. E., & Guetzkow, H. (1964). *A social psychology of group processes for decision-making.* New York: John Wiley & Sons, Inc.

Fisher, B. A. (1970). Decision emergence: Phases in group decision-making. *Speech Monographs, 37,* 53–66.

Hall, J., & Watson, W. H. (1970). The effects of a normative intervention in group decision-making performance. *Human Relations, 23,* 299–217.

Hirokawa, R. Y., & Pace, R. (1983). A descriptive investigation of the possible communication based reasons for effective and ineffective group decision-making. *Communication Monographs, 50,* 363–379.

Hirokawa, R. Y., & Rost, K. M. (1992). *Management Communication Quarterly, 5,* 267–288.

Kanekar, S. (1987). Individual versus group performance: A selective review of experimental studies. *The Irish Journal of Psychology, 8,* 9–19.

Laughlin, P. R., & Ellis, A. L. (1986). Demonstrability and social combination processes on mathematical intellective tasks. *Journal of Experimental Social Psychology, 22,* 177–189.

McGrath, J. E. (1984). *Groups: Interaction and performance.* Englewood Cliffs, NJ: Prentice Hall.

Poole, M. S., & Roth, J. (1989a). Decision development in small groups IV: A typology of group decision paths. *Human Communication Research, 15,* 323–356.

Poole, M. S., & Roth, J. (1989b). Decision development in small groups V: A test of a contingency model. *Human Communication Research, 15,* 549–589.

Poole, M. S., Seibold, D.R., & McPhee, R. D. (1985). Group decision-making as a structurational process. *Quarterly Journal of Speech, 17,* 74–102.

Poole, M. S., Seibold, D. R., & McPhee, R. D. (1996). The structuration of group decisions. In R. Y. Hirokawa and M. S. Poole (Eds.), *Communication and group decision-making* (pp. 114–146) (2nd ed.). Thousand Oaks, CA: Sage.

Poole, M. S., Seibold, D.R., & McPhee, R. D. (1986). A structurational approach to theory building in group decision-making research. In R. Y. Hirokawa and M. S. Poole (Eds.), *Communication and group decision-making* (pp. 237–264). Beverly Hills, CA: Sage.

Ringelmann, M. (1913). Research on animate sources of power: The work of man. *Annales de l'Institut National Agronomique, 2e serie—tome XII,* 1–40.

Salazar, A. J. (in press). Self organizing and complexity perspectives of group creativity: Implications for group communication. In L. Frey (Ed.), *New directions in group communication research.* Newbury Park, CA: Sage.

Salazar, A.J. (1997). Communication effects on small group decision-making: Homogeneity and task as moderators of the communication-performance relationship. *Western Journal of Communication, 61*(1), 35–65.

Salazar, A. J. (1996). Ambiguity and communication effects on small group decision-making performance. *Human Communication Research, 23,* 155–192.

Salazar, A. J. (1995). Understanding the synergistic effects of communication in small groups: Making the most out of group member abilities. *Small Group Research, 26,* 169–199.

Salazar, A. J. (1991). *Assessing the impact of interaction on group decision-making performance: Some conditions and patterns of interaction.* Unpublished doctoral dissertation, University of Iowa.

Salazar, A. J., Hirokawa, R. Y., Propp, K. M., Julian, K., & Leatham, G.B. (1994). In search of true causes: Examination of the effect of group potential and group interaction on decision performance. *Human Communication Research, 20,* 529–559.

Sauser, W. R. (1988). Injecting contrast: A key to quality decisions. *Advanced Management Journal, 53,* 20–23.

Schweiger, D. M., & Sandberg, W. R. (1989). The utilization of individual capabilities in group approaches to strategic decision-making. *Strategic Management Journal, 10,* 31–43.

Shaw, M. (1934). A comparison of individuals and groups in the rational solution of complex problems. *American Journal of Psychology, 44,* 491–504.

Steiner, I. (1972). *Group process and productivity.* New York: Academic Press.

Tuckman, B. W. (1965). Developmental sequence in small groups. *Psychological Bulletin, 63,* 384–399.

ANSWERS TO THE NASA MOON SURVIVAL PROBLEM

4 Food concentrate
11 Two .45 caliber pistols
1 2-100 lb. tanks of oxygen
10 Signal flares
7 First-aid kit also containing injection needles
12 One case dehydrated Pet Milk
8 Parachute silk
2 5 gallons of water
14 Magnetic compass
5 Solar-powered FM receiver-transmitter
6 Fifty feet of nylon rope
3 Stellar map of moon's constellation
9 Life raft
13 Portable heating unit
15 Box of matches

Chapter Eleven Case Study Quiz—Decision-Making

Instructions:
Please read the following case study carefully and select the best answers to the questions. This quiz is an individual assignment. Remember: sharing answers is a form of plagiarism.

Mia is outraged when she finds out there is a group project requirement in her class. She hates working in groups! Her experience has shown that not everyone puts in an equal share and she ends up doing most of the work the day before the project is due. For her current project, she must work with four other people in creating an organization from scratch including the name of the organization, how the organization was founded, and what the values of the organization are. Her instructor randomly picks groups in class one day and Mia spends the rest of that class learning her group members' names and majors. During the next class meeting, the group dives into creating the organization and right away the group members disagree on what the organization should be. Half the members want to create a movie theater/bar and the other half of the members want to create a golf club. After much arguing between Mia and a group member named John, Mia requested that the rest of the group prove why the golf club would be a better organization. John brought in brochures from popular golf clubs, ideas for the organization history, and even suggested that Tiger Woods could be the club's spokesperson. Once Mia could envision the golf club, she decided to give in, let John assume the leader role and the group went forth with the creation of Xanadu Golf Club. Now that the biggest decision was made, they were all comfortable tackling smaller decisions and obstacles.

Student's Name _____

Section Number _____

Section Leader's Name _____

Chapter Eleven Case Study Quiz—Decision-Making

1. Mia's group is trying to create an organization for a class project. The group has spent one class discussing the assignment, and they spent the rest of time discussing possible organizations including a golf club and a movie theater. What type of decision path is Mia's group using?
   a. Unitary sequence path
   b. Complex cyclic path
   c. Solution oriented path
   d. General decision-making path

2. Mia has been randomly placed into a group for this project. During the first class session, Mia voiced her opinion to the group that she wanted to be in a positive group experience and to avoid any bad experiences. The other group members agreed. In what phase of group decision-making is Mia's group?
   a. Orientation
   b. Conflict
   c. Emergence
   d. Reinforcement

3. Mia's group conflicted over deciding what organization to create: the gold club or the movie theater. Once John has shown why the golf club would be a good organization, Mia and the rest of the group have reached a consensus on what to do. In what phase of group decision-making is Mia's group?
   a. Orientation
   b. Conflict
   c. Emergence
   d. Reinforcement

4. Mia did not want to participate in the group project because her past group experiences include others not doing their share of work. This is called:
   a. The Ringelmann Effect
   b. Diffusion of responsibility
   c. Structuration Theory
   d. Additive Task

5. Which of the following is NOT a factor of effective decision-making?
    a. Everyone should be encouraged to participate
    b. Groups should not challenge each other
    c. Effective groups based decisions on reasonable assumptions and facts
    d. The group should define and determine the problem

Chapter Twelve

LEADERSHIP

Franklin J. Boster
Michigan State University

On 25 May 1961 the President of the United States, John F. Kennedy, addressed a joint session of Congress. In his opinion, and in the opinion of many others, the United States faced a crisis. Approximately four years prior to this date Russia had launched a rocket, Sputnik, into outer space. More importantly, on 12 April 1961 they had sent a manned spacecraft into outer space. This spacecraft, the Vostok, had carried Yuri Gagarin in an orbit around the Earth. This dramatic success by our rival superpower caused widespread alarm throughout the United States. It was believed by many that Russia had far more knowledge than the United States in the areas of science and technology. If they could send a man in an orbit around Earth, then they might be capable of even greater feats. Perhaps they could create weapons that would threaten our national security.

President Kennedy's response to this crisis was calm, but firm. The United States would compete in the space race, and we would win. Speaking to the nation that night he said,

> If we are to win the battle that is now going on around the world between freedom and tyranny, the dramatic achievements in space which occurred in recent weeks should have made it clear to us all, as did the Sputnik in 1957, the impact of this adventure on the minds of men everywhere. I believe this nation should commit itself to achieving the goal, before this decade is out, of landing a man on the moon and returning him safely to Earth. No single space project in this period will be more impressive to mankind.

He went on to ask Congress for an appropriation to the space program of approximately one-half billion dollars for the 1962 fiscal year, and for a commitment of an estimated seven to nine billion dollars more for the following five years. His confidence inspired a good proportion of the populace, especially those working in the space program. Soon the United States launched a manned craft into space, and in 1969 the United States became the first nation on Earth to land a man on the moon.

This crisis, and the manner in which Kennedy responded to it, provides important lessons in leadership. Initially, it clarifies three components necessary for leadership to occur (see Wills, 1994). First, **there must be a leader**—President John F. Kennedy in this case. Second, **there must be followers**—in this example citizens of the United States, especially those working in the space program. Third, **there must be a goal,** or vision—in this instance landing a manned spacecraft on the moon, and returning the members of the crew safely.

Without any of these three features it is impossible for leadership to exist. Furthermore, the three are inextricably bound. It is difficult, if not impossible, to understand a leader's action without also understanding his or her followers and his or her vision. Similarly, our leaders say a great deal about us (the followers), and the sorts of dreams which we hold dearly. As Wills (1994) puts it, "Tell me who your admired leaders are, and you have bared your soul" (p. 270). Finally, the rationale for goals, or visions, cannot be understood outside of the context of the leader and the followers who have them. Nevertheless, for the purpose of an analysis of leadership we must separate the three components.

Consider first the leader. When discussing leadership, this component is emphasized most frequently. Typically, the discussion centers around traits possessed by, and unique to or magnified in, the leader. So, for example, a biography of George Washington might focus on his character or his wisdom, arguing that he was more trustworthy or wiser than his peers. Occasionally, discussions of leadership focus on the situation, arguing that features of the economy or society demand that certain persons assume leadership roles. Thus, an analyst reviewing the events leading up to the Nazis' gaining power in Germany in the 1930s might focus on the social and economic forces that made it inevitable that a person such as Hitler would come to power.

From such analyses it is clear that both traits and the demands of the situation affect who emerges as group leader. Leaders, and even effective leaders, differ in their traits. They are more or less intelligent, more or less well-spoken, more or less sociable, and so on. But, some situations demand that the most intelligent emerge as leader, whereas others demand the most courageous, and so on. I shall return to this issue subsequently, and discuss some of the traits and the important situational features that affect the emergence of leadership.

Consider next the followers. Certainly there are more followers than there are leaders. Although most of us assume a leadership role at some time in our life, most of the time we will follow another's lead. And, we need not feel badly about that fact. Because leaders must be responsive to their followers to some extent, and at some point, followers have an important influence on leaders' behavior. In fact, followers can elect to give the leader enormous power, or by withholding support can remove a leader from a position of power. Consider, for instance, the fact that public opinion exerts an important influence on the behavior of legislators and other elected officials (Price, 1992). Leaders must answer to followers, a principle of which most effective leaders are keenly aware.

Finally, consider the vision, or goal. Notice that President Kennedy's goal was very concrete. We would send a man to the moon and return him safely, and we would accomplish this feat by the end of the decade. Concrete goals, such as this one, are verifiable. The followers can assess whether or not they have been met, and in that way can determine the extent to which the leader has been successful. The extent to which the leader has been successful can, in turn, then determine the extent to which the followers will support the leader in the future.

Notice also that Kennedy's goal was reasonable in the context of the times. Much of the technology necessary to meet this goal was already in place, and the Russians had already demonstrated that it was possible to send a man into space. In short, it was a goal in which the public, and especially those working in the space program, could believe as attainable. In contrast, had the President of the United States in 1861, rather than 1961, declared a goal of reaching the moon he would have been criticized as a dreamer, characterized a madman, or worse. Given the state of science in 1860 such a vision would have been viewed as ludicrous by the American public.

To emphasize a point made earlier, these three components must be present for leadership to occur. Recognizing that leadership has occurred, however, is merely a first step in understanding this process. In fact, taking this step raises more questions than it answers. In the pages that follow some of these important issues will be addressed. Specifically, I shall consider four of them: (1) Who is likely to emerge as leader? (2) How effective is the leader likely to be? (3) What factors affect the length of time one is likely to lead? and (4) What is the life of a leader like? I shall begin with a definition.

DEFINING LEADERSHIP

A **leader** is someone a group of followers grants the right to speak for them. The followers grant the leader this latitude because they believe that the leader has a vision of how to reach a future that is more rewarding, and it is this belief that makes the present tolerable for them. Thus, the leader must communicate a vision to those led. The led, in turn, must accept this vision as assuring a future that is more rewarding than the present. Because of the followers' belief that the leader has the ability to chart a course to realize this vision, they agree to conform to the dictates of the leader, and the leader expects that they will do so. The desired end result of this process is to render a future valued by the leader, and for many, if not most, of the followers, more probable. The process of convincing the led to accept the vision, and charting a course toward the realization of the vision, is **leadership.**

Locating a group leader is not always a simple task. Frequently, we associate leaders with a position, such as the Chief Executive Officer of General Motors, the Pope of the Catholic Church, or the President of the United States. Equating the group leader with a position may, however, be an error. Consider, for instance, the common belief that managers, or supervisors, in corporations are leaders. Bennis (1993) challenged this view, and provided some instructive distinctions between managers and leaders. To mention a few of Bennis' distinctions:

1. managers maintain; leaders develop
2. managers rely on control; leaders inspire trust

3. managers have short-range views; leaders have long-ranged perspectives
4. managers ask "how" and "when"; leaders ask "what" and "why"
5. managers concentrate on the bottom-line; leaders concentrate on the horizon
6. managers accept the status quo; leaders challenge it
7. managers are "good soldiers"; leaders are their own people
8. managers do things right; leaders do the right thing

Notice that most of these distinctions (3-8) emphasize that leaders have a vision and managers do not. The first two distinctions, on the other hand, indicate that leaders and managers differ in the manner in which they attempt to influence followers to accept their vision. Clearly, Bennis' point is a compelling one. Having a position does not ensure that one has a vision, and, even if a supervisor does have a vision, it does not ensure that one is able to influence followers to accept and embrace this vision. Thus, the conclusion is clear. Supervisors may be leaders, but the fact that they have a supervisory position does not suffice to classify them as leaders.

An alternative method of finding any group's leader is to ask the group members. Generally, persons will be willing to answer the question, "Who is the leader of this group of which you are a member?" The responses to this question might be very consistent from member to member. Nevertheless, there is a danger in accepting these reports uncritically. Because the term "leader" is ambiguous, for example the members may simply respond with the name of the person in a supervisory position, these reports may be inaccurate.

A more effective method, perhaps the most effective method, of identifying the leader is to observe group members' behavior. If a member performs actions such as orienting other group members toward the task, evaluating the work of others, praising others for their performance, and so on, then that member is likely to be the group leader. Although it is difficult, if not impossible, to specify all actions that are leaderlike, we shall elaborate on this issue subsequently.

LEADERS

Emerging Leadership: Who Becomes Leader?

Given an understanding of how the term "leader" is being used, and how such a person might be located, leadership emergence is the most obvious issue to raise next. Put simply, how might one predict who, from among a set of group members, will emerge as the leader of the group?

Certainly group member traits will be an important consideration. Recent analyses of leadership studies indicate that characteristics such as intelligence, sociability, and dominance play an important role in the process of leadership emergence (Lord et al., Peters et al.). Leaders tend to be more intelligent than the average group member. They tend to be more sociable, and generally possess stronger communication skills. They tend to have stronger needs to dominate than do most group members.

Nevertheless, traits are limited in their ability to help us understand leadership emergence. Consider one important position of leadership, those persons who have been elected to the office of President of the United States, as an example. Presidents both high and low on intelligence, dominance, sociability and other traits can be found readily. For instance, Jefferson was highly intelligent; Harding was not particularly so. Theodore Roosevelt and Lyndon Johnson were dominant chief executives; Grant was low on this trait. Eisenhower ranks as a very sociable president; Polk was very unfriendly. Yet, each of these men emerged as an important governmental leader in the United States.

The fact that traits fail to explain leadership emergence perfectly is not overly surprising, nor is it particularly troubling, because it is likely that situational demands play an important role in leadership emergence as well. One of the ways in which situations affect leadership emergence involves the arena in which leadership takes place. The situation may demand that different kinds of leaders have radically different trait profiles. So, for example, Mother Teresa is certainly a religious leader, or as Wills terms her, a saintly leader (1994, p. 251). Just as certainly Napoleon was a military leader. Nevertheless, one would be hard pressed to find many traits on which these two leaders were similar. A second way in which situations affect leadership emergence involves the different demands that face a particular kind of leader at various points in history. These demands may favor a leader with one constellation of traits at one time, and a leader with a completely different set of traits at another time. For instance, it is plausible that the demands placed upon the United Kingdom of Great Britain and Northern Ireland by Nazi Germany during the late 1930s and early-to-mid 1940s ensured that a person like Winston Churchill would emerge as Prime Minister from 1940 until July of 1945. After the defeat of Nazi Germany new social reform pressures faced this nation, and a very different type of leader, Clement Attlee of the Labour Party, emerged as Prime Minister in July of 1945.

Aside from analyzing leadership on a case-by-case basis, however, is there anything of a more general nature that can be said about the manner in which traits and situational characteristics combine to determine leadership emergence? Certainly Fred Fiedler thinks so. His Contingency Model (Fiedler, 1964, 1978) addresses this question directly, and we shall consider it in some detail.

Initially, Fiedler argues that persons differ in a very important way. He refers to this individual difference as the **assumed similarity of opposites** (ASO). Persons are high on this dimension to the extent that they see opposites as being alike, or put another way, they are low on this dimension to the extent that they perceive opposites to be very different from each other. To illustrate this point suppose that you work in an organization, and that you are asked to report who is your most preferred co-worker and who is your least preferred co-worker. After having done so you are then asked to rate both of these persons on a series of attributes, such as friendliness, loyalty, trustworthiness, and so on. A high ASO individual would rate both the most preferred co-worker and the least preferred co-worker in much the same manner; whereas, someone low in ASO would rate them very differently. Specifically, someone low in ASO would rate the most preferred co-worker very favorably and the least preferred co-worker very unfavorably.

As Bales (1950, 1953) points out there may be more than one type of leader in a group. In particular, Bales argues that groups may have both a task leader and a socio-emotional, or maintenance, leader. Both of these two types of leaders may not develop immediately. Task leaders generally do emerge early, but socio-emotional leaders are expected to emerge later in the history of the group.

The **task leader** focuses on effective completion of the work that the group faces. This type of leader is likely to be seen providing suggestions, opinions, and information

Leadership **249**

to fellow group members, and, perhaps, showing antagonism if they reject them. In contrast, the **socio-emotional leader** focuses on the relationships among group members. This type of leader is more likely identified by behavior which displays solidarity.

Armed with the distinctions between low and high ASO persons and task and socio-emotional leaders Fiedler made a prediction about leadership emergence. Those low ASO persons are likely to become task leaders. They focus on and see differences among members of the group that they lead. So, for example, they have the skills necessary to make personnel and task assignment decisions, skills required of a task leader. On the other hand, those high in ASO are likely to become socio-emotional leaders. High ASOs focus on and see similarities in people. So, for instance, when conflict occurs they are able to help manage it by emphasizing to the participants that the ways in which they agree are more pronounced and important than the ways in which they disagree, skills required of a socio-emotional leader.

Notice that central both to Bales' ideas and Fiedler's perspective is an emphasis on the things that leaders do, specifically the type of communication behavior in which they engage (e.g., giving opinions, displaying solidarity, etc.). Hollander (1958) provides a complementary view of leadership behavior, albeit one peculiar to his view of the leader as the most influential group member. Hollander argues that persons become leaders (i.e., influential) by demonstrating conformity and competence. Each action which conforms to the standards of the members of a group to which one belongs, and each action which demonstrates competence at the task that a group performs, earns what Hollander refers to as **idiosyncrasy credits.** These hypothetical chits can subsequently be employed to influence one's fellow group members.

At least two interesting implications of Hollander's thinking can be derived from the notion of idiosyncrasy credit. First, followers allow themselves to be influenced, or led, only by those who have previously shown themselves to be competent and who have demonstrated their commitment to the basic beliefs, values, and attitudes shared by members of the group. Second, it is exactly the persons who have conformed in the past who are able to lead the group in novel directions. Put another way, those persons with an abundant store of idiosyncrasy credits are able to institute group change, or innovation. They are the only ones in a position to influence their fellow group members to make such changes. Furthermore, if their innovation is successful, then they have demonstrated further competence, and receive from their fellow group members yet further credit to deviate. If, on the other hand, their innovation is unsuccessful, then they may lose all of the credit that they have to deviate in the future.

Hollander's idea may help us to understand several important phenomena. For instance, one rarely observes corporations promoting to positions of leadership those who are perceived by members of the corporation as radical in their approach to the business. Their vision departs too markedly from the consensual vision of the corporate members for them to be trusted to lead. Moreover, Hollander's notion of idiosyncrasy credit can help us understand how Richard Nixon, famous for his anti-communist views, was able to restore friendly relations between the United States and China. His stockpile of idiosyncrasy credits in the area of foreign policy led members of the polity to trust his ability to deal with Communist nations.

The Effectiveness of Leadership: Which Leaders Succeed

When seeking determinants of effective leadership our initial thinking is likely to take the same form that it did when we pursued determinants of emerging leadership. That is, generally one examines effective and ineffective leaders for trait differences. Some progress can be made in this manner. For example, Simonton (1994) shows that a particular profile distinguishes successful and unsuccessful Presidents of the United States. Successful presidents have an extraordinary need for power, strong achievement motivation, and a low need for affiliation (p.131).

Yet, despite this and other examples that we could provide, it is likely that both traits and attributes of the situation will combine to determine leader effectiveness more accurately than either consideration of traits or situations alone, as we saw with leadership emergence. Consider, for instance, the fate of a female (the trait) thrust into a position of leadership that has been dominated traditionally by males, such as an athletic director at a large university (a feature of a situation). Generally, women assuming such roles find it difficult to lead. They tend to be perceived negatively by those in subordinate positions, perhaps because women are perceived negatively when they adopt a "masculine" leadership style—a style which would be demanded of any leader in such a position (Eagly, 1992). Is this outcome fair? Probably not. Is it a common empirical result? The available data indicate that it is.

As with the topic of emerging leadership, Fiedler provides a framework for understanding how traits and situational characteristics combine to affect leadership effectiveness. He asserts that there are three characteristics of situations that are crucial to leadership. The most important of these characteristics is **the relationship between the leader and the followers.** Situations differ in the extent to which followers are supportive of the leader's vision. In some instances the followers are extremely loyal to their leader, and the leader's goals are their own as well. In other cases the followers are extremely disloyal, and few if any of them share any part of the leader's vision. In most contexts the average leader-follower relationship falls between these two extremes.

The second most important situational attribute is **the structure of the task.** On one hand, tasks may be such that group members know what must be done, there is only one way to do it, and they know immediately the extent to which they have been successful in accomplishing the task. Such tasks are said to be very structured. On the other hand, group members may be unclear about what is to be done, there may be multiple methods of accomplishing the goal, and it may not be clear immediately how successful they have been in accomplishing the task. Such tasks are said to be very unstructured.

The third, and least important, situational dimension discussed by Fiedler is **power.** Leaders differ in the extent to which they have the ability to reward and punish group members. When leaders have considerable discretion to reward and punish group members' performance, then they are said to be relatively powerful. When leaders lack this discretion they are said to be relatively powerless.

Combining these three situational characteristics Fiedler claims that the situation is **favorable for leadership** when followers support the leader, the task is highly structured, and the leader's power is strong. Conversely, the situation is said to be **unfavorable for leadership** when followers do not support the leader, the task is unstructured, and the leader's power is weak. Situations may be **moderately favorable for leadership** when one or two of the three situational characteristics are favorable and one or two of them are unfavorable. For instance, when the followers are supportive, but the task is unstructured and the leader's power is weak, then the situation would be said to be moderately favorable for leadership.

Fiedler's claim then is that high ASO leaders will be effective when the situation is moderate in favorableness, but low ASO leaders will be effective when the situation is either high or low in favorableness. Moreover, the results of many of his studies are very consistent with his prediction. Fiedler's rationale for his claim provides insight into these findings.

When the situation is favorable for leadership group members know what to do, how to do it, and how to judge the extent to which they have succeeded. They also like the leader, and know that the leader is able to reward them for excellent task performance or punish them for poor task performance. Under these conditions they tend to be most effective when left alone to perform the tasks assigned them. Low ASO leaders are very task-oriented, and therefore, they recognize that the task is likely to be performed most effectively if they leave the group members to their jobs. High ASO leaders, on the other hand, tend to continue to provide socio-emotional support to the group members, but under these circumstances such supportive communication serves only to distract the group members from the job at hand.

When the situation is extremely unfavorable for leadership the task is unstructured and the leader's power is weak. Low ASO leaders typically respond to these situations by clarifying tasks and increasing and consolidating their power. This increased task direction typically increases performance, and improved performance typically results in higher group morale (Mullen & Copper, 1994). High ASO leaders generally fail to provide the necessary task direction under such conditions. As a result the group tends to continue to be ineffective.

But, when the situation is moderate in favorableness, task-orientation becomes less important than supporting the group members. For example, when the followers are not supportive of the leader, the task is structured, and the power of the leader is strong, the low ASO leader can add very little that would contribute to the effectiveness of the group. By providing socio-emotional support to group members, however, the high ASO leader is able to improve group morale and in this manner make a modest contribution to effective group performance (Iaffaldano & Muchinsky, 1985).

Leader Longevity: Maintaining a Position of Leadership

In many arenas the duration of leadership is brief. Unless they die in office, are impeached, or resign presidents of the United States serve for at least four years. Since Franklin D. Roosevelt, however, no president has served for more than eight years. The chief executive officer of a major corporation may not last as long. Presidents of major universities in the United States serve, on the average, approximately seven years in any given position.

Such has not always been, and is not always, the case. Throughout human history some kings and queens, czars and chiefs, emperors and emirs, and sundry other monarchs have ruled for considerable periods. Catherine II reigned as Empress of Russia for some 34 years. Henry VIII was King of England for approximately 38 years. Louis XIV was King of France for more than 70 years. Of course, these leaders had the force of the state as a means of preserving their longevity. But, in a different leadership arena Robert Maynard Hutchins presided over the University of Chicago for more than 20 years. Harold Geneen served a similar lengthy tenure managing ITT. Even today there are exceptions. Billy Graham is, and has long been, the leader of his evangelistic organization. Nevertheless, these examples are more the exception than the rule.

In some instances departing the leadership role is a matter of choice; in other cases it is forced upon the occupant of this position. For example, Robert Maynard Hutchins left the University of Chicago for a position in the Ford Foundation. Nicholas II, Czar of Russia, was executed. Richard M. Nixon resigned as President of the United States in order to avoid being forced to resign the position. Regardless of the method of departing the role, however, it is clear that maintaining a position of leadership is as challenging, if not more so, than obtaining the position.

From Hollander's work one might conclude that demonstrating competence and conformity would be crucial to maintaining a position of leadership. Although counterexamples can be constructed, such as Churchill losing the 1945 election, short of inheriting a monarchy, there is not much merit to this idea. But, Hollander's thinking is incomplete in this regard. There are special challenges to demonstrating conformity and competence consistently over time.

Specifically, leaders face two important problems relating to time. The first is a **time management** issue. In many contexts in which leadership takes place the leader's time is the most important commodity for the followers. For example, in modern corporate life employees measure their success by how much time they are allowed to spend with the Chief Executive Officer. Thus, obtaining additional time is a major reward, and having one's time reduced or eliminated indicates major career failure. Because time is inelastic, there is a finite amount of it, and because there is so much competition for the leader's time, leaders have very little discretionary time. Moreover, what they have of it they tend to guard carefully.

Second, visions have some **time span.** Some visions are premature, or ahead of their time. As Robert Maynard Hutchins wrote to Thornton Wilder in 1954,

> I discovered in Scotland that in 1648 the General Assembly of the Kirk, in adopting the larger catechism, addressed itself, in Question 145, to the sins included in the Ninth Commandment. One of them is "speaking the truth unseasonably." You will recognize this as a sin I have been committing all my life.

Implicit in Hutchins' remark is that these unseasonable visions tend to fall upon deaf ears, and they tend to result in others labeling the visionary as someone impractical. But, visions can also become dated. For instance, Franklin D. Roosevelt's New Deal gave way to the Fair Deal which yielded to the New Frontier, The Great Society, and many subsequent visions of American presidents. This state of affairs is not unique to American politics, but rather generalizes to other leadership contexts.

The problem for the leader whose vision has become dated appears to have a straightforward solution—generate a new vision. But, inspiring new ideas do not come to mind easily for most of us. Moreover, it is especially difficult for leaders to generate these new visions because **their followers often prevent it.** The fact that the leader's time is an important reward for the followers, and removal of time with the leader is an important punishment, makes it difficult for leaders either to add persons to, or delete them from, the calendar. Thus, leaders may have difficulty being exposed to the sorts of new ideas which would allow them to update, or radically alter, their vision. As a result their tenure of leader is likely to end when the vision becomes dated.

Thus, a central problem of leadership maintenance becomes finding methods of avoiding this trap. In an investigation of successful senior managers Isenberg (1988) suggests some possible solutions. He finds that these successful executives are careful to restrict their agenda so that they pursue only one or two goals at a time. In this way they avoid micro-managing, spreading their time thinly across a number of issues, many of which are likely to be relatively minor. Moreover, they tend to attack only those problems that they believe are able to be solved. This tactic is interesting for at least two reasons. First, it implies that these managers believe that some problems in their organizations are not able to be solved. Restated, even successful leaders are aware that they cannot succeed in eliminating every problem in their units. Second, it implies that, contrary to most of the conventional management wisdom, leaders often let an idea about what constitutes a solution guide the way in which they think about problems. Finally, successful managers take time to sharpen their intellectual skills. Many spend considerable time reading, and their reading is often done in diverse fields. One reason that activity of this sort enhances their success is that it improves their ability to form new visions.

The Life of a Leader

Generally, people view positions of leadership as glamorous. They often report that they are leaders, and even more frequently report that they would like to be a leader. On the other hand, these persons may not have an accurate view of the impact of a leadership role on their lifestyle. Consider some of the by-products of being in a position of leadership.

First, **leaders tend to work long hours, and there are many demands on their time.** It is not unusual for chief executive officers of corporations, university presidents, major politicians, and military commanders to work 70 hour weeks. And, as mentioned previously, little of that time may be discretionary. Much of it is spent serving the followers in one manner or another.

Second, **many leaders expect to, and do, get compensated well for their services.** Some of this compensation may be intrinsic, such as pride in a job well done, but much of it is either directly or indirectly financial. Although there are exceptions, such as the religious leader Dorothy Day, leaders generally expect to be paid well for helping bring about a brighter future for their followers.

Third, as mentioned previously, **job tenure may not be long.** Nevertheless, leaders are remarkably resilient. Chief executive officers move from one corporation to another. Ministers leave one congregation only to begin leading another. University presidents depart one university, and receive job offers from numerous others. Politicians, such as Richard Nixon, lose presidential elections only to emerge victorious eight years later.

Fourth, **leaders must constantly manage their image.** Successful leaders know that followers respond to an image that they have of the leader, and that this image may not be accurate. It is in the leader's interest, however, to present, and to present consistently, an image that appeals to the followers. To do so frequently requires creating a mythology about oneself. This mythology is, by definition, largely inaccurate. For example, John F. Kennedy did not write the bulk of *Profiles in Courage,* the book for which he received the Pulitzer Prize. Theodore Sorensen did. Kennedy received the credit, which helped build the myth of him as an intellectual. The PT-109 incident, for which he was decorated in World War II, served to build the myth of Kennedy as war hero. Nevertheless, there is ample evidence to suggest that the facts of the case were not as portrayed, and that these facts had considerable less flattering implications about Kennedy's military ability. Kennedy did nothing to discourage the mythology, in fact he probably helped promote it. Albeit in less dramatic ways, most leaders find it useful to do the same, and because they find it useful they do so.

Finally, **friendships often suffer.** Becoming close friends with another may mean that it becomes difficult to discard that person when the success of one's leadership role demands it. Presidents generally find it necessary at some point in their administration to ask for the resignation of one of their close advisors. Chief executive officers of corporations, military commanders, and university presidents frequently face the same problem. It is easier to dismiss persons if they are not close personal friends. Most leaders are intuitively aware of this fact, and friendship development suffers as a result.

In sum, the rewards of a position of leadership can be substantial. These rewards may be both intrinsic and extrinsic. Yet there is a dark side to leading. The demands are great, one faces great uncertainty, and one's personal life may suffer. Summing up the benefits and the costs of this activity produces large figures in both columns. Fortunately, subtracting the two produces different results for different persons; positive for some, negative for others. The former assure that we shall continue to have a choice among competing visions. The latter assure an audience for these visionaries.

REFERENCES

Bales, R. F. (1950). *Interaction process analysis: A method for the study of small groups.* Cambridge, MA: Addison-Wesley.

Bales, R. F. (1953). The equilibrium problem in small groups. In T. Parsons, R. F. Bales, & E. A. Shils (Eds.), *Working papers in the theory of action* (pp. 111–161). Glencoe, IL: The Free Press.

Bennis, W. G. (1993). *An invented life.* Reading, MS: Addison-Wesley.

Eagly, A. H., Makhijani, M. G., & Klonsky, B. G. (1992). Gender and the evaluation of leaders: A meta-analysis. *Psychological Bulletin, 111,* 3–22.

Fiedler, F. E. (1964). A contingency model of leadership effectiveness. In L. Berkowitz (Ed.), *Advances in experimental social psychology* (pp. 149–190). New York: Academic Press.

Fiedler, F. E. (1978). The contingency model and the dynamics of the leadership process. In L. Berkowitz (Ed.), *Advances in experimental social psychology* (pp. 59–112). New York: Academic Press.

Hollander, E. P. (1958). Conformity, status, and idiosyncrasy credit. *Psychological Review, 65,* 117–127.

Iaffaldano, M. T., & Muchinsky, P. M. (1985). Job satisfaction and job performance: A meta-analysis. *Psychological Bulletin, 97,* 251–273.

Isenberg, D. J. (1988). How senior managers think. In D. E. Bell, H. Raiffa, & A. Tversky (Eds.), *Decision making: Descriptive, normative, and prescriptive interactions* (pp. 525–539). Cambridge: Cambridge University Press.

Mullen, B., & Copper, C. (1994). The relationship between group cohesiveness and performance: An integration. *Psychological Bulletin, 115,* 210–227.

Price, V. (1992). Public opinion. Newbury Park, CA: Sage.

Simonton, D. K. (1994). *Greatness: Who makes history and why.* New York: The Guilford Press.

Wills, G. (1994). *Certain trumpets.* New York: Simon & Schuster.

Chapter Twelve Case Study—
Power & Leadership

Instructions:

Please read the following case study carefully and select the best answers to the questions. This quiz is an individual assignment. Remember: sharing answers is a form of plagiarism.

In 1878, a young visionary in Menlo Park, New Jersey began a project that would change the world. A young Thomas Alva Edison had been to see a demonstration of carbon arc lighting, whereby a very bright light was generated after passing electricity between a pair of carbon terminals. In concept, Edison viewed the artificial light source to be interesting, but unpractical due to its huge size and overly bright light. Even though others thought he was crazy, he set about with a team of trusted men to develop an incandescent light source which was practical for home use and would be affordable and cost efficient to use. He had previous success with his invention of the phonograph and with his improvements to the telephone, why couldn't he be successful in this endeavor? Although doubtful, investment brokerage J.P. Morgan agreed to finance Edison's research based largely in part on his previous, successful track record. Since funding for Edison's project was limited, Edison had to work efficiently. He divided his group of inventors into specialty groups according to their area of expertise. Some researched animal fibers some researched plant fibers and others researched metallic properties to determine which might produce the strongest filaments for his incandescent light bulbs. After over two years of failure and over 6000 experiments, Edison and his team achieved success. News of Edison's invention spread far and wide very quickly and in 1881, he was invited to the White House to demonstrate his invention to U.S. presidents Rutherford B. Hayes and James Garfield.

Student's Name _____

Section Number _____

Section Leader's Name _____

Chapter Twelve Case Study Quiz— Power & Leadership

1. According to Fiedler's Contingency Model of Leadership and the scenario described here, Thomas Edison best fits the description of a _____?
   a. High ASO, socio-emotional leader
   b. Low ASO, socio-emotional leader
   c. High ASO, task leader
   d. Low ASO, task leader

2. Hollander might say Edison secured financing through J.P. Morgan as a result of using his _____; specifically, because of his proven track record.
   a. Vision
   b. Idiosyncrasy credits
   c. Salesmanship
   d. Power

3. According to Fiedler's claims regarding situational characteristics, circumstances would be favorable in asserting Thomas Edison's leadership when _____, _____, and _____.
   a. Followers support his vision, the task is unstructured, leader power is weak
   b. Followers support his vision, the task is unstructured, leader power is strong
   c. Followers support his vision, the task is highly structured, leader power is strong
   d. Followers do not support his vision, the task is structured, leader power is weak

4. Edison was chosen to present his new invention to Presidents Hayes and Garfield largely in part because of his _____ power.
   a. Coercive
   b. Legitimate
   c. Influential
   d. Expert
   e. Referent

5. Those who did not believe in Edison's vision of an affordable indoor, electric light thought his vision was too ahead of its time. Those who thought so might say that the problem with his vision was its _____.
   a. Time management
   b. Time span
   c. Chronemics
   d. Longevity

Chapter Thirteen

DIFFUSION OF INNOVATIONS: GETTING PEOPLE TO DO NEW THINGS

James W. Dearing
Ohio University

As the last chapter demonstrated, leadership is an important means for getting people to follow and behave in certain ways. In a sense, the diffusion of innovations is a tracing of how followership does or does not unfold by focusing on the process of personal influence in a social system.

American-Style Football in Japan Universities?

Seichi (pronounced SAY EE CHE) was one of my first students at Michigan State. He was from Tokyo, Japan. Seichi had been an undergrad at Keio University, a very old, famous, private university in Japan. When I was an undergraduate, I lived in Japan for one year through a study abroad program. I attended Waseda University, also a very prestigious, private university in Japan. Keio and Waseda are cross-town arch rivals, very much like famous college rivalries in the U.S. such as Michigan-Michigan State, USC-UCLA, and Oklahoma-Nebraska. When Seichi learned one day in my class that I had been a student at Waseda University, he became very excited.

"I hate Waseda," he said.

"Why is that, Seichi?" I asked.

"I am Keio graduate," he replied, smiling with great satisfaction. Immediately I understood this friendly (and familiar) type of conversational game.

"I'm sorry to hear that," I said, trying to make him laugh. "Too bad that you could not be admitted to Waseda." Then Seichi told me what he really wanted to say.

"When I was student at Keio Daigaku (that's "university" in Japanese), Waseda beat us in baseball every year. I was embarrassed very much," Seichi said.

"Yes, Waseda is very strong in baseball," I said as I began to feel proud. My homestay Japanese father, who had attended Waseda University before me, was extremely proud of his university. He had taught me a friendly, but nevertheless passionate, "hate" for Keio University, everyone who had ever gone to school there, their relatives and household pets, their companies and business affiliates, drinking bars near the Keio campus, etcetera (now, of course, I feel the same way about the University of Michigan since I teach at Michigan State University).

"But," continued Seichi, "when I student, we beat you every year in football." In most of the world, the sport of soccer is called "football."

"You mean soccer," I said. "In America, we call your game of football 'soccer.'"

"No. I mean football. AMERICAN-style football!" Seichi said slowly and loudly. I liked Seichi very much, and I could tell that he was delighted that he had taught me something that I didn't know.

"Really. I did not know that Keio and Waseda had American-style football teams."

"Yes! I play four years for Keio. We beat you every year!" Seichi was now so happy to be telling me this news that his enthusiasm was overcoming his limited English language ability. "You losing every time! As for football, Waseda very weak," he added, almost sadly.

Quickly I became curious as to why I had not heard of or seen any American-style football games at Waseda. Baseball, for example, is extremely popular. The Keio-Waseda baseball games are nationally televised. Why had I missed the football games? I had met a Japanese sushi chef who had gone to the University of Wisconsin-Madison in order to play football. He laughed as he told me how shocked he was when he got to the first Badger team tryout and saw firsthand how big the Wisconsin players were (he made third-string, but never played in a Big 10 game). So I knew that some Japanese college students knew about American-style football, and that at least one had almost played in the U.S.

"Seichi," I asked, "is football popular in Japan?" I knew that the answer was 'no.'

"Not yet," he said. "But, it is increase." Seichi went on to explain that recently American-style football had become popular at Japanese universities. He had played for one of Keio's first teams. They drew very few fans. Most Japanese did not yet understand the game.

"How many college football teams are there in Japan? And why is football becoming popular now? Why not before?" I asked him. Seichi didn't know the answers to these questions, but he understood the phrasing of my questions. For someone like me who studies the diffusion of different types of innovations, recent popularity is a sign that an innovation (in this case, football) is diffusing. Diffusion researchers inevitably want to know "when" a new idea or thing is spreading among people, and "why" the new idea or thing is spreading.

"My class project! Football in Japan. Okay?"

I thought for a moment. "Sure, this sounds like a very interesting term paper. First, you must find out when in time each university established a football team. Then, you must discuss why these universities have "adopted" American-style football teams at those points in time," I said. "In particular, I want you to concentrate on the concepts of opinion, leadership and status."

WHAT IS DIFFUSION?

My student, Seichi, had his paper topic: He would conduct a very limited study of when and why American-style football had diffused in Japan. What is diffusion? **Diffusion** is the process by which an innovation is communicated through certain channels over time among the members of a social system (Rogers, 1983, p. 5). When a new music style, hairstyle, or type of automobile—like SUVs—are becoming popular, that's diffusion at work.

Diffusion consists of four main elements: (1) The **innovation,** an idea, practice, or object that is perceived as new by an individual or other unit of adoption; (2) **communication channels,** the means by which messages are exchanged; (3) **time,** or process; and

(4) a **social system,** the structure and function of relations among a set of individuals or other units, such as organizations. Innovations may be new to people in terms of the information they provide, the changed attitudes or behaviors that their adoption requires, and outcomes that would not be possible without use of the innovation.

Diffusion research has been a popular paradigm for scholars in a number of academic disciplines for 40 years. A **paradigm** is an approach to the study of a phenomena (like a sport that is popular in one country and then becomes popular in a second country) that provides researchers with a similar orientation to problems and solutions. For the most part, diffusion research has been conducted using a common paradigm by (1) rural sociologists, to understand why farmers decide to use new agricultural products, (2) public health specialists, to understand how people at high-risk for AIDS or HIV can improve or safeguard their lives, (3) marketing researchers, for understanding customer decisions about new products and services, even "pro-social" products or ideas like car pooling or birth control, and (4) anthropologists, to understand the impact of one culture on another culture. Since diffusion is fundamentally a process of communicating new ideas or things among people, communication scientists can study the diffusion of just about anything because it's the **process** of diffusion, not the particular innovation in question, with which communication scientists are concerned. So communication scientists can study the spread of Total Quality Management (TQM), business consortia (which spread from Japan to the United States in the 1980s), university reform to improve undergraduate education, or notebook computers. Some innovations are primarily ideas and ways of doing things (like TQM or Quality Circles), while other innovations have a distinct physical basis (such as notebook computers or autofocus cameras). To a communication scientist, any of these innovations can be the topic for a diffusion study.

Diffusion scholars sharing this common paradigm have sought to learn when in the diffusion process certain types of individuals "adopt" a certain innovation. Adoption represents a point in time when an individual or group of people makes a choice to buy or make a commitment to learning about and using an innovation. These studies of "innovativeness" (the relative earliness in adopting a new idea), led to categorizing people as either "innovators," "early adopters," or in the "early majority," "late majority," or if they were really late in adopting something, as "laggards." Is it wise to always be an innovator or early adopter? No. Innovators often pay high monetary or other types of costs for their early adoption.

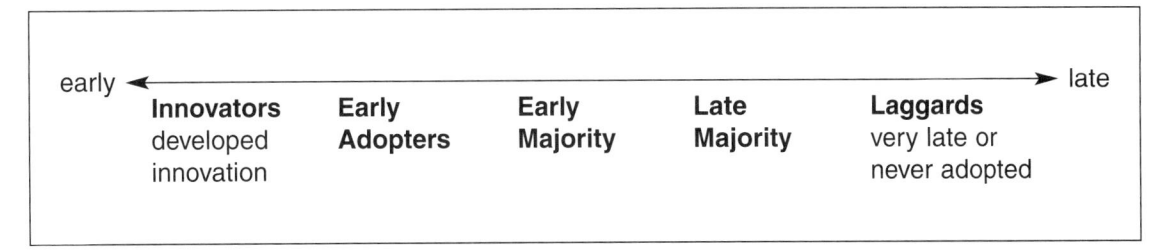

FIGURE 13.1 Innovativeness

early ← → late

Innovators	**Early**	**Early**	**Late**	**Laggards**
developed innovation	**Adopters**	**Majority**	**Majority**	very late or never adopted

Waiting to adopt an innovation can be very wise. In fact, most of the adoption decisions that we make are to not adopt a new idea or thing. Nevertheless, US society tends to share a **pro-innovation bias;** that is, in general, Americans think that "new is better than old." Thus, those people who adopt new ideas and things earlier than most Americans are credited with being smarter or "doing the right thing."

Of course, an individual is not always either innovative or laggardly! For example, my students tell me that I am an innovator or early adopter when it comes to new foods and new ways of cooking, but that when it comes to clothes, well. . . . Most of us are relatively early in adopting certain types of innovations, and at the same time relatively late in adopting other types of innovations.

Besides distinguishing among people depending on when in time they adopt an innovation, an important goal of diffusion researchers has been to understand why we adopt innovations when we do. This goal has led diffusion scholars to study how recent adopters perceived the things that they adopted. These perceptions of adopters have been categorized as "attributes" of innovations. Understanding how people feel about innovation attributes leads to an understanding of why certain innovations spread more rapidly or slowly when compared to other innovations.

For example, the attribute with the strongest relationship to adoption is **economic advantage.** If a product is very expensive compared to other models, it has very low "economic advantage" in the eyes of potential buyers. High prices are usually a disincentive for us to buy. Diffusion scholars have shown that innovations with high economic advantage (those that don't cost much) diffuse rapidly.

Compatibility with existing values, beliefs, and previous ways of accomplishing the same goal is a second very important attribute. Innovations that don't require a great deal of change from past ways of doing things diffuse more rapidly than innovations that have no similarity with previous practices. For example, I studied one innovation that promised great economic advantage, but using it required engineering companies to reorganize themselves into new divisions and teams. This innovation is diffusing very slowly, partly because it is incompatible with the existing structure of work in engineering firms.

A third important attribute of innovations is **complexity.** New things that are very complex and difficult to understand take longer to diffuse among people. Computer software that is confusing does not sell well. Software engineers and programmers spend a great deal of time "reengineering" software after it has been created in order to simplify it. Reducing the perceived complexity of innovations is a frequent reason for holding focus groups with potential customers to consider new products or services.

So, diffusion scholars have concluded that to make an innovation diffuse more rapidly, it should be inexpensive, compatible with previous ways of accomplishing the same goal and with existing beliefs, and it should be easy to understand.

HOW DO PEOPLE REACT TO INNOVATIONS?

A central concept in diffusion is newness and its relationship to personal uncertainty. **Uncertainty** is the degree to which a number of alternatives are perceived with respect to the occurrence of an event and the relative probability of these alternatives. Innovations present us with new possibilities and raise new questions for us. Because we do not have experience with them, we are typically uncertain about how well certain innovations will work. Uncertainty is reduced by the cognitive processing of information about the innovation. After potential adopters first learn of an innovation, and if they perceive that the innovation has some value or attraction for them, they will be inclined to seek out information about it. This information-seeking reduces personal uncertainty about the innovation's usefulness, performance, or implications. More information typically leads to rejection or adoption, either of which reestablish a mental state of cognitive consistency by greatly reducing uncertainty.

Another key concept that drives the diffusion process is **social pressure,** an increasingly strong perception by a potential adopter that nonadoption will meet with peer approval or disapproval. Your peers—classmates, sorority sisters, friends at work, sometimes family members—often have strong influence on your adoption decisions. The cumulative result of different people each being subject to social pressure from their peers is termed the **diffusion effect,** a change in the norms of the social system toward the innovation. Social pressure, felt individually by people in East Lansing, can cause a diffusion effect in the town as a whole with regard to adopting or rejecting an innovation by people who live here.

If you adopt a new idea or thing, over time you usually pass through five mental stages in your exposure to and experience with that innovation: knowledge, persuasion, decision, implementation, and confirmation.

During the **knowledge stage** potential adopters first become aware of an innovation. Most often, potential adopters become aware of innovations through mass media communication, not interpersonal, face-to-face communication. Individuals only perceive the relevance or importance of a small percentage of the innovations of which they become aware. Much of the strategy in disseminating knowledge about an innovation concerns timing, and the extent to which a **change agency** (any organization that is attempting to get you to adopt an innovation, such as Chrysler or Olin Health Center) can frame or promote an innovation as being related to ideas or issues about which potential adopters are already thinking.

During the **persuasion stage** people actively seek out information to reduce their uncertainty about whether an innovation is a good idea, and thus are open to persuasive appeals. A change agency that is able to stimulate information-seeking by potential adopters will experience more rapid innovation diffusion. Persuasive appeals made through interpersonal, face-to-face communication are most effective in leading to adoption.

During the **decision stage** individuals or other decision making units face a "go-no go" point in time when they adopt or reject an innovation. A key distinction that a change agency must understand is who will make the adoption decision, and whether the decision maker will also be the person or unit responsible for implementation of the innovation. When "the user is not the chooser," problems in implementation result.

During the **implementation stage** adopters actually begin to use the innovation. Often, we "reinvent" innovations a bit, to make them most useful for us. When considering the diffusion of innovations within organizations, implementation is a more important time-period than the decision to adopt. Whereas adoption may be a simple discreet mental decision, implementation of an innovation in an organization usually requires behavioral action and adaptation, and may involve various complex activities over time. Organizational members give meaning to an innovation and begin to use it as they implement it. During implementation, people are expected to change existing behaviors as well as attitudes. The presence of the innovation forces people to reconsider and restructure that which they had made routine. When your boss or your professors speak of "organizational change," they are talking about an organization that is implementing an innovation. The innovation may be limited in how many people it affects, such as with a new accounts receivable bill-processing system, or the innovation may affect everyone in an organization, as with the introduction of a vision for a new organizational work culture.

During the **confirmation stage** users actively seek out information from other people that confirms that their decision to adopt or reject an innovation was a correct decision. Use of the innovation becomes seen as normal. The idea, technique, or technology is no longer an innovation when it ceases to be seen as new.

Most research about diffusion has occurred from the perspective of a change agency or "source," and not from the perspective of potential users. Therefore, people or units that are late adopters or actively or passively reject the innovation are viewed as irrational. Yet from a potential adopter's perspective, there are usually very rational reasons for not adopting. It is the responsibility of change agencies to understand potential adopter perspectives prior to diffusion. Understanding potential adopter perspectives requires knowledge of the social system into which the innovation will be introduced. The social system (or "target audience") can either help or hinder innovation diffusion through the application of personal influence.

THE CASE OF CORN FLAKES

One of the first industries that Michigan became famous for was dried, ready-to-eat breakfast cereal. Prior to the early 1900s, millions of Americans ate breakfasts of meat, eggs, potatoes fried in lard, homemade bread that was topped with bacon grease and molasses, and hot cereal with heavy cream. Not everyone thought that this menu represented a healthy diet.

John Harvey Kellogg lived in Battle Creek, Michigan. He was a pioneering medical doctor who sought a solution for his hundreds of patients who developed colon cancer. Kellogg believed that cancer of the colon was due to an unhealthy diet that was high in fat and low in fiber. In 1894, Dr. Kellogg first produced toasted cereal flakes as a breakfast food substitute for his patients. He was not interested in commercializing toasted flakes for people other than his patients, but others, like his younger brother William, were.

With his disinterested older brother, William Kellogg established the Battle Creek Toasted Corn Flake Company in 1906. Competitors had already taken notice of his brother's innovation, and they were beginning to make millions of dollars by moving to Battle Creek and shipping ready-to-eat cereal across the U.S. Battle Creek was the health food capital of the United States, and was known as Cereal City, U.S.A. By 1912, 107 companies were producing cereal in Battle Creek!

William Kellogg knew that he needed help in promoting sales of Kellogg's Toasted Corn Flakes. He decided that while most of the upstart manufacturers were using mass advertising to garner public attention, he would combine mass advertising with the personal influence of trusted friends. He offered a year's supply of Toasted Corn Flakes free to housewives who would work to convince their friends to buy Kellogg's cereal. Without knowing it, William Kellogg was using a key diffusion strategy of achieving high source credibility through the use of homophilous change agents.

After spreading the word about the benefits of ready-to-eat cereal through mass communication (thus leading potential adopters through the knowledge stage in the diffusion process), Kellogg gave away tens of thousands of boxes of cereal in order to persuade consumers of the product's advantages. Giving the innovation away eliminated any monetary disadvantage for potential adopters, and made it easy to judge the product favorably. The giveaways, combined with the personal network of housewives who were "working" for Kellogg's, led to many people deciding to adopt the idea that ready-to-eat cereal was a good innovation and that Kellogg's was the preferred ready-to-eat cereal.

William Kellogg shrewdly associated Toasted Corn Flakes with a status that was desirable to most Americans. Ready-to-eat cereal was promoted as being the breakfast of industry and modernization in America. In effect, consumers were being told that ready-to-eat cereal was a key ingredient in the lives of progressive and successful Americans. Hot breakfasts were portrayed as a thing of the past. The future was with the automobile, talking movies, and dried cereal. This image of Kellogg's Toasted Corn Flakes proved to be very compatible, not only with who Americans wanted to become, but also with their actual lives. More and more Americans did not have the time to prepare, eat, and clean up after a full hot breakfast. In diffusion terms, Toasted Corn Flakes were portrayed as compatible with an image that Americans sought for themselves, and demonstrated relative advantages over hot breakfasts by satisfying real needs of consumers for quicker, less messy breakfast food.

So, the case of corn flakes in US history is a story of successful diffusion. By 1989, Kellogg's had net sales of nearly $5 billion dollars a year.

THE RESULT OF SEICHI'S STUDY OF COLLEGE FOOTBALL IN JAPAN

In agreeing to his idea for a class term paper, I had suggested to Seichi that he concentrate on the concepts of opinion leadership and status in collecting information about the diffusion of American-style football in Japan.

The diffusion of an innovation can usually be graphed on paper as a cumulative curve with a slight S-shape to it, with time represented along the x-axis and the percentage of adopters represented along the y-axis. This curve is a graphic representation of a social process at work—diffusion. Why, in the case of successful diffusion of an innovation, does the plotted data of adoption decisions look like an "S"?

Certain people have more influence within a community than other people. Just as there are innovators—those people who adopt a new thing first—there are also early adopters, people who wait for innovators to take the higher risks associated with going out on a limb in doing something radical, and then quickly decide yes or no about the innovation in question. Early adopters pay careful attention to what innovators do (whereas most of us ignore innovators as sort of weird or bizarre people). Unlike innovators, who are not much respected by most of us, early adopters tend to be opinion leaders for the rest of us. The personal influence

FIGURE 13.2 Graphic Representation of Diffusion

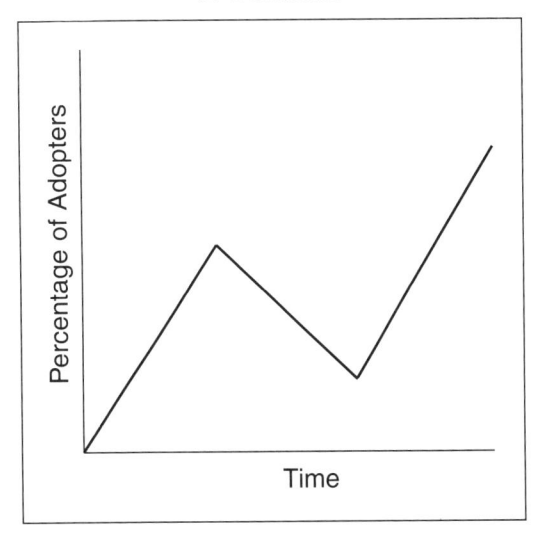

of opinion leaders drives the diffusion process of adoption. **Opinion leadership** is the degree to which an individual is informally able to influence other individuals' attitudes or behaviors in a desired direction with relative frequency. The power of an opinion leader's influence is that it is informal and based on respect, not on positional or formal authority.

Opinion leaders often hold high positions of authority, but this is not a necessary condition for them to have influence over other people. Many diffusion initiatives fail because a change agency mistakenly identifies formal authority figures as opinion leaders. Opinion leaders are at the center of communication networks. They communicate a lot, with a lot of different types of people. So it is the cumulative decisions of opinion leaders within a social system (like in MSU residence halls), occurring relatively early in time, that makes the number of adopters for an innovation really take off and form the characteristic S-shaped curve that graphically describes a diffusion process. Fundamentally, innovations do not diffuse just because they are advantageous, cheaper, or compatible. They diffuse because of the cumulative application of the personal influence of earlier adopters on the decisions of later adopters. Diffusion is a social process.

What Did Seichi Learn?

Near the end of the term, Seichi came back to see me during office hours in the Communication Arts Building. Once again, he was very excited.

"I am finish!" he exclaimed, as he handed me a bound term paper. He had a graph of some data on an x-y chart still in his hand.

"What is this?" I asked, as I began to turn my head and read the plotted data. Seichi knew that I was going to be interested in this chart. There, plain as sushi, was the familiar slight S-shaped curve. Seichi began to tell me what he had done.

"I mark each college's time of establishing a football team. See? You can notice that this is like very bad "S."

I admired Seichi's graph and then, with my finger, circled the part of the curved line where the slope increased the most, early in what looked like the diffusion process. "Why did so many universities begin football teams at this point in time?" I asked.

"That was main problem. I could easily find out when each college started football, but why? I had to talk with many people to learn this." Seichi had found out when each university established a football team from a football association in Japan, but then he had to telephone coaches and university administrators to learn why they created teams when they did. He heard many reasons for creating American-style football teams, but the recurring reason that he heard was that three universities had established teams at the same time, early in the diffusion process. He showed me where on the S-shaped curve the adoption decisions of the three universities were plotted. They occurred just prior to the slope of the curve increasing dramatically. For some reason, as soon as these three universities had created football teams, many Japanese universities did the same. Why? Seichi did not have the names of the universities on the graph, only dots.

"These three universities are most famous in Japan," Seichi said. "All Japanese universities want to be like them!"

Seichi had demonstrated a diffusion process among Japanese universities. The desire for status and social belonging and the effect of peer pressure contribute to cases of successful diffusion, and the spread of American-style football in Japan was no exception. Seichi's graph showed that where a few smaller universities with low national status had adopted football as early as 10 years prior, only when opinion-leading and high-status Tokyo universities adopted the idea of fielding football teams, did the great majority of Japanese universities then decide that they too should play football.

REFERENCE

Rogers, E. M. (1983). *Diffusion of innovations* (3rd ed.). New York: Free Press.

Chapter Thirteen Case Study Quiz— Diffusion of Innovations

Instructions:

Please read the following case study carefully and select the best answers to the questions. This quiz is an individual assignment. Remember: sharing answers is a form of plagiarism.

In 1999, a freshman at Northeastern University started a craze that would shake the music industry. He compiled a slew of songs from various CD's and saved them on a server, allowing him to share songs in an MP3 format with anyone who had an Internet connection. This new capability allowed any user to download music from a server and to burn CD's of their own, saving a listener the money of purchasing multiple CD's. This free service provided by Napster stirred up a "Who's who" of music hornets' nest because royalties were not being paid for their music. Over the last few years, the Recording Industry Association of America (RIAA) has taken Napster, Kazaa and Morpheus to court, citing that these MP3, file-sharing companies are in violation of the Digital Millennium Copyright Act of 1998. The RIAA also alleges that these companies are responsible for a 31% decrease in music sales from 2001 to 2002 because of the ease of MP3 file sharing capabilities (Graham, 2003). The decrease in revenue for recording companies and artists is estimated to be as high as $700 million in fiscal year 2002 (Graham, 2003). Not surprisingly, as profit continues to decrease for the recording industry, MP3 downloaders continue to increase. Word of this capability spread quickly and within a scant few years, hundreds of Napster users turned into an estimated 60 million downloaders in 2002.

Graham, J. (2003) RIAA lawsuits bring consternation, chaos. *USA Today,* September 10, 2003: 4D.
Graham, J. (2003) Hammering away at piracy? *USA Today* September 11, 2003: 1D-2D.

Student's Name _____

Section Number _____

Section Leader's Name _____

Chapter Thirteen Case Study Quiz— Diffusion of Innovations

1. Those users who believe that the new capability of downloading MP3's is better than buying standard CDs, demonstrate what diffusion effect?
    a. The complex compatibility effect
    b. The economic advantage effect
    c. The social system paradigm
    d. The pro-innovation bias

2. Regarding the four main elements of diffusion: The practice of downloading MP3's would be considered the _____, and the Internet would be considered the _____?
    a. Social system / time
    b. Innovation / communication channel
    c. Communication channel / Social system
    d. Time / Innovation

3. The first few thousand users of the Napster download service would best be referred to as _____?
    a. Early Adopters
    b. Early Majority
    c. Late Majority
    d. Laggards

4. At this stage of diffusion, a person would turn to the "Who's who" of music to find out whether or not utilizing Napster downloads is a good idea.
    a. Knowledge stage
    b. Confirmation stage
    c. Persuasion stage
    d. Decision stage

5. At this stage of diffusion, a potential adopter might have seen an ad from a new company called "Napster" on an Internet pop-up ad.
    a. Knowledge stage
    b. Confirmation stage
    c. Persuasion stage
    d. Decision stage

Chapter Fourteen

MASS MEDIA EXPOSURE:

USE, NEGATIVE EFFECTS, AND THEORETICAL EXPLANATIONS

Stacy L. Smith
University of Southern California

Aaron R. Boyson
Michigan State University

The mass media is often criticized. Many are advocating that exposure to images of violence, sex, and stereotyping is contributing to negative effects on this country's youth. To illustrate, consider some of the questions being asked in the popular press: "Should TV share the blame for violence in America?" (*TV Guide*, 1999, p. 35); "Do graphically violent video games desensitize children to violence?" (Flatlin, 2000, p. 1); "Mom, what's oral sex? . . .Who is Monica, and what did the President do with her?" (Wallis, 1998, p. 67); and "*Siege* film engendering anti-Arab hatred?" (National Association of Muslim Journalists, 1999, p.1).

© Reuters NewMedia Inc./Corbis

The purpose of this chapter is to answer questions such as these. To do so, the chapter is subdivided into four major sections. First, mass communication is defined including four general types of effects the media may have on viewers. Second, we turn to examine how much time individuals spend with different mass media. In the third section, we assess the impact of three different types of controversial media content: violence, sex, and stereotypical portrayals. Finally, the theoretical mechanisms used to explain the negative impact of the mass media on individuals' thoughts, attitudes, and behaviors are reviewed.

DEFINING MASS COMMUNICATION AND TYPES OF EFFECTS

Prior to examining the impact of mass communication, it is important to first define exactly what it is. DeFleur and Dennis (1994) offer a six-part definition of mass communication (p. 21). First, **mass communication starts with professional communicators.** These are usually individuals in the entertainment industry that decide to create and disseminate some type of message. For example, producers, writers, and directors would all constitute professional communicators.

Second, the **media messages are created.** Typically, specialists in the entertainment industry are responsible for encoding or creating media messages. The message may be a newscast on *60 Minutes,* a major motion picture such as *Traffic,* or a situation comedy like *Will & Grace.* The process of encoding all verbal and nonverbal aspects of a media message usually requires many industry specialists including but not limited to actors, cinematographers, audio specialists, composers, and graphic designers.

The third stage is **dissemination of the created message.** Dissemination of media messages is characterized by rapid and continuous delivery over time and distance through the use of a medium. In terms of rapidity, mass media in the 21st century is amazingly fast. An event taking place on the other side of the globe (e.g., death of Princess Diana, the Persian Gulf War, the collapse of the Berlin Wall) can be transmitted via television or the Internet almost instantaneously into our homes in East Lansing, Michigan. But even other forms of media (e.g., books, films) are disseminated rather quickly. When completed, movies are sent to theatres across the country for general audience viewing. Another aspect of dissemination is continuousness. As DeFleur and Dennis (1994) argue, media messages are typically scheduled. For instance, the situation comedy *Friends* typically airs on NBC Thursday nights at 8:00 p.m. whereas *People* magazine is available on newsstands weekly.

Fourth, the messages are **received and perceived by diverse audiences.** One aspect relatively unique to mass communication is that the audience is heterogeneous and large being made up of millions of viewers. To illustrate, it was reported that roughly 51 million American viewers tuned in to watch the two-hour finale of the reality show, *Survivor* in August of 2000 (Dini, 2000). Once the show is received, it must also be perceived or attended to by the audience. Not all individuals attend and react to mass media portrayals uniformly, however. There is a great deal of variance in individuals' perceptions of media events.

The fifth stage of mass communication involves **decoding by the audience.** It is here that viewers interpret and make sense of media messages. Given that the audience of the mass media is large and diverse, individuals may interpret the same media message in very different ways. To illustrate, let's take the popular 1970's show, *The Incredible Hulk.* A 4-year old may watch this show and interpret the main character as scary and grotesque looking. This is primarily due to younger children's tendency to focus on striking visual cues such as a character's appearance or dress. A 9-year old, on the other hand, watches the same program and interprets the Hulk's actions as altruistic and helpful. Older children can discount misleading appearances and focus on conceptual attributes of the character such as his/her orientation towards others.

The final stage of mass communication is that the audience is **influenced** or changed in some way. After interpreting the message, the audience is impacted. As an example, let's go back to the two young viewers watching the *The Incredible Hulk.* The younger child watching the show may be extremely frightened by the Hulk's green, monster-like appearance. The older child, however, enjoys the show and cheers for the main character. Clearly, interpretations of media messages influence or mediate the impact they may have on the audience.

The six stages outlined above can be synthesized into a succinct definition of mass communication. According to DeFleur and Dennis (1994), mass communication is defined as,

> "a process in which professional communicators design and use media to disseminate messages widely, rapidly, and continuously, in order to arouse intended meanings in large, diverse, and selectively attending audiences in attempts to influence them in a variety of ways" (p. 28).

Now that we have defined what mass communication is, the next question to ask is "what types of influences or effects might it have on the viewer?" There are four general types of media effects that we will discuss in this chapter. Each of these effects may occur in isolation, or all four may be affected by exposure to the mass media.

First, the mass media can influence a viewer's **attitude.** An attitude, according to Azjen (1988, p. 4), is simply a "disposition to respond favorably or unfavorably to an object, person, institution, or event." Examples of the mass media influencing viewers' attitudes are abundant in the literature. Television violence may influence viewers' attitudes about real-world aggression. Through repeated exposure to TV violence, a viewer may come to like or respond more favorably to acts of violence in society. Advertising can also influence our attitudes. Showing a humorous ad for a product may cause us to like or positively evaluate the brand significantly more than products featured in a non humorous ad.

Copyright © 2001 by John Drury. Reprinted by permission of the artist.

The mass media may also affect our thoughts or **cognitions.** There are a variety of cognitive effects that may occur. For one thing, the mass media may teach us new information. Growing up, many preschool-aged children learn the alphabet and how to count to 10 by repeatedly watching *Sesame Street*. Or, adults may acquire information about the reliability of an automobile on the Internet or by reading Consumers Reports. In addition to learning, the mass media may influence our perceptions and beliefs about the world around us.

Arousal responses can also be influenced by the mass media. Heightened physiological arousal may occur when watching a scary or suspenseful film from the *Jaws* or *Scream* series. In such cases, the intense media message may increase heart rate and perspiration. However, there are also instances when media messages may decrease arousal. When stressed or over excited, watching calming shows (e.g., HGTV) can lower physiological reactivity to more normal levels (Zillmann, 1991).

Last, and perhaps with the most difficulty, the mass media can influence **behavior.** Viewers may imitate or copy something they see or hear in the mass media. Imitation may occur when viewers alter their appearance to be like a media character. To illustrate, young females in the 1980's wore innumerable bracelets, leggings, and lace to model their appearance after Madonna. In the 1990's, however, young males grew their sideburns to reflect the media craze around Dylan McKay and Brandon Walsh on *90210*. Other types of imitation can be more lethal, however. For example, a young 12-year old Florida boy severely injured and killed a 6-year old girl when imitating wrestling moves he had seen on the WWF (Potter, 2001).

In sum, the purpose of this section was to lay a foundation for understanding mass communication and the general types of effects it can have on the audience. Given this understanding, we can now examine how much time society spends with the different types of mass media—the focus of the next section of this chapter.

PATTERNS OF MEDIA USE

Putting DeFleur and Dennis' (1994) definition to work, perhaps it is easier to see how prevalent the mass media are in your life. But what does that mean? Prevalence can be thought of as how much time we allocate to the media, how much money we spend on them, or how much selective attention we devote to different sources of media content. In this chapter, TV gets substantial attention because it has engendered the most research. Other sources are also important to examine, however. Take music, for example. Many of you listen to a song on the radio that is also played on MTV. If you like it, you may buy the compact disc. Undoubtedly, the song is also available on the Internet. From there, it can be digitized to your own CD or downloaded and played on a personal MP3 player. Music, as a message, transcends the traditional media boundaries and is therefore an important potential source of influence. But the Internet, print media, and computer games are also media content that may affect the masses. Therefore, we will investigate how individuals use each of these sources.

Television

Stop and think about television for a moment. Do you marvel at the technology behind recording electronic bits and pieces of information? How about storing those pieces and then casting them over the airwaves or through a tiny cable that pumps information into your TV? Unless you are an electrical engineer, you probably do not. Some scholars would contend that you are numb to the impact of television in your life (Kottack, 1990). This is because you are part of a generation that has grown up in an environment permeated by television. As evidence, TV ranks first as a leisure time activity across the lifecycle after sleep (Kubey & Csikszentmihalyi, 1990).

In the United States, it almost goes without saying that TV is a ubiquitous phenomenon. Ninety-eight percent of American homes currently have at least one television set (Nielsen Media Research, 2000). This has been the case for as long as most of you have lived (i.e., since 1980) (Nielsen Media Research, 2000). Once purchased, TV delivers free content from publicly owned, privately licensed stations. You know these broadcast stations as ABC, CBS, FOX, NBC, PAX, UPN and the WB. The companies that own these networks have all applied for and received licenses from the Federal Communication Commission (FCC) to broadcast programming content across the country. Programming on the networks is received free of charge because the public owns the airwaves the broadcasters use to deliver television content. As such, the Federal government (e.g., FCC) has considerable control over them. In reality, however, this control is seldom used (see Kunkel & Roberts, 1991).

Although television started with the broadcast networks, it has grown far beyond these channels. Cable television began in 1948 as an alternate method of delivery where broadcast signals could not be reached. Only 7% of the American TV audience paid for cable services by 1970. Today, 74% of American households subscribe to cable or satellite television (Nielsen Media Research, 2000). As cable services increased, so did the number of channels. An average of 19 channels were delivered to U.S. homes in 1985. By 1990, the average jumped to 33 different outlets. Today, a majority of the homes in this country receive over 60 different channels (Nielsen Media Research, 2000).

Given all these options, how much time do individuals spend with television? The typical home has the television set "on" for roughly seven and one-half hours per day (Nielsen Media Research, 2000). While this data point is informative, it does not reveal whether individuals are actually watching television. Indeed, the average person reports viewing television about three hours per day (Robinson & Godbey, 1997). There is some variation in daily use by time of year, however. TV viewing decreases slightly in the summer and increases a little during the winter. This probably reflects the tendency for people to get outdoors when the weather is nice, and bundle-up indoors when the mercury plummets.

These simple averages do not tell the whole story, however. At least three variables tend to influence television use. The first is **gender.** Boys watch more TV per day than do girls (Kaiser Family Foundation, 1999). This may be due to the fact that boys are drawn to action and violence, two primary features of animated cartoon programming. As adults, however, the amount of time spent with television reverses for males and females. Women tend to watch more television than do men. This trend can be explained by the fact that more women stay at home during the day as caregivers than do men, and thus have greater access to television programming.

The second factor that can influence television use is **age.** The growing child spends the most time with television as a youngster, reaching a pinnacle just before adolescence. For example, a recent media use survey of over 2,000 children and adolescents found that "tweeners" (e.g., 8- to 13-year olds) watch about 3 and one-half hours of television per day (Kaiser Family Foundation, 1999). Television use among 14- to 18-year olds drops substantially to 2 and one-half hours per day, however. This dip is assuredly due to increases in adolescents' mobility (e.g., driving) as well as the tendency to become involved in a variety of social activities.

The third factor that may influence television viewing is **socioeconomic status,** or SES. Because it is a convenient and inexpensive form of entertainment, you might predict that lower SES homes would consume more television. You would be right. Families earning less than $30,000 per year consume an average of 51 hours of television per week. Those earning more than $60,000 watch an average of 46 hours of television programming per week (Nielsen Media Research, 2000).

Other Media

As mentioned, the boundaries between one form of media, such as music, and another are growing increasingly unclear. This makes "other" media use difficult to measure. To determine radio use, one now has to consider that certain TV stations exist only to broadcast music. Further, the Internet can also be used to listen to radio channels. A recent study found that listening to Internet-only radio stations has tripled during the past two years (Arbitron/Edison Media Research, 2001). Print media, such as newspapers, also have transcended that boundary. Many people choose to get their news from on-line newspapers that were only available in print a few years ago. Due to these and other conditions, it is more difficult to obtain "use" data for other media types.

The Kaiser Family Foundation study (1999) is perhaps the best source of media use information about individuals 18 years of age and under. This is because the authors surveyed not only a representative sample of more than 2,000 children and adolescents but also had certain families fill out media-use diaries with very specific questions. Studies of this nature are extremely costly and rare. Therefore, we will continue to rely on this important investigation in the following section, recognizing its chief limitation is that it only provides information about youth.

The Kaiser Family Foundation study (1999) reveals that young people have a variety of media from which to choose. When asked about their home, 98% of children report having at least one radio, 97% at least one VCR, 90% at least one CD player, 69% at least one video game player, and 69% at least one computer. Much of this technology is dedicated to the growing viewer. In the bedroom alone, 70% of children have a radio, 64% a tape player, 51% a CD player, 33% a video game player, and 16% a computer.

To ascertain use, the Kaiser Family Foundation survey (1999) asked kids to report how much time they spent with each medium. After television, movies, and videos, **music** is by far the most used media by children and adolescents. Music, as noted earlier, may be received on a variety of outlets. In terms of radio, there are 12,932 stations in America, though not all of them play music (FCC, 2001). The recording industry is able to surmount tremendous sales through continuous radio airplay of new music. Last year alone, domestic sales of CDs, tapes, records, and DVDs topped $14 billion (Recording Industry of America, 2001). The largest group of music buyers in the country is the baby boom generation (23%), edging out youngsters between 10- and 19-years of age (Recording Industry of America, 2001). Rock music comprises the largest share of recording sales, or 25%. The Rap/Hip-Hop genre replaced Country music as the second largest segment with 13% of the market due in part to recordings such as "The Marshall Mathers LP" which went platinum seven times (Recording Industry of America, 2001). These sales figures roughly match what children report listening to on a regular basis. The Kaiser Family Foundation (1999) study found that Alternative/Classic rock was most listened to by youngsters, but Rap/Hip-Hop seem to be rivaling that genre in terms of popularity.

The next most prevalent source is the **print media.** Youngsters still report reading for pleasure as a popular leisure-time activity. This seems to contradict the conventional wisdom that children are not reading anymore because of so many other media distractions. In fact, 20% of America's children spend more than an hour reading for fun each day, and the daily average is about 45 minutes. In a typical day, 57% of children will read a book, 51% a magazine, and 31% a newspaper (Kaiser Family Foundation, 1999). While these figures may be surprising, it is important to point out that the introduction of TV in a variety of different countries has been associated with marked decreases in amount of reading (see Condry, 1989, p. 15)

Computers and video games are the next most frequently used media outlets among youth. Computer use seems to be generating loyalty among multiple age groups. Children (Kaiser Family Foundation, 1999) and adults (Aribtron/Edison Media Research, 2000) report that if forced to choose, both groups would rather have a computer with Internet access than a television. This probably speaks to the potential of the Internet to broadcast audio and video, as well as its rapid growth in popularity. In fact, the Internet has experienced a growth pattern similar to that of television. For example, 10% of U.S.

households had a television set in 1950. In less than a decade, all but 13% of American homes had a TV (Nielsen Media Research, 2000). Compare this trend to Internet growth. In 1995, just 5 million households had access to the web. Four years later 50 million homes were connected to the information superhighway (Department of Commerce, 2000). Remember that people can devote time listening to music, reading, or even watching television via the Internet.

Video game systems are also growing in popularity among youth. This may be due to the fact that gaming platforms such as Sony Playstation, Nintendo, or Microsoft's new X-Box have made radical gains in technological sophistication. However, video games are not equally played by all subgroups of youth. Boys seem to play video games more than do girls (Kaiser Family Foundation, 1999). These differences are presumably due to boys increased liking of and attraction to the violence and action in such games. In fact, action, adventure, and sporting games are equally divided as the most popular gaming genres.

It seems clear, then, that children in this country grow up in a media filled environment. For many, a complete media warehouse can be found right in the bedroom. While alternative forms of media exposure seem to be growing, TV viewing still reigns. But TV characters are crossing the lines of traditional media with more regularity now. Celebrities found primarily on TV are establishing their presence in the lives of Americans through a mix of media. Shaquille O'Neal is a primary example. His rise in popularity came primarily from television via sports coverage. Now he produces his own music CDs and is featured in movies, books, video games, and on the Internet in interactive forums. There are many other examples as well. Clearly, TV does not exist in a vacuum. What happens on the small screen influences what happens in other media. This may be more true today than it has ever been. Having said this, keep in mind that the use of media has been presented in a somewhat artificial way. The combination of media content and the context in which it is viewed are important factors that we have almost completely ignored. What we will not ignore, however, is the potential effects of media use—the focus of the next section.

NEGATIVE EFFECTS

Public opinions polls on the impact of the media are constantly being conducted. In one such national survey, *U.S. News & World Report* found that 92% of the Americans interviewed believe that entertainment programming contributes to violence in society (c.f., Impoco et al., 1996). The findings also showed that 90% of those queried are concerned that portrayals of sex contribute to young people having intercourse. Not only are sex and violence issues, but so is stereotyping. A recent survey of Hispanics commissioned by *TV Guide* found that 66% of those interviewed believe that Latinos on most network shows are represented stereotypically (Hanania, 1999, p. 38). The purpose of this section is to take a closer look at these concerns. To this end, we will first document how much sex, violence, and stereotypical content is on American television. Then, we will review what social science research reveals about the effects of such portrayals on youth.

Violence. Recently, a large-scale content analysis of violence on television was conducted. Under the auspices of the National Television Violence Study (Wilson et al., 1997, 1998; Smith et al., 1998), researchers at the University of California, Santa Barbara (UCSB) examined both the amount and context of violence on American television from 1994-97. From October to June each year, the NTVS research team randomly sampled programs across 23 broadcast and cable channels from 6:00 a.m. to 11:00 p.m. to build a composite week of television content from each source. In total, roughly 3,000 programs were sampled and coded for violence yearly.

Five general trends emerged from this massive longitudinal content analysis. First, **violence is pervasive on American television.** Over half of all shows on television are likely to feature one or more instances of physical aggression with an intent to harm, with movies featuring the most (89%) and situation comedies showing the least (37%). Second, **TV violence is often glamorized.** Roughly 40% of all violent interactions on television feature "good" characters that may increase emulation and identification with the audience (Jose & Brewer, 1984). Third, **physical aggression on TV tends to be sanitized.** Over half of all violent interactions on television feature no pain and nearly 40% depict unrealistically low levels of harm. Fourth, television violence is likely to be trivialized. Approximately 40% of all scenes feature humor and less than 20% show any blood or gore. Finally, **violence is rarely chastised on television.** Roughly 40% of all violent programs with "bad" perpetrators fail to show these characters being punished for their aggressive actions. In addition, almost 75% of all violent scenes depict violent characters showing no remorse or penalty for their aggression.

Given that violence saturates the television environment, what impact does exposure to such depictions have on the audience? Since the 1950's, hundreds of studies have been conducted to answer this very question (see Liebert & Sprafkin, 1988). The research community generally concludes that there are three harmful effects associated with exposure to television violence. First, viewing television violence may contribute to **aggressive behavior.** Innumerable studies reveal that viewing TV violence can increase both short-term and long-term aggression (see Smith & Donnerstein, 1998). Second, exposure to violence on television may lead to **emotional desensitization.** That is, viewers who steadily watch violence in the media may grow increasingly numb or insensitive to aggression in the real world. Third, viewing of television violence may **distort viewers' beliefs about becoming the victim of a violent crime.** Repeated viewing is associated with exaggerated fear of falling prey to violence in society (see Gerbner, Gross, Morgan, & Signorielli, 1994).

However, it is also well documented by research that not all types of violent depictions have the same effect on viewers. Some types of portrayals may increase the risk of harm whereas others may decrease such risk. Very simply, **the context or way in which violence is depicted influences how viewers interpret and ultimately respond to televised acts of aggression.** To illustrate this, let's briefly examine two violent films, *Boyz 'n' the Hood* and *The Terminator*. Both movies feature graphic violence liberally throughout. However, the devastating consequences of violence in *Boyz 'n' the Hood* are presented throughout the plot, leaving the viewer with social commentary on the needless violence resulting from gang activity. *The Terminator,* on the other hand, portrayed violence as necessary, humorous, and as a justified means to an end. Thus, viewing a movie like *Boyz 'n' the Hood* may discourage the enactment of aggression whereas watching *The Terminator* may actually glorify it. See Table 14.1 for a complete list of contextual factors found to increase or decrease the probability of learning, desensitization, and fear.

TABLE 14.1 The Impact of Media Violence by Context Factor

	Learning Aggression	Emotional Desensitization	Fear
Attractive Perpetrators	Δ		
Attractive Victims			Δ
Weapons	Δ		
Extensiveness	Δ	Δ	Δ
Graphicness		Δ	
Justification	Δ		
Rewards	Δ		
Punishments	▼		
Realism	Δ		Δ
Humor	Δ		Δ

Outcome Variables

Note: Table 1 is from the *National Television Violence Study*, by Wilson et al., 1997, Newbury Park, CA: Sage.

Δ = an increase of a particular outcome variable

▼ = a decrease of a particular outcome variable

In addition to context, the **type of viewer** influences the impact of media violence. Some viewers are more susceptible to the harmful effects of violent media than are others. Most of the research has been conducted on viewer characteristics influencing the learning of aggression. Studies show that younger children (Paik & Comstock, 1994), boys (Paik & Comstock, 1994), the characteristically aggressive (Huesmann & Eron, 1986), those who fantasize about violence (Huesmann & Eron, 1986), and those who believe television violence is realistic (Huesmann, Moise, Podolski, & Eron, 1998) are more at risk for learning aggression.

It is worth noting that the impact of violence in video games is also receiving a great deal of empirical attention as of late. Like television violence, parents, policy makers, and educators have charged that violent video games may be contributing to aggression in society. Indeed, studies have generally found that playing aggressive video games such as *Doom* and *Mortal Kombat* increases violent tendencies (Anderson & Bushman, in press; Sherry, in press).

Sex. From the sultry *Sex in the City* to the scandalous *Jerry Springer* show, sexual content seems to be the bricks and mortar of television content. Is this really the case? Currently, Dale Kunkel and his research team at UCSB have been attempting to figure this out. Biennially, Kunkel et al. (1999, 2001)

© AFP/Corbis

have examined the amount of sex across 10 broadcast and cable television channels airing between 7:00 a.m. and 11:00 p.m. These researchers found that the prevalence of sex on TV is increasing. Over half (56%) of the shows featured sexual content in 1998 and 68% did in 2000. Much of this increase is due to the amount of sexual talk—not behavior—on television. The study also found that most of the scenes involving sexual intercourse related behaviors involve adults in an established relationship. Yet a growing number of scenes featuring intercourse related acts involve characters in their teenage years. Further, the results from Kunkel et al.'s (2001) study show that very few programs depict the risks and responsibilities associated with sex. Less than 10% of all shows with any sexual content mention the responsibilities (e.g., safe sex, patience) associated with sex and less than 2% of programs strongly emphasize such a mature message.

Unlike television violence, the impact of sexual media content on young viewers' thoughts, attitudes, and behaviors is less clear. Some studies show that children can learn sexual terms and phrases from exposure to educational (Greenberg, Perry, & Covert, 1983) as well as dramatic programming (Greenberg, Linsangan, & Soderman, 1993). There is also some evidence that viewing sexual content can impact viewers' attitudes towards pre-marital sex. For instance, Greeson and Williams (1987) found that adolescents exposed to music videos were more likely to express approval of teen premarital sex than were those who did not see such content. Together, these studies suggest that sexual media may have an impact on adolescent sexual learning and attitude change.

The previous studies have looked at the short-term effects of exposure to sexual media content. Other studies have begun assessing how heavy viewing of sexual portrayals may influence values and perceptions. At least one study shows that repeated exposure to inexplicit sex in the media can alter moral evaluations. For five consecutive days, Bryant and Rockwell (1994) exposed adolescents to three hours of dramatic television content involving either 1) sexual relations among married characters, 2) sexual relations among non-married characters, or 3) content not involving any sexual relations (p. 187). Several days later, the young viewers watched a series of scenes—some featuring sexual indiscretions—and then made a series of moral judgments about the content of the clips (e.g., how bad was the behavior). The results show that adolescents massively exposed to sexual scenes involving nonmarried characters rated the subsequent portrayals of sexual indiscretions as "less bad" than did their peers in the other two conditions (p. 188).

While the previous study used clips from dramatic series airing on broadcast television, other researchers have examined the impact of more explicit portrayals of sexual behavior routinely found on cable outlets. In particular, Linz and his colleagues have examined the effects of repeated exposure to "slasher films" or those movies that commonly juxtapose scenes of sex and violence (Linz, Donnerstein, & Penrod, 1984; Linz, Donnerstein, & Penrod, 1988). In one study, Linz et al. (1984) exposed male college students to a steady diet of slasher films over the course of five days. Immediately after exposure to a single film each day, the men's perceptions of and emotional reactions to the content were assessed. When compared to evaluations of the first film, the results revealed that the last film was rated as significantly less violent, less disturbing, and less degrading to women. The massive exposure also affected men's evaluations of a real-world victim of sexual assault. After watching a documentary rape trial at the end of the study, the men exposed to five days of slasher films rated the victim as less injured and less worthy than did a group of men who did not see any slasher content. Clearly, exposure to sexualized violence can have a powerful desensitizing effect on male viewers.

There is still one unanswered question about sex in the media, however. That is, does exposure to images of sex contribute to early adolescent sexual activity? For obvious ethical reasons, this is a very difficult empirical question to answer. Parents are very concerned about social scientists asking children about their sexual experiences (see Greenberg et al., 1983). To date, only two studies have been conducted on this issue. Yet the findings from these two investigations are mixed (Brown & Newcomer, 1991; Peterson, Moore, & Furstenberg, 1991). As a result, research is needed in this area to more fully understand what impact sexual portrayals in the media may be having on youth.

Stereotyping. The National Association for the Advancement of Colored People (NAACP) recently charged that TV was a "virtual whitewash" (CNN, 2001, p.1). In particular, the NAACP argued that network television does not feature enough minority characters in lead acting roles. Is this true? Does television tend to overlook racial minorities? When it does feature characters from different races, are they presented in ways that are demeaning or negative?

Those interested in the preceding questions have tallied the presence of racial minorities and the manner in which these groups are portrayed through content analyses of prime-time TV. Together, these studies show a few basic trends. The first is that **White characters far outweigh any other race on television** (Gerbner, 1997), thereby supporting the NAACP's concerns. Second, the **presentation of Blacks on TV has grown substantially over the years. Finally, other racial minorities virtually have been ignored by the mass media** (Greenberg, Mastro, & Brand, in press).

The presentation of Blacks on TV has come a long way, in terms of sheer presence. After decades of under-representation, an analysis of the 1996-97 prime-time season found that Blacks occupied 16% of the major and minor roles. At the time, Blacks accounted for 12% of the actual population (Mastro & Greenberg, 2000). This has not always been the case, however. Until the 1990s, research consistently found this minority group to be under-represented compared to their numbers in the real world.

Another important factor to consider is how Blacks are presented when they do appear on TV. Forty percent of all Black prime-time characters appear in crime dramas, while 34% appear in situation comedies (Mastro & Greenberg, 2000). In the past, Blacks were more commonly relegated to roles as supporting or minor characters (Cummings, 1988). These portrayals apparently reinforced many of the negative, stereotypical images developed in early films as well as radio serials (Atkin, 1992; Cummings, 1988). Today, roles seem to be more variant. However, a recent study found that Blacks were more provocatively dressed than Whites, and more unprofessional (Mastro & Greenberg, 2000). In sum, only recently has this group been fairly represented in terms of numbers. Further, the repeated presentations of Blacks as servants and criminals, over time, could have affected how people perceive the reality of this racial minority.

Besides Black characters, other racial minority groups are less fortunate. Asian, Native, and other non-African American groups are virtually nonexistent on television. When minority characters from these groups do appear on TV, they are often relegated to undignified or degrading roles. According to Harris (1999), when Arabs appear on television they are often depicted as terrorists, wealthy oil sheiks, infidels, sexual perverts, or Bedouin 'desert rats' (p. 59-61).

Does exposure to such portrayals contribute to stereotyping among the audience? Research suggests it can. Studies have evidenced a link between exposure to negative images and the development of stereotypes (Ford, 1997; Zuckerman, Singer, & Singer, 1980). Other authors have focused more directly on the news media. This is because content analyses have shown that local and national news programs present more crime stories of Blacks or Latinos than of Whites (Dixon & Linz, 2000; Jamieson, 1992; Romer, Jamieson, & DeCoteau, 1998). A recent study focused on the effects of this tendency. The authors found that exposure to this type of content increased support for punitive approaches to crime and heightened negative attitudes about African-Americans among Whites (Gilliam & Iyengar, 2000). Similarly, another investigation found that prolonged exposure to negative reports of minority crime in newspapers led people to perceive these minorities as more dangerous than if they had read newspapers without these negative reports (Verger, Lubbers, & Sheepers, 2000).

When negative thoughts are cultivated by exposure, there is even some evidence that these attitudes might affect behavior. Valentino (1999) exposed 289 adults to 1) a crime story with non-minority suspects, 2) a crime story with minority suspects or 3) no crime story. Viewers were then asked to evaluate President Clinton. Results found that support for the President suffered the most among subjects who viewed the news story with minority suspects. Further, the reduced evaluation of Clinton spread to other race issues, and to his performance on welfare. The author of the study contends that racial issues are connected in memory and are activated by news coverage that commonly features non-White perpetrators of serious crime (Valentino, 1999). This study also is an important example of a "priming" effect—a process we will discuss later.

At this point, it is important to note that a cluster of cultural factors may influence perceptions of groups of people. Pre-existing prejudice, length of U.S. residence, and proficiency of English were all found to predict Korean Americans' perceptions of fear of crime in Chicago communities (Lee & Ulmer, 2000). This study underscores the need to consider a host of biological and environmental factors that lead to racial prejudice. Though more research is needed, it seems clear that media exposure can be an important environmental influence.

THEORETICAL EXPLANATIONS

In the previous section, the impact of violent, sexual, and stereotypical media portrayals was reviewed. Now, we turn to theoretical mechanisms that explain why such effects occur. Three frequently cited theoretical perspectives on media effects are reviewed below: priming effects, social cognitive theory, and cultivation theory.

Priming Effects. Developed by Leonard Berkowitz (see Berkowitz & Rogers, 1986; also Jo & Berkowitz, 1994), this cognitive theory was created to explain the short-term, transient impact of media violence on aggressive behavior. Much of Berkowitz' theorizing is an extension of memory models developed in psychology. Thus, we will offer a brief and simple review of how memory is conceptualized and then explain how this theory is useful to media effects researchers.

According to Berkowitz (see Jo & Berkowitz, 1994), memory is made up of **networks** (p. 45). Each network contains "**nodes**" which store previous thoughts, emotions, and action tendencies. These networks are joined together by pathways. The memory nodes can be activated or "**primed**" by different types of stimuli. As Jo & Berkowitz (1994) state, "a certain stimulus having a particular meaning 'primes' other semantically related concepts, thus heightening the likelihood that thoughts with much the same meaning as the presentation stimulus will come to mind" (p. 46).

How does this theory relate to media effects? According to Berkowitz (Berkowitz & Rogers, 1986; Jo & Berkowitz, 1994), seeing violent media may "prime" or activate previous aggressive thoughts, feelings, and behaviors stored in memory. Such activation can temporarily alter individuals' 1) interpretations of others, 2) beliefs that violence is justified, and 3) level of aggressiveness (Jo & Berkowitz, 1994, p. 46). Indeed, a whole host of studies have illustrated the short-term immediate effects of exposure to media violence on aggression (see Liebert & Sprafkin, 1988).

Social Cognitive Theory. This theory was developed by Albert Bandura (1994) to explain both the short- and long-term effects of exposure to the mass media. According to this perspective, humans learn through both direct and vicarious experiences. The mass media is one rich source of information through which children or adults can vicariously or observationally learn new behaviors.

Vicarious or observational learning is governed by four distinct subfunctions. First, a viewer must **attend to a media event.** Certain attributes of the message can facilitate viewer attention. Attractive media characters such as Ben Affleck or Brittney Spears are likely to capture the viewer's attention and be potent role models for learning. Other attributes of the message such as its prevalence, relevance to the viewer's life, and vividness can all sway attentional resources.

Simply attending to a message is not enough, however. For learning to occur, the viewer **must retain the media message in memory.** According to Bandura (1994), retention is "an active process of transforming and restructuring information about events for memory representation in the form of rules and conceptions" (p. 68). Retention can be facilitated by repeated exposure to the media message, cognitively ruminating over the depiction, and even fantasizing about the depicted event. Thus, viewers that watch a great deal of television violence and actively think about it may be the most likely to learn that aggression is an acceptable tool for social problem-solving.

Next, a viewer must be able to **reproduce the modeled event.** Reproduction of the media event occurs through "conception-matching." Bandura (1994) argues that media events serve as a guide in the construction and execution of new behavior (p. 68). Viewer characteristics such as physical capabilities and coordination will inevitably affect behavioral imitation.

The last subfunction is **motivation.** Viewers do not imitate everything they learn from the mass media. Rather, they must be sufficiently motivated to do so. Two major types of incentives influence the probability of imitation: direct and vicarious reinforcements. Individuals are more likely to engage in behaviors that will directly result in rewarding outcomes than those behaviors that will be punished or not valued. The same is true for modeled events. Viewers are motivated by others' rewards and deterred by their actions that are punished. Seeing media characters engage in violent behaviors that are rewarded or not punished is likely to encouraging the learning of aggression.

In total, social cognitive theory posits that viewers can learn new behaviors from observing the mass media. Imitation is likely to occur when a viewer attends to a media message, retains it in memory, can reproduce the behavior, and is sufficiently motivated to do so. Although the examples used above pertain to violence, social cognitive theory can also be used to explain learning about sex and sexual intimacy from television.

Cultivation Theory. Developed by George Gerbner and his research team (Gerbner et al., 1994), this theory was created to explain the long-term cumulative effects of exposure to television. In general, there are two basic premises to cultivation theory. First, this perspective argues that television is a cultural **"story teller."** Rather than the family, church, or other societal venues, TV is the major socialization agent of our time. Second, this perspective argues that **television delivers largely homogeneous stories or messages.** Independent of genre, time of day, or channel, the "message" of television is relatively uniform.

Because TV programming delivers similar or uniform content to large and heterogeneous audiences, heavy viewing "cultivates" a shared perspective among otherwise diverse groups. That is, repeated exposure to television cultivates a world outlook that overrides any initial differences due to demographics, personality characteristics, or environment. This enculturation process, according to Gerbner et al. (1994), is called "mainstreaming." Consistent with this theorizing, studies show that heavy viewers of television are more likely than light viewers to perceive the world as a mean and violent place.

Another process in cultivation is **resonance.** In some instances, television offers a "double dose" of reality by mirroring or reflecting viewers' direct experience (Gerbner et al., 1994, p. 27). The result of resonance is that certain cultivation effects will be more pronounced or amplified when fact and fiction match. As Gerbner et al. (1994) state, "the relationships between amount of viewing and fear of crime is strongest among those who live in high crime urban areas" (p. 27).

Cultivation theory can be applied to other areas besides media violence. For instance, repeated exposure to sexual portrayals that do not feature the risks or responsibilities associated with such mature behavior may cultivate in viewers beliefs that safe sex is not important. Or, heavy viewing of demeaning portrayals of racial minorities may cultivate prejudices and negative attitudes towards those from different ethnic groups.

CONCLUSIONS

The aim of this chapter was to examine the impact of the mass media in our lives. The research reviewed above illustrates that we are a media dependent society. Further, exposure to images of violence, sex, and stereotyping in the mass media can have a negative influence on our thoughts, attitudes, and behaviors. Although we focused primarily on the negative effects of exposure, it is important to note that the mass media can also have a positive impact on consumers as well. As such, the next chapter in this text turns to the prosocial or beneficial influences of exposure to the mass media.

REFERENCES

Ajzen, I. (1988). *Attitudes, personality, and behavior.* Chicago, IL: Dorsey Press.

Anderson, C. A., & Bushman, B. J. (in press). Effects of violent video games on aggressive behavior, aggressive cognition, aggressive affect, physiological arousal, and prosocial behavior: A meta-analytic review of the scientific literature. *Psychological Science.*

Atkin, C. (1992). An analysis of television series with minority-lead characters. *Critical Studies of Mass Communication, 9,* 337–349.

Arbitron/Edison Media Research (2001). Internet VI: Streaming at a crossroads. [On-line]. Available: www.arbitron.com/radio_stations/ratings_reports_freestudies.htm.

Bandura, A. (1994). Social cognitive theory of mass communication. In J. Bryant & D. Zillmann (Eds.), *Media effects* (pp. 61–90). Hillsdale, NJ: Erlbaum.

Berkowitz, L., & Rogers, K. H. (1986). A priming effects analysis of media influence. In J. Bryant & D. Zillmann (Eds.), *Perspectives on media effects* (pp. 57–81). Hillsdale, NJ: Erlbaum.

Brown, J. D., & Newcomer, S. F. (1991). Television viewing and adolescents' sexual behavior. *Journal of Homosexuality, 21,* 77–91.

Bryant, J., & Rockwell, S. C. (1994). Effects of massive exposure to sexually oriented prime-time television programming on adolescents' moral judgment. In D. Zillmann, J. Bryant, & A. C. Huston (Eds.), *Media, children, and the family: Social scientific, psychodynamic, and clinical perspectives* (pp. 183–196). Hillsdale, NJ: Erlbaum.

Condry, J. (1989). *The Psychology of Television.* Hillsdale, NJ: Erlbaum.

Cable News Network (2001). NAACP outlines TV diversity options. [On-line]. Available: http://www.cnn.com/2001/SHOWBIZ/News/08/15/naacp.television/index.html.

Cummings, M. (1988). The changing image of the Black family on television. *Journal of Popular Culture, 22,* 75–85.

DeFleur, M. L., & Dennis, E. E. (1994). *Understanding mass communication* (5th ed.). Boston, MA: Houghton Mifflin.

Department of Commerce (2000). The emerging digital economy [On-line]. Available: www.commerce.gov.

Dini, J. (2000, August 24). Survivor finale posts second-highest ratings of season [On-line]. Available: www.thestreet.com/brknews/media/1053408.html.

Dixon, T. & Linz, D. (2000). Overrepresentation and underrepresentation of African-Americans and Latinos as lawbreakers on television news. *Journal of Communication, 50,* 131–154.

Federal Communications Commission (2001, July 13). Press Release: Broadcast station totals as of June 30, 2001. Washington, D.C. www.fcc.gov/Bureaus/Mass_Media/News_Releases/2001/nrmm0107.txt.

Flatlin, P. (2000). Do video games trigger violence? [On-line]. Available: http://www.policy.com/news/dbrief/dbriefarc578.asp.

Ford, T. (1997). Effects of stereotypical television portrayals of African-Americans on person perception. *Social Psychology Quarterly, 60,* 266–278.

Gerbner, G. (1997). Gender and age in prime-time television. In S. Kirschner & D. A. Kirschner (Eds.), *Perspectives on psychology and the media* (pp. 69–94). Washington DC; American Psychological Association.

Gerbner, G., Gross, L., Morgan, M., & Signorielli, N. (1994). Growing up with television: The cultivation perspective. In J. Bryant & D. Zillmann (Eds.), *Media Effects* (pp. 17–42). Hillsdale, NJ: Erlbaum.

Gilliam, F. D. Jr., & Iyengar, S. (2000). Prime suspects: The influence of local television news on the viewing public. *American Journal of Political Science, 44 (3),* 560–573.

Greenberg, B. S., Linsangan, R., & Soderman, A. (1993). Adolescents' reactions to television sex. In B. S. Greenberg, J. D. Brown, & N. Buerkel-Rothfuss (Eds.), *Media, sex, and the adolescent* (pp. 196–224). Cresskill, NJ: Hampton Press.

Greenberg, B.S., Mastro, D., Brand, J.E. (in press). Minorities and the mass media: Television into the 21st century. In J. Bryant & D. Zillman (Eds.), *Media effects* (second edition). Hillsdale, NJ: Erlbaum.

Greenberg, B. S., Perry, K. L., & Covert, A. M. (1983). The body human: Sex education politics and television. *Family Relations, 32,* 419–425.

Greeson, L. E., & Williams, R. A. (1987). Social implications of music videos for youth: An analysis of the content and effects of MTV. *Youth & Society, 18,* 177–189.

Hanania, J. (1999, August 21). White out: Latinos. *TV Guide,* p. 30–32, 38–39.

Harris, R. (1999). *A cognitive psychology of mass communication* (3rd ed.). Mahwah, NJ: Erlbaum.

Huesmann, L. R., & Eron, L. (1986) (Eds.). *Television and the aggressive child: A cross-national comparison.* Hillsdale, NJ: Erlbaum.

Huesmann, L. R., Moise, J., Podolski, C. L., & Eron, L. (1998). *Longitudinal relations between children's exposure to television violence and their later aggressive and violent behavior in young adulthood: 1977–1992.* Paper presented at the annual meeting of the International Communication Association, Jerusalem, Israel.

Impoco, J., Bennefield, R. M., Pollack, K., Bierck, R., Schmidt, K., & Gregory, S. (1996, April 15). TV's frisky family values. *U.S. News & World Report,* p. 58–62.

Jamieson, K. (1992). *Dirty politics.* NY: Oxford University Press.

Jo, E., & Berkowitz, J. (1994). A priming effect analysis of media influences: An update. In J. Bryant & D. Zillmann (Eds.), *Media effects* (pp. 43–60). Hillsdale, NJ: Erlbaum.

Jose, P. E., & Brewer, W. F. (1984). Development of story liking: Character identification, suspense, and outcome resolution. *Developmental Psychology, 20,* 911–924.

Kaiser Family Foundation (1999). *Kids and media @ the new millenium.* Kaiser Family Foundation: Menlo Park, CA

Kottack, C. P. (1990). *Prime time society: An anthropological analysis of television and culture.* Belmont, CA: Wadsworth.

Kubey, R. W., & Csikszentmihalyi, M. (1990). *Television and the quality of life: How viewing shapes everyday experience.* Hillsdale, NJ: Lawrence Erlbaum.

Kunkel, D., Cope, K. M., Maynard Farinola, W. J., Biely, E., Rollin, E., & Donnerstein, E. (1999). *Sex on TV.* Menlo Park, CA: Kaiser Family Foundation.

Kunkel, D., Cope-Farrar, K. M., Biely, E., Maynard Farinola, W. J., & Donnerstein, E. (2001). *Sex on TV2.* Menlo Park, CA: Kaiser Family Foundation.

Kunkel, D., & Roberts, D. (1991). Young minds and marketplace values: issues in children's television advertising. *Journal of Social Issues, 47 (1),* 57–72.

Lee, M. S., & Ulmer, J. T. (2000). Fear of crime among Korean Americans in Chicago communities. *Criminology, 38 (4),* 1173–1206.

Liebert, R. M., & Sprafkin, J. (1988). *The early window* (3rd ed.). New York: Pergamon.

Linz, D., Donnerstein, E., & Penrod, S. (1984). The effects of multiple exposures to filmed violence against women. *Journal of Communication, 34 (3),* 130–147.

Linz, D., Donnerstein, E., & Penrod, S. (1988). Effects of long-term exposure to violent and sexually degrading depictions of women. *Journal of Personality and Social Psychology, 55,* 758–768.

Mastro, D., & Greenberg, B. S. (2000). The portrayal of racial minorities on prime time television. *Journal of Broadcasting & Electronic Media, 44,* 690–703.

National Association of Muslim Journalists (1999). Siege film engendering anti-Arab hatred? [On-line]. Available: http://www.blackjournalism.com/muslim.htm.

Nielsen Media Research (2000). *2000 Report on Television: The First 50 Years.* Nielsen Media Research: NY

Paik, H., & Comstock, G. (1994). The effects of television violence in antisocial behavior. *Communication Research, 21,* 516–546.

Peterson, J. L., Moore, K. A., & Furstenberg, F. F. (1991). Television viewing and early initiation of sexual intercourse: Is there a link? *Journal of Homosexuality, 21,* 93–119.

Potter, M. (2001, January 26). Defense to appeal boy's murder conviction in 'wrestling death' [On-line]. Available: www.cnn.com/2001/Law/01/26/wrestling.death/.

Recording Industry of America (2001). RIAA market reports on U.S. recorded music shipments [On-line]. Available: www.riaa.com/MD-US-3.cfm.

Robinson, J. P., & Godbey, G. (1997). *Time for life: The surprising ways Americans use their time.* University Park: Pennsylvania State University Press.

Romer, D., Jamieson, K., & DeCoteau, N. (1998). The treatment of persons of color in local television news: Ethnic blame discourse or realistic group conflict? *Communication Research, 25,* 286–305.

Sherry, J. (in press). The effects of violent video games on aggression: A meta analysis. *Human Communication Research.*

Smith, S. L., & Donnerstein, E. (1998). Harmful effects of exposure to media violence: Learning aggression, emotional desensitization, and fear. In R. G. Geen & E. Donnerstein, (Eds.) *Human aggression: Theories, research and implications for policy* (pp. 167–202). New York: Academic Press.

Smith, S. L., Wilson, B. J., Kunkel, D., Linz, D., Potter, W. J., Colvin, C., & Donnerstein, E. (1998). Violence in television programming overall: University of California, Santa Barbara. *National television violence study* (Vol. 3, pp. 5–220). Newbury Park, CA: Sage Publications.

TV Guide. (1999, July 10). Hollywood under fire, p. 35–36, 41–42.

Valentino, N. A. (1999). Crime news and the priming of racial attitudes during evaluations of the president. *Public Opinion Quarterly, 63 (3),* 293–320.

Verger, M. Lubbers, M., & Sheepers, P. (2000). Exposure to newspapers and attitudes toward ethnic minorities: A longitudinal analysis. *Howard Journal of Communications, 11 (2),* 127–143.

Wallis, C. (1998, February 9). Eager minds, big ears. *Time,* p. 67.

Wilson, B. J., Kunkel, D., Linz, D., Potter, W. J., Donnerstein, E., Smith, S. L., Blumenthal, E., & Berry, M. (1997). Violence in television programming overall: University of California, Santa Barbara. *National television violence study* (Vol. 2, pp. 3–204). Newbury Park, CA: Sage Publications.

Wilson, B. J., Kunkel, D., Linz, D., Potter, W. J., Donnerstein, E., Smith, S. L., Blumenthal, E. Y., & Gray, T. E. (1998). Violence in television programming overall: University of California, Santa Barbara Study. *National television violence study* (Vol. 1, pp. 1–268). Newbury Park, CA: Sage Publications.

Zillmann, D. (1991). Television viewing and physiological arousal. In J. Bryant & D. Zillmann (Eds.), *Responding to the screen* (pp. 103–134). Hillsdale, NJ: Erlbaum.

Zuckerman, D., Singer, C., & Singer, J. (1980). Children's television viewing, racial and sex role attitudes. *Journal of Applied Social Psychology, 10,* 281–294.

Chapter Fourteen Case Study Quiz— Mass Media Exposure

Instructions:

Please read the following case study carefully and select the best answers to the questions. This quiz is an individual assignment. Remember: sharing answers is a form of plagiarism.

Diane is concerned about her fourteen-year-old son, Jason. He is not involved in extra-curricular activities at school nor does he participate in athletics. Rather, he comes home from school each day and watches hours of television. She has recently read that many of the young kids who have been responsible for school shootings are overexposed to inappropriate media such as violent video games and movies, and song lyrics encouraging young people to be violent. Diane has tried to decrease the amount of time that Jason watches television as well as research the music groups he listens to. However, Jason has begun to rebel against his mother's behavior because his fifteen-year-old sister, Amy, is not subjected to the same discipline. Diane is not as concerned about Amy watching violent television. Instead, Amy is not allowed to watch such shows as "Sex & the City" or the music videos aired on MTV due to the sexual nature of the content. Diane is afraid that Amy will learn many ideals about sex from watching such television.

Student's Name _____

Section Number _____

Section Leader's Name _____

Chapter Fourteen Case Study— Mass Media Exposure

1. Jason's mother should be more concerned about him then his sister because one of the variables that influences television watching is:
   a. Age
   b. Gender
   c. Socioeconomic status
   d. Race

2. There are several trends that discuss violence and television. Which of the following will Jason NOT see on television?
   a. TV violence is often glamorized
   b. Violence is rarely chastised on TV
   c. Violence is pervasive on TV
   d. TV shows more violent talk than violent behavior

3. Diane should not be as worried about her daughter because:
   a. The impact of sexual media content on young viewers is less clear than the impact of violent media
   b. There is hardly any sexual content on TV
   c. Those having sex always use protection
   d. Girls are not influence by TV

4. Social Cognitive Theory explains both short and long term effects from the mass media by describing four key steps. If this theory explained Jason's behavior through his participation in these four steps, which one of the following is NOT a step Jason would engage in?
   a. Attention
   b. Motivation
   c. Resonance
   d. Reproduction

5. According to the theory of Priming Effects, viewing certain media content may activate previous thoughts, feelings, and behaviors stored in individuals' memories. Activating these things may temporarily alter which of the following?
    a. Jason's interpretations of others
    b. Jason's belief that violence is justified
    c. Jason's level of aggressiveness
    d. All of the above

Chapter Fifteen

LEARNING FROM THE MASS MEDIA

Charles K. Atkin
Michigan State University

As dusk falls on the town of Middleville, Norm Johnson takes his dog Bear walking around the neighborhood. It's late October and the leaves are beginning to fall from the trees. This provides a better view into the windows of the houses, and Norm notices that almost two-thirds of his neighbors have TV sets glowing in their living rooms. He had observed only half of the homes receiving a newspaper from the paperboy during his morning walk. Some of the mailboxes are still stuffed with magazines that were delivered earlier in the day. In almost all of the cars passing by, the drivers are listening to the radio.

A curious man, Norm ponders the role that these mass media play in the lives of people in his town. He realizes that Middleville audiences spend most of their time consuming entertainment content, such as TV comedies and radio songs. But Norm also recognizes that there's a sizable amount of **informational content** available: newspaper stories, magazine features, newscasts, public service messages, and educational programs. He wonders whether these more serious types of material have a meaningful impact on the viewers, listeners, and readers. How much of it do they consume? What do they learn? And who learns what things? This chapter examines the patterns of learning exhibited by Norm and his typical American family (wife Norma, preschooler Jennifer, and teenager Jason) and his typical neighbors and co-workers. The Johnson's oldest son, who is away at college, isn't really relevant to this story.

Why does this chapter focus on the learning of typical Middleville Americans, while ignoring the son who's a college student? The main reason is that the way the media influence those living in a college environment simply isn't typical of what happens in the rest of society. When it comes to learning from informational content, students are unique in several respects.

First, exposure patterns are different; students are below-average in viewing TV newscasts, educational programs, and public service announcements, and in reading magazines and off-campus newspapers. Second, students tend to be brighter and more educated than the average person; their greater cognitive capacity enables them to better absorb the serious information that's encountered in the media. Third, students have distinctive reasons for using the media; the typical undergrad is motivated to learn certain types of information (such as sports stories, fashion features, entertainment reviews, campus crime news, and drunk driving PSAs), but other content is less interesting or relevant than it will be later in life (such as local political news, financial investment features, and heart disease PSAs . . . not to mention *Sesame Street* programs).

In exploring the educational effects of the media, this chapter emphasizes audience learning at the **cognitive** level, which encompasses the acquisition of objective knowledge and the formation of subjective images and beliefs. Although attitudes and behaviors are also important, these outcomes are given less emphasis because persuasion is not the main purpose of the informational media and because the persuasive effects are indirectly determined by the cognitions that are absorbed.

The channels of information examined in this chapter focus on the conventional "mass media" that have dominated American society for the past half-century: television, radio, newspapers, magazines. These four media are characterized by a predominantly one-way flow of messages to large audiences; individual-retrieval channels such as internet webpages, library books, or video rental stores will not be covered here.

The chapter provides a series of glimpses into an ordinary day's media use by the Johnson family. Each vignette is accompanied by explanations of what happened and descriptions of the broader patterns in society; concepts and evidence are drawn from mass communication theory and research. The closing section presents strategies for more effective learning from the informational media.

WHAT DO PEOPLE LEARN FROM THE NEWS MEDIA?

As a typical American news consumer, Norm Johnson closely views or reads about twenty stories on this late October day. He actually encounters many more news items, but doesn't pay full attention because much of his evening TV news viewing is merely casual grazing while monitoring for worthwhile stories, and much of his morning newspaper reading consists of simply scanning the headlines. Moreover, there are constant distractions that undermine his attentiveness, especially while the TV is on (eating dessert, talking, clearing the dinner table, and scanning the *TV Guide*). Norm's amount of exposure to news is somewhat lower than five or ten years before, reflecting the steady decrease in both newspaper reading and network TV news viewing in the general population.

Among the stories carried in the news on this particular day are a presidential press conference, a senatorial candidate visit to a school, and an affirmative action protest march. Unlike real events such as plane crashes, congressional votes, and war battles, these **pseudo events** are staged primarily to attract news media reporters and cameras. Manufactured stories are usually more engaging and understandable, which attracts attention and facilitates learning.

Nevertheless, Norm feels that much news content is repetitive and monotonous, and that some of the standard news topics are far from fascinating. He's not really motivated to learn and store away the bulk of what he sees and reads. Instead, Norm primarily consumes news because the experience is mentally stimulating or enjoyable at the moment of exposure. Like junk food, some items produce momentary pleasure, but provide little long-term benefit. Even the high-protein substantive topics such as government affairs or the economy are often consumed and forgotten quickly due to lack of learning motivation.

Suppose Norma asks her husband to recount everything he could remember from the news that day. Norm would able to retrieve only a couple of the stories that he read in the morning paper, and his recall from the recently viewed newscast would perhaps total three items. This low retention rate is typical, because relatively little of what people watch and read sticks in the crevices of the mind.

The **cumulative acquisition** of information over months and years is somewhat greater, due to the thousands of opportunities to learn and the repeated exposure to certain high-profile topics. Which news content tends to be absorbed in the long run? Over the years, Norm has gained considerable knowledge about the space program, gun regulation, and the Arab-Israeli conflict. Norma has learned a lot about the subjects of nuclear power, medical breakthroughs, and Japanese trade policies.

Why are certain types of information learned? The main factor is whether the subject matter is interesting and relevant to the news user. The simple concept of **intrinsic interest** accounts for much of the motivation to consume news and learn it; for example, Norm happens to regard space shots and guns as personally interesting, while Norma is fascinated by Japan and medical research.

The **relevance** concept pertains to the applicability of topical information to one's everyday life; it's the extent to which news can be put to practical use in solving problems, making decisions, or participating in conversations. Because Norma's father has a heart condition, she finds medical news relevant as well as interesting. She's a member of an environmental protection committee, so developments in the nuclear power industry are pertinent to her group's initiatives. Norm can relate to the space program because he's a former pilot; moreover, he recently joined the National Rifle Association, and plans a trip to Israel. When it comes to their favorite topics, Norm and Norma are eager learners.

As for topics that are only somewhat interesting or relevant, individuals absorb much less information but still gain a superficial awareness. While Norm was becoming deeply knowledgeable about his particular specialties, Norma also acquired some vague impressions and assorted facts about space, guns, and Israel along the way: she remembers that the Challenger blast-off was a disaster, she's fairly sure that concealed guns are banned in Middleville, and she realizes that the Israelis and Arabs are continually bickering and fighting. Similarly, Norm knows a few highlights about Norma's favorite topics: he's able to recall the nuclear meltdowns at Three Mile Island and Chernobyl, and he has a notion that Japan drives a hard bargain in automobile trade.

There are dozens of frequently-publicized topics that Norm and Norma regard as quite dull or distant, such as remote conflicts in Africa, dry rulings of the Supreme Court, and routine legislative activities of the Senate. Even though the media give prominent placement to such subjects and try to package the material in an engaging style, the news coverage is largely ignored or forgotten.

Research with news audiences demonstrates that for most of the people most of the time, the amount of learning is narrow, shallow, and short-lived. The main reasons for this limited acquisition of knowledge and beliefs can be traced to lack of audience demand rather than lack of media supply. Except for news junkies, the majority of the population is picky in their topical exposure and attention patterns. Moreover, many people lack the motivation or ability to comprehend and store the incoming information. The paltry amount that readers and viewers retain tends to focus on a subset of interesting and relevant topics, few of which have universal appeal; different segments of the audience tend to specialize in learning certain subject matter. Only with frequent and prominent presentation, over a sustained period of time, do a few key types of content sink into the minds of the majority.

Thus, it's not surprising that Americans score low on "current events" quizzes (especially if there are essay questions about governmental affairs and foreign countries). For example, most people are ignorant or only dimly aware of basic initiatives in Washington regarding social security, economic policy, and energy supply. Americans know even less about other nations; few can identify the leaders of neighboring Mexico or powerful Japan, and few keep track of developments of the United Nations.

The main exception is learning about the president, who receives a phenomenal quantity of publicity. Most people gain some knowledge and images because presidential decisions are frequently relevant to their lives and the personalized news treatment increases interest value. Even so, the amount of learning is far from comprehensive. Rather than absorbing detailed information about policies, the public is more likely to derive personal impressions (that Bill Clinton has character weaknesses or that George Bush isn't very bright), or to retain assorted bits of vivid trivia. Only occasionally does an issue position break through the glaze of daily updates, such as Bush's income tax cut or Clinton's health care reforms.

The national news media have become fixated on misdeeds and moral failings of public officials, and chronicled our leaders' constant maneuvers in the calculated inside game of politics. These unappealing portrayals have contributed to an increasing sense of cynicism about politicians over the past two decades.

Although news media usage is basically a solitary activity, there are clear connections to interpersonal communication. During a mid-morning conversation at the office, Norm brought up a story about gun control that he'd read earlier in the newspaper. Several co-workers hadn't heard anything about this new policy, so he relayed the information to them and added his own opinion about the gun control issue. Norm also got involved in a lengthy discussion with another colleague who already knew about the new policy; the two of them shared their reactions and debated the idea of allowing concealed handguns.

Norm's act of relaying the news story exemplifies the **two-step flow**, where media content indirectly reaches an unexposed person via someone who has seen or read the message. The person who passes on media information can be characterized as an **opinion leader,** especially if they mix in their own viewpoints on the topic. Opinion leaders are not elite members of society, but are average individuals like Norm who happen to be well-informed about a particular subject and who like to talk about it with those who haven't been keeping up. When Norm later exchanges ideas with the colleague who has similar expertise and interest, the process is called **opinion sharing;** in this case, the media message which has been seen by both parties serves as a basis for interpersonal influence that may alter the impact of the new information on attitudes.

As Norm settles down to watch the late evening local newscast, the first story reported on a drive-by shooting in nearby Metropolis. It seemed to Norm that the news always starts off with a murder or mugging; apparently that station followed the dictum: "if it bleeds, it leads." As a result of this continuous diet of TV crime stories, he has long ago formed the image that serious crimes were rampant and on the rise, especially in Metropolis (even though actual crime rates have been dropping substantially since the early 1990's). When he reads newspaper articles dealing with many of these same criminal acts, the impact isn't nearly as strong. The TV portrayals (featuring visuals of the crime scene, the accused perpetrators, the victims and their emotionally distraught friends and relatives) leave a much more vivid impression. Compared to some neighbors who seldom watch the local news, Norm is less inclined to drive in high-crime areas of Metropolis and is more supportive of conservative proposals to build more prisons and hand out longer sentences to felons.

This case illustrates how news produces a **cultivation** effect, which is similar to the impression created by entertainment violence. By repeating the same basic portrayal of criminals and victims, the news media slowly but surely cultivate distinctive stereotypes about who commits crimes, and produce images about what types of crimes occur most often in which settings. Seeing real-life crime stories day after day, the audience gradually develops mental perceptions that murder and mayhem are indeed prevalent in society. This contributes to heightened fearfulness and wider ownership of weapons for protection. Because the news media provide such a credible and compelling window on the outside world, fear and loathing seem to be more closely related to the emphasis on crime in the news than to actual fluctuations in the crime rate.

As a result of the cultivation process, the public tends to have exaggerated perceptions of the prevalence of many other disturbing problems, such as suicides, drug usage, airplane crashes, and supermarket product tampering.

On the national newscast that night, the lead story had described another attempt to reform the health care system. This was the same basic theme that he'd read about on the front page of the morning paper and seen on last night's newscast. In fact, the health care story had been prominent in the news for months. No matter where he turned, Norm saw another news item dealing with the topic. Based on the frequent and sustained coverage, he's beginning to regard health care reform as a very important issue facing the nation.

Norm recalled that several years earlier, the health care story was not so high on the news media agenda. The topic displaced federal deficit reduction, which had displaced the prior #1 topic of the Gulf War. Before that, the media agenda had in turn highlighted the issues of drugs, AIDS, the Iran hostage crisis, inflation, and the environment. Back in the 1960s, the most prominently-covered stories were Vietnam and civil rights. Each one slowly climbed to prominence, attained a couple of years at the top of the topical hit parade, and then faded.

For several decades, public opinion pollsters have asked citizens to identify the most important problems in society that they are most concerned about. The rank order of personally-significant issues closely corresponds with what has been most heavily publicized in the newspapers, newscasts, and newsmagazines during the previous year or so. The public usually attaches significance to a consistently high-profile topic, regardless of whether they possess high or low knowledge about the subject, or whether they hold favorable or unfavorable attitudes toward it. This process is called **agenda setting;** the news media teach people what is important in society by giving continuing front-page or lead-story treatment to the topic. The topic becomes more salient to people, and they discuss it more often. The media don't necessarily tell people what to think, but are quite influential in telling them what to think about.

Status conferral is a parallel process that applies to individual players rather than issues featured in the news. By singling out certain leaders for special attention, the news media confer greater prestige in the eyes of the audience. Leaders whose names and faces receive the most frequent and high profile presentations tend to be perceived as more important. Not only do these spotlighted persons become better known, but they are also seen as more prominent and worthy of consideration.

Which individuals achieve this star treatment in the media and the consequent boost in public prominence? Status conferral is just partly due to the position that the leader holds; it's mostly a function of the person's visible accomplishments, newsworthiness and personal charisma. Thus, certain prime ministers, vice presidents, popes, or auto company presidents become famous, while others who occupy the same role never attain widespread notoriety via the media spotlight.

Another of the newscast items on this October evening describes a congressional hearing on the subject of media violence. Expert critics and senators alike piously attacked TV dramas, movies, and rap music, claiming that fictional entertainment glorifies violence and leads to imitation, desensitization, perceived prevalence, and fearfulness of victimization. There have been repeated attacks by politicians, who calculate that this will impress a crime-weary public seeking scapegoats. The irony in this recurrent news theme about entertainment violence is that informational media presentations (especially local newscasts, tabloid news shows, and real-life police documentaries) may actually exert stronger effects on the masses because of more credible and realistic messages.

The concept of **credibility** plays a major role in determining the impact of the news media. A message is credible if the audience trusts the source or believes that the content is true. Norma Johnson perceives that the local newspaper is biased against liberal leaders and causes, so she tends to discount the validity of political news coverage; she's not as skeptical about the accuracy of articles dealing with other topics. Both Norma and Norm feel that the TV newscasts are trustworthy.

This pattern is typical of Middleville and the rest of the country. Television news is regarded as more credible than newspapers, as TV news viewers tend to trust the newscasters who personally deliver the stories and the visual events that they can see for themselves; moreover, most people regard the broadcast news organizations as non-partisan. By contrast, newspapers feature impersonal journalists, rely on verbal descriptions, and take editorial positions on controversial issues. Nevertheless, newspapers are still given fairly high credibility ratings; people believe most of what they read, as well as view, in the news media.

It should be noted that this chapter has focused on traditional hard news coverage, but news media content can be defined broadly to include additional types of "softer" informational material. Public affairs journalism constitutes only a fraction of the messages in the print media and reality-oriented broadcasts. People usually spend more than an hour per day monitoring the information flow from advice columns and feature stories in newspapers and magazines, from daytime talk shows, evening documentaries, and specialty cable channels on TV, and from offbeat commentators and provocative drive-time hosts on the radio. The average American learns and retains a great deal of practical information about fashion, athletics, diet, weather, relationships, homemaking, childcare, career strategies, travel, sexual matters, and other aspects of daily living from these sources.

Indeed, the amount learned from this rich array of supplemental information sources is typically greater than from standard newspaper and newscast reports of current events. These kinds of "life information" are more relevant and useful, and most people simply have stronger needs for guidance than for keeping track of political maneuvers in the capital or crises halfway around the globe. Furthermore, these alternative forms of information tend to be characterized by a more entertaining style than found in conventional journalism.

WHAT IS THE IMPACT OF POLITICAL CAMPAIGNS?

Because the November election is right around the corner, Norm and Norma have been deluged with a heavy dose of mediated campaigning for many weeks. The candidates running for Governor and Senator appear in the news everyday, and they saturate the airwaves with political commercials. However, the lower-level candidates campaigning for State Representative and City Council have minimal advertising budgets and receive little news coverage.

Neither Norm nor Norma has learned much useful information from the news coverage during the two months of campaign itself; the bulk of their basic knowledge and beliefs comes from the long-term accumulation of news inputs during the previous months and years while the incumbents performed in office. The Johnsons have managed to form some vague new impressions about each candidate's personality, career experiences, and one or two issue positions, but their learning has been restricted by the media's emphasis on the horserace and maneuvering of the competitors and by the dull treatment of candidate policies, along with Norm and Norma's own personal lack of interest in state and local races.

Their rather modest learning from campaign news coverage is typical of most Americans in mid-level elections such as the Senate race, which lack the excitement and significance of presidential campaigns. The news media impact is even weaker in **low-involvement** races for state legislature or local offices, because most voters don't really care enough to seek out detailed information. In many of these minor campaigns, about the only thing the voters glean from the media is greater name recognition of key candidates.

By contrast, the Johnsons and most other citizens of Middleville were highly involved in the last race for President. They followed the campaign news coverage fairly closely on TV and in newspapers; they gained a substantial amount of knowledge, and their beliefs and images were also shaped to a significant degree. Not only do voters learn from the extensive traditional news coverage, but there are secondary informational vehicles such candidate interviews on *Good Morning America, Larry King Live,* and *David Letterman.*

During that presidential campaign, most Middleville voters also watched the candidate debates. The series of TV debates has become the highlight of the campaign and attracts large audiences. Unfortunately, televised debating is not well suited to effectively educating voters about candidate qualifications and issue stands for several reasons: the lengthy format exceeds the attention span of most viewers, the sheer amount of information creates overload for those lacking sufficient prior knowledge, and the debaters craftily express glittering generalities and evasive answers rather than articulating clear-cut policies. The main thing that voters take away from the debates is an impression of the candidates' televised images, as the debaters seek to project personal qualities such as poise, sincerity, intelligence, warmth, and compassion. Even though this type of soft input doesn't enable the viewer to score well on a factual post-debate quiz, the image formation still helps voters to judge whether they want the candidate to lead the nation.

In both local and national elections, the greatest amount of learning probably results from viewing the superficial and annoying **political advertising.** This strong impact may seem surprising, but consider the potency of the candidate commercials. These spots are so frequent and intrusive that even uninterested voters are repeatedly exposed and have ample opportunity to learn. Moreover, the content is rather simple, featuring a readily digestible capsule of imagery, claims, and facts packaged in an engaging manner.

In this year's races, Norma is turned off by the **negative advertising** in which the candidates constantly attack each other. Nevertheless, she has learned some pertinent information about both the attackers and the targets. She interprets accusations against the incumbent Governor's personal life to be harsh and unfair mudslinging; instead of believing the detrimental charges (and consequently disliking the maligned target), she feels sympathy for the "victim" and perceives the attacker to be disreputable and unappealing. On the other hand, one Senate candidate attacked the opponent's position on the issue of welfare reform and presented evidence to back up the claim; Norma believed that this was a valid point and added it to the increasingly negative pool of information she had acquired about the target.

These divergent outcomes illustrate how negative advertising can be a double-edged sword. Some attacks provoke a backlash, which results in a counterproductive **boomerang effect;** the challenger who attacked the Governor ended up losing support. By contrast, the Senate candidate effectively used the TV spot to convey a piece of information that undermined support for the targeted opponent. In the typical campaign, the rate of success in attacking the opponent isn't much higher than 50-50. Because it's a risky strategy that frequently backfires but may also provide a crucial breakthrough, negative advertising is more often used by an underdog who has little to lose and who needs to drag down the frontrunner in order to catch up.

DO PUBLIC SERVICE INFORMATION CAMPAIGNS WORK?

Like most teenagers, the Johnson' son Jason largely ignores the news reporting and tunes out the political campaigning, but he does watch the usual two or three hours of TV programming each day. Among the clutter of commercials appearing during the program breaks, there are two PSAs that catch his eye. One informational message preached against drunk driving, and the other spot warned of the dangers of marijuana. Jason displayed divergent reactions to each message, based partly on the differing quality of the persuasive appeals and partly on his own set beliefs and attitudes.

When Jason attends drinking parties, he's careful to make designated driver arrangements with his friends because of concerns about getting caught by the police and smashing his car. The drunk driving PSA employed a standard fear appeal depicting a wrecked car and asserting that an intoxicated driver is far more probable to have a crash. Although this was hardly a new revelation to Jason, the familiar theme served to remind him of the serious consequences that were likely to occur if he drove drunk. The message heightened his concern about crashing and further solidified his intention to avoid drunk driving. This effect illustrates the concept of **reinforcement,** where incoming information serves to strengthen a pre-existing inclination.

By contrast, Jason resisted being influenced by the marijuana PSA. He has become a frequent user of pot, and doesn't believe that he's experienced any adverse consequences. While viewing the TV spot, Jason counter-argued against the claim that pot would impair brain functioning, and selectively tuned out the portion that cited scientific evidence. Like other marijuana messages over the past year, this one had no influence on him.

As this example demonstrates, health campaigns achieve varying degrees of success. For a few topics such as drunk driving, tobacco, cocaine, and safety belts, research shows that comprehensive campaign efforts have been moderately effective. In most cases, however, there has been minimal impact. **Three sets of factors determine whether a campaign is successful: audience receptivity, message potency, and the environmental situation.**

First, the target audiences that campaigns seek to influence have differing degrees of **receptivity** vs. resistance. People are more receptive to learning information when the recommended behavior is easy to perform (buckling safety belts), or when the benefits are highly advantageous (safe rides with a designated driver). Some campaigns succeed because they're aimed at segments of the population who are generally susceptible to influence (young children rather than teenagers), or for whom the sacrifice is rather minor (recreational cocaine users rather than hard-core addicts). On the other hand, many campaigns face a tough sell because people are asked to forgo highly pleasurable pursuits (fatty foods, addictive cigarettes, suntanning, casual sex), or to exert considerable effort (exercise, medical checkups, condom use). In these more common cases, the typical unhealthy person will resist learning new information and complying with the unpalatable advice.

Second, campaigns vary in the quantity and quality of messages. The **quantitative** aspect of **message potency** encompasses the sheer frequency, repetition, and prominence of message presentation; this helps to increase levels of exposure and awareness. Significant progress has been made in a few problem areas (drunk driving, AIDS, cocaine, and tobacco), primarily because so many messages have been disseminated on prime time TV and in numerous other channels over a period of years. By contrast, only a trickle of messages reaches the public in most cases (even for important health problems such as breast cancer or heart disease).

Qualitative message factors are essential to achieving the more central goals of attracting close attention, facilitating in-depth knowledge gain and belief formation, and motivating the audience to perform the behavior. A high-quality campaign presents compelling persuasive incentives (such as fear appeals) supported by credible evidence and packaged in an understandable, relevant, and engaging manner. This is a difficult task, and campaigners often struggle in vain to create the perfect messages. In the history of real world campaign messages, the highly-potent "silver bullet" is a rare achievement.

The third key to success is a conducive social and media **environment** which will complement the public service messages. There is an extensive array of non-campaign forces that shape the individual's behavior, including positive and negative inputs in the domains of entertainment, advertising, social influence, and legal policies. For some topics, these environmental factors nicely complement the campaign, while in other cases the campaign may be undermined because the individual's environment doesn't support the recommended behavior.

Consider the problem of teenage drunk driving, where interpersonal influences are crucial. Friends typically provide contrasting social inputs; there's peer pressure to drink alcohol, but widespread disapproval of drunk drivers. Parental influences are quite varied; some parents try to prohibit their teens from attending beer parties, while others take a lenient attitude. Campaigners seek to alter this social environment by aiming messages at these **significant others** as well as the targeted teens; one thrust of a drunk driving campaign would attempt to discourage pro-drinking peer pressures and to stimulate parental restrictiveness.

Drunk driving campaigners may also try to shape other environmental factors by educating and persuading an array of small but influential audience segments: government agencies (to make stricter rules against youth-targeted beer commercials), Hollywood producers (to feature designated driving themes in prime-time programs), police forces (to aggressively enforce drunk driving laws), alcohol retailers (to avoid selling to minors), the clergy (to preach against the evils of alcohol), and legislative bodies (to reduce consumption by raising the alcohol tax).

In a comprehensive environmental approach, campaign messages are used to directly influence key players who impinge on the teenager; this in turn serves to indirectly restrict the teen's drinking or drunk driving opportunities or to generate additional educational inputs.

IS EDUCATIONAL PROGRAMMING EDUCATIONAL?

At 9 am on that October morning, four-year-old Jennifer turns on the TV to watch *Sesame Street*, produced by the Children's Television Workshop (CTW). Like most preschool

© Bettmann/Corbis

children, she watches this program two or three times per week. Jen is attracted by the entertaining mix of muppets, caring adult characters, cartoon segments, and music. Interspersed throughout the hour-long show are brief snippets of educational material: numbers, letters, shapes, and sizes, along with prosocial lessons involving harmonious relationships with other people.

When she was just three years old, Jen mastered the most frequently-repeated content on *Sesame Street:* the alphabet and counting from one to 20. Although preschoolers in earlier generations managed to learn these simple elements without the benefit of televised instruction, those growing up with *Sesame Street* tend to pick it up a bit earlier. This rote learning impresses parents such as Norma, who believe *Sesame Street* provides a wonderful educational service.

The evidence collected by researchers isn't quite so impressive. The testing shows that children who regularly watch *Sesame Street* do gain cognitive skills, but the degree of impact is rather modest. The program is good for kids, but far from great. Furthermore, critics have attacked the show for producing several minor negative consequences: young viewers are trained via repetitious memorization rather than learning creative thought processes; they come to expect that education involves slick production values rather than the dry instruction displayed in schoolrooms, and they develop short attention spans due to the fast-paced and varied segments in the televised magazine format.

One of the main controversies focuses on which subgroups of children are benefiting from *Sesame Street.* One of the original goals of the show was to provide disadvantaged children with a boost in cognitive skills before entering school, in order to help them catch up with middle class children raised in a more educationally stimulating home environment.

Norma has helped Jen learn from *Sesame Street* by watching the show with her and reinforcing the lessons that are presented. This form of **parental mediation** reflects Norma's middle class value for early education, and her part-time job allowed her to be home with Jen in the mornings. Unfortunately, children from disadvantaged homes are less likely to benefit from parental co-viewing and reinforcement. Thus, poor and minority children tend to learn slightly less from the program, and this contributes to a widening gap between the haves and have-nots. Although the disadvantaged children are making gains, they actually fall relatively further behind the predominantly white middle class children.

In the 35 years since the apparent success of *Sesame Street*, there have been numerous attempts to produce other educational programs. However, none have attained the same level of popularity. CTW created the *Electric Company* to teach reading skills, *3-2-1 Contact* to teach science, and the *Infinity Factory* to teach math. This type of program employed the same "magic formula" pioneered with *Sesame Street:* an entertaining style of presentation, high quantity of episodes and frequency of repetition, and reliance on adult supplementation. In each case, these shows targeted older children who are generally less interested in the subject matter than are the avid preschoolers; kids who are 8- or 10-years old prefer straight entertainment programming, and their parents are less apt to co-view the CTW programs once their children are older. As a result, the viewership levels are far lower and the shows narrowly appeal to those kids who are already motivated to learn the particular subject matter. For older viewers, it appears that the "magic formula" achieves less-than-magical impact on home viewers.

In an attempt to overcome this problem, some elementary schools have used classroom feeds of these shows, with the teacher reinforcing the educational message. Test scores indicate that students exposed to the reading, math, and science programming do make modest gains, and some viewers do have their interests stimulated. However, the degree of impact is rather limited in terms of the amount of learning and the proportion of children who benefit.

WHICH PEOPLE LEARN THE MOST?

Not everyone in Middleville learns equally from the informational media. Several sociological and psychological theories account for differences in learning among various segments of the audience. According to **social categories theory,** responses to media messages depend on one's demographic position in life. For example, males tend to learn more about world affairs and women learn more about health. Teenagers gain the most information about celebrities, while the elderly tend to become knowledgeable about political candidates. When it comes to hard news, those with higher socio-economic status gain considerably more knowledge than persons with less education and income.

Uses and gratifications theory provides a more precise and comprehensive explanation of differential learning. This theoretical model encompasses the individual's background characteristics, social interaction patterns, and personality factors. Each person develops distinctive interests and needs resulting in different motivations for using the media. The audience's choices of which messages to read and view and their selection of which content to learn and retain is determined by utilitarian motives such as surveillance and decisional guidance.

Learning also depends on the individual's basic intelligence and his or her specific knowledge structures, which are called **schema.** Those who are brighter tend to absorb more information, especially hard news content and other complex material. Those who already possess an elaborate schematic structure for a particular topic can more readily integrate new information.

For example, consider a person who is familiar with the way that Congress operates, who recognizes the names of key leaders, and who already has detailed understanding of the bills under deliberation. When a news story describes the legislative debate on a new policy, this person will be far more likely to be exposed to the message, to comprehend the content, and to retain the basic facts in memory.

Thus, there's a tendency for those who already know the most to subsequently learn the most new information: the "information rich" get richer. Over time, the subset of persons with greater prior knowledge about politics or health or the alphabet (or Hollywood celebrities, for that matter) become steadily more knowledgeable about that basic topic area than do other segments of society. While the majority is making some modest gains from the media, the well-informed segment acquires the new material at a faster rate. This leads to a **knowledge gap** that gradually widens over months and years. Instead of uniformly informing all strata of society, the media contribute to an uneven distribution of knowledge, as occurred with the *Sesame Street* audience.

In What Ways Is Learning Biased?

As in any community, the citizens of Middleville have widely differing attitudes about politics, sex, drugs, and numerous other issues. When the media present messages on a particular topic, the nature of what is learned is partly determined by the attitudinal predispositions, just as the amount of learning depends on utilitarian needs, intelligence, and schema frameworks.

The learning process is biased by how the person feels about the subject. Because of a preference for maintaining cognitive consistency, audience members tend to avoid reading or watching discrepant messages that challenge their prior attitudes while seeking out reassuring messages.

This form of bias is called **selective exposure.** For example, Republicans will be more exposed to news stories favorable to the Republican candidate; smokers will defend themselves from disconcerting health warnings by selectively avoiding anti-tobacco PSAs. If this first line of defense is breached by a compelling message, then **selective perception** may kick into operation. People tend to interpret message content in a biased fashion by dismissing certain facts, mentally refuting certain arguments, and distorting certain portrayals. As a result of this partisan processing, most of the audience resists significant change in their viewpoints and the messages end up reinforcing their predispositions. Again, people typically learn what they want to learn.

HOW CAN YOU LEARN MORE FROM THE INFORMATIONAL MEDIA?

As the Johnsons drift off to sleep one by one, it's time to tabulate how much time they've spent with the media and how much they've learned. Television has been the dominant medium on this typical day. Being a typical couple, the Johnsons have averaged slightly less than four hours each in front of the TV set, but only a portion was informational programming. Because he's a teenager with a greater amount of both pleasant and unpleasant distractions, Jason watched less than his sister or his parents.

Both parents spent about a half-hour reading the newspaper, and somewhat less time looking through magazines. The children didn't read any non-assigned materials on this typical day. Jason had the radio and CD player on for several hours, but seldom paid close attention to any verbal content. Both parents also logged considerable listening time, primarily background music on the radio rather than informational messages.

What do the Johnsons have to show for their day's media use in terms of meaningful learning? Not very much, considering the time investment, but more than nothing. After all, family members did gain some new fragmentary bits of knowledge about current events, political candidates, health risks, and the alphabet. But they certainly could have made more effective use of the informational media resources available to them, if only there was a set of guidelines that they could utilize. It's too late to help the Johnsons, but here are a few tips to facilitate your learning from informational messages:

It's surprisingly difficult to learn substantive information from the news media, especially during political campaigns. Because TV newscasts and newspaper front pages typically chronicle event-based daily snapshots rather than illuminating fundamental developments and issues, the "informed citizen" needs to make a special effort to gain additional perspective by seeking feature stories and commentaries. Furthermore, the sophisticated news user must first develop a basic understanding of the key players, policies, and philosophies in order to adequately comprehend and integrate new tidbits of information each day. Weekly newsmagazines provide an excellent basis for gaining perspective and making sense of recent trends and developments, thus enabling better comprehension of the daily coverage.

When reading newspapers or watching TV newscasts, be alert to several subtle types of bias that characterize news media coverage. Due to the norms of contemporary journalism, editors and reporters provide a distorted picture of the world in their selection and treatment of topics. Because it's unlikely that these news-gathering practices will improve, the savvy consumer should understand the biased nature of news presentations. Here are some things to take into account in interpreting the stories that are encountered.

Recognize that journalists are highly selective in their choice of topics to cover. Newspapers and newscasts carry only a tiny fraction of all events, which tend to be unique cases that aren't representative of the real world. The OJ Simpson trial is not typical of all trials, nor is an Anthrax terrorist attack an ordinary event. This form of bias will cultivate a distorted impression of reality unless the news consumer realizes that "newsworthy" items are far from commonplace. In particular, the news media overplay or exaggerate threats to society, such as street crime, nuclear powerplant meltdowns, and killer viruses. These stories should be critically scrutinized to determine if they are sensationalized or overplayed. Otherwise, the images that are formed may be unduly alarming and depressing.

Regarding news about foreign countries, there are two key factors to consider. Our newspapers and newscasts ignore much of what's happening in the rest of the world; the U.S. news media carry fewer international stories than are found in almost any other country. When foreign news is covered, negativism is generally manifested with an emphasis on disasters, conflicts, political crises, and other assorted problems. It's easy to perceive foreign countries as unimportant and unpleasant (especially in the third world), so the enlightened news consumer must strive to overcome the potential for ethnocentrism by learning about the rest of the world from specialized sources as a supplement to network newscasts and the local paper.

An essential quality of news information is credibility, the extent to which the material can be trusted. The consumer must judge whether the source is credible: the mainstream media (network newscasts and prestige press) tend to be most accurate, while tabloid news shows and radio talk shows require a healthy dose of skepticism. Although most people rely on the "seeing is believing" rule, one should realize that visuals can be as readily manipulated as words; in forming judgments, it's wise to focus on hard evidence rather than seductive pictures.

In still another form of bias, the news media present predominantly negative treatment of almost any high-profile leader. News about the president's achievements is far outweighed by coverage of his mistakes and personal failings; likewise, there's more emphasis on Congressional wrangling and scandals than legislative progress. Based on the news, it's tempting to believe that politicians are immoral incompetents and that government agencies are ineffectual. In order to resist becoming overly cynical and apathetic, remember that this fundamental tilt toward the negative side is not a representative reflection of reality.

During election season, considerable diligence and vigilance are needed to compensate for the superficiality of daily reports from the campaign trail and the partisan biases of certain media outlets. The TV networks and news magazines tend to be even-handed, but newspapers often tilt toward the Republican or Democratic side; check which candidate the newspaper supports on the editorial page before relying on the front page news stories. When reading campaign news reports, be conscious of which candidates the newspaper favors and opposes so your natural defenses can kick into gear. In general, it's a good idea to utilize multiple news outlets in order to derive a balanced picture and to overcome the limited coverage from any single medium. Rather than focusing attention on the horserace updates or analyses of candidates' tactical maneuvering, much more useful information can be learned by seeking out the in-depth examination of issues.

In order to evaluate the deluge of messages generated by the candidates in their news appearances, ads, and debates, the rational voter should try to distinguish between substantive information about core philosophy and leadership qualities vs. self-serving rhetoric and imagery. Utilize selective exposure and selective perception to screen out the posturing and petty attacks; hone in on the material that offers insights into the candidate's traits and illumination of how the candidate will perform in office. In particular, look for evidence that's offered to support impressive claims, such as the track record of past policy implementation and professional accomplishments. This essential information can be extracted from a broad variety of sources; 30-second spots (even negative ads) and MTV snippets can be a more valuable resource than the standard televised debates and lengthy print essays.

Regarding health campaigns, most of the messages contain advice that's "good for you" because it can actually improve your life. The information is certainly more beneficial than the vast majority of entertainment and advertising that's carried in the media, so make an effort to seek out this type of content, pay close attention when the messages are encountered, try to make sense of the material, and store away the ideas for future reference. Even if the style of presentation is dull or complex, or even if the producers haven't done a good job in making the topic relevant, attempt to extract the useful material.

Too many young adults fall into the trap of defensively denying that the recommended health behaviors apply to them, especially when a disturbing fear appeal is presented. Individuals should carefully consider whether the threat is indeed valid, by evaluating the severity of the harmful outcomes along with the likelihood of suffering the consequences.

Because brief broadcast spots are better suited to raising awareness or arousing emotions than providing detailed "how to" guidance, it may be necessary to actively search for pamphlets, books, magazines, or webpages in order to learn sufficient information about these health topics.

Not all health communicators are well intentioned, however. When the beer companies advocate "responsible drinking" or the tobacco industry states that "smoking is an adult habit," the messages have the appearance of a public service campaign. It's wise to be skeptical about the motives of private sector sponsors offering health information, because they may be seeking to cleverly promote their products or to subtly gain public relations points.

Finally, remember that information provided in the media should give pleasure as well as educational payoffs in the form of knowledge gain or decisional inputs. Similar to entertainment, people primarily consume the informational content for purposes of personal enjoyment; they achieve gratifications from mental stimulation, emotional arousal, and relaxation during exposure rather than using the media for utilitarian purposes such as learning. Thus, don't devote too much time and energy to school-like absorption of names and places, facts and figures, and concepts and advice; narrow your learning focus to the material that you really need or want to know, and just enjoy the rest. It won't be on the midterm.

REFERENCES

Backer, T., Rogers, E., & Sopory, P. (1992). *Designing health communication campaigns: What works?* Newbury Park, CA: Sage.
Berry, G., & Asamen, J. (1993). *Children and television.* Newbury Park, CA: Sage.
Bryant, J., & Zillman, D. (2002). *Media effects.* Hillsdale, NJ: Lawrence Erlbaum.
Dominick, J. (1996). *The dynamics of mass communication.* New York: McGraw-Hill.
Graber, D. (1993). *Mass media and American politics.* Washington, DC: Congressional Quarterly Press.
Jeffres, L. (1994). *Mass media processes.* Prospect Heights, IL: Waveland Press.
McQuail, D. (2000). *Mass communication theory: An introduction.* Newbury Park, CA: Sage.
Pfau, M., & Parrott, R. (1993). *Persuasive communication campaigns.* Needham Heights, MA: Allyn & Bacon.
Rice, R. & Atkin, C. (2001). *Public communication campaigns.* Newbury Park, CA: Sage.
Robinson, M., & Levy, M. (1986). *The main source: Learning from television news.* Beverly Hills, CA: Sage.

Chapter Fifteen Case Study Quiz— Learning from Mass Media

Instructions:

Please read the following case study carefully and select the best answers to the questions. This quiz is an individual assignment. Remember: sharing answers is a form of plagiarism.

In 1990, students were unpacking and reunions were taking place as students awaited for classes to begin at the University of Florida. The campus was part of a small and quiet community in Northern Florida and at a time when students should only be concerned with class schedules and what bar had the best "happy hour" specials, tragedy struck the small community. The bodies of two female students were found inside their apartment, strangled and badly mutilated. As news of the deaths spread nationwide, reporters from local, state and national news companies flocked to the campus to report. The town became a media circus as it became clear that a serial killer was loose on campus once the murder of a third student was announced. Reporters demanded information from police around the clock and to satisfy such requests, the police held two press conferences a day to update interested parties. Some reporters went as far as questioning residents in the same building as the third victim to learn her name. The victim's name was broadcasted nationwide before police could notify the next of kin. His relatives learned of his death from a radio broadcast and another relative of the fourth victim learned of her daughter's death from a co-worker. Further, when students would hold candlelight prayers, the media was there with cameras in their faces and rumors were spread about the police covering up other murders. Many students were pulled out of school by their parents, gun sales increased from 1-2 a week to 25 a week, and over seven people were blamed for the serial murders. When the media received criticism for their practices in this case, the public was blamed for not being patient in receiving the news. Media officials who spoke out stated that their media coverage of the Gainesville murders was fair and that they were just answering the requests of their news company's audience. Police did find the man responsible for the murders of Christina Powell, Sonja Larson, Christa Hoyt, Tracy Paules, and Manny Taboada. Edward Rollings was sentenced to death for each murder.

Wilkening, D. (1992, March 7). When the media circus came to town. *Editor & Publisher*, 125, 48-52.

Student's Name _____

Section Number _____

Section Leader's Name _____

Chapter Fifteen Case Study Quiz— Learning from Mass Media

1. A woman heard news of Tracy Paules death from the media. She then informed Tracy's mother of her death. What does this exemplify?
   a. Two-step flow
   b. Agenda setter
   c. Campaign
   d. Intrinsic interest event

2. The press conferences serve as:
   a. Message potency
   b. Pseudo events
   c. Political advertising
   d. Opinion sharing

3. Millions of people watched as the Gainesville case unfolded. Students watched the news as a way to gain information while others watched the intriguing case as a form of entertainment. The reasons for why people watched the television news coverage of this case can be explained by what theory?
   a. Uses and Gratifications
   b. Social Categories
   c. Social Cognitive
   d. Agenda Setting

4. Students at the University of Florida tuned into the news each day to gain updates on the serial murders and assess their safety on campus. This is an example of:
   a. Credibility
   b. Relevance
   c. Opinion Sharing
   d. Media function

5. During the serial murders, the media was focused on the city of Gainesville. Other stories might have been neglected or downplayed because of the seriousness of the case at the University of Florida. In this case, the media is telling people what to think about. This is called:
   a. Uses and Gratifications Theory
   b. Message Potency
   c. Social Categories Theory
   d. Agenda Setting

Chapter Sixteen

THE ART OF SPEAKING IN PUBLIC

Monique M. Turner
University of Maryland

Lisa L. Massi Lindsey
Centers for Disease Control and Prevention

Leslie M. Deatrick
University of Oklahoma

Public Speaking is Important

It has been said, "You are what you communicate". That is a simple truthful sentiment, but there is more to the importance of communication. What you communicate is the foundation of how other people see you. However, what you communicate might not be an accurate representation of the person you really are. You might be a tremendous genius, but unable to communicate your genius to the world. Essentially, other people only know *what they know* about *who you are* from what you communicate to them. If you want your ideas to go beyond bouncing around in your pretty head and out into the greater world, you need to learn how to effectively communicate those ideas. Public speaking is not to be feared more than death; it is to be seen as a wonderful opportunity to show the world your talents and passions.

This course is intended to teach you how to show off your insight and charm using the one of the few channels at your disposal: public speaking. It is the humble wish of this chapter, to be helpful in showing you how to use public speaking for good and wholesome goals. It is important to remember that *speakers should speak with integrity, passion, skill, and implication.* This chapter will flow along and develop those themes.

Public Speaking Defined (Generally)

Endless examples of public speaking exist all around us each and every day. Generally speaking, speeches are either (1) read from a prepared text, (2) recited from memory (i.e. the speech was written in advance and memorized), (3) delivered impromptu or without any immediate preparation, or (4) delivered extemporaneously, where a speech is prepared and practiced in advance, but only brief speaking notes are used during a presentation.

While many speaking situations share the same purposes: (1) to inform others, (2) to persuade others (therefore influence and change the world), (3) to entertain an audience, and (4) to express a person's ideas and identity, public speakers generally focus on only one of the four purposes of public speaking. However, it is important to keep in mind that while a good speech may only focus on one of the four purposes, it will also do the other four as well. If someone does a good job of informing, they are probably entertaining and persuasive as well. If a person is communicating effectively, they are also conveying their self (identity and ideas) to others. The next time you go to church, attend a lecture, or see a politician give a speech, watch and listen to see if they incorporate the four purposes of public speaking. Did they manage to do all four? How could they have been more informative, persuasive, entertaining, or conveyed their ideas and/or beliefs better? Did you have a better understanding of who the speaker was after the speech? Was your impression and evaluation of the speaker positive? *Speakers should speak with skill.* One of the ways we learn a new skill is by looking and listening critically. As you learn about public speaking watch and critique those around you to help develop your idea of what a good public speaker sounds like.

Public speaking goes beyond making speeches. It involves being able to present oneself in a skillful and eloquent manner. Public speaking is more structured and more formal than the conversations we are accustomed to having. Speakers usually have set time limits and often allow questions and commentary only after they have finished speaking. Public speakers try to avoid excessive slang, jargon, and improper grammar. As well, public speaking requires a different form of delivery than normal speech. Conversation often contains spacers or interjections like "you know" or "like," and the use of vocalized pauses such as "uh" and "um." Effective public speakers keep things like spacers and vocalized pauses to a minimum while adjusting their voices so that they may be heard clearly by all of their audience.

Ethics

Speakers should speak with integrity. Whether or not a public speaker actively tries to inform, persuade, or entertain his audience, public speakers should attempt to act in an ethical manner. Ethics in public speaking require that the speaker respect his or her topic and audience. Lucas (1992) suggests that speakers should act ethically by being well-informed about their topic; being honest when presenting information; using reasonable evidence; and using valid reasoning. Conscientious public speakers ask themselves, "Will my audience receive any benefit from my speech?" and "Does my audience want to know about my topic/information?" In many cases speakers have to decide whether or not unwanted, but important information should be given. In such cases, speakers try to have plausible, believable, and accessible answers to the questions and concerns that they might raise by their speaking. Lastly, ethical public speakers, like writers, avoid plagiarism. Public speakers are careful not to take credit for words and ideas that are not their own by telling their audience where they got their information and who inspired their words.

Be Not Afraid: the Fear of Public Speaking

Speakers should speak with skill. It is said that people fear public speaking more than death. Can we give a perspective to this fear? Death and public speaking are similar because all people have a contract with the universe to at some point in their lives (abet death) do both. Yet, there is a distinct difference between public speaking and death; while to quote Hank Williams "you won't get out of this life alive," you will come out 99.99 % of public speaking engagements ALIVE, which for most individuals is a GOOD thing.

Public speaking is a terrifying experience for most people. Even the most outgoing individuals, when in front of a group of their peers (or strangers), feel their knees shake and their palms begin to sweat. They may never say the word "um" in any other conversation, but when standing up in front of others they hear themselves say it over and over. They may blush, talk too fast, forget their speech, or even worse, no one will laugh at their jokes! One student even passed out after his speech because he was so nervous that he forgot to breathe!

It is common for public speakers, even those with considerable experience, to feel nervous about speaking in front of a group. Communication apprehension comes in many different forms and in different degrees of severity. A little nervousness is a very common and natural occurrence. The best way to deal with your apprehension is to acknowledge your nervousness, prepare carefully for your speech, and practice your speech first in front of a mirror and then later in front of some friends who will give you an honest, but kind, appraisal. Practice is the best way to reduce or avoid speech anxiety.

The fear of public speaking is mainly because standing in front of an audience triggers the flight or fight response. This surge of adrenaline can actually make your speech better. Being nervous should not be suppressed; it just means you care about your speech. Why bother standing up if you do not care about your speech? Acknowledge specifically what scares you about the situation. Knowing is half the battle. Once you have figured out what the particular fear is, you can take steps to address it. Deal with your fear of public speaking and get out there and be heard!

The best advice for dealing with speech anxiety is to practice, practice, and practice. It may seem uncomfortable and very silly at first, but practicing a speech in front of the mirror can be very beneficial. First, you are your own worst critic and will better see errors than a friend who listens to your speech. However, it is also useful to practice giving your speech in front of friends as well. Make sure that they will give you constructive feedback. Second, practice in the room where you will be giving your speech. Many times classrooms are open early in the morning and in the evenings. Make time to go into the classroom when it is free so that you can close the door and practice your speech undisturbed.

Are you afraid of failing? What is the worst thing that can happen to you from speaking in public? You could fail and embarrass yourselves in front of people whose opinions matter to you. While not ideal, the pain of that will go away with time. Trust us. No one but you still remembers when you tripped at the 5th grade recital. Shed your ego centric assumptions that other people are constantly thinking about you and your failures. Other people are much too busy being concerned with their OWN failures and fears of public speaking. Your audience is not there to criticize you; they are much too happy that it is you up there speaking instead of them. Face the fact that you may fail, but visualize success. What is important to remember when giving a speech is that everyone is nervous. Some people may seem like a "natural" when they give their speech, but if you were to ask them, they would say that they were nervous, too. Professors even get nervous. Anytime you talk in front of a group of people it can be scary. Don't feel like you are alone when you are up in front of your audience; everyone else in the room is nervous about their speech as well.

Movement can help with nervousness. If you feel your knees shaking, take a couple of steps. The movement will help you work out some of your nervous energy.

Look for encouraging people in your audience. You may have some idea before you give your speech which people have been good audience members for other speakers. But, if you don't, look around just before you start and try to make eye contact with a couple of people. Doing so will make you more comfortable, and serves as an invitation for these individuals to listen to your speech. If for some reason your audience does not seem encouraging, don't be discouraged. They are not trying to be mean, they are simply thinking about their own speech. Just keep trying to make eye contact with as many of them as possible. If you catch someone's eye he will be more receptive to you.

Keep in mind that speakers tend to feel much more nervous than they actually appear to the audience. For example, when a student was asked to rate how nervous her audience perceived her to be, she believed that she appeared to be a 7 out of 10 (10 being the most nervous speaker the audience had ever seen). When audience members were asked to rate how nervous the same speaker appeared, they only rated her as a 3 out of 10. This example illustrates that even when we feel nervous, and even though we may think we look very nervous, often times the audience will not pick up on it. In general, with practice it is easy to control the external factors that make us look nervous, even though we may not be able to control how we feel inside.

Also, picking a topic that you are really interested in can make giving the speech much easier. If you ask a professor whom you really like why she teaches, she will most likely tell you that she really enjoys working with the students, the material, or both. If you love what you do or talk about what you love, it shows on your face. You do not have to force it or make yourself emphasize certain points; that will come naturally.

Good can come out of public speaking, even public speaking failures. Successfully conveying your ideas can make changes in the world around you. A quality public speech can communicate who you are to others. Only by risking your "social face" speaking in public, will your good ideas ever be credited to you or see the light of day. If you mess up a speech, generally people will sympathize with you and like you because you will seem more loveable and vulnerable as human beings often are. While we learn from success, failure is our greatest teacher. You can learn lessons that will make you a better speaker in the future. Remember, if you make a mistake in a speech, keep going. In most cases your audience will have no idea you made a mistake. Few audiences have a text of your speech in front of them. Move past your mistakes without drawing attention to them. Count your mistakes as good lessons and avoid the same mistake in later speeches.

Finally, remember that the fact that you are trying to become a better speaker is courageous. It is one of the hardest, but most valuable, communication skills you can learn. You have chosen to put yourself out there and that is honorable. Again, think of this as a process, learn as much as you can, and build on what you learn.

So, be yourself, have fun, and remember, BREATHE! The most important thing to remember is that if you are nervous about giving a speech, you are not alone. You may see others give the most dynamic speeches you have ever seen, and even they are nervous to some extent. Public speaking can be scary. Reading this book or taking a class in public speaking is the first step in overcoming this anxiety. It takes a great deal of courage to face a fear and overcome it, so bravo!

RESEARCH

Personal Research

Speakers should speak with implication. What you say should have relevance to the world and have value. Good research can explain the implication of your topics. This section will discuss research that individuals gather for their personal use to be presented to others for such presentations as classroom research assignments and work projects. This section will cover gathering research, credibility of research, processing research, and citing research.

Gathering Research

Gathering research can use up most of your allotted preparation time for a project if you are not efficient about the process in the first place. The first key to research is knowing how to focus on what information you are looking to gather. Topics which are too general guarantee you a long difficult general research mission. Topic selection will be explained later in the chapter, for this section understand that you need to narrow your topic in order to establish a reasonable search area.

Once you have a specific topic, brainstorm a list of vocabulary terms related to your topic. It is also helpful to look up critical terms in the dictionary so you understand your topic area better. This term list can help you in your database searches. Keep the term list nearby as you research. As you read the research you gather, you can add new words to your term list to help in further searches. If you want to recreate your database searches, it helps to have a list of terms that you used. You can also make notations on the word list about which databases and resources you used in case you need to return to get new copies of articles or get other articles.

There are several places to get research information. First, understand that the internet is not the only research resource! If you are in college and have not visited the campus library to get research, feel ashamed, then go to your university library. There are many places to gather research in the library. Check out current copies of journals in the area of your topic and skim the table of contents. You can also check out the bookshelves in your topic area for information. Do not sit in the stacks and read whole books! Look through the indexes of books to see if relevant topics are discussed. Your word list discussed above can help in this process. Did someone write in the book before you? Remember writing in library books is not ethical, but if those in the past did it and were seemingly smart, important information may be highlighted for you. Go to seminal texts in your area and check out the references of those books. It could lead you to other valuable sources. Many libraries have government document sections that may provide a great source of information depending on what topic you are researching. Talk to librarians; they can direct you in your search and save you a large amount of time.

Electronic databases and internet searches are good to get lists of articles. You should try to get an actual hardcopy of the articles you use. Select databases that are specific to your topic area if possible. Key word searches, using the words on your term list, get the best results. General databases that provide good searches are Proquest and Lexis-Nexis. Sometimes Google searches can also be helpful. Try not to cite information directly from the internet unless it is from an established credible source. As stated, get the original hard copy of the information from the library. If you must cite information from the internet, and there are topics where this is appropriate, have more than just internet sources. Once you reach college, the expectation of research is higher. If you are quoting a quote of a quote, try to get the original source of the quote. It might be misquoted or taken out of context in the second source.

Credibility of Evidence

The credibility of the research that you cite in your work reflects upon your personal credibility. Choose evidence from sources that is worthy to be cited in university level work. There are several tests of good evidence: relevancy, recency, source identification, source credibility, contextual accuracy, external consistency, and internal consistency.

A piece of evidence that meets the test of *relevancy*, is one that proves or supports the attempted argument well. Evidence that meets the test of *recency* is evidence that describes today, by being recent and reflecting the knowledge known up to the present. For evidence to meet the test of *source identification*, it must have the source/author fully identified. The test of *source credibility* asks whether or not the source is credible. There are several considerations within the test of source credibility: geographical and/or chronological proximity (is the evidence from a first hand source?), source objectivity (is there a bias of the source that makes the source unfair?), and expertness (does the source have the knowledge to be believed?). There are three types of expertness: experience (what has the source done to gain their knowledge and for how long?), training (where did the source get their training and for how long?), and position (what is their job? i.e. staff writer or fellow at the Brookings Institute?).

The test of *contextual accuracy* is met with evidence that is understood in the context that the author intended. Quoting information out of context violates this test, so it is important to go to the original source of the information to make sure that you are quoting the evidence as the author originally wrote it. The test of *external consistency* asks if the evidence quoted is consistent with the views of other people in the field. The test of *internal consistency* asks if the evidence quoted is consistent with other writings from the same source.

The best cited evidence will meet the requirements of all these tests of evidence. To gain credibility with your evidence, it is sometimes appropriate to mention how your evidence meets the tests of evidence. For example, cite the impressive qualifications of the source to show that your evidence is of good quality.

There are different types of evidence pieces. Evidence can provide *examples* of your argument, including statements of facts or statistics. Examples of example evidence also include evidence which supplies narratives, stories, art, humor, quotations, charts, or pictures to support your argument. Evidence can include *statements or claims* to support your argument. Statement or claim evidence usually follows the format: "if x occurs then y will occur." Usually the reason for this statement is not in the piece of evidence, just the claim. The last type of evidence provides a *warrant or analysis*, explaining why a statement supporting your argument is true. The best evidence answers the "why" question, giving justification for the logic of the claim.

Processing Research

Processing information or reading the materials you have gathered is important to organizing your thoughts and presentation. There are many techniques for reading information, and not all of them work for everyone. Find a process of sorting through information that works best for you. The technique discussed here comes from competitive policy debate, and is called "blocking and briefing". The briefing part is optional but can help on large assignments. With practice the technique gets easier.

"Blocking" is the process of reading research literature. To start, when you get a copy of an article or book, make sure you have a complete citation. This is critical because if you have evidence without proper citation and can not retrieve the citation, you can not use it in your work. Write the citation on your copy of the article or chapter. Read the article. With a pen, if this is your copy of the material, put brackets around "cards". A card is simply a quote from the text that makes an argument or statement relevant to the topic you are writing about. You can also underline or highlight the important sentences in the card, but err on limiting your underlining.

In the margin, next to the card, write a short "tag line" about what the card is saying (an explanatory fragment statement, less than 10 words, in small handwriting, using symbols and abbreviations). Tag lines are usually the argument that you would use the piece or evidence, called the "card", to prove. Cards should make statements of information. Good quality cards also have "warrants", or reasons why the statements in the card are true or why the statements in the evidence have an implication. Remember that speakers should speak with implication. Using evidence that supports the importance of your topic and explains why your topic is important, assists you in speaking with relevance. At the end of the card, or bottom of the paragraph you "bracketed", in parenthesis write in the page number that the card appears on. This will become important during the briefing and citing process.

Once you have "bracketed" the material, you can "brief" the material. While this can be a large amount of upfront work, it can help you organize your thoughts. Visual learners may benefit from this process. Briefing becomes easier the more you practice doing it. First, type out the citations for each source you have. Number the citations, one number per source. Count the number of cards from each source and copy/paste enough copies of the citation so that each card is linked to the citation it comes from.

Cut the cards out of the article (including the tag lines in the margins, the page number written at the end of the card, and only if you have one sided copies). On the back of the cut out card, write the number that corresponds with the citation of the article. Attach a copy of the citation to the card that links to the citation. This is why it is important to write the cite number on the back. A stack of cards can get mixed up and you might forget where the evidence card came from. On a sheet of typing paper, write out the tag line in a complete sentence that makes an argument. Tape the cite and card that the tag refers to onto the paper, below the handwritten tagline. You can use these "briefs" to write your paper or speech. They can be spread out on a table and organized according to your outline. Save your briefed cards for future projects!

Citing Research

Citing other people's ideas and work is critical to researching with integrity. Any time you use evidence to supplement or inform work that you wish to present to others you must cite where the information originated from. In the communication field, the American Psychological Association guidelines are the citation rules that are followed.

Professional Research

The communication field is rich with research in the areas covered in earlier chapters of this text, as well as some new areas. Michigan State University, the first department of communication in the country is a leader in the field. Many of the strong professionals in the field are graduates of Michigan State's communication department or students of students of Michigan State University. Michigan State's influence is far reaching! University communication departments that focus on research usually fall within two types of research: qualitative and quantitative. Qualitative research techniques include case studies and interviewing. Quantitative research techniques include experimentation and surveys. Michigan State's communication department is highly respected as one of the best programs in quantitative research, with a greatly published faculty. Department faculty and graduate students are very busy researching for publication and thesis/dissertations.

COM 100 is a good pool to gather research participants and data. The research requirement of the course rewards research participation, but we do not want you to participate in research just because we need subjects. There is value in getting first hand research experience. Once you have been exposed to research, journal articles about research will make more sense to you. Also participating in research gives you a taste of what professionals in the communication field do with the knowledge they gather.

Research articles are published in journals. The parts of a quantitative journal article are the abstract, introduction, literature review/background section, hypothesis section, method section, results section, discussion section, and reference section. The *abstract* section summarizes the article and the sections of the article. The *introduction* explains why the research issue is one worthy of study and previews the rest of the article. The *literature review/background* section summarizes the previous research in the area of the research topic. The background section also explains why the study is being done and how the research project is moving the knowledge gathered in the area further. The *hypothesis* section of the article outlines the predictions about the phenomena the research project wanted to observe. Research questions, questions asked if the researchers can not make a specific prediction but still want to answer are also asked in this section. The *methods* section explains how the research was done, including: demographics of participants, experimental design, and scales of measurement. The *results* section summarizes the findings of the study, usually in statistic form and how the data supported or did not support the hypotheses. The *discussion* section explains what the findings mean and provide possible explanations for the findings. Problems with the study and future directions for research are also in the discussion section. Not every article follows this format, but usually the same information is still in the article just presented differently. Understanding research articles can help you in research for your speeches and papers as well as inform how you see research you participate in here at Michigan State.

TOULMIN MODEL OF ARGUMENTATION

Speakers should speak with skill and that involves using strong argumentations supported by research of good quality. There are many ways to structure an argument. The Toulmin Model is a helpful model of argumentation developed by British Logician Stephen Toulmin. The Toulmin model provides a wonderful format of the components of a complete argument which will aide your speeches and any papers you may have to write. There are several components of an argument: the claims, the grounds, the warrant, the backing, qualifiers, and the rebuttal (Rybacki & Rybacki, 1996). The *claim* is the beginning of an argument and is a statement of your opinion on the topic you are discussing. A claim is developed based on the knowledge you gather on a topic. The second part of the model is the *grounds*. Since claims are merely opinion, it is important to explain the proof you used to derive the opinion, this is the purpose of the grounds part of an argument. Grounds provide what evidence supports the claim, but does not explain why this evidence supports the claim. The third part of Toulmin's model, the *warrant*, provides the explanation of why the grounds support the claim. Think of this as the implication statement. The warrant suggests the logic behind making the conclusion of the claim when you see the evidence of the grounds. The warrant states that "if the grounds are true, then by logic the claim is true." In every strong argument the first three parts of the model must be present.

There are several parts of the model which function to further strengthen and clarify the argument. The *backing* is the next part of an argument in the model and is not always present. The backing provides an explanation of the reliability of the warrant. The backing gives further support to the logic of the warrant. The *qualifiers* indicate how strong the argument is by stating the cases in which the argument is true. The *rebuttal* anticipates objections to the claim and answers them before they can be raised.

Example:

Claim: Michigan State University is a great university to attend in Michigan.

Grounds: Michigan State University has a great (insert athletic team).

Warrant: Generally, a school with a great (insert athletic team) is more enjoyable to attend because there is more school spirit.

Backing: Research has shown that students attending a school with school spirit tend to rate the school more favorably.

Qualifier: Except for students who do not pay attention to school sports, most students enjoy having a winning team.

Rebuttal: Of course teams might not be successful every year, but students still remember past victories and retain their spirit.

SPEECH CONSIDERATIONS

Speech considerations are issues about your speech that you must consider before and while you write your speech. Speeches do not exist in a vacuum. All speeches have: an *overall goal and purpose,* a specific *topic* discussed to accomplish the overall goal and purpose, a specific *audience* to cater to in order to accomplish the overall goal and purpose, and a *context* in which to accomplish the goal and purpose. A good outline will have the speech considerations identified. The more you think and plan your speech, the better your speech will be and the easier it will be to connect with your audience. Even if you don't plan to write the speech considerations in your preparation materials, take the time to think about these issues to direct the construction of your speeches. Figure 16.1 illustrates the first page of an outline, answering the speech consideration questions.

Suppose you are a member of the local school board. You wish to pass a proposal to make condoms available in the local high school without parental consent. You have been asked to present your position to the high school parent-teacher association. Figure 16.2 applies the first page of an outline, the speech consideration section, to this example.

Overall Goal and Speech Purpose

Speakers should speak with implication. Implication refers to the value and ramification of what is being said. Everything you say should have a purpose and accomplish something. Why are you speaking? What do you hope to achieve with your speech? What are your goals for the speech? How will you assess that your goals have been accomplished? Pointless speeches, or speeches without clear objectives, waste the time of the speaker and audience. Purposeful speeches accomplish the goals of the speaker and are more memorable.

In the school board member example, the overall goal of the speech would be to persuade the parent-teacher association to support your condom distribution proposal. The requested action to the audience would be to ask for an endorsement for the proposal from the organization. The goal is one which could be accomplished with a speech and

FIGURE 16.1 Speech Considerations (first page of an outline)

Title: List your catchy speech title.

Overall Goal and Purpose: Write a statement that outlines a goal which can realistically be achieved during a speech. Write another statement explaining how you plan to evaluate whether or not you accomplished your speech goal.

Topic: List the specific topic and why discussing this topic will accomplish your speech goal.

Audience Analysis: Who is the target audience for your speech? A good speech is aimed at the needs, wants, aspirations, and interests of the audience.

    A. Demographics:
        1. Describe the characteristics or your audience.
        2. Explain how your speech is affected by the demographics or your audience.
    B. Psychographics:
        1. Describe the biases of your audience, and how your speech is affected by their biases.
        2. Describe the knowledge level about the topic of your audience, and how the audience knowledge level affects your speech.
        3. Describe the mood type of your audience, and how the disposition of the audience towards your topic affects your speech.
        4. Describes the goals/needs/wants of your audience related to your topic, and explain how your speech meets the audience' goals/needs/wants.
    C. Are there any special nonverbal considerations you need to make for this audience? Why do you feel you must make these considerations? How will the nonverbal considerations make your speech better?
    D. Are there any special verbal considerations you need to make for this audience? Why do you feel you must make these considerations? How will the verbal considerations make your speech better?

Speech Context:

    A. Is the speech formal or informal? What considerations will you have to make to meet this expectation?
    B. What is the location of the speech, and how will the speech be affected by the location?
    C. What is the external political context that will affect the speech? How will you construct your speech to respond to the external context?

limited discourse. Knowing precisely what your goal is, you can include information in your speech that will further your cause, focusing what you will discuss.

As we mentioned earlier, public speaking, in fact all speaking, involves being able to inform, persuade, and entertain. Although public speeches in general have such purposes, your individual speech must also have a specific purpose. A purpose statement is one, clear, concise statement that says what you want to accomplish in your speech. It should be result-oriented; it should reflect a change in the audience, not in the speaker. For instance, "To inform my audience why the drinking age should be lowered" reflects

FIGURE 16.2 SAMPLE "Speech Considerations"

Title: Protect our children

Overall Goal and Purpose: To persuade the parent-teacher association to support a condom distribution proposal for the local high school. I will ask for an endorsement from the organization.

Topic: Condom distribution. Sexually transmitted infections and pregnancy are a problem in our community and distribution of condoms would solve the problem.

Audience Analysis: The high school parent-teacher association.

  A. Demographics:
   1. The audience is composed of parents and teachers of the high school students. The audience is around the ages of 35-50. The socioeconomic level of the audience members is suburban middle class. The organization is 75% female, 25% male.
   2. I will try to use examples from the community that will be relevant to the audience.
  B. Psychographics:
   1. Many of the members of the PTA will not like to face the potential that their children are sexually active. I will need to prove there is a real risk that their children are sexually active. Some people believe that sex education increases sexual activity. I will have to provide evidence that the opposite is true.
   2. The members of the PTA should all have a general understanding of the issue, sexually transmitted illnesses, pregnancy, and that condoms can prevent these consequences. I will have to provide evidence that these issues threaten our community and that the program will work.
   3. The audience is a mixture of hostile, negative, undecided, and positive orientation to this issue. I will have to provide information that connects to each of these groups.
   4. The need of this group is to do what is in the best interest of their children. My speech will point out a threat to the wellbeing of their students and a reasonable proposal to solve the problem.
  C. I need to appear professional for this audience. I need to establish my credibility with this audience since the speech topic is controversial. The audience will take my recommendations more seriously if I appear knowledgeable.
  D. I need to avoid jargon. Speaking in a conversational way to the audience using narratives, will help the audience be more sympathetic to the cause. If I can connect to them as another parent, they will feel less adversarial.

Speech Context:
  A. The speech is in an informal setting, but the subject matter should be presented in a more formal way. I will dress in business casual clothing, but make a formal presentation.
  B. The speech is going to be in the high school library. I will be able to talk to individuals one-on-one during the break to clarify my position.
  C. The external political climate is that abstinence only sexual education is supported by the current school district. The community is liberal, but the school district has not caught up yet. I will have to appeal to the audience that this is a step in the right direction to protect our children's health.

a change in the audience, where "To explain why the drinking age should be lowered" only reveals that the speaker has accomplished something. In this instance, the audience is not involved and may be completely unchanged. Although neither the speaker's general purpose nor their specific purpose statement are usually presented in the delivery of their speech, they are essential to the development of a clear, well-focused message. Writing out a purpose statement and a thesis statement essentially lays the foundation of the speech. A good purpose statement is specific, realistic, and results-oriented. A specific purpose is most often one statement that explains exactly what the speaker hopes to accomplish. It focuses a speech on just one aspect of the topic. For instance, a good purpose statement would not focus on "relationships," but possibly "the initiation of a relationship." A general topic, "skiing," and its purpose may involve any of a number of different subjects, for instance "the cost of skiing," "dangers of skiing," and "skiing fashion," but a specific purpose only focuses on one specific subject or topic. A specific purpose statement limits the speaker to what might possibly be achieved given the speaker's time constraints. It is not possible to inform your audience about the awards of the Academy of Motion Picture Arts and Sciences, the Oscars, in five or 6 minutes, but you could inform them of the history of the awards or one of the award categories. It is not possible to persuade your audience to start a business, but you could persuade them to consider the benefits of being self-employed.

A good purpose statement is results-oriented. It states what change the speaker expects in his or her audience. Writing a results-oriented purpose statement includes the audience, whom you want to change in some way, and how the audience is to change. For example, your audience might be more informed about the American Bison; persuaded to believe that university students need to wear uniforms; or maybe persuaded to sign a petition calling for welfare reform. Good purpose statements should not be written in the form of a question. For example, "Is the food in the cafeteria good?" is not appropriate. Good purpose statements avoid vague and figurative language. It is not clear or specific what "many reasons for gun control," "awesome book," or "would be terrible" mean. On the other hand, "The top three reasons for gun control," "informative and easy-to-read book, " or "would result in the loss of human lives" are better because they do not leave questions in the minds of audience members about what the speaker is referring to. Lastly, a good purpose statement lays the groundwork for a good thesis statement.

Topic Selection

Speakers should speak with passion. Select a topic that is important to you. Select a topic that is relevant to the results you want to achieve with your speech. Trying to persuade the parent-teacher association to support condom distribution requires a specific topic and relevant information: the risk of sexually transmitted infections and pregnancy in the community youth population, the consequences of sexually transmitted infections and pregnancy to the community youth population, and a proposed solution of distributing condoms to the high school students. The speech topic of the example is one that if conveyed well will accomplish the goal of gaining support for your proposal.

One of the first steps in giving a good speech is choosing a topic that interests you. While the vast majority of public speakers have their topic dictated by the situation and occasion, it is customary for students learning about public speaking to have the luxury of choosing their own topic. Interestingly enough, many students of public speaking find this first step the most difficult. With practice, choosing a speech topic becomes one of the shortest and easiest parts of public speaking. There are several ways to choose a topic; five of them are: knowledge, interest, brainstorming, free-association, and reference.

The most obvious subject to talk about is one you already *know* a lot about. People speak best when talking about subjects with which they are familiar. Your knowledge will lend you credibility and allow you to be more confident when speaking. Moreover, the more complete your knowledge the less research you will have to do on your topic. People often think that they do not know any topics that their audience might be interested in, but this is not true. The average person knows many topics of interest. Students have given talks about their adjustment to school, exotic pets, and experiences with the law, internships, and family businesses that were both exciting and knowledgeable. Do you know how to scuba dive, price a thoroughbred, make an ice sculpture, plan a wedding, or refinish a dresser? Chances are that not everyone in your audience will know how to do these things, and would not only be interested in learning how, but may also be persuaded to give them a try.

A topic you know a lot about might also be one you are *interested* in. For instance, you might know a lot about and enjoy baseball, crossword puzzles, working at the local animal shelter, or even shopping the day after Thanksgiving. Choosing a topic because it interests you is almost always a good idea. If you are not interested in your speech topic it is unlikely that your audience will be. Boredom and unhappiness in a speaker can usually be detected by the audience. Choose something that interests you so that you will be a motivated and excited speaker. Think about how impassioned some preachers and salespeople can get. Their excitement can often be contagious. Don't be afraid to put energy and excitement in your speech. If you have chosen a topic that interests you, you are halfway there.

Brainstorming, free-association, and use of a reference book are three methods to find topics that interest you and that you might know something about. *Brainstorming* is the uncritical suggesting of ideas. Suggest idea after idea without judging the acceptability of each idea as a speech topic until after you have developed a long list of possible topics. People usually brainstorm about places, people, things, and events; or activities, problems, natural events, laws/policies, and goals (like graduation). *Free-association* is when you begin with a topic and move to related topics until you come up with one that interests you. For example, I might think of television, then Nick at Nite, then the sitcom Bewitched, to the Salem witch trials, to the State of Massachusetts, to Boston, to the Boston Celtics basketball team. Free-association allows your mind to wander along normal pathways that are filled with topics you know a lot about and that interest you. Finally, if neither of the above work, you might want to get a *reference source*—encyclopedias or the New York Times Index are far better than dictionaries—and open the book to any given page. Look at the page and see if any of the topics interest you. For instance, if you opened a book to "H" you might find higher education, highways, hijacking, hiking, and Hinduism. Inspiration comes in many forms. Trying to force a topic tends to be counterproductive; instead take time out, read a magazine or watch television, search the internet, talk to other people, search textbooks, listen to National Public Radio, and let your ideas coalesce and put themselves into a hierarchy of interest. The right topic is there, you just need to let it emerge. There are many different ways to choose a good speech topic; just keep in mind that what is important is that you find a topic that will interest both you and your audience.

Audience Analysis

When preparing your speech it is critical to have an idea of who your audience is going to be. Good public speakers are always oriented toward their audience. They ask the questions of "To whom am I speaking?" "What changes am I asking for?" and "What is the best way of presenting my speech to get that result?" Good speakers tailor their message to their audience. The more tailored a message, the more likely it is that the audience will understand and accept the speaker's ideas. People in advertising and marketing do intensive research to find out what customers want. Similarly, politicians and political scientists spend enormous amounts of money to research what the public thinks about a candidate and their stance on an issue. Although most public speakers will not spend nearly so much time and money investigating the attitudes and beliefs of their audience, they should still gather information about the demographics and psychographics of their audience.

Demographics and Psychographics

Demographics are the external variables people possess: most often age, sex, ethnicity, religion, amount of education, and amount of income. Psychographics are internal variables such as one's attitudes, beliefs, and needs for inclusion, control, and affection. After a little thought, it becomes readily apparent why demographics and psychographics must be considered. A group of 6th grade Catholic school children will no doubt be different from a group of middle-aged college professors in an Alcoholics Anonymous meeting. It is possible to have similar demographic characteristics, but very different psychographic characteristics. For instance, consider young Republican or Democrat meetings, or a fraternity house and a group from the women's center. Similar age and education do not necessarily make for similar attitudes and beliefs. Public speakers should be careful not to make too many assumptions based on demographic characteristics, but to instead ask questions, do some research, and make careful observations that will reveal how the audience might react to the speaker's topic.

A good public speaker not only considers his audience's demographics and psychographics, but also the audience size, situation, and physical setting as well. Generally speaking, the larger the audience the more formal the speech and the more nervous the speaker. However, every situation calls for a slightly different treatment, and every speaker has his or her own style. Groups as small as three or 4 may be considered very formal, while groups of a hundred or more might be very informal. The audience situation is an often overlooked, but very important factor. Are the people in your audience there because they want to be or because they are required to attend? Is it a business meeting or the local Parent-Teacher Association? Are you speaking at 8 a.m., after lunch, or at a dinner assembly? Are you speaking in a classroom, lecture hall, or cafeteria? Different situations and locations often change the psychological make-up of an audience and what they expect of a speech or presentation. Your audience's expectations are especially important when you are speaking to persuade. Take the time to do a little groundwork and you'll be able to adjust your speech content and delivery to present a far stronger speech.

To carry on the school board member example, understanding your audience can inform the arguments you choose, the political slant you give your speech, word choice, the persuasion technique, and the information you provide.

Audience Disposition

It is very important to understand your audience's attitude toward your topic. This is important because the strategies that you should use to persuade your audience depend a great deal upon whether or not your audience agrees with the position that you are advocating. There are three basic phases of influence that represent the degree to which the audience agrees or disagrees with the topic: discontinuance, conversion, and deterrence. The specific goals that the speaker adopts depend upon which phase their audience is in.

Sometimes the audience is very hostile toward the position that the speaker is advocating. When this occurs, the audience is in the discontinuance phase. For example, a speaker may be trying to convince an audience of feminists that a woman's place is in the home or an audience of pro-choice advocates to outlaw abortions. In either case, the speaker will be dealing with a hostile audience. Speakers should be aware of this hostility ahead of time and set their goals accordingly.

There are three basic goals when dealing with a hostile audience. First, the speaker should reduce overt opposition. For example, the speaker should reduce the volume of catcalls and hisses being received. However, overt opposition should not be a problem for most classroom speeches. The second goal is to reduce private opposition. The speaker could create doubts in the minds of the hostile receivers by providing some type of factual evidence. The final goal is to reduce discontinuance and create genuine indecision. Although you will not be able to convince a hostile audience to adopt your point of view, you may be able to reduce their hostility and make them less sure of their previous point of view. A speaker who makes a hostile audience indecisive and more receptive to alternative points of view has given a successful persuasive speech.

Sometimes the audience will critically listen to the speaker's message. The audience may disagree, not care, or not have an opinion about the topic, but they are still willing to listen to what the speaker has to say. In this case, the audience is in the conversion phase. There are three basic goals when dealing with critical receivers. One goal is to convert the disbelievers. An audience may disagree with the speaker's message, but they are willing to listen to what the speaker has to say. The speaker needs to provide strong arguments in order to modify the attitude of this audience. A second goal is to convert the uninformed and apathetic. For example, if the audience does not care about organ donation, the speaker would need to present messages that make organ donation more relevant to the audience and then form the appropriate attitudes in the audience's mind. A third goal is to convert the conflicted. For instance, the audience may have received a lot of information about the candidates in an upcoming election. This audience may also be very interested in this election, but cannot decide whom they will vote for because they have received so much discrepant information. The speaker would then have to deal with this discrepant information and present it in such a way that it favors the desired candidate and forms the correct attitude in the audience.

Sometimes the audience already agrees with the speaker's attitude. Further, the audience may already be behaving in ways that are consistent with this attitude. When this occurs, the audience is in the deterrence phase. There are four basic goals when dealing with sympathetic receivers. First, the speaker needs to reinforce these favorable attitudes in the audience. Phone companies often use television advertising to reinforce their customers' attitudes. Although these commercials often advocate switching to a particular company because they offer the better rate, the real goal in these commercials is to keep existing customers loyal to that company. Therefore, they are trying to keep people from changing their attitudes. A second goal is to activate favorable attitudes. Sometimes it's important to have people who privately support a position exhibit some type of public commitment. Although an audience may support organ donation, this means nothing unless they have placed an organ donation sticker on the back of their driver's licenses and discussed their decision with family members. In order to activate the audience's favorable attitude, the speaker needs to provide these stickers to the audience and encourage them to take the appropriate steps to become an organ donor. A third goal is to increase behavioral commitments. This involves persuading individuals who have already given some type of behavioral commitment to give even more. An example would be to persuade someone who is already an organ donor to encourage others to become organ donors. Also, some religions encourage their members to recruit new members. Not only does this increase the size of the religion, but it reinforces the attitude of the existing members by increasing behavioral commitment. A final goal when dealing with sympathetic receivers is to maintain high levels of attitudinal and behavioral commitment. It is important to reinforce high levels of commitment in order to maintain this high level.

As the above discussion illustrates, the goals that a speaker adopts are highly dependent upon which phase of the influence process the audience is in. An obvious problem is that the speaker may be dealing with a mixture of hostile, critical, and sympathetic audience members. If the majority of the audience is in one particular phase of the influence process, the best solution would be to adopt the goals of the phase which most of the audience members are in. Otherwise, the speaker will have to balance the different goals in order to deal with different audience members who are in different phases of the influence process. In either case, the speaker will have to adequately analyze his or her audience before he or she can determine which goals need to be accomplished in his or her speech.

In the parent-teacher association example, the audience could be considered to hold mixed dispositions. Some members may be hostile to the idea of condom distribution for religious reasons; other members may disagree with the policy because they believe condom distribution increases sexual activity in teens. Other members might be undecided about the policy, while others could be very supportive. The more controversial the topic, the more widespread the audience orientations are to the issue. With a mixed audience, it is strategic to address the concerns of each group within the audience, or to target the groups who are more likely to be persuaded.

Speech Context

Understanding the big picture your speech fits in can help you write an appropriate speech for the context. *Political context of the speech:* What is going on in the world to influence how your speech will be received? What are the ramifications and implications of your speech? In the example of condom distribution, perhaps the issue of sexual education is a current hot topic with other districts implementing similar programs. You could mention these examples to provide an "everyone else is doing it" mentality in your audience. *Environment of the speech:* Where is the speech occurring (conference, to a company, in front of your boss, at your friends wedding)? The location of the speech can influence what you put in the speech, the visual aids you use, and more. The type and size of room can affect how you give your speech. Suppose the local sports team just won a championship, can you work that into your speech? Paying attention to the news of the place you will be speaking and tie it in. When is your speech occurring? Being the first to speak can make your speech be received differently than if you were the last one to speak. Take advantage of the context of your speech to make the speech better and wow the audience with your ability to see the big picture and anticipate needs. If the speech to the PTA is occurring in a school library, perhaps your access to visual aide equipment is limited or the setting might be casual and you would need to speak to be appropriate in the setting.

Word Choice

Verbal communication is the use of words and language. Sometimes this aspect of a speech is the most overlooked. Individuals often want to write a speech in the same way that they talk to their friends; however, this conversational style may make the speech more difficult for the audience to understand. *Speakers should speak with skill.* With regards to the language you should use when you are preparing your speech, two aspects of verbal communication are important: jargon and slang.

Jargon refers to technical language that is specific to a given area. For example, a physician may say that a patient had a myocardial infraction, but the patient's wife would say that he had a heart attack. Often when giving a speech it is easy to forget that your audience may have a significantly different background from you. Using too much jargon can cause you to be perceived as smug. Therefore, it is important to identify and define all terms that you think your audience may not understand.

Slang refers to the language that individuals use when among friends. Often when individuals spend a great deal of time together they develop a way of speaking that is unique to their specific group. When speaking to a diverse group of individuals it is important to not use slang since your audience may not understand you. In order to reduce your use of slang in your speech, write your note cards in formal English and try to not stray from them too much. You can also tape yourself giving your speech and play it back. When you review the tape, take note of any words that you should avoid using.

The best advice in terms of verbal considerations is as follows: In order to be perceived as a good speaker you need to speak better than you usually do. Learning how to use language to your benefit is perhaps the hardest but most important skill a public speaker can develop. In order to effectively communicate, sometimes simple clear language is the best way to get a message across to an audience. Descriptive, vibrant language can increase audience excitement about your topic. Use words the audience can understand and not find offensive. Choose words that will best convey the message, connect with the audience, and set a good tone for your speech.

A GUIDE TO INFORMATIVE SPEAKING

What Are the Goals of Informative Speaking?

Once you know and understand the occasion for which you are speaking, you need to consider the purpose of your speech. In general, the purpose of informative speaking is straightforward: it is to inform your audience. However, this is not to be confused with your specific purpose statement (e.g., informing your audience about how cheese is aged). We can further break down the goals of informative speaking into more specific goals. Speaking to inform generally emphasizes one of the three following areas: (1) communicating new and unfamiliar information, (2) extending what the audience already knows, and (3) updating old information (Kearney & Plax, 1996). Let's discuss each separately.

Communicating New and Unfamiliar Information

We live in a growing, fast-paced information age. We are constantly being bombarded with new information, especially with the increased use of the internet and electronic mail. This brings us to the first reason we might give an informative speech—to communicate new information. You might not know about the latest computer virus, the most recent outbreak of Tuberculosis on the west coast, or a rare cancer that has just been discovered by doctors at Johns Hopkins University. These situations result in a need for us to acquire new and unfamiliar information in order to better understand each issue. Doctors, researchers, and mechanics provide us with good examples of speakers who often have to provide their audience with, and explain clearly, new information so that we can understand it.

Extending What the Audience Already Knows

Speakers can also inform others by adding to the knowledge the audience already possesses. For example, a few years ago at Michigan State University, a keg ban was placed on tailgating activities. One could give a speech extending the information students have about kegs at tailgating parties by informing the audience of the rules regarding kegs before the ban, and how the rules have changed as result of the ban. This goal of informative speaking might also be used by government officials who have to relay information to their staff on a regular basis. A government official might first communicate new information to her staff, and subsequently extend that information in later presentations by providing additional information.

Updating Old Information

As the years go by, old information can become disproved or irrelevant. Therefore, a final goal of public speakers may be to update this old information. Speakers can add a new perspective to a topic by reinterpreting it, or explaining new research. For example, while once it was commonly believed that a way to rid someone of disease was to place leeches on a sick person's body, we now know this is untrue. When this discovery took place, it is likely that doctors had to give public speeches addressing this new information. Doctors are often faced with giving speeches such as these. As medical research continues we are often finding that "truths" we all once believed are not true.

A GUIDE TO PERSUASIVE SPEAKING

Persuasion is prevalent in everyday communication. People are bombarded with persuasive messages when they watch television, listen to the radio, or listen to a presentation at work. Persuasion also occurs in more interpersonal contexts such as when your friends try to convince you to go out to the bar on a school night. Persuasion is the process of using communication to modify a target audience's attitude or behavior toward some topic. This definition implies that, in order for persuasion to occur, some discrepancy between the position that the speaker is advocating and the audience's attitude must exist. The specific goals and purpose of the speech will largely depend upon the viewpoint of the audience.

Purpose of Persuasive Speeches

The purpose of giving a persuasive speech is to modify the attitude of your audience. An attitude consists of three different components: beliefs, opinions, and values. Beliefs are notions of whether something is true or false. These beliefs represent an individual's view of reality. "It is raining outside right now," is an example of a belief. All you need to do is go outside to determine if this belief is true or false. Similarly, the belief that "the resources in this country are being depleted" can be verified by researching the topic or by consulting experts. Opinions are notions of whether things are good or bad. "It is good that it is raining outside," and, "it is bad that the resources of this country are being depleted," are examples of opinions. Values also represent notions of whether things are good or bad. However, values differ from opinions in two important ways. First, values are more enduring than opinions. These values take many years to develop and are usually resistant to persuasion. Second, values guide our behavior in many different contexts because they control many of our opinions and behaviors. For instance, values are often linked with attitudes about religion and abortion.

It is important to keep in mind that some components of an attitude are more difficult to change than others. Beliefs are probably the easiest component of an attitude to change. In general, you need only provide people with additional information to change their beliefs. If someone does not believe that the sun causes skin cancer, providing them with evidence to the contrary should alter their beliefs. Opinions are more difficult to change than beliefs. Simply providing information will not change how people feel about the issue. Finally, values are the most difficult component to change. However, when values are altered, this change will last a long time and will control many opinions and beliefs.

It is also important to target the right component when you are trying to persuade your audience. It is a common mistake to target an audience's beliefs when either opinions or values should be targeted. For instance, a speaker may try to persuade her audience that abstaining from sexual intercourse will decrease their chances of contracting HIV. Since most people already know this, the speaker will not be very persuasive. Instead, the speaker should target the audience's opinions and values. Another common mistake is to target an audience's opinions or values when beliefs should be targeted. For example, most people believe that taking office supplies from work does not cost the organization a thing. Most people also think that stealing is bad. Therefore, a speaker would have to convince people that stealing office supplies from work hurts the organization in order to make their opinions and values about stealing relevant to the situation. In sum, you need to find out what your audience's attitudes are in order to make sure you target the right level.

Persuasive Devices

Aristotle identified three different approaches that can be used to persuade an audience: logos, pathos, and ethos. Logos refers to appeals to the audience's logic, pathos refers to appeals to the audience's emotions, and ethos refers to appeals to the speaker's credibility. Although these three appeals were developed long ago, they still provide an effective means of persuading the audience.

Appeals Based on Logic

A speaker can appeal to the audience's logic by using evidence. Evidence consists of all examples, statistics, and personal testimony that are used to support the main points. Every point a speaker makes should be backed up with evidence in order to persuade the audience. There are a few guidelines that should be followed for the evidence to have the maximum persuasive impact (Lucas, 1995). First, the evidence should be stated in specific rather than general terms. In a speech about bike safety, for instance, it would be less effective to say, "lots of students will be involved in a bike accident." Instead, the more specific claim that, "one out of ten students on this campus will be involved in a bike accident," would be much more effective. Second, evidence that the audience has never heard before will be more persuasive than evidence that the audience already knows. Sometimes it is difficult to discover something that the audience does not know, but the effort will pay off in the long run. Third, all evidence should come from credible sources. Rather than using testimony from your friends and family, go to the library or consult experts on the topic. Finally, make sure that the evidence is clearly related to the point you are trying to make. Don't assume that your audience will figure out what you are trying to say. It is the speaker's job to make sure the audience reaches the desired conclusion.

Appeals Based on Emotions

Emotional appeals are often used to enhance the message of the speech. These appeals are designed to generate a specific emotion in the audience such as anger, compassion, fear, joy, reverence, or shame. Audience members will be more motivated to change their beliefs, opinions, and values after experiencing this emotional reaction. Examples of emotional appeals are prevalent in television advertising. For instance, the familiar "this is your brain on drugs" commercial uses a fear appeal to get the message across. There are some techniques that the speaker can use in order to generate an emotional appeal in the audience. These techniques include using emotion-laden words, using vivid examples that will personalize the speech, and speaking with sincerity and conviction.

Appeals Based on Source Credibility

Source credibility is a powerful communication tool. Source credibility affects whether or not your audience listens to you and believes what you have to say. When an audience believes the speaker has little credibility, they will often tune out everything the speaker has to say. Even if the audience does listen to the speech, they are unlikely to be persuaded by a speaker with low credibility. Conversely, a highly credible source will captivate the audience and be very persuasive. Source credibility is probably one of the best predictors of persuasive success. Any speaker can develop the necessary skills to be perceived as a highly credible speaker. Speakers can enhance their credibility through careful preparation. For example, using logical and easy-to-follow main points, citing good evidence to support those points, and referring to previous experience with the topic are all ways to increase a speaker's credibility. Other techniques that can be used to enhance a speaker's credibility will be discussed later in this chapter.

MONROE'S MOTIVATED SEQUENCE

People need to be motivated to change their beliefs, opinions, and values. Although there are several ways of organizing persuasive speeches, only one method effectively boosts the audience's motivation and involvement. This method was developed in the 1930s by Alan Monroe and is known as Monroe's Motivated Sequence. Monroe's Motivated Sequence is a five-step organizational scheme that moves the audience through the persuasive process.

The Attention Step

The first thing you need to do is gain the interest and attention of your audience. This can be accomplished in a variety of ways. For instance, you can make a startling statement, tell a joke, use a visual aid, tell a dramatic story, ask a series of questions, or relate the topic to the audience. Almost anything can be used to gain the attention of the audience as long as it is directly related to the topic of your speech. A speaker who shouts at the top of his lungs right before he gives his speech will gain the attention of the audience, but will lose a lot of credibility unless this is somehow relevant to his speech. You also need to make sure that your attention grabber is ethical and does not violate any laws or regulations. For instance, if the topic of your speech is gun control, you might get in trouble with the local authorities if you have your friends dress up as terrorists, wave real guns at the audience, and fire blanks into the air. (Don't laugh—this actually happened in a classroom speech.) Remember that the whole point of the attention step is to get the audience interested in your topic. Attention grabbers that are either irrelevant or extreme will not accomplish this goal.

The Need Step

Your audience should now be interested in your topic and ready to hear more about it. Now what you need to do is to make the audience feel that there is a need for a change. The audience is not going to change their attitudes unless they think there is a good reason to do so. It is up to you to provide a reason to alter their beliefs, opinions, and values. This can be accomplished by clearly explaining the problem to your audience. For example, a speaker advocating gun control would have to convince his audience that the absence of strict laws is causing serious problems. You should make the problem vivid by providing a lot of details and citing specific examples. By the end of this step, the audience should believe that the problem is serious and somehow affects them.

The Satisfaction Step

Now that your audience feels a need for change, you satisfy this need by presenting your solution to the problem. If you made the audience feel a need to recycle, tell them exactly how they will accomplish this. Providing a lot of details about your solution will help the audience understand how this solution works. Tell your audience exactly what can be recycled and where they need to take their recyclables. You also need to provide evidence that your solution is realistic and will actually solve the problem. Let your audience know how easy it is to recycle and how much it will help the environment. Any research or statistics you can find to back up your solution will help.

The Visualization Step

It is not enough to tell the audience what they need to do to solve the problem. You also need to motivate them to actually implement your solution. This is done by having the audience visualize your solution in action. The audience should have a clear mental picture of how your solution will satisfy their needs. For example, a speaker who advocates a regular exercise routine could ask his audience to imagine what they would look and feel like after they have been working out regularly. Advertisements for fitness centers often do this by showing extremely athletic models and claiming that you can look just like them in no time. The audience should be able to clearly picture how they will benefit once they adopt your solution.

The Action Step

This final step calls for the audience to take some sort of action. You should tell the audience exactly what you want them to do; the more specific you are the better. Whenever possible, have the audience fulfill this action step right after your speech. For example, if you are trying to persuade your audience to support some policy (such as gun control, prayer in the classroom, or the legalization of marijuana) you could encourage your audience to sign a petition that would support this policy, and distribute this petition at the end of your speech. Although it is not always possible to get your audience to implement your solution right away, you should still have them take some sort of token action or small step toward your solution. This will increase your audience's behavioral commitment and they will be much more likely to adopt your proposed solution. You should conclude your speech by reinforcing your audience's commitment to take action.

ORGANIZING A SPEECH

Introduction

Writing an Effective Introduction

Once you have finalized your topic and know the considerations of your speech, you need to begin developing your speech. Writing an effective introduction is key to being an effective public speaker. How many times have you turned on the TV and within seconds became bored with the channel you were tuned into? Don't allow this to happen to you. Your introduction should pull in your audience, and make them desire to listen to you. When you publicly address people you desire for them to listen to you, and to recall what you have said. Obviously, this will not occur if you have failed to gain their interest in the first place. Ideally, the introduction, transitions, and conclusion should all be in the same theme to tie the speech together and flow well. Parts of the speech are related and reflect each other. In general, the introduction of your speech serves four purposes: (1) to capture the audience's attention. (2) To deliver the thesis statement. (3) To gain credibility from your audience. (4) To preview your main points.

The Attention-Getter

It is clear why capturing attention is so important, but how do you do it? There are several effective techniques for gaining someone's attention. The attention step should accomplish two goals: (1) to capture the audience, and (2) to set the tone for your speech. This is important to remember because you do not want to pick an inappropriate attention getter. Just think how awkward it would be to tell a joke as an attention getter before giving a speech about leukemia. In addition, your attention getter should be relevant to the topic. For example, once I listened to a speaker who opened her informative speech entitled "Abortion: Let Freedom Live" by playing a clip from the movie Annie Hall. The audience enjoyed the clip and laughed at Woody Allen. After they quieted down, the woman gave her speech. Unfortunately, the effect of her attention getter did not last;

FIGURE 16.3 Effective Attention Getters

- Tell a joke
- Ask a question
- Use a visual aid
- Recite a famous quote
- Cite a startling statistic
- Tell a story
- Tell a startling or strange fact
- Use an emotional appeal

within minutes the audience's attention was gone. In this case the woman would have been much better off using an emotional appeal related to freedom or abortion. That way, when she received the audience's attention, they would have been prepared to listen to a speech about abortion. Figure 16.3 provides a list of effective ways to gain an audience's attention.

A Good Thesis

Your thesis statement is the one central idea of your speech. A good thesis is a statement, not a question or phrase. Similar to a purpose statement, a thesis should not include slang, figurative language, or vague words, but unlike a purpose statement, a thesis statement is usually delivered to the audience. It is important to note that your thesis is: (1) what your audience will remember when you are finished speaking, (2) a concise statement of what you intend to say.

Because of this, a good thesis is both clear and specific. For example, if you were giving an informative speech about date rape, your thesis might be, "If the other person says 'No' it is rape," or, if skiing was your topic, your thesis might be, "There are three types of skiing: downhill, cross country, and water skiing." It is clear from these theses that the speaker will discuss what constitutes rape, not how rapists are prosecuted or other aspects of rape; and what the three types of skiing are, not the cost of skiing or what type of skis he or she prefers. While some of these issues may be covered in the speech, they would be subpoints used to complete and complement the information contained in main points that relate directly to the thesis statement. The thesis reflects the content of the speech and every point and subpoint should be related to it in a logical manner.

The Preview Statement

In order to keep your audience organized it is important to "say what you are going to say." More specifically, while your purpose and thesis statements provide the audience with clear and concise information regarding the intent of your speech, the preview statement provides a clear list of the specific main points you will discuss. In essence, this list acts as a road map by providing each of your main points, in order, so that the audience has a picture in their mind of what you will talk about. It helps the audience follow the organization of your speech in their minds, because they know what you will talk about next.

In addition to providing a mental road map for your audience, the preview statement also provides a smooth transition from your introduction to your first main point. Since the preview statement appears at the end of the introduction, it sends a signal to the audience that you are ready to move to the body of your speech.

Transitions

As noted earlier, the preview statement acts as a mental road map for the audience. Likewise, transitions serve to signal when the speaker is moving from one point to the next, linking two different ideas or issues together. Specifically, a transition provides a conclusion to the point the speaker is currently discussing, and provides a segue into the next point. Transitions help the audience follow the organization of the speech, and help the speech to flow more smoothly.

Think of transitions as the connections between cars on a train. If the entire train is to make it to its destination, the links between cars must be strong. For a speech to flow easily from section to section the transitions need to be strong, clear, and concise.

Transitions should state both the idea the speaker is leaving and the one s/he is moving to (Lucas, 1998). Here are a few examples of effective transitions:

> **Example 1:** While downhill skiing is one type of skiing that many people enjoy in the winter, cross-country skiing is another popular type.
>
> **Example 2:** Now that we have examined why each of us should sign an organ donor card and discuss the decision with our families, let us explore what steps we can take to become organ donors.
>
> **Example 3:** In addition to organizing a clear, cogent speech, practicing your speech will also help you to become a good public speaker.

Transitions can also simply be used to indicate what you are going to talk about next. Examples of this type of transition are as follows:

> **Example 4:** Next I am going to discuss cross-country skiing.
>
> **Example 5:** Finally, let's explore the steps we can all take to become organ donors.
>
> **Example 6:** Now I will explain how practicing your speech will help you to become a better speaker.

Transitions do not need to be complex. In fact, the simpler they are, the better. It may seem difficult to think of transitions at first, but when you are giving your speech you will be glad that you did. It will make your speech flow smoothly and your audience will not get confused about what you are talking about and why.

Signposts

Signposts are words or phrases that signal the importance of what you are going to say. Signposts signal to your audience that they need to listen to and remember what you are going to say next. You can use words to put an emphasis on certain areas of your speech by saying something like:

If you remember anything that I discussed today, it should be the following...

The key to success in public speaking is . . .

Using words that emphasize the importance of what you are saying can be effective, but it is the nonverbal emphasis you put on the words that can make the audience pay attention. Take the last example, "The key to success in public speaking is..." If you emphasize the word "key" you will be telling the audience that what you are saying next is significant. If you put the emphasis on the words "public speaking" you are telling the audience that what comes next is important, but only to public speaking situations. Your words and voice are powerful tools; use them to your benefit.

Body

To begin writing your body, you will need to consider how the speech will be organized, and how your supporting evidence will be researched and developed. The first aspect you need to consider is how to organize your main points. There are many ways to go about doing this, four of which will be considered here: (1) time patterns, (2) space patterns, (3) problem-solution patterns, and (4) cause-effect patterns (Adler & Rodman, 1994).

Time Patterns

Arranging a topic chronologically is probably the most popular way to organize a speech. This form is particularly popular if you are discussing an event of some sort. For instance, if your speech is on the history of American Art, your main topics can easily be broken down by time.

A. Early American Art refers to art created prior to the 1600s.

B. The next period of American art I will discuss is the period from 1600–1775.

C. Modern American Art refers to the art created from 1800–present.

Using this type of pattern is also useful if you are discussing steps one needs to take to accomplish a task. For an instructional speech, a time pattern is most often appropriate. For example, consider writing a speech on baking a quiche.

A. Step one is purchasing the ingredients for the vegetable quiche.

B. Step two is cutting and preparing the vegetables.

C. Step three is mixing and preparing the egg mixture.

D. Step four is baking and filling the crust.

Topic Patterns

A topical pattern is based on types or categories. It is appropriate for most informative speeches. For your main points, the categories into which you break your topic should be well-known or very original; either has its own advantages. For instance, if you are giving a speech on baseball, you could break up your topic like so:

A. It is most important for pitchers and catchers to communicate effectively in baseball.

B. Outfielders engage in the least amount of communication.

C. Infielders must remain aware of the communication occurring between the pitcher, the catcher, and the coach.

If you desire to use original or unique kinds of categories and/or topics, you will need to define the category. It is important that your audience understands exactly what you are talking about. Consider this example of types of graduate students.

A. Anal-Retentives are the graduate students who begin each project the day they receive their syllabus.

 1. These students have their desks clean at all times, and file every piece of paper work.

 2. Organization is their key to life.

B. The Clowns are the graduate students who entered graduate school because they are afraid of the "real world."

 1. They would write their papers on time, but they can't find their syllabuses.

 2. After receiving their Ph.D.s, most intend on finding a new graduate program to enter.

C. The Mixers are graduate students who have a good balance between hard work and good fun.

 1. Their work is done in a timely manner.

 2. When they are finished, they usually can be found in local pubs.

Problem Solution Patterns

As the name suggests, with problem-solution organization, your first main point breaks down what the problem is. Your second main point suggests a solution.

A. The Problem: There is not enough parking at Michigan State University.

B. The Solution: We need to write a federal grant allowing funds toward building three parking ramps on campus.

Cause-Effect Patterns

Cause-effect patterns are very similar to problem-solution; however, with this type of format you begin by talking about the cause of an issue. Hence, your second main point is built around discussing the effects of this problem. This speaker wrote a speech about receiving bad grades in college.

A. There are several causes for receiving poor grades.

 1. Professors using monotone speaking voices can lead to poor grades.

 2. Professors testing on material the class has never visited cause bad grades.

B. The effects of receiving poor grades.

 1. Cannot receive a job interview because G.P.A. is too low.

 2. Student goes on academic probation due to low grades.

 3. Parents find report card with low grades and become angry.

A second consideration one should make when writing the body of your speech is supporting material. You will need to consider definitions, statistics, stories, visual aids, and/or quotations you will use to flesh out your speech.

Conclusion

Just like the introduction, the conclusion is central to your credibility as a speaker. The conclusion is the last aspect of your speech that your audience will recall. It should leave a lasting mark of what kind of speaker you are, and what you desire your audience to recall about your speech. Thus, the conclusion to your speech serves two purposes: (1) to review the main points, and (2) to say some pertinent closing remarks. Reviewing your main points is where you "say what you said." Many speakers have a hard time following this form because they feel they are being overly redundant. This is not true. Remember, your audience has never heard your speech before, so it is important to keep stressing to them what point(s) you are attempting to make. Repeating the key points also keeps the listeners organized. Finally, restating the main points can serve as a signpost telling the audience you are concluding. Below are some examples of how to review your main points in an effective manner.

Example 1: I would like you all to recall the main points covered in today's speech. They were _____, _____, and _____.

Example 2: In sum, there are three key elements to becoming a good public speaker: researching your topic well, making sure your speech is well organized, and practicing your speech ahead of time.

If you do not like being so straightforward, try this technique:

Example 3: Today, I discussed the importance of _____, which has an enormous effect on _____. Finally, I encourage you all to not forget_____.

Making closing remarks is not as simple as reviewing your main points. Use your creative juices to put together a final statement that will not only sum up your speech, but will leave a lasting remark on your listeners. Many closing statements are remarkably similar to attention getters. Therefore, when you write your close, do not use the same technique as you did in the introduction unless absolutely necessary. For example, if you used a statistic as an attention getter, use a story for the close. Yet try to use the same theme for the conclusion as for the attention getter. Here are some examples of excellent closing remarks:

Example 4: When I think back to my times at Michigan State I will always remember what my first year art teacher said to me. "Creativity is not a destination, it is a journey."

Example 5: Look to your right. Now, look to your left. By the time you graduate from college, it is likely that those two people will be addicted to drugs.

Example 6: Close to 5000 people will die from Lupus this year. Let's bring an end to this painful disease.

Remember, the introduction and conclusion are key to how you will be viewed as a speaker. Particularly, in regard to your conclusion, it is the last thing the audience will recall about you. Do not end abruptly. Make sure that you develop your conclusion fully, and have a well thought-out closing remark. You do not want to end by saying "And, well, that's it." Do not babble. Again, your conclusion should be concise and clear. Make your ending definite. Do not introduce new points. One of the worst things you can do to lose credibility is to say "Oh, and I forgot to mention . . . " or "And my speech didn't even cover all of these key events . . . " Even if you forgot a main point, don't mention it in your conclusion. Do not ever apologize. I can't count how many times I have heard students say "I'm sorry, I was so boring . . . " or "I was so nervous, sorry." This will only make you look weak and non-credible. Simply end as if you are very confident that you did a good job.

Outlining

The most effective way to organize your speech is to write an outline. An outline is simply a skeletal version of your speech. It helps you focus on when certain points will be stated, and how much information you have to relay to the audience. You may realize after you write your outline that you have too much information (or too little), or do not have enough pertinent examples. There are many kinds of outlines; for the purposes of this class, only the basic speech structure will be taught. Figure 16.4 shows the formatting of an outline. Good advice regarding public speaking is "Say what you are going to say, say it, and then say what you said." The basic speech structure emphasizes this old saying. Thus the standard format for such an outline is:

I. Introduction

    A. Attention-getter

    B. Thesis Statement

    C. Preview Statement

II. Body

    A. Main Point #1

        1. Statement

        2. Evidence or warrant why the statement is true.

        3. Transition to the next main point.

    B. Main Point #2

        1. Statement

        2. Evidence or warrant why the statement is true.

        3. Transition to the next main point.

    C. Main Point #3

        1. Statement

        2. Evidence or warrant why the statement is true.

        3. Transition to the conclusion

FIGURE 16.4 How to Correctly Label the Components of an Outline

> I. Title of First Section—The title of each section of your speech should be identified with roman numerals.
>   A. Main Point #1—Main points should always be identified with capital letters.
>   B. Main Point #2
>   C. Main Point #3
> II. Title of Second Section
>   A. Main Point #1
>   1. Subpoint #1—Subpoints should always be enumerated with standard numbers.
>   a. Sub-subpoint #1—These are identified with lowercase letters.
>   b. Sub-subpoint #2
>   c. Sub-subpoint #3
>   i. Sub-sub-subpoint #1—These use lowercase roman numerals.
>   ii. Sub-sub-subpoint #2
>   2. Subpoint #2
>   B. Main Point #2
>   C. Main Point #3
> III. Title of Third Section
>   A. Main Point
>   B. Main Point
>
> Remember: You should never have an A without a B, a 1 without a 2, an i without an ii, etc. In other words, no point may stand alone. You must always include at least two!

    III. Conclusion

        A. Review Main Points

        B. Implication Statement that explains how the main points prove your thesis and accomplish your speech goal.

        C. Closing Statement

In a sense, outlining is a language. It has rules and standard formats that must be followed in order for it to be understood. In order to understand this "language" we must know the differences between main points, subpoints, and sub-subpoints. A main point is a major point that you are attempting to make through your speech. A subpoint contains relevant and pertinent information to support your main points. Subpoints are often facts, statistics, and other supporting evidence. Finally, sub-subpoints help to clarify the subpoints if necessary. Stories and examples can make great sub-subpoints. Each of these points has a standard format that must be adhered to in an outline. Every formal outline that you put together needs to follow this format. In outlining there are two aspects in that need to be paid attention to: indenting and complete sentences. Under each type of point (e.g., main points), the next point (subpoint) is indented. This is a central part of the standard format that cannot be ignored. Moreover, the outlines you put together should employ full sentences. That is not to say that your outline should have full paragraphs and be wordy. Rather, your outline should have one concise, full sentence for each point. This will help you remember exactly what you meant to say when you give your speech.

It is not only necessary to understand the correct outlining format, it is also necessary to follow the rules of division and parallel wording.

The Rule of Parallel Wording

The rule of parallel wording deals with writing your outline in a consistent manner. Notice that when you write papers for college courses you would never begin writing in the third person and complete the paper in the first person. Similarly, you wouldn't write half of a paper in a computer language and the rest of the paper in standard English. This illustrates the rule of parallel wording. All of your main points need to be written in a consistent and similar manner. That is, if one of your main points is written in a complete sentence, then all of the main points need to be written in complete sentences. The same is true for subpoints, sub-subpoints, and so on.

The Rule of Division

In order to understand the rule of division, grab the most recent copy of the State News. Think of it (metaphorically) as a main point in your outline. Now, take that main point and rip it in half. How many subpoints (the newspaper halves) do you now have? Two, right? This illustrates the rule of division. In formal outlines you will always have at least two main points (subpoints, sub-subpoints etc.) for every topic. Just like the newspaper, if you break up any point in your speech, you will always have at least two parts. Hence, the rule of division states that you never have an I without an II, never an A without a B, and so on.

DELIVERING A SPEECH

This section of this chapter will give you some tools for becoming a better speaker. As you develop these tools or skills you will find that you are less nervous and that your speeches will flow better. Giving a good speech is a skill that relatively few people possess. It is a skill that can set you apart from others in your college career and in any future vocation.

How to Write Out Ideas on Notecards

In the business world the following is commonly stated, "If you fail to plan, you plan to fail." Organization can make you successful; the lack of it can hurt you. When writing out notecards you are accomplishing two things: first, you are making it easier to give your speech; and secondly, you are helping yourself memorize the speech by repeating it. Also, notecards are better to use than paper because if you get nervous in front of your audience you may start shaking; then the paper will also start shaking, your audience will know that you are nervous, and they will start paying attention to how much your paper is moving and not to what you are saying. Figure 16.5 is an example of an effective notecard and an ineffective notecard.

But how should you write out notecards? It is important when writing out notecards to try to do the following:

1. Put all of the information that you need on the notecards.
2. Do not put too much information on each card.

The information that goes on the note cards comes from the outline which you create for your speech. You can actually write out exactly what is in the outline on the cards so that you do not forget any important information. Also, it is important to include transitions on your note cards. Transitions connect one idea to the next, and are discussed further in the previous section.

FIGURE 16.5 Effective and Ineffective Note Cards

[Smile and look at audience!!!]

Effective Notecard

I. Having a pet can make a difference in your life.
   A. I have a cat named Sprinkles and he is the light of my life.
      1. He is big, fat, and orange, and lays around all day.
      2. But, when I come home at night he is always happy to see me.
   Transition: Do any of you have pets? This leads me to my next point. . . .

Ineffective Notecard

I. Having a pet can make a difference in your life.
   A. I have a cat named Sprinkles and he is the light of my life.
      1. He is big, fat, and orange, and lays around all day.
      2. But when I come home at night he is always happy to see me.
   Transition: Do any of you have pets? This leads me to my next point. . .
   B. Animals have been shown to have a beneficial effect on their owner's health.
      1. Simply holding a pet can lower your blood pressure.
      2. Also, playing with a pet dog or cat or other animal can reduce stress.
   Transition: Have you ever felt really lonely? A pet can help you not feel alone.
   C. Pets help people fight off loneliness and depression.
      1. Retirement communities have individuals bring in pets to help the elderly individuals fight depression and loneliness.
      2. My Aunt Gladys lived alone and would have been very lonely and depressed had it not been for her cat. She even taught him how to dance!
   Transition: Not only can pets help people fight off sickness and loneliness, some pets have even saved lives!!

When creating your note cards you can highlight areas of your speech on which you want to put a special emphasis. You can also draw smiling faces or something which will remind you to smile or look at your audience during your speech. Some people have even written positive affirmations in the margins of the cards to tell themselves that they will survive the speech. Remember, the cards are to help you.

One very common problem that occurs is that too much information gets put on the cards. This is primarily a problem because the speaker then tends to read the cards and not to use them as a guide. Also, when too much information is put on one card it is easy to lose your place; this can make a speech even more challenging.

The Figure 16.5 includes examples of effective and ineffective note cards:

The first example note card is effective because it reminds the speaker to look at his or her audience and to smile. People often forget to do either of these so it is good to remind yourself. Also, the speaker included one set of ideas and used big lettering that is easy to read. This will make it easier on the speaker when she looks up at her audience and then back down at her cards. She will easily find her place in the speech so that she can continue without interruptions.

The second note card is ineffective because it has too much information on it. This will force the speaker to read off of the cards and he will forget to look up at his audience. Also, it is easy to get lost with smaller letters, more words, and so many different ideas put together on one card. Try to keep one idea or similar ideas together on one card with a transition telling your audience (and you) where you are going next.

Whatever your topic is and however you organize your ideas, your note cards can either benefit you or hurt you. When you write them out, try to think about how you can write them so that they can make your speech easier.

Nonverbal Communication

Nonverbal communication has been defined in various ways. Burgoon, Buller, and Woodall (1989), describe the following categories of nonverbal communication: kinesics, vocalics, proxemics, chronemics, physical appearance, and artifacts.

Kinesics

Kinesics is the study of body movement. How individuals walk or move their arms when they speak relates to kinesics. In your speech you want to learn to use your natural body movements to your advantage. You also want to identify what body movements you make that will be distracting to your audience. For example, if you gave your whole speech leaning on your right leg with your left hip thrown out, your audience would focus on your stance and wonder how long you could stand that way without falling over. Or, say you are using a podium, and all your weight is on the podium and you begin to kick your legs in strange directions. Both of these are real examples of body movements that students did not anticipate and thus occurred during their speeches. The audience stayed interested in them because their movements seemed so unnatural, but the audience did not pay attention to the speeches.

Appropriate body movements are those which make the speaker seem comfortable and conversational, yet formal. This is a difficult mixture to get right. Think about David Letterman. He does an excellent job balancing these. He gestures in ways that are unique to him, but he does not throw his arms up in the air or do strange movements, unless he is doing so to make a point. He also stands up straight, even leaning slightly backward.

He gives the audience the appearance that he is giving a formal presentation (by standing up straight) but does so in a comfortable, welcoming fashion. He walks around and sometimes even runs (this would not work for your speech, however), but again, not through his entire presentation. He uses these movements to do something or show the audience something. He is a master of using nonverbal behaviors to make his presentations interesting and funny.

So, how do you use body movements to help you illustrate your points? Practice giving your speech in front of friends or a UTA or TA who will give you pointers. Try to gesture the way you would if you were describing the ideas in your speech to another student, but as if you were doing so sitting next to them and not standing in front of them. Let your personality show, but find out if you have nervous movements that come out when you stand in front of others to speak. If you find that you do exhibit nervous movements you can write a note to yourself on your note cards to remind yourself to watch for these movements.

Also, another method for controlling some nervous nonverbals is to take a couple steps to the right or left or toward your audience and back. This movement will help with your nervousness and will also keep your audience interested. Be careful not to pace, however, and this is tough to control as well. Although, when you give your first speech give yourself a break. If you use some strange body movements or start to pace, do not get frustrated or angry with yourself. You have to start somewhere, and the next time you will do it better. David Letterman did not start out with a perfect delivery and making millions of dollars on television. He probably gave monologues in dives and maybe even got booed. You will not get booed, but you may not start out with the same ability you will ultimately develop with more experience speaking in front of people.

Face movement is also included in the study of Kinesics. For the purposes of this section, eye contact will be included with facial movement. Facial movements and eye contact may be the most important aspects of your entire speech. For example, think about someone whom you have met who did not look you in the eye. You may have not liked that person right away. Increasing eye contact tells someone that you like her/him. Also, when someone makes eye contact with you when they are talking to you, you will look back at them. Often speakers complain of an uninterested audience when it was the speaker who did not try to keep the audience involved.

By establishing eye contact with as many people as possible during your speech, you make your audience feel as if you are talking to each of them. A trick that you can do is to pick out people that you already know before you give your speech. Start your speech by looking at them for encouragement. Sometimes it is even fun to walk toward and look directly at an individual who is not paying attention. This individual may have tuned out because she is thinking about her own speech, and when you make an effort to include her in your speech, she may begin to be more involved. When you are making eye contact with an individual, try to maintain it for at least five seconds. This seems as if it would be an easy thing to do, however, during a presentation five seconds can seem like five minutes. An easy way to accomplish this is to maintain eye contact through an entire sentence that you speak.

Along with eye contact, smiling can be a key aspect to the presentation of your speech. Even when giving a speech on a very serious subject, there will be times when you would naturally have smiled if you were talking to someone else. When beginning a presentation the best way to warm up your audience is to smile at them. This tells your audience that you are a nice person and that you are happy to be there. Studies have also shown that the more an individual smiles, the more attractive they are perceived to be.

For an example, think of David Letterman and think about how boring he would be if he never smiled. Also, watch a political debate closely. Watch for how often the speakers smile. For example, former President Bill Clinton has been considered to be a great orator, and he frequently smiles at his audience.

The bottom line is this: be a friendly speaker and your audience will be receptive to you.

Vocalics

Vocalics refers to the way individuals speak. This has to do with the rate, pitch, tone, or loudness of your speaking voice. Vocalics can be the most difficult aspect of your speech to control. Your rate of speech can be very difficult to monitor while you are presenting your speech. It is common for individuals to speak much faster when they give their speech than they did when they practiced it. The best way to control the rate at which you speak is to remind yourself to slow down. Try to force yourself to speak more slowly than feels natural, and you will not speak as fast. Speaking at a slower, natural pace is important because it allows your audience to better understand you.

Another aspect of vocalics which can make a speaker difficult to understand is the loudness of an individual's speaking voice. If your audience cannot hear you, they cannot understand you. It is important to try to speak more loudly than normal when giving a speech. For many people this is a major hurdle because they naturally do not speak loudly. A way to make yourself speak loudly enough to be understood is to go to the room in which you will be speaking and practice there. Have a friend sit in the back of the room and tell you if he or she had a hard time hearing any of your speech. Also, for softer speakers it is even more important that you do not look at your note cards a lot during your speech. When your audience cannot understand you they will look at your mouth to try to "lip read." If they cannot see you forming the words they will remain confused. Therefore, it may be beneficial to have parts of the speech memorized so that you can maintain good eye contact with your audience.

The pitch of an individual's voice refers to the high or low sounds in his speech. For example, I once knew a girl who had a very high voice, like a mouse. She was very painful to listen to because she always seemed to be whining, even when she was not. She even received the nick-name of "Squeaky Toy."

The varying of the pitch of your voice can be a great asset to a speaker. For example, one of the most powerful speakers of our time, Dr. Martin Luther King, Jr., had a deep and strong voice. Listen to his "I had a dream" speech to feel the power of varying pitches in a speech. He spoke softly in parts and angrily in others. He used his voice to reach millions of individuals. You can hear his speeches without seeing the videotapes and still be moved by his voice alone.

Of course, you cannot expect yourself to be as skillful as speakers who have had years of experience. Simply make the effort to vary your voice as you speak to sound conversational and to keep your audience interested.

Lastly, there is the tone of your speech. The tone of your speech refers to the manner in which you deliver the information to your audience. For example, are you being sarcastic, funny, or serious? It is important to set the tone from the beginning of the speech. If you are talking about a national disaster it would be inappropriate to tell a joke at the beginning of the speech. Relate the manner in which you speak to your audience as well. If the audience is comprised of individuals about the same age as you, it would be inappropriate to speak down to them, even if you are an expert in your field. If you are talking in front of a reputable and respected board of directors for a corporation it would be important to be respectful, but confident, about that which you are speaking. Adapt the tone or manner of your speech to the topic and audience you are addressing.

Proxemics

Proxemics refers to how individuals use space. During your speech it is important that you not stand in the back of the room, far away from your audience. Try also to avoid standing too close to one particular individual. Stand toward the middle of the area reserved for speakers, and then stop worrying about proxemics.

Chronemics

Chronemics is the use of time. Timing yourself is important so that you finish within the required amount of time. Often individuals will speak faster when presenting a speech, so when you practice, try to make your speech go as long as the maximum time limit. This will ensure that your speech will not go over the maximum time limit, and you can be certain that you will reach the minimum time requirement.

Physical Appearance

Physical appearance refers to how you present yourself in terms of clothing. When you are preparing to give a presentation, think about how you can dress to gain the respect of your audience before you even begin to speak. Dress in comfortable clothing that is nicer than you would usually wear to class. Some individuals dress as if they are going to an interview, and this is very impressive. Dressing professionally for your speech is also good practice for those individuals who plan on entering a career which may require that they make formal presentations.

Although wearing a baseball hat is stylish, you should avoid wearing a hat because the audience will have a difficult time seeing your eyes. Also, remember to take off your jacket before giving a speech. When an individual stands up to give a formal presentation in a ski jacket, the audience wonders if the speech is about skiing or if the speaker really wants to get the heck out of there. Clothing such as this may limit a speaker's credibility, so be sure to avoid wearing clothing items that can detract from your presentation.

Artifacts

Artifacts are the visual aids that individuals use to help them present the information within their speech. These often can make a speech topic "come to life" for an audience. For example, one student did a speech on motorcycles and brought in color transparencies. He used an overhead projector and showed his audience the color pictures as he was talking about specific bikes. This helped make the aspects of the motorcycles, which he was trying to emphasize, clear to his audience. The two most important issues to remember when using visual aides are that they must be clear and uncluttered and you need to practice using them. Just like note cards, visual aids can a speech easier or more difficult.

Overall, you have a lot to think about when it comes to the nonverbal aspects of your speech. The best advice we can give you is to practice, practice, practice. Practicing will allow you to determine what you do well, and what you need to improve. After you give your speech, read your instructor's comments regarding any specific nonverbals you need to perfect. Try to improve on those for the next speech. It is important for you to realize that learning to be an effective public speaker is a process. Be gentle with yourself and do not expect too much. Try to improve your skills with each speech, and you will ultimately develop a strong ability to speak in public.

Preparation

There are a few steps of preparation that will help your final speech product.

1. Answer the speech consideration questions.

2. First main edit: Once you have a draft of your speech, be it in outline form or completely scripted, read the speech aloud to yourself and edit it.

3. Second main edit: Get critical feedback from someone else. Try to get as many people as possible to evaluate your speech. Have the person hearing your speech ask cross-examination questions about your speech. Practice defending your speech. Edit the speech based on the feedback you receive.

4. Plan appropriate visual aides. Visual aides should help the flow of the speech, progress the speech forward, not distract too much from the speech content, and supplement the information provided. You should also plan how you will handle the visual aides and practice using them. Make sure that the speech venue has all the necessary equipment for your speech.

5. Plan gestures and where to stand and move strategically in order to emphasize parts of your speech. And example of strategic moving would be to present the introduction in the center of the front of the room, move to the left side of the front of the room for the first main point, cross to the right side of the room for the second main point, return to the center for the third main point, step forward for the conclusion. Write your non-verbal plan on your speech notes as if you were blocking a drama or play.

6. Practice giving the speech to become familiar with the wording of the speech. Knowing your speech well will reduce fillers and improve the general flow of the presentation. Circle words your wish to emphasis, strategically planning the terms you want the audience to focus on. Indicate where you will pause in your speech for effect on your notes.

7. Time each section and the entire speech. Therefore if you are pressed for time, you will know how long each section takes and be able to edit yourself as you speak. Keep in mind that often speakers speak faster in front of an audience. So include extra information or examples in your speech that can be added if your have extra speaking time, yet could also be left out if you did not have the time. Sometimes it helps to have two similar versions of the speech: the short and the long versions to be selected as time permits. Mark "SLOW DOWN" on your notecards to remind yourself if you need to.

8. Make sure to bring some speaking "tools" with you to the speech. Bring several copies of your speech (located in different places of you materials) so if you forget a copy on your desk, you have a back up copy in your backpack, etc. Get a

timer with large numbers that counts up and down so that you can watch your time. For the COM 100 class, make sure the instructor has timecards to display so you know how much time you have remaining. Bring your visual aides and handouts ("the dog ate it" does not work in the real world). Bring overhead pens, tape, scissors, paper, a highlighter, and easels if necessary. Bring the technology that you need and what the venue can not provide. Bring water to drink. Carry along a good luck charm if you need it!

Presentation

To Use or Not to Use the Podium

It is easy to understand why people want to use a podium when they speak for the first or second time in front of a group. The podium can make you feel as if you are somehow protected from your audience. However, if you are going to use a podium you need to be aware of a few issues. The following examples are indicative of what can happen when you misuse a podium:

Driving the Podium. This is the most common mistake. "Driving" occurs when a speaker puts each of her hands on the edges of the podium and holds on tightly. She then starts to move the podium while speaking, rocking it or turning it. Although it may be entertaining to picture this happening to someone else, you don't want this to happen to you.

Holding onto the Podium for Dear Life. Sometimes an individual will hold on to the podium so tightly that his knuckles turn white, and the audience watches to see how long the speaker can hold onto the podium without feeling pain.

Laying Down on the Podium. Sometimes when a speaker wants to reach her audience but is afraid to come around the podium and face them, she will lean forward onto the podium so much that she is practically laying on top of it. Not only is this incredibly distracting, but laying down on the podium will make it harder for people in the back of the room to see you. Again, the audience will be spending most of its attention on your posture and not on your speech.

Using the Podium as a Percussion Instrument. Often when a speaker is nervous he will tap his note cards, fingers, or fists on the podium. Some speakers also bump the podium with their knees or feet in a rhythmic fashion. These acts may demonstrate the musical and rhythmic abilities of the speaker, but mostly serve to distract the audience from the speech. In addition to being a distraction, banging on the podium can make it difficult for the audience to hear what you are saying.

Just like visual aids, podiums can help or hinder you. If you are going to use one it is extremely important that you practice using one before the day of your speech. Try to use it only to hold your note cards, and also try to take a step to the side of the podium to seem more intimate with your audience. Do not use the podium with the purpose of hiding from your audience. This is perhaps when the greatest mistake is made. When speakers hide behind a podium they also tend to put their cards down and read from them. When they do this, they are looking farther down than they would have if they were holding their cards in their hands, and the audience cannot see the speaker's face at all. It is natural to want to use the podium as a comfort device, but instead think of it as a tool. The key word is: PRACTICE. You can prevent mistakes from happening in your speech if you are comfortable using the podium before the day of your speech.

CROSS-EXAMINATION

Speakers should speak with skill and be able to defend the ideas that are presented. It takes great courage to face a firing squad of questions. With practice and by really knowing your topic, being cross examined is not to be feared. A questioning period is important to clarify information, to test the validity of the information that is presented, and to establish credibility. Concepts that were not clearly explained can be asked about and be further clarified by the speaker. An actively participating audience should not take what a speaker says to be the ultimate truth. Critical thinking and questioning is a good way to test that the information presented is logical and empirically sound. Speakers and questioners can establish credibility via the question answer period: speakers by intelligently answering questions and defending their ideas; and questioners by asking smart questions that show they are looking at the big picture of the presentation.

There are several tips for asking good questions. Ask your questions slowly, deliberately, and loud enough for others to hear. Ask questions to clarify concepts you do not understand. Listen to other questions to avoid asking a repeat question. If you are asking a question to challenge the speaker, get the speaker to defend a position that is clearly wrong. If you are asking a question that questions the logic of the speech, know the answer before you ask the question to avoid surprises. Take notes during the speech so that you can directly quote the speaker in your questions.

Defending your ideas is important. Speakers being questioned should not get defensive or appear shaken. Sound confident with your answers (even if you are not really confident). Remember that cross-examination is where you must defend your credibility. If you do not know an answer, admit it and offer to get the answer to the questioner when you find the answer. Be polite. Know your own evidence and arguments well. Defer questions that are only relevant to the single questioner to after the speech or during the break if the answer will take awhile to say. Understand that the better prepared you are, the easier cross-examination becomes an opportunity to supplement your speech and impress your audience.

POST SPEECH

After your speech, reflect on the success and failure of the speech. Did you accomplish a speech of integrity, skill, passion and implication? What did you do in the speech that you were proud of? What could you have improved in the speech? What actions could you have taken to make the improvements? Save your speech. You might be able to adapt the speech and/or research for a later assignment or presentation. Could your speech be videotaped for post analysis? Watching yourself on tape is a great way to get a different perspective on how you present speeches.

Seek out information to improve your speech writing and presentation skills. Read books and internet sites on public speaking. Listen to speakers you admire and pay attention to their speaking style. Critique other speakers. How would you improve others' speeches? Join a speaking organization such as Toastmasters. Volunteer for speaking opportunities. The more chances you have to hone your public speaking skills, the better speaker you shall be.

SPEECH TYPES

Public speaking opportunities are everywhere and difficult to avoid. There are speeches necessary in the workplace and professional life. There are several personal occasions where a public speech is required. In the civic community, those wishing to get involved better be prepared to speak in public. There are also forms of public speaking that are purely for your personal pleasure, such as performance speeches. Time constraints prevent us from shaping you into a public speaking super hero, but hopefully this course and chapter can expose you to the speech types and give you some tips that will help you survive and excel in your public speaking (and maybe score a good grade in this course as well).

For purposes of this chapter, the types of speeches are listed in four categories: professional, civic, personal, and entertaining. This list is not exhaustive, but a good start. Some of the speeches cross categories, try not to get too stuck on that issue or read into the order too much. Yes, some of the definitions of the speeches are tautological, do not worry too much about that either. Use a dictionary if you need more detail and depth.

Professional Speeches

Address of Welcome. This is a speech that welcomes guests and members to the meeting/conference.

Introductions. These are the speeches given before another speaker is to speak, where you introduce the speaker to the audience.

Closing Remarks. This speech thanks those involved in putting together the meeting/conference and ties the theme of the meeting/conference together. The speech also says goodbye and dismisses the audience.

Awards. This type includes speeches that present awards and accept awards.

Job Talks and Interviews. These are speeches given to get hired and to hire individuals.

Job Training. These are speeches designed to educate members of your organization in information they need to know in order to perform their jobs. Training. I am often asked by students what kinds of jobs they can get with a communication degree. One of the most common careers for communication majors, though not often considered, is training. One can train someone else to use a computer, do sales, play soccer, or serve drinks. Training develops people's communication skills, use of theory, teaching skills, and team work. Training is typically done with smaller groups and is more individually based.

Process Analysis Speeches. This type of informative speech tells the audience how to do something (a process). In the introduction of the speech explain why the process is important to your audience and what steps you will be covering. In the body of the speech explain the steps of the process. Make sure the audience is following what you are saying and can ask questions if they become confused. If you lose your audience at one of the steps, the remaining process steps will most likely not make sense either. Review the steps briefly in the conclusion.

Demonstrations. Frequently speakers are asked to show groups of others how to do something. These how-to speeches are focused on providing others with information about a particular activity or object. Cooking shows provide an excellent forum for demonstration speeches. Typically, the demonstration lasts only a few minutes; any longer than that and the instructions may appear too complicated and overwhelming.

Presenting News (Good versus Bad). When good or bad events or information affects an organization, someone must be the messenger. There are different strategies to present important information based on what type of information it is.

Briefings. Often people are asked to inform others on a certain action that needs to take place. This kind of informative speech is known as a briefing. A briefing specifically focuses information and analysis on what the receiver needs to know immediately. For instance, if a tornado hits East Lansing, it is likely that news broadcasters and journalists will be asked to brief the locals.

Reports. If you have not experienced presenting reports, you certainly will before you graduate from college! Often as students and professionals we are asked to report on information that we know well. For example, in the Department of Communication at Michigan State University, an in-depth study of talk shows was completed (Greenberg et al., 1995). After this research was completed, the primary researchers were asked to travel all over the country presenting the results. They were even asked to attend the New York Talk Show Summit!

Small Groups. Presenting to a small group occurs at work, in volunteering, in school, and in the home. Often small groups are casual, but some work groups can be more formal. It helps your small group audience if you provide an agenda of your presentation for them to follow and take notations on.

Conventions and Conferences. Professionals give presentations on their area of specialty and participate in panel discussions at conventions and conferences in their field.

Sales Presentations. These speeches are designed to sell a product or skill. There are two types of these speeches: direct and indirect.

Speaking to Other Cultural or International Groups. When speaking to an international audience, it is important to be aware of the cultural expectations and language issues of the audience. Violating a cultural norm could offend your audience and make them hostile to your information. If a translator is involved, be aware that some words do not cleanly translate and that can hinder understanding.

Retirement Speeches. When you retire from a position, often there is a party in your honor. Retirement speeches are given by the person retiring and as toasts by the guests about the person retiring.

Civic Speeches

Dedications. This type of speech is where one dedicates a ship, building, park, statue, etc. This type of speech is important in establishing community relationships and a sense of belonging to the community members.

Nominations. These are speeches where you nominate someone for a position or office.

Installation Ceremonies. This speech formally installs individuals into positions or offices.

Elections. This is a persuasive type of speech, where the goal is to get yourself or the one you are speaking in support of elected into a public office.

Appeal for Funds. This is a speech that asks for money from the audience for your group or organization.

Court Testimony. As a witness in a trial or hearing, the goal of this form of speaking is to give facts and evidence which judges, lawyers, and juries can use to make decisions.

Incident Reports. Incident reports are given when you witness an event first hand.

Impromptu. Speeches given on the spot without much preparation are called impromptu speeches. Impromptu speeches occur in many contexts, such as in business meetings or community meetings or religious meetings. Many times in response to a discussion, individuals are compelled to add their opinions in the form of a speech. Since it is more of a "heat of the moment" situation, little preparation has been done.

Activism or Religious. Speeches which are said to drum up excitement for a political issue or belief or religion fall in this category. Often the speaker's goal is to persuade the audience to support their cause, be it political or religious.

Debate. There are many forms of debate: policy, Lincoln-Douglas, and parliamentary. There are public speaking competitions in these types of debate and real world applications of the techniques. Policy debate discusses the means and ends of policy choices. Lincoln-Douglas debate is a one versus one format that debates issues. This form of debate is usually found in campaigning. Parliamentary debate is done with the rules of parliament and can be found in many governing bodies. A critical term in all debate is "clash", which means that the arguments being made are in response to each other. Poor quality debates are between two sides which never directly refute each other. To avoid this, take notes during your opponents' speeches and answer all of the arguments made.

Personal Speeches

Graduation Speeches. These speeches are presented at graduation ceremonies.

Eulogies. This type of speech is given in praise of a person. Usually eulogies are given or written in event of someone's death, but they can be given any time someone is being honored.

Happy Birthday or Anniversary. These are specific toasts given in honor of birthday or anniversary of a person. Cake is usually involved.

Toasts. Toasts are given at special events, usually when there is a meal or drink involved in the special occasion.

Roasts. Roasts are given in honor of someone. They usually are dinner parties. People give humorous speeches about the guest of honor, "roasting" them over the hot coals of embarrassment.

Entertaining Speeches

Narratives and Storytelling. Narratives are stories told in the first person. Not all stories are told from that perspective. There are many opportunities to tell stories: campfire, parties, with friends, as an attention getter for a speech, to children, to explain a concept.

Dramatic Interpretation. Acting selections from plays, prose, and poetry in public is a form of dramatic interpretation.

Lectures. Frequently, when people become very adept at what they do they are asked to lecture others on it. As a college student you are asked to listen to lectures nearly every day. Lectures commonly employ the use of visual aids, such as slides, movies, and graphs. In addition, lectures are more likely to make use of interaction with the audience and conversational speaking styles. Finally, lectures sometimes combine question and answer periods.

INTO THE WORLD YOU GO

This chapter has provided a summary taste of how to inform and persuade using ethical public speaking, tips to deal with the fear of public speaking, how to research and cite evidence, considerations of an effective speech, tips for delivering a speech, and a list of different speeches you might encounter. We encourage you to seek more information about this important area and be thoughtful when you speak. If you live and speak with integrity, implication, passion, and skill you will have great success in your endeavors. Use these skills wisely. Good luck.

REFERENCES

Adler, R. B. & Rodman, G. (1994). Understanding human communication. (5th ed.). New York: Harcourt Brace.

Burgoon, J. K., Buller, D. B., & Woodall, W. G. (1989). Nonverbal communication: The unspoken dialogue. New York: Harper & Row.

Greenberg, B. S., Smith, S. W., Ah Yun, K., Busselle, R., Rampoldi-Hnilo, L., Mitchell, M. M., Sherry, J. (1995). The content of television talk shows: Topics, guests and interactions. Executive Report, Kaiser Foundation: Menlo, CA.

Kearney, P. & Plax, T. G. (1996). Public speaking in a diverse society. Mountain View, CA: Mayfield Publishing Company.

Lucas, S. E. (1992). The art of public speaking (4th ed.). New York: McGraw-Hill.

Lucas, S. E. (1998). The art of public speaking (6th ed.). New York: McGraw-Hill.

Lumsden, G. & Lumsden, D. (1996). Communicating with credibility and confidence. Wadsworth: Belmont, CA.

Montalbo, T. (1984). The power of eloquence: Magic key to success in public speaking. Englewood Cliffs, NJ: Prentice-Hall.

Osborn, M. & Osborn, S. (1994). Public speaking (3rd ed.). Geneva, IL: Houghton Mifflin.

Rozakis, L. (1999). Public Speaking (2nd. ed.). New York: Macmillan.

Rybacki, K.C. & Rybacki, D.J. (1996). Advocacy and Opposition: An introduction to argumentation (3rd ed.). Needham Heights, MA: Allyn and Bacon.

Verderber, R. F. (1996). Communicate! (8th ed.). Belmont, CA: Wadsworth.

Workbook

Leslie M. Deatrick
University of Oklahoma

Alysa A. Lucas
Pennsylvania State University

Lisa L. Massi Lindsey
Centers for Disease Control and Prevention

Monique M. Turner
University of Maryland

Homework Assignments 361

Speech Materials 369

    Informative Speech 369

    Persuasive Speech 377

Working Toward Good Study Habits 385

Key Terms/Concepts 389

Chapter Exercises 397

Section Leader Activity Profile Evaluations 427

Homework Assignments

Personal Goals: Part One

PURPOSE OF ASSIGNMENT:

This assignment is designed for students to identify what aspects of their own communication they would like to improve, and to tie class content to future goals.

Requirements:

Write at least ONE page assessing your personal goals for the semester as a public speaker. Your response should contain answers to the following:

1. In which areas of communication (public speaking, interpersonal communication, group communciation, organizational communication) do you think you need the most improvement and why?

2. What aspects of your public speaking would you like to improve? Perhaps you simply want to be more comfortable in front of an audience, or maybe you want to improve your eye contact or speak at a slower pace. Please identify two or three things you'd like to improve.

3. Indicate two benefits you expect to attain in your academic, professional, or personal life as a result of improvement in these areas of communication?

This assignment should be typed and double-spaced. Hand-written assignments will not be accepted. Please include on the paper:

Your Name
Your Section number
Your SL's name

Grading:

Graders will be looking for the following:

- Meets the requirements as listed above
- Answers the questions and provides insight
- Assignment is organized and clear
- No spelling or grammatical errors

This assignment is due:

Special Occasion Speech

PURPOSE OF ASSIGNMENT:

This assignment is designed to give the students experience writing and presenting a small, informal speech that students may be asked to give at some point in their lives. Further, the goal of this assignment is to get students more comfortable presenting in front of other people.

Requirements:

Students will select ONE type of Special Occasion speech to present in their small recitation section. Speeches that meet the criterion include: toasts, eulogies, introductions, or nominations. Please see next page for speech descriptions.

Students will turn in a complete manuscript of their Special Occasion speech. Note: The student MUST bring an extra copy if they want to speak using the written speech as their final version is due at the beginning of recitation.

Limit your speech to 1 1/2-2 minutes. One point will be deducted for speaking under or over the time limit.

This assignment should be typed and double-spaced. Hand-written assignments will not be accepted. Please include on the paper:

> Your Name
> Your Section number
> Your SL's name

Grading:

- Graders will be looking for the following:
- Meets requirements listed above
- Clear distinction of type and topic
- Word choice
- Effective eye contact, body movement, volume, rate, use of space and within time limits

This assignment is due:

Special Occasion Speech
Speech Description

Toasts: These are used for momentous occasions such as weddings, birth of a baby, reunion of friends, successful business ventures, and anniversaries. The toasts can be personal or generic, are usually accompanied by raising glasses, and are generally short.

Eulogies: Speeches that deliver tribute when someone has died. The speaker should mention unique achievements of person to whom you are paying tribute AND to express loss. Further, the speaker should turn to living and encourage them to transcend their sorrow, sense of loss, and instead to feel gratitude that the dead had once been among them.

Note: Eulogies can be about self, pet, famous person, or family member.

Nominations: Nominations involve noting the occasion and significance of award, office, etc. The speaker should explain clearly why the nominee's skills, talents, and past achievements serve as qualifications for the award or position.

Introductions: An introduction is similar to an informative speech. The purpose is to provide the audience with information about the speaker and to ultimately, trigger interest in the speaker. The main elements include gaining attention of the audience, building the speaker's credibility, and introducing the speaker's subject.

Note: Both nominations and introductions should be about a real person, but they can be a famous person or a person you know personally.

Other Elements:

- Special Occasion speeches may be formal or informal so the word choice and language should fit accordingly. For example, some slang may be appropriate in a toast, but not in a nomination. However, the entire audience should be able to follow the speech and not be offended.

- Think about the characteristics of the audience when writing this speech. The people in the audience may affect the way you write and present the speech. For example, parents and grandparents would be present at a wedding so stories about drinking or other controversial topics may not be appropriate in a toast.

PRO/CON Speech

PURPOSE OF ASSIGNMENT:

This assignment is designed to research a current controversial issue, to respond in an argumentative format to a controversial issue, and to practice parts of the Toulmin Model of Argumentation.

Requirements:

Students will work in pairs to formulate a PRO and CON stance on a controversial issue. One student will present the PRO stance and the other student will present the CON stance. Please note: only one student will present each PRO and CON stance on each controversial issue. There will be no duplicate speeches in a small section.

Students can work together to discuss the PRO/CON stances to the controversial issue, but the grading for each student will be independent from each other.

Write a **full text** written speech in response to the controversial issue selected.

Follow the Toulmin Model of Argumentation presented to you in recitation by your TA.

Limit your speech to 1 1/2 to 2 minutes. One point will be deducted for speaking over or under the time limit.

This assignment should be typed and should follow the format described below. Hand-written assignments will not be accepted. Please include on the paper:

> Your Name
> Your Section number
> Your SL's name

Cite TWO sources that informed your speech in the actual text of the speech and on a References page. See the APA Style Guide or your TA. After each source, write a Test of Evidence you think the source/evidence meets and WHY you think it meets this requirement of credibility. Refer to chapter 16 in your textbook for a list of Tests of Evidence.

Format:

Give a thesis statement (your PRO or CON stance)

Give two reasons why the thesis statement is true:

Argument 1

1. Provide a Claim
2. Provide a Grounds for the Claim (a piece of evidence or example to support thesis statement)
3. Provide a Warrant (a reason for why once you know the Grounds, you can logically assume the Claim)

Give a transition statement.

Argument 2

1. Provide a Claim
2. Provide a Grounds for the Claim (a piece of evidence or example to support thesis statement)
3. Provide a Warrant (a reason for why once you know the Grounds, you can logically assume the Claim)

Summarize your original thesis statement.

Possible PRO/CON Topics:

1. Free parking ought to be available to students.
2. All students should have to complete a senior thesis to graduate.
3. The United States was justified in going to war in Iraq.
4. The death penalty should be legalized in all states.
5. Marijuana use should be legalized.
6. Abortion should be banned.
7. Campus noise violators should be given lighter punishments.

Grading:

Grader will be looking for:

- Meets requirements as listed above
- Follows format listed above
- Two sources are cited and includes Tests of Evidence
- Argument is clear and concise
- Word choice and appropriate presentation of a controversial topic
- Effective eye contact, body movement, volume, rate, use of space and within time limits

This assignment is due:

Personal Goals: Part Two

PURPOSE OF ASSIGNMENT:

This assignment is designed for students to assess the goals they met over the semester and what goals they may work on in the future.

Requirements:

Write at least one page about how you feel your communication skills have improved over the course of the semester. Please answer the following questions:

1. What is the most important information about communication that you will take away from either lecture or recitation?
2. Did you improve in the areas of communication you felt that you needed the most improvement? How?
3. Considering the second question on your original personal goals statement, what improvements did you make in your public speaking communication skills? Comment on the improvements you saw in your public speaking across the semester.
4. What improvements in your public speaking skills will you continue to make as you continue to develop your speaking ability?

This assignment should be typed and double-spaced. Hand-written assignments will not be accepted. Please include on the paper:

Your Name
Your Section number
Your SL's name

Grading:

Graders will be looking for the following:

- Meets the requirements as listed above
- Answers the questions and provides insight
- Assignment is organized and clear
- No spelling or grammatical errors

This assignment is due:

Media Analysis

PURPOSE OF ASSIGNMENT:

This assignment is designed to challenge students to critically analyze the role of the media in daily life.

Requirements:

Please select ONE of the following concepts from lecture and/or textbook to analyze through the lens of the media:

1. Gender Roles
2. Relationship Values
3. Conflict
4. Culture
5. Decision-making
6. Self-concept (i.e., body image)

Please choose ONE of the following media outlets in which to analyze the chosen concept:

TV, film, magazine, advertising, music, books, Internet, or video games

Turn in at least ONE page written analysis. Please indicate in the analysis what media (i.e., TV, film) and what type of specific media (i.e., "Friends," Maxim magazine, or *Pirates of the Caribbean,* etc.). Answer the following questions:

1. What specifically are we learning through the media regarding your chosen concept?
2. Are there benefits for the audience learning this concept through the media?
3. Are there problems with the audience learning this concept through the media?

Attach a copy of any article, advertisement, web site, book excerpt, etc. used in the analysis or include a detailed account of examples, lyrics, or parts of script.

This assignment should be typed and double-spaced. Hand-written assignments will not be accepted. Please include on the paper:

Your Name
Your Section number
Your SL's name

Grading:

Graders will be looking for the following:
- Meets the requirements as listed above
- Answers the questions and provides insight
- Assignment is organized and clear
- No spelling or grammatical errors

This assignment is due:

Speech Materials

Informative Speech: Tell Us about Your Hometown or Home State

PURPOSE OF ASSIGNMENT:

This assignment is designed to help students inform an audience about something unique to them, which will help build rapport between the speaker and the audience. Also, students will have an opportunity to improve skills in speaking before a small group of people.

Topic:

Students will select an interesting or unique characteristic of their hometown or home state to inform their audience about. For example, someone from the Upper Penninsula of Michigan could talk about copper mines, interesting tourist attractions, or unusual wildlife unlikely to be seen in other parts of Michigan.

Requirements:

Each student will complete a written speech outline and a 4-6 minute in-class speech.

The speech outline must follow the format shown in the textbook and it must be typed. Hand-written outlines will not be accepted.

There should be **at least** TWO references cited in the outline and speech. The reference page must follow APA style. See the APA Style guide or your TA.

Note: Students must turn in a copy of the outline to their TAs prior to giving their speech. An additional copy of the outline may be used during the delivery of the speech.

Grading:

Please review the grading forms for the requirements.

This assignment is due:

COMMUNICATION 100—INFORMATIVE SPEECH GUIDELINES

THIS IS WHAT YOUR OUTLINE SHOULD LOOK LIKE
(The things that are bold are what you should actually have on your outline)

Your name and Section #

Title: Be Creative!

Topic: What is your speech about—this can be very brief (e.g., Wildlife in the Upper Penninsula of Michigan). Make sure you cleared your topic with your SL.

Purpose Statement: To inform my audience about . . .

Audience Analysis: You will have about two sentences per sub-point (A., B., C., D.) here. *The rest of the speech will have only one complete sentence per point.* In your audience analysis always include WHY the fact is relevant to your speech.

- **A. Demographics.** Describe the characteristics of your audience. How will your speech be affected by the demographics of your audience?
- **B. Psychographics.** Describe the biases, knowledge level, mood, for example: sex, age, ethnic background, group memberships, etc. and goals/need/wants of your audience. How will these factors affect your speech?
- **C. Verbal Considerations.** Describe the verbal considerations you will need to make, specific to your speech and audience. Why will you make these changes?
- **D. Nonverbal Considerations.** Describe the nonverbal considerations you will need to make, specific to your speech and audience. Why will you make these changes?

I. **INTRODUCTION:** No actual sentence needed here.
   - **A. Attention getter:** Write what you intend to say to get your audience's attention. Examples: story, fact, startling statement.
   - **B. Thesis Statement:** this should be a clear and specific rewording of your purpose statement.
   - **C. Preview the main points:** Tell us what three or four main points you will be making in your speech.
     1. Main point 1
     2. Main point 2
     3. Main point 3

Connective: Insert a statement linking your introduction to the body of the speech.

II. **BODY:** No sentence needed here
   A. First main point-remember only one sentence.
      1. Sub-point (You can use a definition, an example, or evidence to support your main point.) Be sure to cite your sources in your sub-points.
      2. Sub-point. Don't forget that these need to be complete sentences. The second sub-point could be an example.

Connective: Insert a comment linking your first main point to your second main point.

   B. Your second main point goes here.
      1. Just like in A (could be a definition).
      2. Could be an example like in A.

Connective: Insert a comment linking your second main point to your third main point.

   C. The last main point
      1. Again, complete sentences describing the main point
      2. Your final sub-point

Connective: Insert a comment linking the body of your speech to the conclusion.

III. **CONCLUSION**—no sentence needed here
   A. Restatement of Thesis
   B. Summary of main points
   C. Closing statement: wrap up your speech with a memorable point- you could refer to your attention getter, or use a story, fact, quote to end your speech.

Be sure to include your reference page, correctly formatted in APA style.

WHAT TO REMEMBER FOR YOUR SPEECH

1. **You should have three main points—remember to use a pattern that makes sense when you organize them. (Ex: if you are talking about something chronological, keep events in order.)**

2. **Your speech needs to be 4-6 minutes so plan to speak for 5 minutes. Anything less than four minutes or more than six minutes will be penalized.**

3. **Your outline must be typed or it won't be accepted.**

4. **Remember to bring your grading forms on speech day- all your grading forms are in the textbook. You will lose 10 points from your speech for failure to bring your grading forms on the day of your speech.**

5. Make sure to practice your speech. You will be more nervous than you think on the day of your speech!!

6. If you need help be sure to contact your TA or SL before the speech. We are here to help!!

Persuasive Speech: Support a Cause

PURPOSE OF ASSIGNMENT:

This speech assignment is designed to help students learn about presenting to a group through a persuasive format.

Topic:

This speech focuses on persuading the audience to join a group or complete some request made by a group.

For example, the Humane Society might persuade people to donate money or Locks for Love may encourage people to cut their hair as a donation to the organization. Perhaps the National Organization for Women encourages an audience to become members of their group or to support some critical issue.

Requirements:

Each student will complete: a speech outline with a reference page, a relevant visual aid, and a 5-7 minute speech in front of their small recitation section.

The speech outline MUST be in the Monroe's Motivated Sequence format as discussed in recitation and in Chapter 16 of the textbook.

The speech outline MUST be typed and the visual aid must look professional. No hand-written outlines will be accepted.

There should be at least FIVE references cited in the outline and speech. The reference page must follow APA style. See the APA Style guide or your TA.

Grading:

Please review the grading forms for the requirements.

The assignment is due:

COMMUNICATION 100— PERSUASIVE SPEECH GUIDELINES

THIS IS WHAT YOUR OUTLINE SHOULD LOOK LIKE

(The things that are bold are what you should actually have on your outline)

Your name and Section #

Title: Provide a short title for your speech. (e.g., "Give Life, Give Blood")

Topic: List the non-profit organization and the issue (e.g., The American Red Cross, blood shortage).

Purpose Statement: Your purpose in this speech is to persuade. You need to provide once sentence here that describes the action you want your audience to take. (e.g, Please donate money or blood to your local Red Cross.)

Audience Analysis: You will have about two sentences per sub-point (A., B., C., D.) here. The rest of the speech will have only one complete sentence per point. In your audience analysis always include WHY the fact is relevant to your speech.

   A. **Demographics.** Describe the characteristics of your audience. How will your speech be affected by the demographics of your audience?
   B. **Psychographics.** Describe the biases, knowledge level, mood and goals/need/wants of your audience. How will these factors affect your speech?
   C. **Verbal Considerations.** Describe the verbal considerations you will need to make, specific to your speech and audience. Why will you make these changes?
   D. **Nonverbal Considerations.** Describe the nonverbal considerations you will need to make, specific to your speech and audience. Why will you make these changes?

I. **INTRODUCTION:** No actual sentence needed here.
   A. **Attention getter:** Write something catchy to interest the audience. (e.g., a startling statistic, a personal narrative, a joke, etc.)
   B. **Thesis Statement:** this should be a clear and specific rewording of your purpose statement.
   C. **Preview Statement:** (e.g., "Specifically, I am going to discuss...")
      1. You need a sentence describing your *need/problem step*. (This is the cause of the organization)
      2. You need a sentence describing your *satisfaction/solution and action steps* (This is the request.)

In the informative speech outline above, we would like the insertions to be formatted this way.

II. **Need/Problem Step:** You need one sentence here that summarizes the cause of the organization. You are going to have to provide two good arguments and/or statements about the problem the group is trying to solve.
   A. **Main Point #1**
      1. Sub-point. (You can use a definition, an example, or evidence to support your main point.) Be sure to cite your sources in your sub-points.
      2. Sub-point. Don't forget that these need to be complete sentences. The second sub-point could be an example.

Transition Sentence.
   B. **Main Point #2**
      1. Just like in A (could be a definition).
      2. Could be an example like in A.

Transition Sentence.
   C. **Main Point #3**
      1. Again, complete sentences describing the main point.
      2. Your final sub-point.

Transition Sentence.

III. **Satisfaction/Solution: Satisfaction/Solution Step:** You need one statement summarizing your solution. You will have two general suggestions for audience action. Give an overview of an organization working to solve the problem described in the need step. Tell us when they were founded, by whom they were founded, and why they are interested in this problem.
   A. **Suggestion #1** for how to help the organization (e.g., you should donate blood every chance you get.)
   B. **Suggestion #2** for how to help the organization (e.g. financially support the Red Cross with a donation each year.)

Transition Sentence.

IV. **Visualization Step:** Write one sentence motivating your audience to act on the issue. Describe benefits the audience will receive from action.

Transition Sentence.

V. **Action/Conclusion Step:**
   A. Make a specific request that the audience can do today. (e.g., sign a petition, take membership information home, donate money—but don't actually collect it...)
   B. **Summary of Main Points:** Name the organization again and the two main points of the problem/cause.

C. **Implication Statement:** Explain how the main points prove why the cause is important enough to warrant action.
D. **Closing Statement:** Finish with a wrap-up statement that ties into your attention grabber.

WHAT TO REMEMBER FOR YOUR PERSUASIVE SPEECH

- The student must use the Monroe's Motivated Sequence format (Attention, Need, Satisfaction, Visualization and Action).

- The outline must be typed or it will not be accepted.

- Bring extra outlines to speak from (if needed).

- The outline must be at least one page (not including the reference page).

- There must be at least FIVE sources in the outline. They must be cited in your outline correctly. See example handout, APA Style Guide, or ask your TA.

- Be creative and try to use emotional, logical, and credibility appeals in the speech. See chapter 16 of your textbook for more information.

- The speech must be 5-7 minutes. There will be penalty going over or under the time limit. The best way to avoid penalty is to practice, practice, and more practice.

- The tabs and indents should look identical to this outline. Suggestion: Turn off auto-formatting on Word or Works.

- PROOFREAD! Points will be deducted for spelling and grammatical errors.

Study Guide

WORKING TOWARD GOOD STUDY HABITS

The number one reason why students test poorly in their courses is poor study habits. Often, when students come to our offices and look at their old exams, we hear comments such as "I didn't think of the question that way," "I didn't think we had to know that," or "I just read that, but didn't study it." Therefore, we decided to put together this compilation of ways to improve your study habits, not just for this class, but throughout your college career.

I. **Don't just read the chapter; take notes on it.**

   Often, people think that by just reading a chapter they are learning it. Although this may be true at times, it isn't in general. When reading through your chapter, I suggest this:

   A. Write out all of the definitions for bolded, highlighted, or italicized terms. More than likely, you'll need to know them.

   B. Write out an outline of the chapter; sometimes by seeing how the chapter was arranged it is more obvious what the author was getting at.

II. **Study in groups if possible.**

   Although I've heard from different students that studying in groups is either good or bad, I generally feel that it facilitates learning. Here's why:

   A. You'll be less likely to miss a certain topic/ definition, etc. when put more than one head to it.

   B. When you discuss the topics, you may sometimes discover a discrepancy between what you think a topic means and what our peers think it means. This will alert you that you need to ask your T.A. about it.

   C. When you study in a group, there is more pressure to study. It is much easier to blow off studying when you're the only person you're letting down.

III. **Teach the concepts to each other.**

   You may be saying "teach this? I am not the teacher, you are . . . " The reason I suggest this is because when you have to explain a subject to another student it forces you to understand the topic. Here are some suggestions:

- A. Come up with real life examples, similar to the ones your instructor uses. When you do this, you'll be more prepared for the exam because application questions are often used.

- B. If you are confused about a topic, choose to teach it to your friend; that way you have to try to sort it out. If you can't, you'll realize you need to ask about it. Maybe your friend will understand it and can help explain.

IV. Make flash cards.

Flashcards are very handy because they are brief, to the point, and can be taken anywhere. Here's how to make them effective:

- A. Every concept, definition, etc., should get a card.

- B. Simply write the concept on the front of the card and the definition on the back.

- C. Take the cards with you to your classes; flip through them before class. Flip through them while walking to class, during commercials, or when you are relaxing.

V. Take notes on more than just the overhead.

I often see people put down their pencil in class when examples are being given. This can be detrimental because examples are what help you apply the concepts to your life. Also, you may see those examples again, so if you do not remember them, how can you answer them correctly on the exam? Here are some suggestions:

- A. When examples are being given, write down the ones that make the most sense to you.

- B. If you miss the example because someone was speaking too quickly, ask a peer or the instructor after class.

- C. If you aren't sure how a certain example applies, ask.

VI. Use mnemonic devices.

Some of you are probably wondering why you would ever use a mnemonic device—some of you most likely do not know what they are, but I guarantee that they will help some of you. They are in most simple form made up words or sayings that will help you remember things for class. For example, if you needed to remember a list of animals, maybe "dog, cat, elephant, iguana," you could use the phrase "Dan could eat ice-cream." This phrase is easy to recall.

Dog: Dan

Cat: could
Elephant: eat
Iguanas: ice-cream

VII. Don't study where there is a lot of background noise.

Many of you may study in front of the TV, and although you may say that you've been doing it for years, research has shown that those who study with background noise do much worse than those who study in silence. Study in a comfortable place where you will be able to concentrate.

HOW TO USE STUDY GUIDES

To improve your performance in class each week, we have designed study guides for each chapter. The study guide for each chapter has two parts—Word Power and Communication Concepts.

Word Power is a listing of words that are used in the textbook chapter that may not be familiar to you, especially in the context in which they are being used. That is, the word itself might be familiar but you've never thought about it in the way it is utilized. Therefore, it is important that you clearly understand these words. When you look at Word Power words, and find words that you cannot easily define, you should look them up in a dictionary. You should do this before you read the chapter. This may help you on the exams, because some of these words may be used in exam items.

Communication Concepts is a list of the major ideas from the textbook chapter. After you have read the chapter, look at the Communication Concepts list. You should be able to define and explain each concept on the list. (Note: this list is not exhaustive; it does not contain all concepts, but it is a useful sampling of ideas from the chapter). If you read a chapter, then discover that you do not know all of the concepts in list, then you will know that you need to study the chapter more intensely.

We hope that you enjoy reading this text and find these study guides useful. They are intended as an aid to your independent studying efforts.

Key Terms/Concepts

Chapter One

Word Power
Psychological
Interference
Ambiguous
Biases
Arbitrary
The Global Village

Communication Concepts
Respect, Preparation, and Control
Connection
Information Exchange
Encode
Noise
Feedback
Channels
Messages
Impact
Influence, Information Exchange, Meaning, and Symbolic Language

Chapter Two

Word Power
Congregate
Morse Code
Phonemcs
Morpheme
Indexing
Pragmatic
Arbitrary

Communication Concepts
Inherited Communication
Learned Communication
Phonemic
Semantic Rules
Morpheme
Indexing
Pragmatic
Speech Act Theory
Norms
Characteristics of Language
Connotations and Denotations
Coordinated Management of Meaning
Semantic Triangle
Symbolic Interactionism
Speech Community Theory
Language Intensity
Sapir Whorf Hypothesis
Sexism
"I" statements
Language and Accountability
Language and Clarity
Code Switching
Communication Accomodation Theory
Effective Communication

Workbook **389**

Chapter Three

Word Power
Androgyny
Sociological
Schema
Extrovert
Inference
Physiological

Communication Concepts
Selective Exposure
Input Processing
Stages of, and Guidelines for Input Processing
Output Processing
Stages of, and Guidelines for Output Processing
Communication Plans
Social Cognition
Gender
Biological Sex
Selective Attention
Decoding
Communication Plans

Chapter Four

Word Power
Subjective
Residual
Validation
Psychodynamic

Communication Concepts
Self Concept
Self Esteem
Roles and Self Concept Development
Residual self
Social Learning Theory
Cognitive Development Theory
Self Monitoring
Culture, Roles, and Family
Gender Development

Chapter Five

Word Power
Paradigm
Consummate
Synchronous
Differentiating
Stagnation
Novelty

Communication Concepts
Types of Families:
    Closed
    Random
    Synchronous
    Open
Distinctions of Friendship
Sternberg's Triangular Theory of Love
Types of Marital Relationships:
    Independents
    Separates
    Traditionals
    Mixed
Stages of Intimate Relationships
Kinds of Lovers
Predictors of Relational Success
Reasons to Form Interpersonal Relationships
Johari Window
Altman and Taylor's Social Penetration Model

Chapter Six

Word Power
Socialization
Facilitating
Normative
Imparting
Cognitive
Solidarity
Inculcating
Sequential
Disjunctive
Investiture
Divestiture
Erroneous

Communication Concepts
Social Roles
Knowledge, Ability, and Motivation
Agents of Socialization
Contextual Strategies
Outcomes of Socialization
Peripheral Tasks
Disjunctive Socialization

Chapter Seven

Word Power
Compensation
Inevitable
Attributional

Communication Concepts
Conflict
    about Values
    about Beliefs
    about Resources
Interdependency
Benefits of Conflict
Drawbacks of Conflict
Stages of Conflict
Singular Perspective
Hidden Linkages

Chapter Eight

Word Power
Paradox
Languid
Ethnocentrism
Collectivism
Polychronic
Monochromic
Rival Hypothesis
Avoidance
Cognitive Dissonance
Accommodation
Convergence
Divergence

Communication Concepts
Culture
Intercultural Communication
Stages of Adjustment
Culture Shock / Culture Re-entry Shock
Group Orientation
Individualism and Collectivism
Power Distance
Tests of Culture
Uncertainty, Interaction, and Power Orientation
In-group versus Out-group
Uncertainty Avoidance
Uncertainty Apprehension
Host versus Home Culture
Low and High Context Culture
Negative and Positive Face
Implicit Personality Theory
Independent Self-Construal
Interdependent Self-Construal
Universalist Theories
Indigenous Theories
Integrationist Theories

Chapter Nine

Word Power
Volition
Coercion
Affective
Consonant
Dissonant

Communication Concepts
Persuasion
Attitudes
Beliefs
Behaviors
Balance Theory
Cognitive Dissonance Theory
Source Effects:
    1. Credibility
    2. Likability
    3. Ethos
    4. Pathos
Mere Exposure
Learning and Reinforcement
Contagion
Emotional Appeals
Motivational Appeals
Message Composition

Chapter Ten

Word Power
Reciprocity

Communication Concepts
Basic Management Models
    Holding Company
    Strategy and Oversight
    Active Leader Involvement
    Command and Control
Communication Structure
    Upward, Downward, Horizontal
Communication Links
Communication Roles
Network Analysis
Liaison
Rules
Coordination
Leadership

Chapter Eleven

Word Power	Communication Concepts
Inevitable	Ringelman Effect
Modified	Diffusion of Responsibility
Emergent	Additive Tasks
Duality	Intellective Tasks
Unitary	Eureka Tasks
Contingencies	Demonstrable Tasks
Implicit	Expert Judgment Tasks
	Stages of Decision Making
	Duality of Structure
	Abilene Paradox

Chapter Twelve

Word Power	Communication Concepts
Inextricable	Components of Leadership
Ambiguous	Distinctions of Leaders
Subsequently	Assumed Similarity of Opposites (ASO)
	Idiosyncrasy Credits
	Situational Characteristics
	1. favorable
	2. unfavorable
	3. moderately favorable

Chapter Thirteen

Word Power	Communication Concepts
Innovations	Diffusion
Advantageous	Paradigm
	Innovators
	Early Adopters
	Early Majority
	Late Majority
	Laggards
	Pro innovation bias
	Economic advantage
	Compatibility
	Complexity
	Reactions to Innovations
	Stages of Diffusion

Chapter Fourteen

Word Power
Arousal
Physiological
Decoding
Dissemination
Cultivation

Communication Concepts
Six Stages of Mass Communication
Four Types of Effects
Five Trends on Violence on Television
Three Harmful Effects of Exposure to TV Violence
Social Cognitive Theory
Four Sub Functions of Observational Learning
Priming Effects Theory
Three Cognitive Effects of Priming Theory
Cultivation Theory
Mainstreaming
Resonance

Chapter Fifteen

Word Power
Cognitive
Acquisition

Communication Concepts
Pseudo Events
Cumulative Acquisition
Intrinsic Interest
Relevance
Two-Step Flow
Opinion Leader
Opinion Sharing
Agenda Setting
Cultivation
Status Conferral
Low Involvement
Boomerang Effect

Chapter Exercises

Chapter Two

Meanings Are in People, Not in Words

It is important to realize that in lieu of roots, stems, and Latin and Greek derivations, the meanings of words are highly symbolic and arbitrary. One lesson to be learned is that the meaning of any word lies within the individual and his/her experience.

The goal of this exercise is to see how one word can bring many meanings to many people. Your UTA will write a word on the board within your quadrant. After the word has been written, each student will write down what that word brings to his/her mind. After all the words have been written, the class will discuss individual meanings and how they differ among individuals.

Potential words:

Love	_____
Freedom	_____
Dog	_____
Dope	_____

Try to come up with other words you believe would work in this exercise and discuss them with your classmates. Try and understand why there were so many meanings for the same word.

Chapter Three

Conversation Scripts

Chapter three teaches us how social knowledge and schemas work to affect our lives. In this exercise you will work with a partner developing a conversation script. Write the dialogue for a "typical" conversation that you would expect to hear in one of the following situations. Write down what each person in the "conversation" would say, as it would appear in a transcript.

Situations:

1. A conversation between a man and a woman who are strangers to each other, and are studying in a cafe. Imagine that the man is interested in the woman.
2. A conversation between a parent and an adult child who has just come home on college break.
3. A conversation between co-workers during a coffee break.
4. A conversation between a parent and the new date that a teenage child has brought home.
5. A conversation between a boyfriend and a girlfriend, in a situation in which one of them suspects the other of having an affair.
6. A conversation between two people who are strangers to each other, but are trapped on an elevator during a power outage.

Choose two members of your group to role play the parts, reading your group's script to the class.

Questions to be answered and discussed following the role plays. These are based on information in chapter three.

1. What kinds of social knowledge did you use to determine what the conversation would be like?
2. What types of schema did you have to tap into in order to write the script?

Workbook

Chapter Four

Connecting to Develop the Self

This exercise is oriented at helping you look within yourself and monitor the amount of "I" or "Me" behavior (as learned in lecture) that you exhibit.

Students will be split into groups of 4 or 5. The instructor will give each group a copy of an excerpt from a talk show, a cartoon, a book, or some other form of media. One good example is the movie *Annie Hall* with Woody Allen.

Read the transcript, and among the group assign each other roles to play. For your role, read the dialog carefully and assess whether the character has a weak sense of "me," a weak sense of "I," both, or neither. Make sure you are able to defend your answer. Below, write down your answers to the above questions.

_____
_____
_____
_____
_____
_____
_____
_____

After you are finished with analyzing your character for "I" and "Me" behavior you will be asked to act out your scenario in front of your classmates.

If time allows, discuss the characters which clearly have a weak sense of "I" or "Me." Discuss how you know the individual has an "I" or "Me" issue and what strategies the individual(s) can use to overcome the problem.

Chapter Five

Connecting to Develop Relationships

The following scales tap into the amount of relational satisfaction you have in a romantic relationship and what kind of love style you use in this relationship. If you find that your relationship is very satisfied, think about what kind of love style you use and if it is consistent with your partner's. Likewise, if your relationship is unsatisfactory it may be an effect of inconsistent love styles. Have fun!!!

Relational Satisfaction Survey:

Most persons have disagreements in their relationships. Please indicate below the appropriate extent of agreement or disagreement between you and your partner for each item on the following list.

The scale is as follows:

    1 = Always agree
    2 = Almost always agree
    3 = Occasionally disagree
    4 = Frequently disagree
    5 = Always disagree

1.	Handling finances	1	2	3	4	5
2.	How to have fun	1	2	3	4	5
3.	Religious matters	1	2	3	4	5
4.	How to be affectionate	1	2	3	4	5
5.	Friends	1	2	3	4	5
6.	Sexual relations	1	2	3	4	5
7.	Proper ways of behavior	1	2	3	4	5
8.	Philosophy of life	1	2	3	4	5
9.	Dealing with parents (or in-laws)	1	2	3	4	5
10.	Aims, goals, and things considered important	1	2	3	4	5
11.	Amount of time spent together	1	2	3	4	5
12.	Making major decisions	1	2	3	4	5
13.	Household tasks	1	2	3	4	5
14.	Leisure time interests and activities	1	2	3	4	5

HOW TO SCORE THE RELATIONAL SATISFACTION SCALE:

Add your scores from questions 1–14 and divide that score by 14. This will give you your average score on how much you agree with your mate. *The lower your score, the better off you are!* If your score is a 1 or a 2, this indicates great amounts of agreement in your relationship. A score of a 3 indicates that you disagree at times, but there is no reason for alarm. A score of 4 or 5, however, indicates that there is much disagreement in your relationship.

LOVE STYLES PROFILE*

Place the number that best represents your attitude in the space next to each statement.

    1 = Strongly agree
    2 = Agree
    3 = Neutral
    4 = Disagree
    5 = Strongly disagree

_____ 1. My lover and I were attracted to each other immediately after we first met.

_____ 2. My lover and I have the right physical "chemistry" between us.

_____ 3. Our lovemaking is very intense and satisfying.

_____ 4. I feel that my lover and I were meant for each other.

_____ 5. My lover and I became emotionally involved very quickly.

_____ 6. My lover and I really understand each other.

_____ 7. My lover fits my ideal standards of physical attractiveness.

_____ 8. I try to keep my lover a little uncertain about my commitment to her/him.

_____ 9. I believe that what my lover doesn't know about me won't hurt her/him.

_____ 10. I have sometimes had to keep my lover from finding out about other lovers.

_____ 11. I could get over my love affair with my lover pretty easily and quickly.

_____ 12. My lover would get upset if s/he knew of some of the things I've done with other people.

_____ 13. When my lover gets too dependent on me, I want to back off a little.

_____ 14. I enjoy playing the "game of love" with my lover and a number of other partners.

_____ 15. It is hard for me to say exactly when our friendship turned into love.

_____ 16. To be genuine, our love first required caring for a while.

_____17. I expect to always be friends with my lover.

_____18. Our love is the best kind because it grew out of a long friendship.

_____19. Our friendship merged gradually into love over time.

_____20. Our love is really a deep friendship, not a mysterious, mystical emotion.

_____21. Our love relationship is the most satisfying because it developed from a good friendship.

_____22. I considered what my lover was going to become in life before I committed myself to her/him.

_____23. I tried to plan my life carefully before choosing a lover.

_____24. In choosing my lover, I believed it was best to love someone with a similar background.

_____25. A main consideration in choosing my lover was how s/he would reflect on my family.

_____26. An important factor in choosing my lover was whether or not s/he would be a good parent.

_____27. One consideration in choosing my lover was how s/he would reflect on my career.

_____28. Before getting very involved with my lover, I tried to figure out how compatible his/her hereditary background would be with mine in case we ever had children.

_____29. When things aren't right with my lover and me, my stomach gets upset.

_____30. If my lover and I break up, I would get so depressed that I would even think of suicide.

_____31. Sometimes I get so excited about being in love with my lover that I can't sleep.

_____32. When my lover doesn't pay attention to me, I feel sick all over.

_____33. Since I've been in love with my lover, I've had trouble concentrating on anything else.

_____34. I cannot relax if I suspect that my lover is with someone else.

_____35. If my lover ignores me for awhile, I sometimes do stupid things to get her/his attention back.

_____36. I try to always help my lover through difficult times.

_____37. I would rather suffer myself than let my lover suffer.

_____38. I cannot be happy unless I place my lover's happiness before my own.

_____39. I am usually willing to sacrifice my own wishes to let my lover achieve his/hers.

_____ 40. Whatever I own is my lover's to use as he or she sees fit.

_____ 41. When my lover gets angry with me, I still love her/him fully and unconditionally.

_____ 42. I would endure all things for the sake of my lover.

*Taken from Hendrick and Hendrick (1990a).

HOW TO SCORE THE LOVE STYLES PROFILE

Add your ratings for statements 1–7. This is your score for love of beauty or passionate love. Your total for statements 8–14 is your score for game-playing or playful love. Your total for statements 15–21 is your score for friendship or companionate love. Your total for statements 22–28 is your score for realistic love. Your total for statements 29–35 is your score for obsessive love. Your total for statements 36–42 is your score for altruistic love. Mark your total score for each of the six types of love in the space provided below. Next, read the accompanying description. In general, the lower your score, the more positive your attitude is toward that type of love. A score of 7 reflects strong positive attitudes; a score close to 35 reflects strong negative attitudes toward this type of love. *In fact, the love style with the lowest score is your overall love style.*

_____ **PASSIONATE LOVE** (score on statements 1–7):
Passionate love is an ideal love of beauty. It is intense, immediate, and powerful. It involves physical intimacy, touching, and emotional peaks and valleys.

_____ **PLAYFUL LOVE** (score on statements 8–14):
Playful love is a love of games. It involves challenging and conquering. The reward is winning the prize. The player tends to be confident and independent. The player also desires good times and may be lacking in commitment.

_____ **COMPANIONATE LOVE** (score on statements 15–21):
Companionate love is love that grows naturally and peacefully. It involves affection, friendship, stability, and predictability. Partners are less likely to be preoccupied with one another, and the relationship can become too dull.

_____ **REALISTIC LOVE** (score on statements 22–28):
Realistic love is love based on compatibility, practicality, planning, and logic. The role of feelings is minimized, and partners tend not to be able to adjust easily to changes.

_____ **OBSESSIVE LOVE** (score on statements 29–35):
Obsessive love is addictive love. The lover can be the object of dependency and manipulation. It is possessive, all consuming, and difficult to satisfy. It is characterized by high emotional peaks and valleys, and can generate pain and jealousy.

_____ **ALTRUISTIC LOVE** (score on statements 36–42):
Altruistic love is unselfish, patient, kind, generous, and reciprocal. An altruistic lover is rarely demanding, but too much concern for the other can become a relational problem as it can be stifling.

Chapter Seven Exercise

Trying to Keep Things under Control: Communication and Conflict Management

Although Chapter Seven does illustrate some of the negative effects of conflict, in general it is good and healthy to confront conflict and try to manage it. This exercise will help you hone your conflict management skills.

1. Think of the most recent conflict that you had and make a list of all the emotions you felt. For example, you might have felt angry, betrayed, disrespected or hurt. Why do you think you felt this way?

2. Think of how the conflict began and how it escalated. Try to remember with as much detail as possible and script the conflict episode on a separate piece of paper.

3. Now, think of all the potential emotions that the person you were in the conflict with might have felt. List them.

4. Why do you think that the person you were fighting with felt those emotions? Try your hardest to put yourself in his/her shoes. Try to make sense of the conflict from his or her point of view.

5. Your UTA will break up into pairs. Now, with your partner, reenact each other's conflict episode, but have your partner act out the part as YOU, and you act out the part of the person you actually fought with.

Often when we put ourselves in other people's shoes, it becomes easier to see why the conflict developed and how it might have been avoided. With your partner, discuss how you might better handle such a situation in the future.
Conflict Management 1

Chapter Eight

Appreciating Cultural Differences

This exercise illustrates the concept of stereotypes in intercultural communication. Often, when we have been stereotyped or have stereotyped others, it becomes difficult to accomplish the task at hand. Think of the stereotypes you may have about people from other cultures and how these may hinder your working with them.

Tools Needed:

1. Transparent tape
2. Marker
3. Construction paper

Instructions:

1. Break up into groups of five.
2. Assign each member of the group a job as described below. Each member is instructed to carry out his duty to the best of his knowledge.
3. Each member is to carry out his/her job while acting as he or she would in a normal committee meeting.
4. After each job has been assigned, give each member a different head band with labels on them. The other committee members are instructed to treat the member exactly as the headband states.

Committees:

1. The first member is the Top Manager (TM) of the committee. The TM is in charge of insuring each job is accomplished with precision and detail, and is also in charge of making sure the committee's decision is realistic and creative.
2. The second member of the committee is in charge of finances. He or she is accountable for making sure the committee can attain the monies it needs to achieve its goal. In addition, this person is in charge of making sure the plan accounts for all of the money needed.

Workbook **409**

3. The third member is the secretary of the committee. He or she is in charge of making sure all of the decisions made by the committee have been accurately recorded. In addition, the secretary is in charge of making sure all the persons who need to be contacted, in order to see the plan through, are contacted.

4. The fourth member of the group is the salesperson. The salesperson is in charge of "selling" the final idea to the administration of Michigan State University. Remember, just because a plan has been constructed does not mean that it will be instituted. The committee also needs to have a plan on how to sell it to the university.

5. The fifth member of the group is the politician. This member is in charge of making sure that the plan can be carried out. For example, your group may want to construct a petition to be signed by university students in order to reveal how many students agree with your plan. Alternatively, you could hold a vote or a rally. Remember, you may want to work closely with the salesperson because what you find out what will help him or her sell the idea.

Ideas for headbands:

1. I am INCAPABLE—ignore me.
2. I am STUPID—do my work for me.
3. I am just a JOKER—laugh at me.
4. I am POWERFUL—defer to me.
5. I am UNTRUSTWORTHY—don't believe what I say.

Discussion questions:

1. How did being stereotyped affect your work ability?
2. Did being treated in a stereotyped manner make it difficult to act like yourself?
3. What kinds of actual stereotypes about other cultures do we have, that match the ones you were given?

Chapter Nine

Persuasion

For this exercise, pick out any advertisement to analyze. It can be a newspaper ad, magazine ad, poster, etc. Look at the ad carefully and answer the following questions using the concepts from chapter nine.

1. Is the ad persuasive? Why or why not?

2. What kinds of source cues does the advertiser use to be persuasive?

3. What kinds of audience(s) would be most susceptible to this ad?

4. Which of the theories in Chapter Nine would explain the success of this ad?

5. Is this ad attempting to change an attitude, a belief, or a behavior? Defend your answer.

Chapter Ten

Coordination and Organizational Communication Structure

Most corporations in America utilize "downward communication patterns." Two of the biggest failures in downward communication content are (1) lack of feedback about performance, and (2) lack of information about the organizational procedures and practices. This exercise will demonstrate just how frustrating these failures can be.

The class will break up into groups of five.

Each group is to pretend it is a small organization. Part of being an organization is to have your own communication style (downward, upward, formal, informal etc.). In addition, you will have rites and rituals. As a group, decide how your organization will operate in the following areas:

1. Communication style most frequently used:
2. How meetings will be operated (formal, informal etc.); be specific.
3. What are your formal rules?
4. What are your informal rules?
5. What are your content rules?

After your organization has decided how the above matters will be handled, have three of your members leave the group and join another, and have three members from a different organization join yours. Conduct a meeting with your new employees, but do not tell them what your rules are. In addition, do not give them feedback on whether or not their behavior is deemed appropriate. After the meeting is concluded, answer the following questions:

1. What kinds of "inappropriate" behavior did the new employees do?
2. (To be answered by the new employees) Was it difficult to join the meeting, not knowing in what format the meeting was being held?
3. What kinds of feedback would have been helpful in this situation?

Chapter Eleven

"Sinking Ship" Group Decision-Making Activity

You are the officers aboard the U.S.S. Titanic II bound for the South Pacific. It is the maiden voyage for the ship. Suddenly you hit an old World War II mine, and a huge explosion occurs, killing everyone on board except 12 of you. Your radar shows a small, uninhabited island off in the distance. Your have only one lifeboat on board which will hold six passengers, yet you have 12 passengers. The ship's radio equipment is not working, and since you are off course, you expect these six passengers to be stranded indefinitely (maybe forever). You are sinking FAST; whom do you choose to make the trip in the lifeboat to the island?

Passenger List and Limited Information:

1. Ben Holmes, age 33. He owns a construction company. He is an expert woodworker and is always building something in his free time. He is nearsighted.

    Reasons in favor:

    Reasons against:

    Decision of committee:

2. Edward Justman, age 43. He is a judge and a politician. He is predicted to be the next nominee to the Supreme Court of the United States.

    Reasons in favor:

    Reasons against:

    Decision of committee:

Workbook 415

3. Demi Moore, 38. She is a movie star who got her start posing nude in *Penthouse.* She is a high school dropout. She has two young children at home, and is divorced. She most recently earned $12 million for a single motion picture.

   Reasons in favor:

   Reasons against:

   Decision of committee:

4. Hui-Jung Yeh, Ph.D., age 26. She is a plant scientist at a major research university in Taiwan, currently studying the nutritional value of plant materials of the South Pacific. Her English is not very good and, as a result, she has trouble communicating with the other passengers.

   Reasons in favor:

   Reasons against:

   Decision of committee:

5. Jason VanEss, age 25. He is a gourmet chef. He is married to Dr. Yeh. He is also a musical genius. He sings and can play any instrument he picks up. He tends to be a hypochondriac.

   Reasons in favor:

   Reasons against:

   Decision of committee:

6. Ann Rodriguez, age 31. She is a fourth year medical student, and bisexual. She is in good health.

   Reasons in favor:

Reasons against:

Decision of committee:

7. Ralph Brooks, M.D., age 75. He is a medical doctor. He has a bad heart and his prognosis is limited to no more than four years to live.

   Reasons in favor:

   Reasons against:

   Decision of committee:

8. Bethany Kaufman, age 65. She is a lifelong inventor and entrepreneur. She has invented everything from containers to plumbing systems.

   Reasons in favor:

   Reasons against:

   Decision of committee:

9. Randy Brooks, age 11. He is the grandson of Dr. Brooks. He is a Boy Scout and loves to explore and camp out. He has a twin sister, Ebony.

   Reasons in favor:

   Reasons against:

   Decision of committee:

10. Ebony Brooks, age 11. She is the granddaughter of Dr. Brooks. She has recently recovered from Leukemia and is looking forward to attending school again. Ebony is considered to be the smartest child in her class. She has a twin brother, Randy.

    Reasons in favor:

Reasons against:

Decision of committee:

11. Eric Weaver, age 23. He is a textile worker. He is an expert weaver and tailor. He spends his free time with his herd of sheep which he shears and spins his own cloth. He has two drug convictions on his record.

    Reasons in favor:

    Reasons against:

    Decision of committee:

12. Marcy Bitterman, age 55. Until recently, Marcy was a hermit who lived in a cabin in the mountains of Vermont. She is an expert hunter and knows how to live off the land, but she hates being with anyone else. She has spent the entire voyage locked in her room. She was on her way to the South Pacific because she needed a change of climate and had bought a place 100 miles from her nearest neighbor.

    Reasons in favor:

    Reasons against:

    Decision of committee:

"Sinking Ship" Group Decision-Making Activity Worksheet

1. What decision did your group make?

2. Describe the type of decision-making process which your group followed?

3. What type of leadership style was evident in your group?

4. How effective was your group at making a decision? What could have made your group more effective?

Chapter Twelve

Leadership

In America's history there have been several leaders who took steps to change the lives of many. Your instructor will show you a video or provide you with a written excerpt; read the excerpt (or watch the video) and answer the following questions. Example speakers to use for this exercise include Dr. Martin Luther King, Jr., President John F. Kennedy, Kweisi Mfume, Reverend Jesse Jackson, Pope John Paul III, and Billy Graham.

1. What kind of leader (from the types listed in the text) do you think is exemplified in this speaker?

2. What kinds of speech acts or overt actions does this leader perform which lead you to answer as you did in question one?

3. Do you believe this leader has the power to change numbers of people? Why or why not?

4. What qualities, as discussed in the chapter, are illustrated by this leader?

Chapter Fourteen

Media Use

A portion of this chapter examined the average American's use of the mass media (Kaiser Family Foundation, 1999; Nielsen Media Research, 2000). For this exercise, take an objective look at your own use, by medium, to see how you compare to other consumers. Analyze your time spent by medium, and the top three content preferences within each.

1. Estimate the amount of time you spend with each outlet:
   a. Television time per week   _____
   b. Music time per week   _____
   c. Print media time per week   _____
   d. The Internet time per week   _____
   e. Video Game time per week   _____
   f. **Total** _____ (per week); **Total** _____ (per 16 week semester); **Total** _____ (per year)

2. List your favorite content within each medium (choose only your top three).

   a. Television Content -

   b. Music content -

   c. Print content -

   d. Internet content -

   e. Video game content -

3. Do you notice any trends in your viewing preferences? If so, what type of negative effects do you think you are most susceptible to (e.g., learning of aggression, desensitization to violence, fear, unprotected sexual intercourse, early sexual activity, or negative stereotyping)?

Chapter Fifteen

Public Service Announcement (PSA)

Subject of PSA: Last year there were only three babies born in the United States. The birth rate needs to dramatically increase or there will be severe economic problems. Develop an idea for a PSA that will persuade radio listeners to have more babies. Assume that everyone has been using some type of birth control, so you need not encourage having sex, but to stop using birth control and encourage having babies!!

Before writing the PSA, analyze the audience, source, and message. Write your answers out in complete sentences.

1. **Type of Radio Station:** _____

2. **Audience analysis:** Consider the type of audience that would listen to the broadcasts of the radio station. List **FOUR** characteristics that would describe the typical listener.

    a.

    b.

    c.

    d.

3. **Source analysis:** Who are typical advertisers on this station? What are the call letters of the station? What type of language is typically used?

4. **Message appeal:** What persuasive techniques would reach this audience? (e.g. jingle, humor or fear appeal, spokesperson-who?) Come up with **THREE** and explain the rationale for choosing these for your audience.

    a.

    b.

    c.

5. **Types of evidence:** Why should this audience care about the problem? What evidence would appeal to them persuasively?

6. Write out the entire commercial. Provide details about background music or sounds. Then, practice your PSA to perform for class!!

Evaluations

SECTION LEADER (SL)

ACTIVITY PROFILE EVALUATION

(MIDTERM)

*Turn this form into your TA (NOT YOUR SL) at the midterm exam.
This form evaluates the performance of your SL to this point in the course.*

SL's Name: _____

Rating Scale: 1 = Never   2 = Rarely   3 = Often   4 = Always

1. Encourages class discussion.　1　2　3　4
2. Explains clearly the class assignments.　1　2　3　4
3. Provides goals for class sessions.　1　2　3　4
4. Shows a genuine interest in the students.　1　2　3　4
5. Helps relate material to the "real world".　1　2　3　4
6. Has a good sense of humor.　1　2　3　4
7. Treats students with respect.　1　2　3　4
8. Encourages students to ask questions.　1　2　3　4
9. Manages class time well.　1　2　3　4
10. Admits when he/she makes a mistake.　1　2　3　4
11. Tells students when they are wrong.　1　2　3　4
12. Tells students when they are right.　1　2　3　4
13. Illustrates class material with examples.　1　2　3　4
14. Asks open-ended questions with many possible answers.　1　2　3　4
15. Asks questions that have one definite answer.　1　2　3　4

16. Debriefs class activities well.	1	2	3	4
17. Effectively encourages participation.	1	2	3	4
18. Emphasizes conceptual understanding.	1	2	3	4
19. Grades fairly and consistently.	1	2	3	4
20. Makes him/herself available.	1	2	3	4

Please write any additional information on the back of this form.

Evaluations

SECTION LEADER (SL)

ACTIVITY PROFILE EVALUATION

(END OF SEMESTER)

Please turn in this form to your TA (NOT your SL) at the end of semester. This form evaluates the performance of your SL throughout the course.

SL's Name: _____

Rating Scale:	1 = Never	2 = Rarely	3 = Often	4 = Always
1. Encourages class discussion.	1	2	3	4
2. Explains clearly the class assignments.	1	2	3	4
3. Provides goals for class sessions.	1	2	3	4
4. Shows a genuine interest in the students.	1	2	3	4
5. Helps relate material to the "real world".	1	2	3	4
6. Has a good sense of humor.	1	2	3	4
7. Treats students with respect.	1	2	3	4
8. Encourages students to ask questions.	1	2	3	4
9. Manages class time well.	1	2	3	4
10. Admits when he/she makes a mistake.	1	2	3	4
11. Tells students when they are wrong.	1	2	3	4
12. Tells students when they are right.	1	2	3	4
13. Illustrates class material with examples.	1	2	3	4
14. Asks open-ended questions with many possible answers.	1	2	3	4
15. Asks questions that have one definite answer.	1	2	3	4
16. Debriefs class activities well.	1	2	3	4

17. Effectively encourages participation.	1	2	3	4
18. Emphasizes conceptual understanding.	1	2	3	4
19. Grades fairly and consistently.	1	2	3	4
20. Makes him/herself available.	1	2	3	4

Please write any additional information on the back of this form.

Evaluations

SECTION LEADER (SL)

ACTIVITY PROFILE EVALUATION

(END OF SEMESTER)

Please turn in this form to your TA (NOT your SL) at the end of semester. This form evaluates the performance of your SL throughout the course.

SL's Name: _____

Rating Scale:	1 = Never	2 = Rarely	3 = Often	4 = Always
1. Encourages class discussion.	1	2	3	4
2. Explains clearly the class assignments.	1	2	3	4
3. Provides goals for class sessions.	1	2	3	4
4. Shows a genuine interest in the students.	1	2	3	4
5. Helps relate material to the "real world".	1	2	3	4
6. Has a good sense of humor.	1	2	3	4
7. Treats students with respect.	1	2	3	4
8. Encourages students to ask questions.	1	2	3	4
9. Manages class time well.	1	2	3	4
10. Admits when he/she makes a mistake.	1	2	3	4
11. Tells students when they are wrong.	1	2	3	4
12. Tells students when they are right.	1	2	3	4
13. Illustrates class material with examples.	1	2	3	4
14. Asks open-ended questions with many possible answers.	1	2	3	4
15. Asks questions that have one definite answer.	1	2	3	4
16. Debriefs class activities well.	1	2	3	4
17. Effectively encourages				

	participation.	1	2	3	4
18.	Emphasizes conceptual understanding.	1	2	3	4
19.	Grades fairly and consistently.	1	2	3	4
20.	Makes him/herself available.	1	2	3	4

Please write any additional information on the back of this form.